This book is lovingly dedicated to my wife and kids,
and to all the filmmakers we've lost too soon.

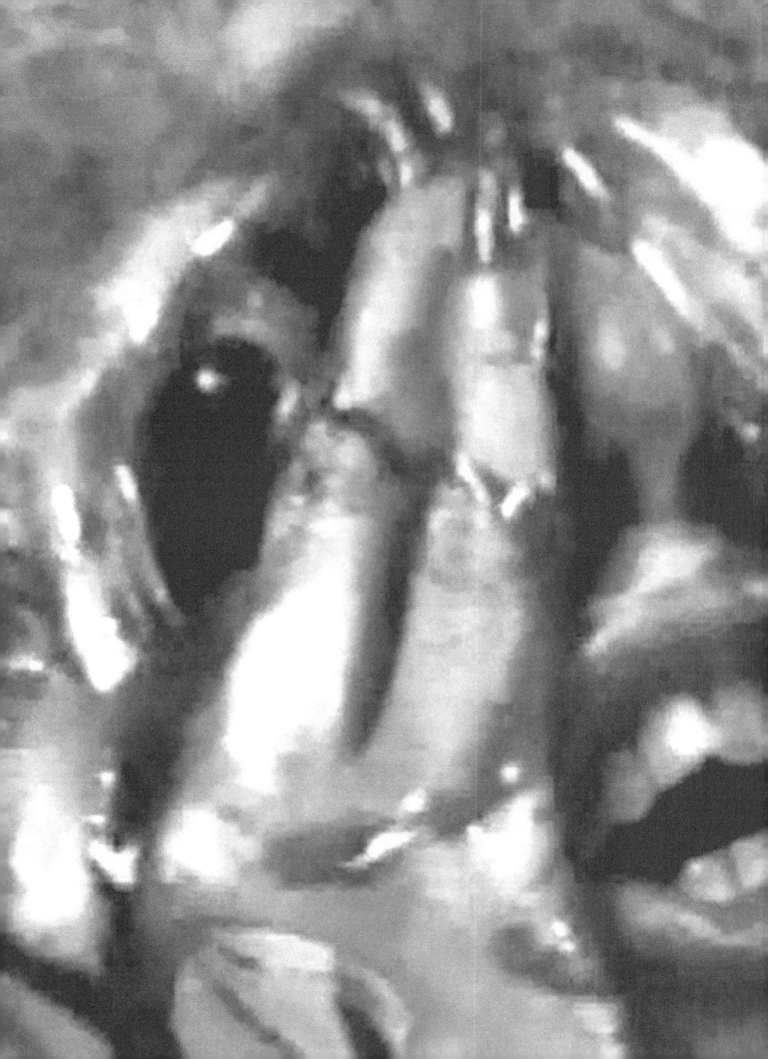

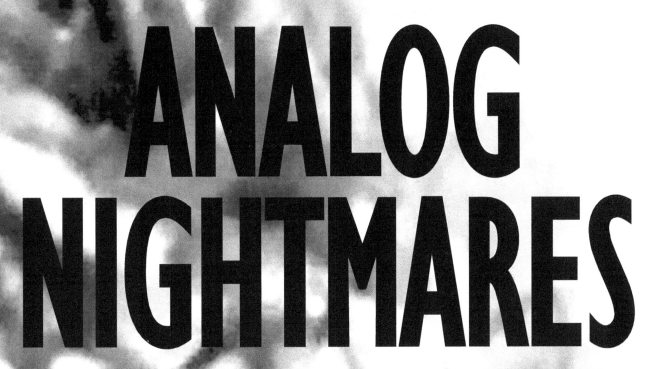

ANALOG NIGHTMARES

THE SHOT ON VIDEO HORROR FILMS OF 1982-1995

RICHARD MOGG

ISBN 9781999481704

This book would not be possible without the incredible help of some invaluable contributors. Whether it was an interview, a film title or a suggestion, your efforts will forever be appreciated. Thank you!

Tim Boggs, Andrea DeLesDernier, Mark Polonia, Donald Farmer, Tim Ritter, Doug Stone, Joel D. Wynkoop, Nick Millard, Walter Ruether, Gary Whitson, Dave Castiglione, Phil Herman, Eric Stanze, James L. Edwards, Todd Jason Cook, David "The Rock" Nelson, Ron Bonk, Michael Felsher, Ross Snyder, Tony Masiello, Tony Newton, Chris Yardley, J.R. Bookwalter, Todd Sheets, Doug J. Barry, Drew Marvick, Andreas Schnaas, David Sterling, Joel Shanahan, Ben Warren, Vince D'Amato, Nicki Hancock, Chris Hartley, Jimmie Gonzalez, Kristofer Von Winter, John Ward, Jeff Kirkendall, Becky Lee, Nick Weaver, Matt Tull, Mickey Cardoni, Daniel Carlson, Mac Brewer, Aaron Clift, Fangoria, VHS Collector, Bleeding Skull, Massacre Video, Saturn's Core Audio & Video, Camp Motion Pictures, SRS Cinema, Intervision, Synapse Films, Slasher // Video, W.A.V.E. Productions, Cult Movie Mania, Code Red, Troma Entertainment, The Sleaze Box, Screamtime Films, Cinema Home Video

A BL MOVIE CORPORATION PRODUCTION · A TIM BOGGS FILM

BLOOD LAKE

INTRODUCTION

This book is several years in the making.

In 2011, I had the pleasure of interviewing Tim Boggs: director of the 1987 shot on video classic *Blood Lake*. The interview was through correspondence where I sent him 11 detailed questions about the making of the movie. We chatted back and forth via email while I patiently awaited answers, ready to hear his behind-the-scenes secrets. This was an exciting time for me, *Blood Lake* unquestionably my most favorite shot on video horror film. But also for Tim, who had seldom (if ever) commented on the making of the movie. *Blood Lake* was the one and only film he ever directed. I could only imagine the stories he'd share.

And share he did.

To my astonishment, Boggs delivered a 22-paged memoir in my inbox. He detailed events in his life, the production itself, personal struggles he underwent (many unrelated to *Blood Lake*) and his ultimate perspective on the film today. I was floored. And for the first time, I questioned whether I was genuinely ready to learn the secrets behind the movie. Tim said that he *"wanted to finally get everything written down,"* and that this *"seemed the best time to do it."* But through the memoir, I was given a warts-and-all perspective into the film I adored. It was both fascinating and terrifying because as much as I craved the secrets, they were demystifying the magic. Were some films best left unexplained?

There is something of a wonderful innocence when it comes to shot on video (SOV) horror. Some films enjoyed extremely limited releases in their time; regionally circulated on small video labels. Some were only available through exclusive mail-order requests (and often for a limited time only). Therefore an extreme rarity exists within the SOV horror genre, making some films untraceable with information scarce. They were made and sold typically without regulation or Motion Picture Association of America (MPAA) classifications. Most were crafted by untrained artists eager to spill blood onscreen. And because of this, many SOV titles often presented an uneasy quality to the viewer.

Were they even safe for human consumption?

Throughout the 80's and 90's, many SOV movies suddenly appeared on video store shelves adorned with eye-catching garish covers. They were designed to get your attention; but you really didn't know what the movie was until you watched it. Could some SOV tapes actually be someone's family's vacation? Might they contain a killing spree caught on tape? Maybe even a real snuff murder? No one knew until you popped in the tape and pressed PLAY. That was the dangerous magic of SOV horror, never knowing what they contained. But one thing was sure: they were incredibly entertaining. Learning their backstories may indeed shape how you see them today, but I also hope it may enhance your appreciation of them as independent films in their truest form.

The goal of this book is to share the SOV love. The majority of films contained within these pages were made with little to no money, crafted by untrained individuals who used guerrilla-style tactics while making them. But what they lacked in experience, they made up for in heart. These were the true renegade films of independent cinema and with their horrors, the people involved created humor, nightmares, shocks, scares, adventure and (yes) boredom on analog cassette. In some cases, they did it simply because no one else had done it before. SOV horror was made with love.

With the support of several invaluable video collectors and filmmakers, I have worked to catalogue as many SOV feature-length horror films as possible between 1982-1995. Films were hunted down, viewed and reviewed with detailed information added throughout. And I lovingly present them here; not as a traditional review book, but as a tome dedicated to their analog format. I have also interviewed the people behind the films when possible, provided the filmmakers' intimate thoughts as offered. Finally, I present this collection to you in chronological order, beginning with the first SOV horror film ever made: 1982's *Boardinghouse*.

So gear up those top-loaders and slide in those cassettes! Because heads are going to roll, static is going to play and dudes are going to get wasted. This is SOV horror at its bloody best.

Let's dream in analog!

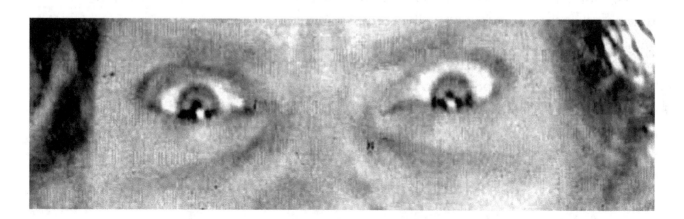

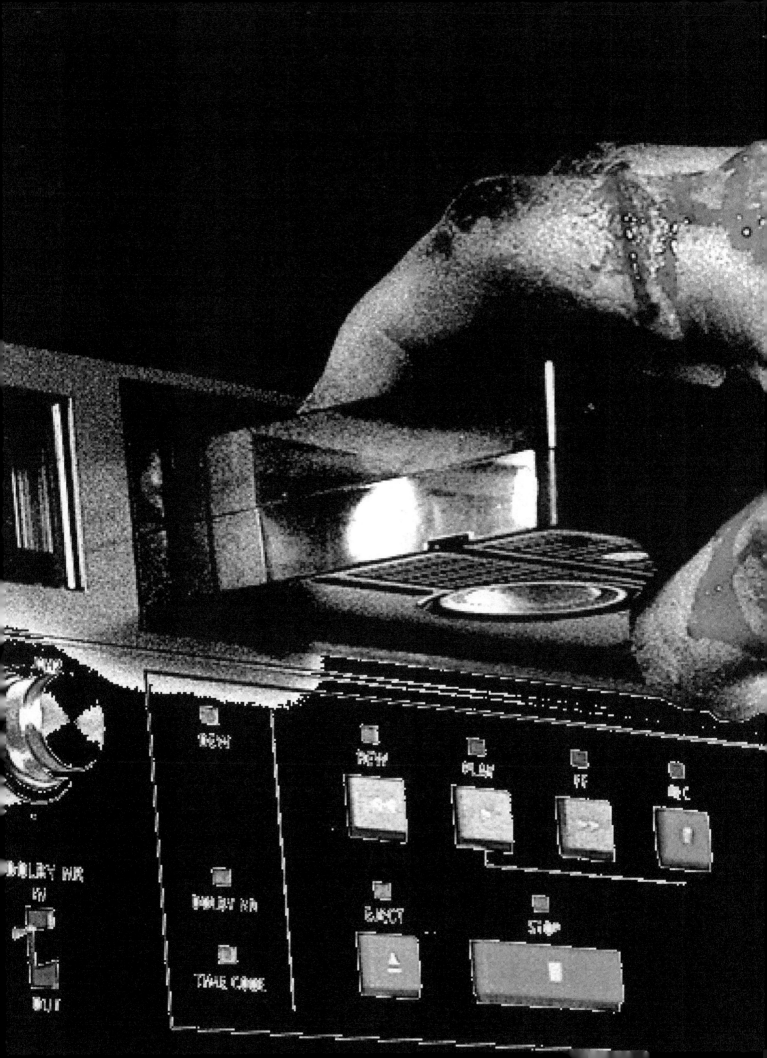

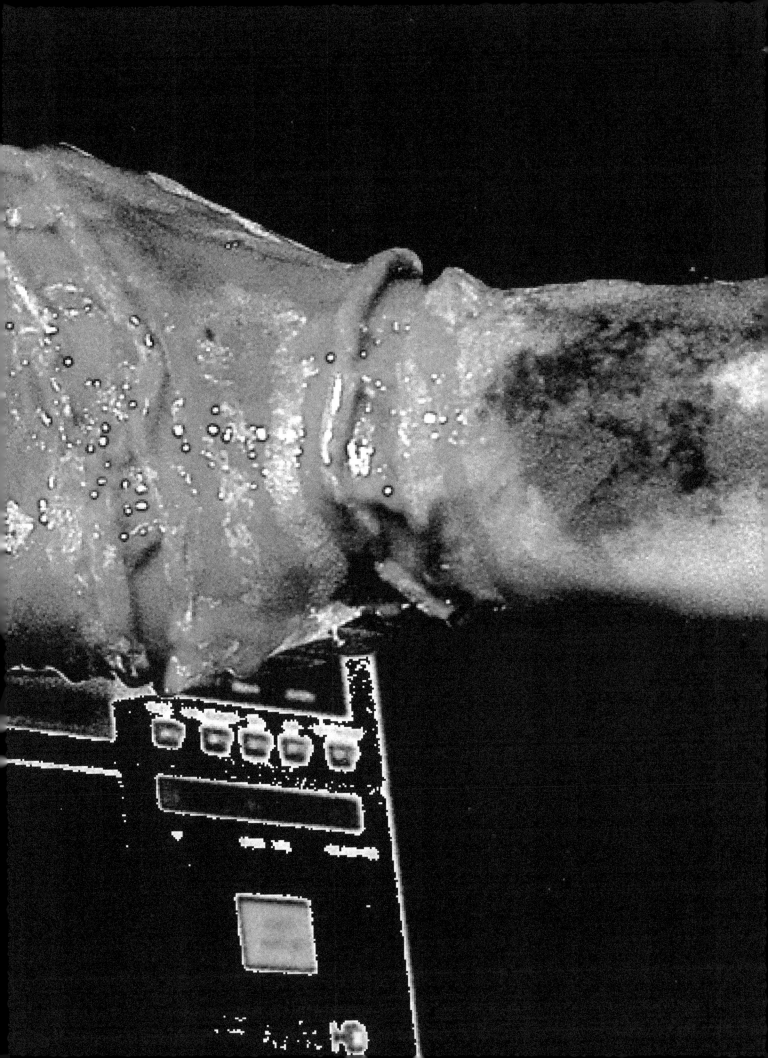

TABLE OF CONTENTS

Chapter 1
THE VIDEO REVOLUTION

From the day I learned to walk, my parents were taking me to the video store. My father was a video enthusiast so trips were frequent. This was before store franchising; before Blockbuster. I was born in 1981 and throughout my early years, video stores were unique and diverse. They were family businesses. Mom & Pop owned. They operated in communities where neighbor knew neighbor and it was a magical time. Stores were gaining popularity then; new ones opening across town at an incredible rate. I recall the store nearest to my home was dark in color, situated at the far end of a large strip mall. From the outside, it looked like something of a candy store.

But inside was a different story...

The walls were painted white. Homemade shelves built on every available inch. Fake wood paneling appeared sporadically and posters were hung on the front and back of windows. Partitioned island-like units stood freely throughout the floor and cardboard standees popped out from every cranny. It was a video combat zone; a feast for the eyes and a knockout to the senses. And the strangest bit of hilarity were the five potted plants hung decoratively above the cashier's counter. Remnants of another world? Yet amongst this arena of chaotic home craftsmanship were **movies**. Movies on videotape. VHS and BETA, lovingly sharing shelf space in (what was then) perfect harmony. I was too young to realize the difference between them, only to know that we didn't rent the smaller boxes (we were a VHS family). But smaller boxes weren't the ones that caught my eye.

Comedy was the store's largest section but its Horror space was legendary. Kept in an alcove (as if banished from the "normal" films), the horror films available were the epitome of nightmares. Oversized big-boxes of bodily dismemberment, flesh-eating aliens and demonic possession. Films so shocking, they forever burned their box art into my brain. But films so equally gruesome, my parents would never knowingly rent them. Well, almost never.

But after being allowed to rent one of these films, a strange thing happened. I brought the tape home and immediately slid it into our top-loader player. It played, reels spinning. And unbeknownst to me, the film was not fully rewound to the beginning.

Onscreen, a man was sitting cross-legged on a desk in his underwear, staring at me. I was  petrified. I stopped the tape and looked around. No one had seen what I saw. So I tethered courage to curiosity and played the tape again. The man returned; back on his desk and back in his underwear. But something looked weird (much weirder than the film's own natural weirdness). It looked like a television show - like my Mom's daytime soap opera. Was there something wrong with the tape?

I eventually rewound and watched the movie from the beginning. Sure enough, the weirdness was still there. Everything moved... smoothly? And then I realized I had seen this strange smoothness before. The year was 1985 and my father had rented a camcorder for my sister's 3rd birthday. That video looked like this video!

Was the movie I rented actually someone's home video?

Ultimately (and many years later), I learned that the movie I watched had actually been produced on videotape. That the man sitting cross-legged on a desk in his underwear was John Wintergate, and the film's title was *Boardinghouse*. But *Boardinghouse* wasn't just a movie that happened to be shot on video, it was actually the first feature-length horror film ever shot on the format. And several hundred films followed. Understand that film stock, production equipment and post-production facilities were an incredibly expensive venture to produce movies on film. 16mm or 35mm? Only the wealthiest of companies seemed to undertake it. But with its growing availability and dramatically cheaper cost, the introduction of home video in the 1980's changed the moviemaking landscape forever. It made camcorder cameras available to consumers with a durability and ease that had never existed before. And it put the ability to make movies into untrained hands, if only they dared to imagine. True, some were still shooting on Super8 film by the 1980's, but video was totally unbound. And no one could have predicted how far imagination and determination would go without boundaries. After all, video was not your grandpa's 8mm reels needing developing or a projector to play. Video was the future.

But things didn't change immediately.

Boardinghouse was produced in 1982 using broadcast video equipment, not camcorders. In August of 1982, Sony released its first professional camcorder named the Betacam, a large and heavy unit containing both the camera and tape recorder together as one (cameras and recorders were previously two separate items connected via cable). Betacam eventually became the standard for broadcast news, particularly as video's instant playback meant no time wasted on film development. Video played the moment it was recorded.

In 1983, Sony released the first consumer camcorder: the Betamovie BMC-100P. Large and best rested on shoulders when not on tripod (as with the professional Betacam), the BMC-100P differentiated itself by promising big studio abilities to an untrained public. It was the camera designed for home use, not professional, advertising as *"taking all the trouble out of making home movies."* JVC followed with their own camcorder in the same year, but most early SOV movies still originated from broadcast equipment. For making movies on very little money, it was simply easier to make deals with broadcast equipment companies rather than buy new expensive camcorders. Shoot with someone else's equipment in exchange for part ownership. Plus the quality was nicer. But the tides were turning as consumer grade equipment quickly grew in both accessibility and popularity.

And we're getting ahead of ourselves.

As long as Hollywood has tried to control and regulate filmmaking, independents have sought to free it. This is ultimately the struggle between unionized productions working in an established system (Goliath), and non-union independents struggling to produce through informal means (David). Union productions have strictly controlled crews, secured funding and established industry credentials with media recognition. Independents do not. This often results in an imbalance of quality between union and non-union productions. Generally, independent filmmakers do not have the financial resources or technical

expertise that union members do. So while union productions may be able to hire appropriate people or use money to solve problems, non-union independents must be intuitively
creative and ready for the unknown. Quite simply, independent talent has to overcome
limitations to impress and be recognized. George Romero, Wes Craven, Tobe Hooper,
John Carpenter - some of the biggest names in modern horror cinema all had to astound
audiences with heart stopping masterpieces before Hollywood took notice. And Hollywood
eventually recognized them because it had to. Almost singlehandedly, these men had each
changed the face of horror by pushing boundaries beyond where Hollywood seemed willing
to go. They were all non-union but the unions wanted in on their productions. Footage
from 1974's *The Texas Chain Saw Massacre* was recently aired during the 2018 Academy
Awards (though Hooper himself was left out of the obituaries). Yet *The Texas Chain Saw
Massacre* was a totally independent film created far away from the Hollywood scene.

But for every Carpenter, Craven, Hooper or Romero, there are far more filmmakers who
have continued to remain professionally unrecognized. Herschell Gordon Lewis, famously
credited for making the first "gore" picture *Blood Feast* in 1963 (in full color), was never
officially acknowledged for his work or brought into the Hollywood class. Others pushed
the boundaries of violence in films (some impressively so) yet Hollywood seemed more
interested in copying rather than celebrating. Perhaps there are several reasons behind
Hollywood's lack of inducting particular individuals, but the strongest contrast between
union to non-union productions lies in the horror genre. The nature of horror is to challenge
society's norms, which is likely the confounding issue. Hollywood overwhelmingly offers
"happy endings" in their films, giving comfort to the audience that everything is solved
before the credits end. "Happy endings" also ensure probable repeat viewings,
guaranteeing a bigger financial return. But the most effective horrors are the ones that
challenge complacency. Craven's *Last House On the Left,* Romero's *Night of the Living
Dead,* Carpenter's *Assault On Precinct 13* - three films that bend the standards of
acceptable horror by introducing characters capable of both good and evil acts. And they
end pessimisticly. But they were independent films that struggled to stand out by using

incredible style and design. Yet independents have always struggled to have their work recognized, particularly when existing alongside Hollywood's. Hollywood has resources. Hollywood can advertise on television. In theory, theaters should be indiscriminate when screening films (shouldn't all films be allowed to reach an audience?). But most theaters tend to favor Hollywood, in part due to conglomerate ownership and/or studio-mandated arrangements that shut independents out. Drive-in theaters were somewhat more balanced (and often independently owned), but declined in popularity as home entertainment, video recorders and movies on videotape entered the marketplace.

By 1980, televisions had already been in homes for decades, presenting episodic serials and other programs to a viewing audience. But as video recorders and movies on video became popular, something fundamentally changed about the way people watched movies. Movies were no longer being discovered only in theaters (on grandiose scales) in a place you had to go *to*, but also now on television *in the home*. Then gradually, movies started entering the home in a physical sense, contained on videotapes unlocked by video players. Movies were suddenly commodities. And as the world of home entertainment grew, a new type of store was created to help fill the incredible demand for content that followed.

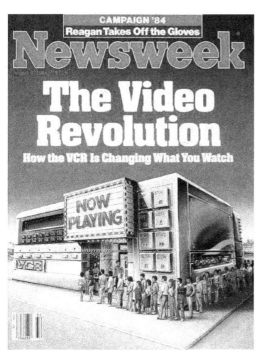

One cannot underestimate the influence of movies on video. For nearly a century, movies were seen only in the theater. Be it classic movie houses or drive-ins, movies were transformed by light shining through a projector onto a screen for audiences to see. Then came television and eventually movies aired on television networks. Movies played in the home. But networks often censored language and sensitive material for audiences, interrupting with commercial breaks. Nevertheless, movies would air and be seen. They would play during their arranged time, end and be missed by audiences not presently watching the screen. Then came video recorders (VCRs) and everybody lost their minds. Studios panicked. With VCRs, people could now record movies directly from television, possibly infringe copyright and seriously jeopardize future profits from reruns. And to an extent, VCR owners did just that: they recorded and kept television-aired movies on video to watch (and re-watch) at leisure. As wonderfully described in Joshua M. Greenberg's book *"From Betamax to Blockbuster,"* VCRs were initially marketed as a "time shifting" device.

WATCH WHATEVER WHENEVER.

With Sony's Betamax SL-8600 video-recorder, you can see any TV show you want to see anytime you want to see it.

Because Betamax, which plugs into any TV set and is easy to operate, can videotape a show up to three-hours long (with the L-750 videocassette) while you're doing something else—even while you're out of the house, by setting the electronic timer.

It can also videotape something off one channel while you're watching another channel.

And remember, Sony has more experience in videorecorders than anyone (over 20 years!). In fact, we've sold more videorecorders to broadcasters and industry than any other consumer manufacturer. We even make our own tape.

For years you've watched TV shows at the times you've had to. Now you can watch them at the times you want to.

SONY

SONY BETAMAX

They were machines that could record programs for playback at the customer's schedule rather than the network's. VCRs literally "shifted" the time one could watch a program by recording and saving it for you. Videotapes were also initially sold as blank components to the VCR and everything was geared towards recording. And Hollywood cried foul. In a statement delivered to US congress in 1982, Jack Valenti (president of the MPAA) said *"the VCR is to the American film producer and the American public as the Boston strangler is to women home alone."* Valenti argued that VCRs were an unlicensed *"wild animal"* in the marketplace, and should be removed. But thankfully the court upheld the VCR under fair use grounds, declaring it legal in 1984. Then pre-recorded videotapes arrived and people scratched their heads. What good was a pre-recorded tape?

Of course it didn't take long for pre-recorded tapes to take off. They quite literally were movies already recorded for you, albiet studio sanctioned. Many VCR owners had already discovered tape duplication by this time, hooking one VCR up to another (or to many) so that a tape could play and be copied. But owners only had copies of network airings. Pre-recorded videotapes (movies on video) promised unedited, theatrical versions of films uncensored for language or content. They were expensive but of higher sound and picture quality than duplicates. And for the connoisseur, pre-recorded videotapes allowed the customer to "own" a movie legally. ("Own" is an interesting concept because the physical parameters of a pre-recorded versus blank cassette are exactly the same. An intuitive understanding had to be reached that a pre-recorded cassette possessed intangible content that the blank cassette lacked. Therefore "owning the movie" actually meant "owning a cassette authorized to contain" copy of said movie, much like a record album). But buying pre-recorded movies was costly and early consumers were selective in their purchases, particularly with lesser-known titles.

Enter the rental business.

After wrangling some legal issues, pre-recorded videotapes were deemed legally rentable for a fee without infringing copyright. Like books in a library, the argument was successfully applied to movies on videotape, meaning 3rd party entities could purchase and then rent videotapes to another. And so the video rental business was born. Across the United States and Canada, a new type of store started appearing at an almost daily rate. Called Video Rental stores, they were essentially large rooms filled with shelves holding various videotape boxes. Movie posters and other movie related items typically decorated the walls, while popcorn was often sold alongside other candy snacks. The earliest designs of most video stores largely resembled theaters (complete with blinking marquee lights), likening the experience of visiting to that of visiting the cinema. But their biggest draw was

that they offered hundreds of titles to view. For the cost of membership and the rental itself, customers could bring pre-recorded tapes home, watch and return them later. This became the standard practice for renting movies, lasting (incredibly) for nearly 30 years. From the early 1980's to the late 2000's (and particularly for those raised during this time), watching movies on video was how most people discovered movies. Videotape became the home video standard, even though it wasn't the first or only medium for consumer choice. And the 30 year dominance of the video store became its incredible legacy, only tragically ending as the concept of movies changed again with its separation from physical media. But in the early 1980's, customers couldn't get enough and rentals were flying off the shelves. Almost everything would rent as customers hungered for new content to enjoy. Even non-VCR owners got in on the act, renting VCRs themselves for an additional fee. And video stores often struggled to keep product on the shelves thanks to demand. It was a gold rush. Basically if a movie was on video, it would turn a profit. But what if a customer wanted a movie already rented? How could other customers be equally satisfied? Stores addressed this by purchasing two (or more) copies of the same title, if popularity demanded. But they also tended to stock shelves with similar movies of similar content.

Similar movies of similar content?

Buckle up, this is where our journey begins. Employees often noticed that if a certain film was popular (say an alien film), customers would often rent similar movies with similar storylines. Often films by the same director or featuring the same actors would rent too, sharing a communal popularity. For some, a title was less important than the subject matter. Customers often came in asking for *"a scary movie"* rather than specifics, and there was always more demand than content. The major studios were slow releasing titles, initially hesitant that movies on video meant drops at the box office or widespread bootlegging. *E.T. The Extra-Terrestrial* famously wasn't released on North American video until October 1988, and only after green components (and a hologram) were added to the cassette to combat piracy. Studio concerns were valid, but stores plainly needed more movies to rent and they needed them fast.

Enter the independents.

With the growing introduction of consumer grade camcorders and the incredible demand for stores to fill shelves, a handful of maverick filmmakers pushed video in ways that had never been conceived before. They were innovative and took risks. They poured their hearts, souls, savings and (often) blood into their work and tried to rise above personal limitations. They were home-grown independents. They made art (however cheap or derivative it may have looked) and they did it on their own terms on the only format available to them at the time: home video. They were working on inexpert equipment, crafting visions of horror on analog without any prior experience. And only with determination (and a whole lot of heart) did these men and women succeed in making their own movies for the video market. And the movies were ugly.

Video was an analog medium at the time, complete with hopelessly fuzzy details, bleeding colors and overall cheapness. Yet with its undressed, unprofessional look came a realism that film could not duplicate. Video looked real and film looked rehearsed (the elephant in the room being that video also looked like porn). But the road to making video an origin source for feature-length movies did not begin with confidence or design.

It began with luck.

American Cinematographer

International Journal of Motion Picture Photography and Production Techniques

JUNE 1981/$2.00

RAY HARRYHAUSEN

TALKS ABOUT THE FILMING OF

CLASH OF THE TITANS

Chapter 2
VIDEO MOVIES AND THE FUTURE

The year was 1981.

Ozzy Osbourne had bitten the head off a dove, IBM released their first personal computer (the IBM PC5150) and *Raiders of the Lost Ark* was the biggest and most popular movie at the box office. It wasn't that long ago. Desmond Davis' *Clash of the Titans* adorned the June issue of American Cinematographer, a professional magazine of industry reports and equipment resale opportunities (officially known as the International Journal of Motion Picture Photography and Production Techniques). And as fate would have it, one article in particular caught the eye of LA based assistant casting director Elliot Van Koghbe:

"The Emerging New Film/Video Interface" by Bob Fisher.

It was an interesting piece. At six pages long, Fisher opened with *"sophisticated new equipment yielding spectacular quality transfer at the film-to-videotape interface"* and continued with *"growing interest in the development of new methods for making tape-to-film transfers."* Yet the most intriguing details came from Image Transform, Inc. president Robert Ringer, quoted stating *"with the improving technologies for transferring film to tape and vice versa, the interfacing of the two media is fast becoming an everyday reality."*

An everyday reality?

This was exciting news for Van Koghbe (alias for Shazer Everquar), who had colleagues looking to produce their own movie on a minuscule budget. Creative partners John Wintergate and wife Kalassu Kay had been focused on starting their own production since 1978, after spending years in the Hollywood music scene. They wanted to create something truly their own but the cost of film was realistically unattainable. They knew video was cheaper, but video lacked the quality necessary for theatrical exhibition (and theatrical exhibition is where you made money). But suddenly, Fisher's article suggested a bridge between formats.

> *"There is a time for film and a time for tape,*
> *and now there is a time to interface both media."*

Van Koghbe contacted his colleagues and shared what he had read. The article's focus was on film-to-video transfers, but there was enough to suggest that the reverse was possible too. Could video be printed to film? Video was of interest to Wintergate, as he already had access to editing equipment thanks to his music studio connections. And key to the article's persuasion, it also included a list of post production companies capable of doing the transfer. Together, the men researched further into the technical aspects of printing video-to-film (likely with producer Howard Willette's involvement) and found that an attempt was already in progress.

In 1980, *Monty Python Live at the Hollywood Bowl* was filmed live on a specially made analog video system called Image Vision. The video was then transferred to film (first 16mm, then blown-up to 35mm) for theatrical play. *Live at the Hollywood Bowl* would eventually enjoy theatrical release in June 1982, but Wintergate now knew enough to get the ball rolling. A script was written within a week and production started after a short casting call for friends and associates. Wintergate embraced video, shooting multiple takes and an abundance of footage *"since we knew it might take many takes to get the right weird (off the wall) flavor to the scenes."* His goal was to create something *"far out, over the top, tongue & cheek, outrageous and insane"* and *"to be innovative and do it in video format."* Wintergate added a metaphysical aspect in the film, hoping to give it a *"deeper scope somehow and also make it more emotionally intricate as well as a bit more crazy."* And it worked.

Boardinghouse was released theatrically in late 1983 on an unsuspecting public. Producer Howard Willette paid for the video-to-film transfer (after insisting the film be re-edited as a straight horror outing) and the film became the first feature-length horror film shot on video. Recalling *Live at the Hollywood Bowl's* Image Vision (and infusing their own William Castle vibe), Willette presented *Boardinghouse* in Horror Vision: whereas a gloved hand and sound would play before excessive violence appeared onscreen. Of the theatrical transfer, Wintergate recalls it *"did not turn out quite as well as we had hoped, but we thought it was good enough for an innovative cult type film and the distributor agreed."*

The film eventually found a home on videotape, available in almost every video rental store across North America (thanks to Paragon Video's vast distribution reach). *Boardinghouse* soon became a cult oddity favorite amongst viewers and marked the history books for its unique analog origins. But this was only one beginning.

The cultural impact of *Boardinghouse's* use of video was hard to measure on the filmmaking community, largely due to its theatrical exhibition. People saw this movie on film. It was a strange film, edited strangely and given a theatrical look that was... strange. But the film passed from consciousness as other new films released each week. *Boarding-house's* innovation (and ingenuity) wasn't fully realized until it came back to video, playing on the format it originated from. Meanwhile across town, another man had an idea...

The year was 1983. For seven days in September, David A. Prior attempted to make a film with the only equipment available to him at the time: broadcast video. Hungry to direct since appearing as a background actor in 1978's *Halloween*, Prior reached a deal with a local production company. In exchange for part ownership of the movie, he was permitted to shoot and edit with company equipment. They agreed. But knowing that he didn't have many resources, Prior decided to do *"the simplest story I could write and make cheap."* Something he could finance *"easily under $10,000"* and above all, something he could produce quickly. *Sledgehammer* was born.

FLESH TEARS
BONES SHATTER
THE NIGHTMARE HAS BEGUN

Starring his brother and shot entirely inside their shared apartment (save exteriors), *Sledgehammer* was a straight-forward slasher with a supernatural twist. A male-dominated group of friends are stalked and killed by a masked sledgehammer-swinging apparition. But after completing photography and assembling the footage, Prior realized his runtime ran short. The movie wasn't as long as it needed to be. So he creatively stretched certain sequences into slow-motion, added music over lost dialogue and therefore lengthening the picture's duration. Prior completed *Sledgehammer* and eventually moved onto other projects, but the film didn't find distribution immediately. Only during negotiations for Prior's second film (1985's *Killzone*) was *Sledgehammer's* rights included, bringing the video movie to market a year or so after completion. *Sledgehammer* would eventually be recognized as the first horror film made and distributed on videotape, but it took time to get there.

The details of *Boardinghouse* and *Sledgehammer's* productions are both incredible and unique. That anyone would have the idea to take video (a format totally relegated to family home use, daytime television and news broadcasts at the time) and use it to produce a feature-length motion picture is impressive. But that it was achieved in style by outsiders to the Hollywood system, is truly remarkable. With limited resources, these creative mavericks took the chance and bet the farm on an unknown outcome. Could video work? Without guarantees, they were the early few who adopted an unconventional format and unknowingly creating a new type of movie. And soon, they weren't the only ones.

1983 also saw the creation of other shot on video features. The Missouri based revenge-thriller *Copperhead*, featuring live snakes and light animal abuse. The UCLA film student (and self-described anarchist) James Robert Baker's teen rebellion-shocker *Blonde Death*. The Swedish slasher/stalker *Blödaren* (*The Bleeder*). And the student produced British nasty *Suffer Little Children* concerning a demonic girl leading underage tots to kill. Video was even used as a tool to help sell other films with the Charles Band produced *Filmgore*. Indeed by the early 80's, video was increasingly becoming commonplace in the genre. More productions followed with Chester Novell Turner's 1984 Chicago-based sleaze epic *Black Devil Doll From Hell*, Mexico's *El Monje Loco* (*The Mad Monk*) and Emmeritus' television slasher *Deadly Pursuit* the same year. But it wasn't until 1985's *Blood Cult* by Christopher Lewis that a production so boldly advertised itself as being made specifically for the video market.

It's important to note that since *Boardinghouse's* beginnings, video was being used in productions primarily due to its low cost and availability. *Sledgehammer*, *Copperhead* and certainly *Boardinghouse* would all likely have been shot on film, had the cost been cheaper. But for the first time, a production was marketing itself with its video origins as forefront news. With an advertisement campaign reportedly costing between $75,000 to $100,000, *Blood Cult* gleefully announced it was *"the first movie made for the home video market,"* gaining notoriety in the process. Note they didn't state that they were the first movie made *on* the video format (as most incorrectly

recall), though confusion is understandable. As more and more shot on video films released, the video look quickly became the eyesore of low budget movies. It was the look of a production's cheapness. And soon the notion of films shot on (or made for) video was a deterrent to customers looking for quality entertainment. But as customers rifled through store shelves, shot on video titles were situated next to bigger movies shot on film, with no way to tell them apart. Bloody box art looked just as gory as the next, and pictures on the back didn't necessarily mean they came from the movie itself (several actually had no pictures at all). Only titles and plot summaries remained, leaving SOV entries like *Pieces of Darkness* typically found next to John Carpenter's *Prince of Darkness* on the video shelf. You just never knew what you were going to get.

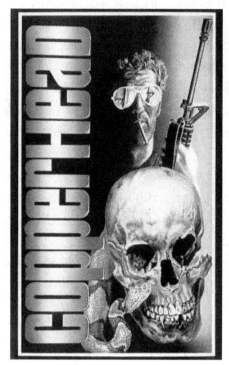

VHS confusion between shot on video Copperhead and Ray Dennis Steckler's celluloid cheapie The Chooper (Blood Shack)

But 1985 became something of a watershed year, releasing more shot on video horror films than ever before. And this cycle continued throughout the 80's until sadly, customers caught on. Complaints mounted over the films' low-fi quality and stores stopped stocking them. Movies shot on video became overwhelmingly frowned upon and regarded as bottom of the barrel crap. Some titles stood out positively, but most were forgotten. Yet early shot on video films continued to thrive as larger video chains bought out smaller ones, ingesting old stock onto new supply. The movies continued to rent. But titles produced throughout the 90's continually had to find new ways to reach an audience.

When selling to distributors ceased and direct sales to stores evaporated, producers found new ways of advertising in horror and independent filmmaking magazines. Dubbed the mail order business, producers would place adverts in magazines offering films for sale. Customers could then request an order, mailing cash (or some form of payment) to the provided address. Some of the most recognized titles sold this way were Carl J. Sukenick's mind-bending *Alien Beasts* (1991) and the entire library of Gary Whitson's W.A.V.E. Productions. Whitson in particular seemed to defy odds as several adult stores also agreed to carry his films. But the occasional shot on video entry still managed to hit rental stores, notably 1995's *Feeders* by John and Mark Polonia and Jon McBride.

After re-editing and adding new material, McBride and the brothers found themselves in the right place at the right time with Blockbuster Video. In 1996, the chain was looking for something similar to the recently released mega blockbuster *Independence Day*. Blockbuster picked up *Feeders* and immediately stocked the title for rent. *Feeders* became *"the #1 independent rental of 1996"* thanks to its alien similarity (and charming hilarity), breathing new life into the low budget moguls of *Splatter Farm* and *Woodchipper Massacre*. And though John Polonia tragically passed in 2008, brother Mark has continued directing films to this day. Whitson is still at it too, shifting his distribution model (as most independents did) from print magazines to the World Wide Web.

When I started writing this book, I approached shot on video horror as its own genre. I didn't classify films based on subject or style, but only as films sharing a unique shooting format. Some may have been broadcast, 3/4 inch or even Hi8 - but they were all video. In 1995, digital video (DV) launched and camcorders became increasingly more sophisticated. Digital video quickly became popular in the family home and new cameras were shooting incredibly detailed images beyond what was previously imagined. Video, as it was once known, was no longer the smeary eyesore. And as technology grew, video incredibly rivalled film as the superior format. But another development during the mid-90's drastically and forever changed the video industry, again altering the way people watched movies: the incredible creation known as the internet.

Though it had been around for decades, the internet (as we know it today) truly took off during the latter half of the 1990's. At an unprecedented rate, information could now be shared instantaneously with people all across the world. Websites such as the Internet Movie Data Base (IMDB), could catalog and share details of films as readers posted their own personal reactions. Other sites such as YouTube, eventually hosted videos of films themselves. And together with sites offering movies for sale, users now had access to an incredible resource for uncovering lost or forgotten films.

Developments in home video technology surpassed VHS too, particularly with the late 90's introduction of DVD. With its higher quality, recordability (on blank media) and common-place adoption of special features, DVDs were marketed as *"Home Theater Quality"* for the home. VHS could not compete and the format officially ended production in 2006.

But while the internet has enhanced the possibilities of what we can now watch, it has simultaneously killed the physicality we once tied to it. Movies were no longer just on VHS (or Laserdisc, or DVD, or Blu-ray); movies were now unbound. Movies today are available at the click of a computer button; watched or downloaded as intangible files. Movies are still shot on video, but in a completely different world than before. High definition (HD) cameras are as common as cellular phones, allowing everyone the ability to upload videos online. This is both good and bad for independent filmmakers. For the first time ever, independents have unlimited access in reaching an audience. But there is immeasurable competition in getting that audience's attention. And now, the major corporations want control of the internet too.

The one constant is the independent spirit, continually striving to succeed and stand out.

Behind the scenes on Prehistoric Bimbos In Armageddon City (1992)

And that spirit is here, in this book, contained in the interviews between these pages. As you will soon learn, these incredible filmmakers, writers, producers, distributors and actors all fought an uphill battle to succeed in making their own movies and getting them out there. Let their stories inspire you. Determination indeed, perseveres.

The focus of this book is feature-length shot on video horror films produced for videocassette, before digital photography and the internet killed it. 1982 to 1995: thirteen years of SOV productions from the opening moments of *Boardinghouse* to the introduction of digital video. Hundreds of films, several lost to the limbo of time, many of which were only released to VHS. Some were sent through mail order advertisements. Some were singlehandedly given to buyers directly. Some were distributed nationally while some may not have been distributed at all.

How in the hell do we do this?

Thankfully, I'm a fan first. I've been buying and trading movies for the better part of three decades, so a sizeable collection of SOV oddities was already at my fingertips. I joined various horror film websites and pillaged through every bit of content available. I explored the deepest reaches of the internet and made connections with incredible like-minded individuals. Together we've shared trivia, laughs and title suggestions. And everything shared resulted in a list bigger than I could have ever expected.

A list of MOVIES.

But still, each movie had to be rigorously investigated (difficult when no information exists).

THE RULES

The movies had to be acquired, viewed for review and possibly eliminated when revealed to have been shot on film. In researching, I have discovered several so-called shot on video horrors that actually weren't. Titles like *Fatal Exposure, Death Magic, Hollow Gate, Lunchmeat, The Newlydeads, The Porn Murders, Dreamaniac, Mayhem, The Abomination, Forever Evil, Deadly Love, Hell Spa, Epitaph, The Last Slumber Party, Iced, Dead Meat, Mirror of Death, Video Murders* - many titles that were actually shot on film, then transferred to video for post production editing. People often confuse direct to video as shot on video, and it's understandable. The production values between the two are often overwhelmingly similar, but this book isn't about post production. Shot on video should mean exactly that: video in and video out. So any movie that was actually shot on film had to be eliminated.

Another decision had to be made concerning short films, a seemingly larger group as countless shorts did not officially gained distribution during the period. True, nobody really knows how many feature-length horror films were shot on video prior to 1996, but shorts? Shorts could be completely untraceable. This book would never finish! So the decision was made to focus exclusively on features (with occasional exceptions).

I was also aware that some movies produced within the timeframe were unfinished until decades later. Titles like *Church of the Damned, Nightmare Vacation* and *Channel 13* (which also contains material produced after 1995). I have decided to include these with specific notations where applicaple.

Lastly, consideration was given as to where certain films should be chronologically catalogued. Donald Farmer's *Savage Vengeance* was produced in 1988 but released in 1993. I have tried to be as accurate as possible cataloguing movies by production year in most cases, but date discrepancies appear within reviews when necessary.

Certain films have also undergone re-edits over the years, so special mention has been made about alternate versions too.

Tim Ritter on Creep (1995)

In short, I have attempted to do something with SOV horror that has never really been done: cataloge and place them within a timeframe of historical importance. SOV films are a wholly unique group; largely ignored by Hollywood and generally unknown to the independent filmmakers of today. And no one really knows how many there are! These are the must-see treasures destined for every trash movie lover's hit list, and their stories can't stay buried any longer. This is their time.

What you hold in your hands is a tome dedicated to the greatest films of analog's yesteryear, extensively researched and featuring the most complete collection of SOV horror films between 1982 and 1995 ever compiled. Special chapters have been added concerning Canadian television's Emmeritus company, and how video was adopted into an educational (and profit making) tool for the genre. Most importantly, I have interviewed several of the men and women responsible for these films, sharing their unique stories and inspirational wisdom for do-it-yourself productions. And as an added bonus, testimonials and recommendations from some of SOV horror's biggest fans have been added too. This has truly been a labor of love.

So what are you waiting for? Get the popcorn ready and let your eyes adjust the tracking. Hold your breath and turn the page! Because you're in for the wildest ride of your life...

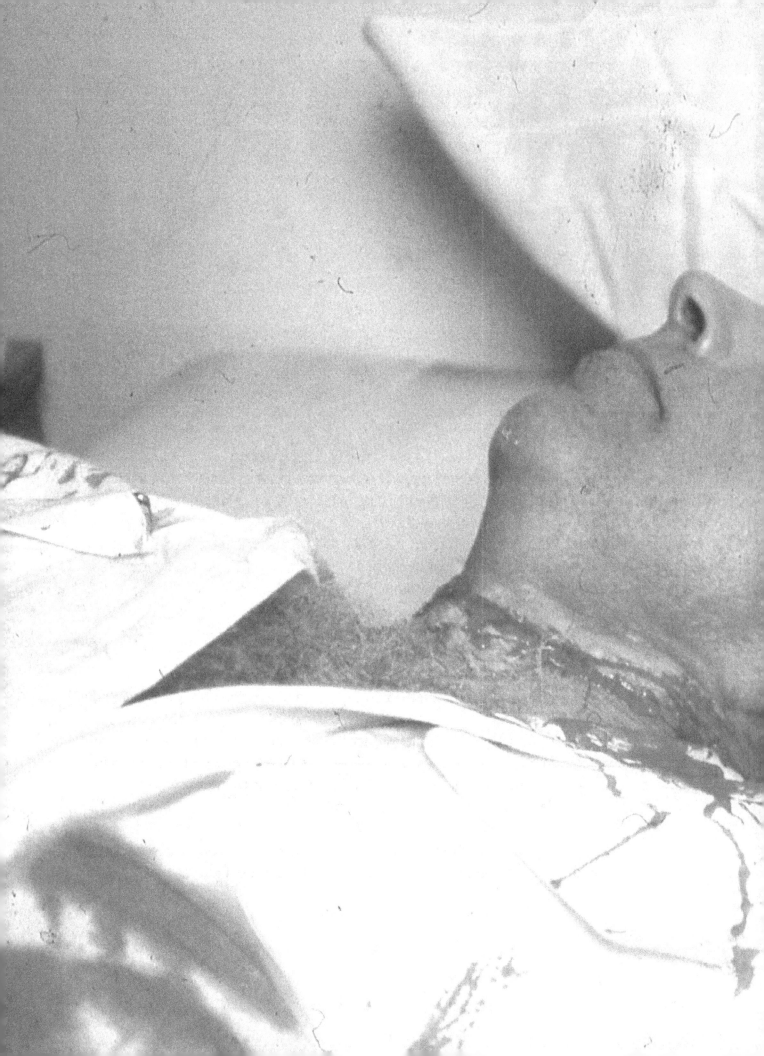

WARNING!!!

The following reviews are the personal responses of the author only. They may not reflect the views of other readers.

In attempting to compare these films (and to find commonality throughout the genre), I have tried to hold each picture to a basic set of norms. Is the story original? Did the film entertain? Was there any standout gore, action or knockout nudity? My findings should not be absolutes. Some titles are more positively reviewed than others, but this does not distract from the genuine effort involved in making them. Every film is important and deserves viewing.

Track them down!

BOARDINGHOUSE

...Where The Rent Won't KILL YOU.
but something else WILL !

IN HORROR VISION
HORROR VISION GLASSES
ONLY A STRONG HEART!

HOWARD WILLETTE Presents 'BOARDINGHOUSE'

STARRING

HANK ADLY · KALASSU · ALEXANDRA DAY

Chapter 3
IT ALL BEGINS WITH BOARDINGHOUSE (1982)

BOARDINGHOUSE
1982, Color, 98 min
STARRING: *Hawk Adley (John Wintergate), Kalassu Kay, Alexandra Day, Joel Riordan*
DIRECTOR: *John Wintergate*

Jim Royce, an 80's punk businessman (with a flair for telekinesis) inherits a large house cursed with the history of its previous dead owners. Naturally, Jim turns the home into a boardinghouse. "Girls, girls, girls" soon surround him, spending their days in bikinis by the hot tub. But one of Jim's tenants is actually the evil offspring of those previous owners, and she has a temper for jealous bitches. Eye gouging, slutty seductions and hypnotic telekinesis ensues.

BOARDINGHOUSE - Where the rent won't kill you, but something else will.

 What a premiere entry for shot on video horror! By all accounts, this film is nuts. It's positively bonkers in the most endearing way (and I mean this sincerely; newcomers should know what they're getting into). Also known as *Housegeist*, the film has an easy to follow narrative that happily breaks from the physical world. Characters behave crazily, then return to normal in following scenes. A psychedelic image of a gloved hand making fists appears throughout (warning of impending gore) then later, the film showcases Adley naked and levitating a bar of soap in the bathtub. Everyone looks like they sniffed a line of coke and food is constantly thrown across rooms. And there's more! A drunk falls on a golf course, a cop looks straight out of 1970's porn, and one girl calls another *"Cindy,"* then screams *"your name's been Cindy ever since I've been here!"* after being told it's Sandy. I still recall the first time I saw *Boardinghouse* (specifically the image of Adley sitting on his desk in his underwear) and thinking it was a genuine porno. It just HAD to be. With its rich mahogany walls, its shag carpets and those bikini babes who were flashing skin so often, it just had that look that made you think porno.

That *video* look.

Incredibly (and as described in the previous chapter), someone had the crazy idea to lens this masterpiece of mystical terror in broadcast video. For the first time in history, videotape was the medium used to shoot a feature length fright film. And it wasn't done for television access, but simply because *"it was the cheaper way to go."* Indeed Wintergate still had

 intentions of bringing the movie to theatrical release, which he eventually did after the picture was transferred to 35mm film. In his 2008 DVD commentary, Wintergate states the film had a *"$30,000-$40,000 budget with an additional $45,000-$50,000 cost for 35mm blow-up"* (however, IMDB suggests that the film had an estimated $10,000 budget, which I suspect is more accurate). Unbilled producer Howard Willette paid for the transfer after insisting on cuts to make the film *"less spoofy,"* and securing an R rating from the MPAA. Its theatrical run proved successful with *"a couple hundred prints all over America,"* playing opposite *Jaws 3D* in 1983 and eventually bringing in an estimated $390,000 in North American gross. Some video releases used the 35mm transfer (resulting in choppy play with crushed blacks), yet the majority of home video copies have been made from the original video, which looks fantastic. Movement on screen is smooth and crisp thanks to video's interlaced 29.97 frames per second (compared to film's 24, video's extra frames are what makes motion look so smooth). The film apparently only took a week to write and two to shoot; remarkable considering its multiple characters and situations. And being the earliest SOV horror feature, *Boardinghouse* doubles as a video time-capsule for the 1980's in the very best way.

Shooting the movie on analog instantly dated the production. Analog captured technology as it was in its current state in 1982, recording actors in locations with the same visual feel as a family vacation. *Boardinghouse* would have already been a wacky trip of bizarre pop culture had it been shot on film, but thanks to video's photography, the film literally becomes a product of its time. The movie forever plays like 1982, turning the picture into an artifact  from a metaphysically different and distant period. Videotape showcases *Boardinghouse* in a completely unique presentation that hadn't yet been recognized as a format except for television or home use. Its monumental impact and resulting surge of shot on video titles were soon to come, but we can recognize *Boardinghouse* today as the first real success of SOV horror. It was motivated as an inexpensive way to achieve film exhibition, but it became an innovative, unique and personally loved film for the annals of analog infamy.

 Countless viewings later, *Boardinghouse's* lasting experience is like riding a haze of drugs while coming out of a gas chamber. It grooves with electrifying rock while drilling your head with incessant breathing & orgasmic screams. And just when you've grasped the plot, it pulls a fast one and throws you back in the tub (or the bed) with Adley. It's totally hypnotic. You can watch the film endlessly and still feel like it's the first time. Several memorable moments are laugh out loud with lines delivered in deadpan glee. Food flies across the room daily and characters never think it strange. And the notion that Adley surrounds his house (and himself) with a harem of bikini-clad girls should announce his scumbag status, but he's

actually the rat-tailed hero of the story! The film is tightly edited with a good use of cutaways. And then we have Kalassu, singing and rocking everything she's got in a triumphant ending of heart-ripping gonzo breathing. Cue smoke! *Boardinghouse* has it all. Nudity is frequent (and classily understated), blood is generously thrown around and a bloody tampon is pulled from the mouth of a fantasy-pig's head. It's a scene, man.

 It goes without saying that *Boardinghouse* comes with my highest recommendation. This is required viewing for fans of horror, sleaze, 80's excess and bizarre analog video. Viewing is still preferred on an original videocassette (Paragon for me), but the film is also available on DVD. Interestingly, a Director's Cut commissioned in 1999 was released in 2010 featuring a considerable amount of additional footage. Never before seen sequences and alternate takes were re-inserted back into the film, with several scenes moved around. The new footage is interesting (and allows for more comedy) though it unnecessarily bloats the film to 2 hours and 37 minutes! And its criminally filled with highly inappropriate 90's-era digital fades and swipes. Why? Only Wintergate knows. Stick with the theatrical release.

Jonema (Wintergate) and wife Kalassu in their band Lightstorm

FLESH TEARS
BONES SHATTER
THE NIGHTMARE HAS BEGUN

SLEDGE HAMMER

Chapter 4
THE NIGHTMARE HAS BEGUN (1983)

SLEDGEHAMMER
1983, Color, 87 min
STARRING: *Ted Prior, Linda McGill, John Eastman, Jeanine Scheer, Doug Matley*
DIRECTOR: *David A. Prior*

A young boy kills his mother and her lover with a sledgehammer before disappearing.
10 years later, a group of friends stay in the same cabin where the murders took place.
The boy (who also appears as a 6 foot tall man) and his sledgehammer return to finish
the job.

Flesh tears... bones shatter... the nightmare has begun.

 It's unclear if David A. Prior was aware of Wintergate's *Boarding-house* from the previous year (and likely not, as *Boardinghouse* released direct to cinema) but *Sledgehammer* owes its existence to the same factors. Namely, it was the first film from a director hungry to make a movie and video was the cheapest format. But similarities end there because while *Boardinghouse* felt like a coke-fuelled telekinetic porno, *Sledgehammer* is more mushroom trip on the barren floor. The cabin (which was actually Prior's apartment) is nothing but white floors on white walls, a white mattress with white sheets and big white couches. I guess they wanted to emphasize the blood. But if the dead white doesn't get to you, just wait for the extreme slow motion. A shot of two characters walking in the yard turns into an absurd art-house exhibition as they float at 0.3 frames per second. And the effect is only heightened by the soundtrack's repeated low bass. Creepy! Prior states that the film was written in a couple days, shot over a week in September and brother Ted drew the box art. The slow motion sequences were actually done later to extend runtime, after noticing that the film ran short. And the final result? This movie is a definite trip! Prior wasn't the biggest horror fan but he liked the genre enough to do *"the simplest story I could write and make cheap."* No official budget was tallied but Prior claims it was less than $10,000.

Yet it's these oddities that makes *Sledgehammer* stand above countless other slashers from the time. White visuals! Deadening bass! And shot on video in 1983! Broadcast video again brought that time-capsule feeling, but with a completely unique, otherworldly (and medicated) quality not found in *Boardinghouse's* zaniness. Equally stand-out is the dynamic between the male characters, drinking and belching like careless teens when they're clearly decades older. The men (led by Ted, one-time Playgirl model) are extreme

 body builders with biceps the size of bowling balls. They treat their girlfriends terribly; bouncing beer cans off their heads while generally disregarding anything they say. One poor girl even gets licked chin-to-eyebrow as a slobbery joke! The men seem far more comfortable with each other, constantly falling and pretending to kiss, giving the film a strong homoerotic vibe. And the killer (Matley) is BIG. Big like the sledgehammer itself (which is very phallic).

Wait, what was this movie about again?

The impact of *Sledgehammer* as a shot on video feature is hard to trace. The movie released straight to video in 1984 with little fanfare and was quickly forgotten. Recent years have been more kind though, recognizing it as the analog trailblazer that it was. Officially, it is the first feature-length horror film shot on and released to video.  However, *Sledgehammer* has come back into consciousness with the 2011 DVD and VHS release from Intervision (a division of Severin Films). It is a release of spectacular quality and filled with well-deserved extras. *Sledgehammer* is an uncomfortable but pleasant watch of analog horror, historic in existence and genuinely entertaining for both newcomers and experts to the genre. Plus it also contains one hell of a food fight! Required Viewing.

Behind the scenes on Sledgehammer (1983)

THE BLEEDER (BLÖDAREN)
1983, Color, 80 min
STARRING: *Sussi Ax, Ake Eriksson, Eva Danielsson, Mia Hansson, Maria Landberg*
DIRECTOR: *Hans G. Hatwig*

An escaped lunatic terrorizes an all-girl rock band after their bus fails in the woods.

A Swedish slasher produced by the editor of pop-magazine OKEJ, *Blödaren* was an attempt to capitalize on American horrors popular at the time. Swedish censors were notoriously stringent in the 1980's, so Hatwig approached *Blödaren* with sensibilities that would please. In other words, the film couldn't be excessively violent or bloody. But it thankfully compensates with enthralling performances and wild chase sequences.

Eriksson as the balding long-haired maniac impresses, flicking his tongue at wayward babes before throwing them into his large baby carriage. The character's eyes bleed throughout (the result of some type of blood disease) but his creepy dilapidated houses are the real star. *Blödaren's* runtime mostly features neon-clad rockers exploring real abandoned mansions with trash and peeling walls to great effect. And later while being chased, panic builds because these locations are really dangerous! In addition, the film is incredibly well shot. Wide angle lenses mix with point-of-view inserts as the killer stalks his victims. And indeed, Hatwig did his homework. The film technically impresses beyond American counterparts and the opening sequence wonderfully sets the tone. But the lack of gore stands out. The music is a direct riff on Carpenter's *Halloween,* and the film feels like a *Friday the 13th / Texas Chainsaw Massacre* amalgamation (with shades of *Anthropophagus*). Hilariously, one of the doomed girls has several bells on her boots which ring everywhere she goes! But these are small complaints. *Blödaren* is a fun stuck-in-the-80's woodsy slasher, highly recommended to horror fans everywhere.

The film was apparently shot with only one camera, impressive considering the photography and 1983 production date. And *Blödaren* was slightly re-edited in 2005 for a DVD release, shortening the girls' band performance (though their essence is still intact). But incredulously, Hatwig initially rumored that Gene Simmons from KISS was cast as the maniac to help boost audience interest. Rock & Roll!

BLONDE DEATH

1983, Color, 98 min
STARRING: *Sara Lee Wade, Jack Catalano, Scott Ingram, Linda Miller, Anne Kern*
DIRECTOR: *James Dillinger (James Robert Baker)*

Teenage southerner Tammy moves from Mississippi to California with her abusive father and religious stepmother. Bursting with rebellion, Tammy inexplicably finds herself home alone and quickly lets ambitions fly: dancing in her underwear and watching non-stop MTV. But after spending a day at the beach with her eye-patch wearing friend (a lesbian constantly making advances), the girls return home to find an escaped inmate has broken into the house. Now held hostage, Tammy turns the tables on the escapee by grabbing his gun while he takes a shower. And Tammy's demand? *"I want you to kiss me!"* Soon the two have a simmering romance as they tie-up and kill Tammy's parents and other random bystanders.

Oliver Stone must have loved this movie.

Bursting with hilarious one-liners like *"they filled my mind full of crazy thoughts like running nude through a Kmart, or sitting on Richard Gere's face,"* Blonde Death is a zinger. Technically more black comedy than horror (though the premise is ripe with exploitation), *Blonde Death* stands as a great piece of endless nihilism from director Baker, whose previous short "Mouse Klub Konfidential" revolved around a Disney Mouseketeer turned gay bondage photographer. Baker's anti-Disney motif continues here as the film ends with a mass poisoning inside the Disneyland park itself (filmed without permit, naturally). But what's truly impressive is the feel-good humor throughout. We actually care about these characters and want them to succeed. The subject matter (abusive parents, murders, eye gouging) could easily have been offensive, but a joyful glee permeates thanks to witty dialogue and charismatic performances. The film portrays religion as ineffectual quotes of rhetorical nonsense, and I'd wager that's Baker's intention. *Blonde Death* is ultimately making a statement against the norms of society, most of which are designed to control the masses. This film, while providing endless belly laughs, asks the viewer to question norms or die trying. Disney may own the land, but we live in it. An excellent example of analog hilarity and a winning SOV thriller. Highly Recommended.

Meet Tammy, the Teenage Timebomb

18 years of bottled-up frustration are about to explode!

BLONDE DEATH

A video by

JAMES DILLINGER

with music by the Angry Samoans

COPPERHEAD

1983, Color, 95 min
STARRING: *Jack Renner, David Fritts, Gretta Ratliff, Marianne Blaine, Daniel Schell*
DIRECTOR: *Leland Payton*

A crooked, bible-thumping family move into an abandoned church deep in swampland. Soon they begin feuding with their young neighbor (a wildlife lover) after killing a copperhead snake in his presence. The feud continues as more snakes settle on the land and tensions grow, leading to mass paranoia. Snake bites and gun blasts fill the screen. Hundreds of snakes die. A twist ending reveals that another character was seeking revenge by planting serpents on the property.

Lesser known among shot on video enthusiasts, *Copperhead* (or *Copperhead: The Snake Movie*) stands out mostly for its unflinching killing of snakes onscreen. Repeatedly shown and often in slow motion, snakes can't catch a break as they're literally blown to bits by gunshots. "No animal was harmed during the making of this film" - a credit nowhere to be found, but the film genuinely works as a tension builder. The family leader (Renner in a wonderfully crazed performance) is intensely religious; spouting gospel and only interested in vigilante justice. He is clearly the villain. His young neighbor is an easy-going forgiving man with no religious convictions and is clearly the hero. This ultimately presents religion as a trait of evil within the film; a tool used to control the weaker minded. Renner's character repeatedly uses religion to control his family, getting them to carry out his dastardly wishes. It's an interesting perspective that I wish held more weight in the story (everything's dropped when the twist comes into play). Numerous films have shown religion blatantly perverted into mind control, but seldom has religion itself been critiqued. And it seems far too easy to blame Renner as evil and write him off, which Payton clearly tries to do (allowing the rest of the family a scapegoat). But Renner's character is likely the product of upbringing, directly tied to the religion he preaches. The film may not be interested in arguing for religious validity, but it sure does play with the building blocks.

Copperhead visually resembles more of a staged play than an actual movie, with doses of animal violence throughout. The direction doesn't do much with the format itself, but the film was apparently intended to be blown-up for theatrical distribution (ala *Boardinghouse*). It never happened. But still, it's a fun ride. Recommended.

SUFFER LITTLE CHILDREN
1983, Color, 76 min
STARRING: *Colin Chamberlain, Ginny Rose, Jon Hollanz, Nicola Diana, Mark Insull*
DIRECTOR: *Alan Briggs*

A mute girl is abandoned and left at a children's orphanage. Though welcomed by the group, problems arise when random fights erupt and a handicapped boy falls violently down the stairs. Suspicion leads to the new girl, who reveals herself to be demonic. Lead by Satan, she convinces the other children to kill.

Though apparently a 1983 production, *Suffer Little Children* purports to be a re-enactment of events from August 1984. To this end, the film presents itself in a quasi "caught on tape" manner with static shots from staircases and hallways. Performances are fairly believable as upper-crust Brits in the 1980's (this is a UK production), but one pop-singing character feels quite out of place. A rock star visiting an orphanage? And he's a main character! *Suffer's* paranormal aspects (flying plants, sliding desks) are handled well and bring chills as the children turn evil. But unfortunately many sequences appear staged. Only the bloody knife attacks impress (thanks to the youngsters involved) and Nicola Diana as the demonic mute is adequate, but she's no Linda Blair. Hilariously, loud trash-metal blares every time something evil is about to happen. And the ending (featuring Jesus!) contains sound effects straight out of *Godzilla*. The film ran into some trouble when it was initially released without BBFC certification (lambasting it as an immoral work of depraved violence), but its origin was actually drama school students looking to showcase talent. *Suffer Little Children* is nonetheless recommended for a good fright.

They had no
experience and
no money, just
determination and guts.

BLACK DEVIL DOLL FROM HELL

Chapter 5
HERE COMES THE PAIN (1984)

BLACK DEVIL DOLL FROM HELL
1984, Color, 87 min
STARRING: *Shirley L. Jones, Marie Sainvilvs, Ricky Roach, Keefe L. Turner*
DIRECTOR: *Chester Novell Turner*

Helen Black is a God-fearing woman. Church on Sundays, a Bible in every room and won't let a man see her naked (until they are good and married). But all that changes when a cursed marionette doll unlocks her repressed sexuality. Helen lusts for it, showering and exploring her naked body as the doll watches. Then the doll comes alive. It attacks her, belching white smoke and raping her until she begs for more. Helen is confused but aroused enough to fall in love. And now she can't get enough...

"Are you ready for the pain, bitch?"

This is where SOV horror goes completely off the rails. Whatever technical sophistication *Boardinghouse* and *Sledgehammer* shared is totally out the window here. This is handheld, point-and-shoot quality (completely hilarious, highly offensive as it is) but of real interest to independent fanatics - it doesn't get any more backyard than this. Originally titled *The Puppet* and shot in Turner's Chicago home with people he knew, *Black Devil Doll From Hell* is the most unapologetic example of camcorder misuse I have had the pleasure of viewing. Obviously filmed with off-the-shelf equipment and scored entirely on a Kasio keyboard, *Black Devil Doll* worms its way into your heart like your first dirty magazine. It's forbidden... but you can't stop looking! Jones plays Helen Black with extreme reservation before turning totally sex-crazed, fucking a doll and then bed hopping with men she hopes will equally satisfy her. But only the doll can satiate her newly awoken lust. And one hasn't lived until seeing and hearing this doll in action. Fully dressed with Rastafarian dreads and painted black, the doll resembles a miniature Rick James. It licks Jones' body, dripping mayonnaise from its mouth and blowing foul smoke in her face. And it constantly yaks about how it's going to fuck her, finally doing so in a grotesquely hilarious and frighteningly uncomfortable scene. Damn!

Once again, *Black Devil Doll's* video quality captures surroundings like a documentary time-capsule of the early 80's. It's horrendously cheap, allowing the film to feel like someone's actual home movie (and a very dirty one at that). But the picture was actually produced on a $7,000-$8,000 budget, half of which was spent on the camera equipment itself. And Turner got into some trouble when the Pastor appearing at the beginning wanted to be edited out, but had already signed a release. So a rumor was spread that Turner was using the footage for an X rated film! Police apparently investigated, but backed off after all signed releases were produced and nothing was out of line. There are moments of laugh out loud hilarity in *Black Devil Doll From Hell*, but it's wonderfully balanced with extreme perversion and doll nastiness. And a bizarre eroticism permeates the film that has yet to be duplicated. Truly a trip with strong recommendation.

The film (along with Turner's 1987 follow-up *Tales From The Quadead Zone*) was rescued from obscurity by Massacre Video in 2013. Now readily available on DVD, the disc contains both the original release and the preferred director's cut.

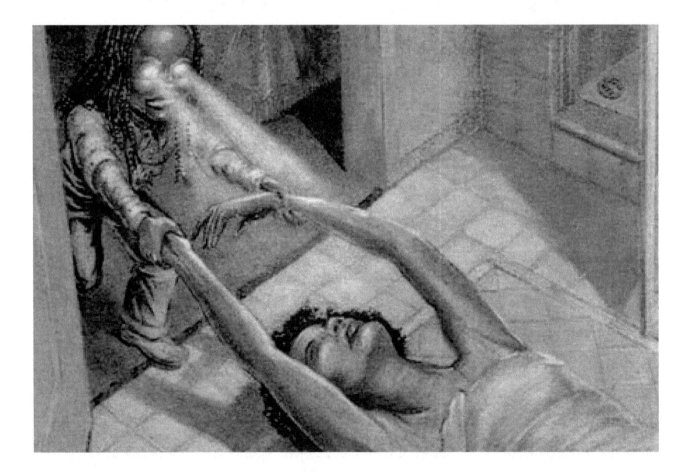

THE MAD MONK (EL MONJE LOCO)
1984, Color, 77 min
STARRING: *Julio Aldama, Julio Augurio, Luz Maria Rico, Queta Lavat, Paco Pharrez*
DIRECTOR: *Julio Aldama*

A one-eyed monk semi-hosts two tales of despair. The first is about a priest torn between loving a woman and the love of God, while the second is about a farmer's bad luck wishing over a gardening fork.

This is no *"Tales From the Crypt."*

A Mexican production seemingly devoid of logic, *El Monje Loco* feels like a hasty assembly of two shorts (which indeed, it is). But it's actually the retelling of a 1937 radio play and a 1940 film. A one-eyed monk aimlessly strolls through a desert. A ping-pong ball covers his right eye. The monk disappears and we spend 40 minutes listening to Father Martin pine over a girl named Carmela. Ping-pong monk returns laughing and the second story begins with a title. The film is extremely pedestrian. Emphasis is placed on religion, temptation and spiritual debt as we're introduced to stiff characters wanting to sing. Seriously, three songs are sung in *El Monje Loco* and two of them are duets! But interest peaks when Father Martin freaks, trying to rape Carmela but knocking her off a roof instead. Is he el monje loco? Then the Father enters a shouting match WITH GOD HIMSELF after being stabbed with a rubber knife (sounds better than it is). "The Cursed Talisman" (the 2nd story's title) equally fails as a farmer wishes for money upon a gardening fork (a retelling of "The Monkey's Paw"). The ping-pong monk returns laughing and... wait, is he el monje loco? Turns out they both are; the first story was the monk's origin.

There's very little horror here. One character resurrects with a facial injury, but *El Monje Loco* isn't interested in terrifying the audience. This is a film designed to get people praying. God is everything and veering away from the church only brings despair. An unimpressive soap opera.

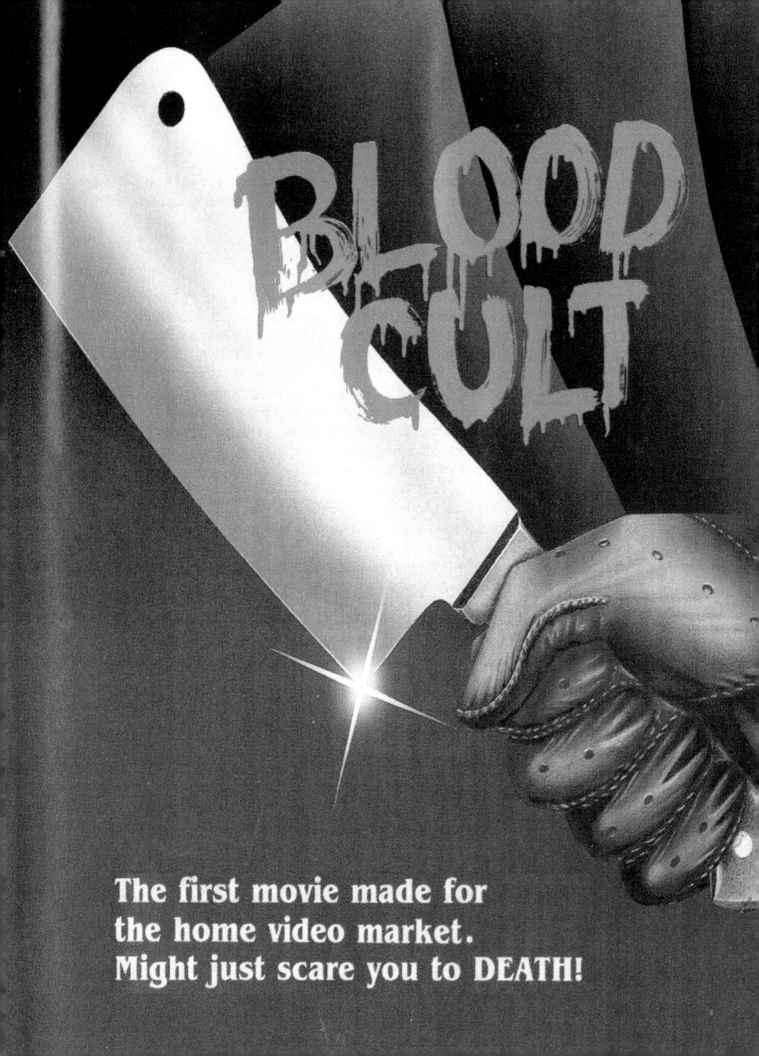

Chapter 6
THE FIRST MOVIE MADE FOR HOME VIDEO (1985)

Before 1985, video was the tool of underfunded movie visionaries. It was the format used because it was inexpensive; cheap in cost but also in look. And had budgets been higher, these films likely would never have been on video at all. Would *Sledgehammer* have been shot on film if Prior had the ability? Perhaps. Would *Boardinghouse?* Almost certainly. But video was used, largely because it was the only available format at the time. And the same is true for the other films discussed in the previous chapters.

But a change in perspective was on the horizon. Video entertainment had exploded into a gold rush of popularity (and immediate profit). VCRs and camcorders were being increasingly marketed to consumers and video stores were soaring in business. Video wasn't just a fad, it was a revolution. VCRs and the way they unlocked content for audiences became top news stories, adorning magazine covers such as Newsweek and Time by the end of 1984. And the demand for new content continued to grow.

Executive produced by Bill F. Blair and directed by Christopher Lewis, 1985 saw the production and release of *Blood Cult*. Dubbed *"the first movie made for the home video market,"* Blair and Lewis publically embraced video as no one had before. They held notices in Variety and worked the business from within. Maybe they weren't the first movie made for the market technically, but they bolstered themselves loud and proudly enough to gain attention. And it worked. For the first time, a movie seemed honored to have been shot on video and produced for video distribution (though *Blood Cult* did not claim to be the first shot on video movie). *Blood Cult* had intent, and it used what other productions kept secret to become headline news.

More films were produced in this timeframe too, making 1985 the biggest SOV horror year yet. Canadian television's Emmeritus Productions came into their own, video continued as an educational tool and early feature productions from Tim Ritter, Joel D. Wynkoop and Mark & John Polonia arrived (though the Polonias' work would not see release until decades later). But what's incredibly apparent about 1985's productions is their sense of trial and error. Filmmakers were experimenting; testing the waters. More individuals were turning out and making their own movies than ever before. Emmeritus worked to timed perfection (making films on a television schedule) while independents began articulating themselves. Films such as *Bikers Versus the Undead*, *Twisted Illusions* and *Church of the Damned* were only possible thanks to video's growing accessibility in 1985. And though video production was still a few years away from total consumer dominance, this was the start.

The match had been lit and there was no going back.

BLOOD CULT

1985, Color, 89 min
STARRING: *Charles Ellis, Julie Andelman, Josef Hardt, James Vance*
DIRECTOR: *Christopher Lewis*

A series of gruesome murders on a college campus peaks the interest of the local sheriff. The victims have all been hacked to death with a meat cleaver. Certain body parts are missing and strange gold coins are left in their place. With the aid of his librarian daughter, the sheriff connects the crimes to a secret cult.

Is this the first movie made for the home video market?

 Not really, but it was one hell of a marketing ploy. By the mid 1980's, video was a booming business. Rental stores were a goldmine; clearing profits with practically every title stocked. But demand was constant and more films were needed. VCRs had already lowered in price (so most middle-income families could afford) and camcorders were continually marketed direct to consumers. As more people bought equipment, more people rented videos. And though it wasn't commonly stated, the general public now possessed the tools necessary to make a movie. Visionaries and underfunded producers had already achieved this, but it was unadvertised. Films shot on video usually kept their format a secret and early titles (such as *Boardinghouse* and *Sledgehammer*) were just hitting videocassette. Apparently, no one had yet recognized video as a selling point. Some television was shot on video; game shows and the news too. But movies? The idea of using video as a source for motion pictures was still alien to the majority of consumers, aside from the few mentioned in previous chapters.

The public needed a guide.

Boldly billed as *"the first movie made for the home video market,"* *Blood Cult* embraced its format and came out swinging. Its producers may not have known about *Sledgehammer*, *Black Devil Doll From Hell* or *Copperhead* (titles that were just starting to hit video too), but *Blood Cult's "made for the home video market"* claim spiked a great flag into the home entertainment landscape and gave video legitimacy. *Blood Cult* made other video-shot movies  fashionable, because it tied its own "video look" directly into its marketing. This was video for video's sake and *Blood Cult* had intent. Famously, director Lewis credited Bill Blair as *"having the idea of making the movie direct for the video market"* if it was possible under a $100,000 budget. Blair seemingly anticipated the home distribution market throughout the late 60's and 70's by acquiring films and their nontheatrical rights into his company United Films. By the 1980's, Blair was selling movies on video and licensing content to cable networks, renaming the company United Video (and eventually VCI Entertainment). Blair was set to produce *Blood Cult* and Lewis wanted to direct, so he pitched a complete production cost of $25,000 (though $27,000 was spent) with an additional $70,000 on marketing. Lewis managed to secure two Betacams plus editing equipment from Sony, for the then-low sum of $1000. It was an incredible deal. Shot in March, production lasted 9 consecutive days in Tulsa, Oklahoma under its original title *The Sorority House Murders*. Some colleges would not allow photography on their campuses (subject matter concerns with the occasional rumor that this was actually a porno) so Blair gleefully claimed *"so grue-somely realistic, it was banned from two mid-western campuses!"*

Blood Cult released direct to video in August of 1985 at the sell-through price of $59.95 per cassette. And while sleazy, *Blood Cult* wasn't your possible porno or filthy sex doll fantasy (referencing *Black Devil Doll From Hell*). Lewis tried doing things respectably, and it shows in the work. Cranes were used for establishing shots. Camera angles were artistic. Tracking shots were smooth. In short, the movie feels like a professional film. The cast (largely Tulsa locals) do a fine, though occasionally theatre-level job. And humorously, the sheriff is played by an elderly man with a visible hearing aid while his librarian daughter is ruggedly in her forties. Not typical heroes for a teen slasher. The best of the bunch is Hardt's Medical Investigator, radiating with home-style comfort and deadly menace throughout. Blood and guts are wonderfully showcased too; technically the most impressive seen in a SOV horror to date. From the opening murder of a girl in the shower, we know we're in for a bloody good time as her severed arm lands with a rubbery THUD in the blood-spattered bathtub. And the hits keep coming with beheadings, bloody cleaver hacks and severed fingers lost in a cafeteria salad. The film doesn't stray from its basic storyline (borrowing heavily from *Blood Feast*), letting *Blood Cult* work as an easy introduction to the world of SOV horror. Required Viewing!

A 16mm sequel came in 1986.

ATTACK OF THE KILLER REFRIDGERATOR

1985, Color, 16 min
STARRING: *Lori Regonini, Christina Murphy, Lori Carson, Michael Savino, Mark Veau*
DIRECTOR: *Michael Savino*

An old fridge launches a murderous rampage after its ice-filled freezer is chipped clean the night before.

Though this book is focusing on features, Savino's short *Attack of the Killer Refridgerator* attained video release in 1990 on the legendary Donna Michelle label, so respect is due. Paired with another short *The Hook of Woodland Heights*, *Killer Refridgerator* is best regarded as the first of a two part anthology. Beyond the synopsis above, nothing much happens in *Killer's* 16 minute runtime. People's limbs are bitten off by a fridge. Whole characters get sucked in. Even those standing beside it aren't safe, as the door handle harpoons unsuspecting visitors. What more could you want? Hilariously, the fridge even sucks in a cat! It's short and sweet but also charming. Plus it never gets old. This really feels like a party tape gone wrong.

BIKERS VERSUS THE UNDEAD

1985, B&W, 61 min
STARRING: *Jim Greenway, Jerry Anderson, Larry Bruce, Joni Barborich*
DIRECTOR: *James R. Buick*

A gang of chopper-riding bikers fight against a horde of resurrected zombies, brought to life by a rich man's radioactive serum.

Shot throughout Arizona, *Bikers Versus the Undead* is a fun time-waster. A rich man named Speed forces a scientist to create a serum (hilariously using radioactive materials which no one knew was radioactive) to combat bikers. Why does Speed hate bikers? No clue, but damn if he does. The biker/zombie fight commences early, then spends 40 minutes meandering before having another go towards the end. Guys drink while girls sing. We wait for something to happen. A subplot about a biker's best friend becoming a zombie distracts (he spends the whole movie saying *"you just need medical help"*) but it goes nowhere. These are pretty nice bikers too, asking for police involvement as soon as shit hits the fan. But too bad the cops aren't interested. The film contains an impressively large cast and some nicely done makeup, furthering proof that the 1980's really were the best time for zombies. But the ending feels rushed, saying Speed must have gotten away before credits roll with a Speed theme song (I kid you not).

CHURCH OF THE DAMNED
1985, Color, 61 min
STARRING: *Mark Polonia, Todd Smith (Todd Rimatti), John Polonia, Matthew Satterly*
DIRECTOR: *Mark Polonia, Todd Smith (Todd Rimatti), John Polonia*

A satanic cult committing murders baffle detectives in a small Midwestern town. An amulet found at one of the crime scenes lead detectives to the killers' hideout, but not before the cult's long-dead leader is resurrected in demonic form.

 Though filmed in the winter of 1985, *Church of the Damned* didn't see completion (or release) until 2013. Therefore it is difficult to calculate what impact the film might have had on the burgeoning SOV market of the time. Ultimately I believe it would have been profitable; influencing countless would-be filmmakers because the film is riddled with promise and ambition. *Church of the Damned* is the first feature length attempt by teenaged filmmakers John and Mark Polonia (twin brothers) and friend Todd Smith; all still in high school. Everyone appears as their pre-adult age (regardless of role) and yes, much of the violence seems teen fantasy driven. A detective drills a hole through a suspect's head for kicks! But passion is here, baked into the unmistakable sense that everyone is trying and having fun. Gore is highly impressive, particularly an in-camera autopsy on a dead cult member. And some of the plot is unintelligible, likely because the original production was never really finished. *"We abandoned the project,"* explains Mark during an introduction. *"It was our first foray into video."* The film was finally assembled in 2013 using modern editing equipment, with efforts made to keep a 1985 mindset. But results occasionally feel a

bit too savvy for teenagers using analog. There are clean cuts and fades throughout. So one can't help but wonder what could have been if assembled 30 years ago, but the fact that we have this at all today is a miracle (and I'd definitely rather have it than not).

Church of the Damned's most striking aspects are its obvious influence (*Blood Cult*) and the impressive originality the boys brought to the project. Todd and the brothers were already crafting 8mm shorts when they attempted this on video, and the trio finally found commercial success with their 1987 gorefest *Splatter Farm*. But here's where it all began. Recommended!

   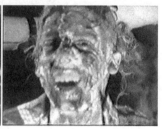

DEADLY TRIGGER
1985, Color, 88 min
STARRING: *Audrey Landers, Judy Landers, Wayne Allison, Jan Fedder, Joe Martinez*
DIRECTOR: *Joe Oaks*

Singing sisters Polly and Ruth Morrison move from New York to Germany, where they are raped and beaten in a parking garage. Ruth suffers a miscarriage and attempts suicide. Polly plots revenge. Turns out the rapist is the son of a powerful businessman so Polly orchestrates a money theft scheme, setting the scoundrel up for police.

 Starring long-time television stars Audrey and Judy Landers, *Deadly Trigger* is mess of convoluted ideas. Also known as *Deadly Twins*, the film wanders from one plot device to the next as the Landers' pursue justice. The film climaxes with an endless parade of car chases and musical numbers (and in the worst way). After performing a wonderfully dreary ballad, the girls are confronted by four men in a parking garage. Four, yet the girls are only vengeful against one. Regardless, Ruth miscarries and leaps from a hospital window shortly therafter. But she survives. She's confined to a wheelchair and is also (hilariously) thrown down some stairs in the climax, but she lives to fight another day. On the other hand, sister Polly is the one blackmailing and setting up the rapist while splitting her time seducing the assigned detective on the case. The romance dominates the second half of the film, wining

and dining the audience with nudity-free love scenes. Then *Deadly Trigger* launches into its unbelievably long chase sequence. Cars, motorcycles, bulldozers and a helicopter come into play, and end narration tells us everybody went back to their lives (and unbelievably, Ruth is walking again!)

Though using the rape/revenge setup, *Deadly Trigger* contains little horror. Instead we get a movie-of-the-week melodrama with a couple short flashes of skin. Violence is largely off-screen and action randomly appears without reason. Audrey Landers as Polly escapes mostly unscathed, delivering a relatively compelling performance and looking great. But the film is frankly forgettable.

THE RIPPER
1985, Color, 102 min
STARRING: *Tom Schreier, Mona Van Pernis, Wade Tower, Andrea Adams, Tom Savini*
DIRECTOR: *Christopher Lewis*

A college professor obsessed with Jack the Ripper finds a ruby-embedded ring that once belonged to the infamous killer. When he puts it on, gruesome murders occur. Is the ring possessed with the Ripper's spirit?

 Released a mere six months after *Blood Cult*, *The Ripper* is director Lewis' second SOV horror feature - and it's a winner. An improvement on almost every level, *The Ripper* is a fun who-done-it gorefest with endearing characters and charming performances. The movie opens in a Victorian-like set piece involving horse-drawn carriages and elegant costumes, then quickly dissolves into modern 80's fashions of flashy colors and big hair. To call the opening ambitious is an understatement, but ambitions don't stop there. Throat slashings and disembowelments occur fully in-camera, there's solid camera use with crane shots (as there was in *Blood Cult*), a car explodes and a mini aerobics video beats out by dance students. See, Lewis had $75,000 and 2 weeks to shoot here (not $25,000 and only 9 days as before). But what's really impressive is how well it gels. Schreier and Van Pernis give good performances with strong chemistry. And Tower and Adams steal the show

as romantic youngsters tragically planning their futures together. Likeability is somewhat rare concerning characters in SOV horror, making *The Ripper* all the more enjoyable (and more shocking when Adams meets her untimely end).

But (of course) what demands mention is the film's coupe de resistance: Tom Savini as the Ripper. Savini was in his prime in 85, having just provided special makeup effects on *Day of the Dead* (arguably his most triumphant work to date). And along with his outstanding effects on *Dawn of the Dead*, *Friday the 13th*, *Maniac* and *Creepshow*, Savini was a household name. To cast Savini must have sounded like a genius marketing plan, but it's disappointing to see he's only an actor here. *The Ripper's* violence is impressive with hearts cut-out and throats slashed, but Savini's name is used more like a gimmick. He only appears at the end for 5 minutes, and had nothing to do with the make-up. *"Now I have to get on my knees and apologize to everybody who sees this. I'm forced to be more selective these days,"* says Savini now, who nabbed $5000 for less than a day's work (and hilariously, top billing). But Savini's cameo is just one of the great marketing ploys common to low-budget movies, much like Bela Lugosi in *Plan 9 From Outer Space*. The film plays well without him, but enters infamy due to his seemingly-random appearance in the final act. This is a perfect example of a high quality SOV horror that hit at the right time and made an impact. Required Viewing!

  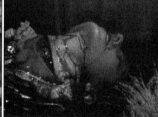 

SOUTHERN SHOCKERS
1985, Color, 74 min
STARRING: *Mike Gordon, Robert Harrell, Tom Hatcher, Eric Shusterman, Tammy King*
DIRECTOR: *David Coleman*

An anthology of three tales. A priest delivers a sermon predicting the death of three men. The first ("RX") involves a doctor with strange healing powers arriving at a small town. The second ("Moonshine") has poisoned booze turning men into zombies. And the third ("King of the Road") details a driver pursued by a hearse and a demon.

US made but apparently only distributed in Spain (titled *El Espiritu del Zombie*), *Southern Shockers* is nothing to write home about. Seemingly produced for television, Coleman

*Andrea Adams and Wade Tower
in The Ripper (1985)*

crafts a film devoid of nudity, scares or basic tension. Placid music and zingers overrun the film, wiping natural sounds off the soundtrack completely. Some impressive effects occur (courtesy Chris Witherspoon) but their not until the halfway point. Where's the hook? Spain must have been hungry.

TRASHCANS OF TERROR
1985, Color, 72 min
STARRING: *Chuck Handy, Terri Heater, Les R. Rigwood, Larry Frampton*
DIRECTOR: *Chuck Handy*

An alien queen and her army of trashcans invade Earth looking for her missing pouch. Only a drifter and his blonde babe girlfriend can stop them.

Absolutely bizarre and full of comedy, *Trashcans* is smarter than it looks. Opening with the dedication *"to everyone that has found themself [sic] behind schedule over budget or traped [sic] in a silly plot,"* Handy's *Trashcans* knows how silly it is. One scene involves Handy and Heater kissing for 3 minutes - and an onscreen timer clocks it out! Actors constantly burst into laughter and everyone looks straight to camera for direction. The cameraman's no better, giggling throughout and spiking takes with his hand popping in to adjust focus. But it all adds up to honesty. There's a wonderfully drawn out "fight sequence" as Handy hilariously fake-punches surly patrons from a bar, Heater magically turns silver to Hulk-out, and everyone gets to throw trashcans across a field. But that's not all! The entire plot is told through narration and action climaxes when Heater is abducted and tortured for *"a thousand orgasms per minute."* Say what?!? But she survives because hey, she's from California. A really wonderful video that apparently was shot over 3 weeks for $300. Highly Recommended.

TWISTED ILLUSIONS
1985, Color, 64 min
STARRING: *Joel D. Wynkoop, Holly Tate, Al Nicolosi, Colleen Foley, Jerry Zel, Tim Ritter*
DIRECTOR: *Tim Ritter, Joel D. Wynkoop*

An anthology of random skits and stories. The film opens with Ritter and Wynkoop eagerly pitching project ideas to a comatose producer. From there, we're treated to a mother who inadvertently vacuums her own baby, a health-nut who curses his friend before falling to his death, a mad scientist and a cob of corn, a deadly game of Truth Or Dare and other such ventures.

The premiere release for young friends Ritter and Wynkoop, *Twisted Illusions* is packed full of energy and enthusiastic ideas. Indeed the pair seem so excited, they attempt some ideas twice with two versions of the same story! Ritter and Wynkoop bounce off each other like a slapstick comedy duo. It's heartfelt and charming. The stories themselves have more humor than horror; a favorite being a wife who seduces her husband, then kills him behind a closed door for 3 minutes (we see the closed door and just listen). The Truth Or Dare segment was later expanded upon for Ritter's 1986 breakout feature *Truth Or Dare? A Critical Madness*. But it's Ritter and Wynkoop's charismatic breakout here that make things memorable. Recommended!

Twisted Illusions was remastered in 2000 with extended sequences, then later assembled with footage from its 2004 sequel (dubbed *Twisted Illusions: The Ultimate Edition*).

Interview
MARK POLONIA

One of the most well known video filmmakers still working today, Mark and his twin brother John actually started making Super8 shorts in their pre-teens. Fearless and ready to try new things, the brothers moved into video with their first feature-length film *Church of the Damned* in 1985. Critical success followed with their 1987 SOV gross-out *Splatter Farm*, and financial success came with their 1996 alien release *Feeders*. Over 30 years in the business (and after just as many productions), the brothers continue to inspire as independent filmmaking giants. John sadly passed in 2008 but Mark has continued with his never-ending love for moviemaking and monster movies.

Mark, thank you for giving your time to this interview!

Absolutely! I love talking to fans and I like spreading the Polonia gospel, so to speak!

In 1985, you made *Church of the Damned* while still in high school. How did that project come about? What made you want to attempt a feature?

That's a great question! We had just finished a Super8 movie called *Halloween Night Part 2* in November. We took it to school and showed it. We always would take films to school (that's why we never had girlfriends) but my dad had just got a video camera. Now people have to understand that video cameras were new back then. We had seen *Blood Cult* and we're like *"this is shot on video and it's everywhere. Let's shoot a movie on video!"* I think over a weekend we came up with the idea and it emulates *Blood Cult*. There's a cult, there's cops and really it was a bad idea. It wasn't a bad idea to shoot on video, but it was a bad idea to do it the way we did. We should have made a slasher movie about kids, instead of us trying to play adults. It absolutely fails on almost every level. Although there's a few good scenes in it (primarily the one where they go to investigate the house. I think that's a pretty good scene). But again, we we're reaching beyond what we were capable of doing. Why we did that still defeats me. We should have stuck to something a little more grounded in our reality and it would have made it a better movie. But that's where that came from. We shot almost all of it in 2 and a half months and we didn't finish it. We had a couple more scenes to film and we did alter it; for years I had the shooting script and it listed every shot. But we never edited it because (at that point) we had no access to editing videotape. So we left it and moved on to something else. It was great to be able to shoot something and look at it immediately, but we were so used to economizing that we would shoot movies on video like they were movies on film. We would shoot a take, then move the camera and get another thing instead of filming it all the way through. We were still trying to shoot in-camera. And that was something we had to learn not to do. It didn't hurt our production because we still knew how to shoot and put it together to make it look like a movie - and *Church of the Damned* (as awful as it is) still looks like a movie. If there were adults in there, it would look like a below average SOV movie but it would still be a movie. We were 16 but I wish we used a little common sense, you know *"let's do a movie out in the woods about a slasher killing skiers"* or something. Again, why did we do what we did? We thought we could make it work and it just didn't work. It was a bad idea. But years later when I got all the footage and started editing (despite the fact that we're kids playing adults) it came together pretty well. I was amazed that at that early age, we had a pretty good mastery of cinema and what it would take to put a scene together. Even though we didn't shoot a lot of footage, it all cut together pretty easily. I was surprised that it actually looked like a real movie. It had a beginning, middle and end. We probably should have finished it. After I cut it together, I regretted not finishing it because we probably could've done something with it.

Did you immediately jump into *Hallucinations* after that?

Hallucinations would have been a few months later. We were going to regroup, get back on our feet and do something obtainable. *Hallucinations* was really an experimental kind of thing. We had an outline from beginning to end, but we had no real script. We shot it in order and we were really stranded in our location. We shot in the winter and we just kept adding to it. It's like a dream; a zero budget *Phantasm*. It's linked together by imagery and these three characters and it jumps in and out of reality. Technically, it's pretty shoddy. But there's something about it that really captures a feeling, an essence or a mood that we were not cognitive of at the time. I don't think we were setting out to do that, it just kind of developed as we made it. That's the neat thing about filmmaking as you develop your style. We remade it as *Lethal Nightmare* and it's amazing how some people like the original over the new one. But I think it was the first step in the right direction. It was a regroup, a refocus. It was a story that we could do. We had those props, we had that house, it was snowing out, there was atmosphere, and we edited that in a sort of professional place. Edited only on weekends (so it took forever) but we were able to do cuts and slow-motion. Sound is not good, but it is what it is. And it has some creepy things in it that people remember.

When you finished, was the intent to start shopping it for distribution?

Yeah, we actually did. There was a company in California who was sort of interested but then they got cold feet. And it just never happened. So we just put it on the shelf and moved on. This would have been 1986-1987. The season changed and we went out to California for a little bit right after we graduated. Then we came home and made *Splatter Farm*.

And then you made *Splatter Farm*!

Splatter Farm was born out of *"what do we have at our disposal?"* We had tons of horror props and access to a farm, so we sat down and thought. It was originally going to be called *The Degenerates* and it was going to be our *Last House On the Left*. We were going to make our mark and hopefully propel our career. So we based a lot of it on different serial killers and some of the sick things that they would do. And we shot the movie over 3 months. We were out of school but we had jobs and we had to work around our schedules. And we took time making it. We didn't rush through and it really has something, like a car wreck. Once you look at it, you can't take your eyes off it. The title's great too. My brother came up with the title and it's fantastic. If it was made in 1975, it probably would have made millions of dollars!

How did you convince Marion Costly to be in it?

We just told her what we were doing and she agreed to do it. She didn't put up a fuss. But had she not agreed to do it, it would have been a completely different movie. A lot of times we may not have been forthright with what the end result was going to be, but she liked the movie when it was done. She saw it, she laughed and thought it was funny. It's probably the most over-the-top picture we ever made. But we were struggling to get a foothold in the market and the version that got released was really a rough cut. But that film did well for the distributor. It was all over the United States; it was everywhere.

Splatter Farm was drastically recut for its DVD release. Why did you want to recut it?

Well that was really an assembly cut released on video, where we took everything we shot and put it together. So we sent that out to distributors to see if there was any interest. The idea was if there was interest, we could cut it down to what we wanted. And we cut that with equipment that wasn't as technically advanced as what we cut *Hallucinations* on. We had issues with sound and things like that. But the company just wanted to release it the way it was. And they did. We should have said *"no"* and recut it but we were young and naive. But I look at the original cut now and it almost reminds me of that *Blair Witch* reality, like you're living it. It's crudeness works for it.

Do you think the original version would ever be released again?

Probably not. Professionally, I would not want to do that again. The version released on DVD is what I would call the definitive version. [A limited VHS edition of the original cut has since been released by Camp Motion Pictures]

Splatter Farm was your first big distribution deal. Did it pay off financially?

Here's a funny story. The distributor also sold *Cannibal Campout* and that really put them on the map. I don't think *Splatter Farm* did as well as *Cannibal Campout*, but it did very well. We got a $420 check that bounced. I still have the check in a folder somewhere. It's funny now but it wasn't at the time. The distributor had one more release after ours and then they closed their doors. I think it was because people were trying to sue them.

Was *Hellspawn* the immediate follow-up?

So after *Splatter Farm* there was *Saurians* (on film), then *Lethal Nightmare* (on film) then *Hellspawn*. *Hellspawn* would have been made in 1992, maybe 1991. One day I'm going to have to sit down and figure out the timeline.

Why were *Saurians* and *Lethal Nightmare* shot on film?

Well ultimately with *Saurians*, I was going to be using stop-motion animation. And there was no way I could edit frames on video. So I used film and went back and edited and added stuff to it. But the VHS release was the final edit. And I ended up using more puppets than stop-motion so I should have just shot it on video.

Was *Hellspawn* co-directed by both you and John?

Yes. Now the version you saw was probably on that DVD 4 pack? Well the movie's really not that bad. I don't particularly like it because we had a lot of problems shooting it. The two actors we had had complicated schedules and they didn't always give their best. It was frustrating. And the monster itself was a big letdown. But it has some neat scenes (like the end when they're fighting in the water). There's some production value but the sound is bad. I don't know what happened when they transferred that movie but there's a buzz in almost all of it. I don't ever recall that sound on any of the master. I wish they came to us first if there was an issue (I probably could have filtered some of that out) but they didn't care. They just put it out and it hurts the movie. *Hellspawn* was a struggle to make for a lot of reasons. We we're using a better camera, we shot on a huge SVHS camera that was cumbersome and the batteries always gave us issues. So it's a step up in equipment but with that came a learning process. I haven't watched the movie in a long, long time. Maybe I'd like it if I did, but it's probably (of all the movies I've made) one of my least favorites. I don't think it's any better than *Church of the Damned* really. My brother wrote it and it was based on the Jersey Devil. We had that mask and I think we rushed some of it. I think it could be much better. It's a pretty expansive movie, there's a lot going on but we didn't handle certain aspects of it properly - and one of those is the creature. We really should have done something different. But when you make a movie, you never see it the same way as other people do. Later we used footage of *Hellspawn* in *Bad Magic* out of necessity, and the mask in *Terror House* too. It was such a giant yard sale. But *Hellspawn* does have a couple cool scenes. There was supposed to be a big bar scene (that got truncated) and I think it has some decent lighting in it.

You can almost sense John's influence or your influence in certain films. As if John sided with demonic horror while you enjoyed lighthearted dinosaurs.

I think you're correct. Even though we were twins and shared a lot, we did have different ideas when it came to movies. There were certain times where he would go for the gut and I would probably hold back. But then when you get older and have kids, you get more mature and your ideals change. Part of making movies is putting yourself into movies. Part of who you are spills into the movies you make.

How did *Hellspawn* ultimately find distribution?

It was sold in a package with a couple of other movies we made. But by that time, the market had changed and it was harder to get shot on video stuff out there. So a lot of these productions just sat on the shelf. But instead of giving up, we'd say *"let's do another one"* knowing that one day there'd be some kind of a market or pipeline. And some of our stuff got released because that pipeline was multi-packs. But even as a kid shooting

Church of the Damned, I always knew to keep making them because some day there would be an avenue to sell them. And I was right. In high school, I would just write movie title after movie title and say *"we should make every single one of these!"* We should have done that, just cranked them out. But that's how I felt. So what if no one likes *Hellspawn*, let's just make another one.

And then you tried comedy with *How To Slay a Vampire*.

When we were in 11th or 12th grade, we had a class called Supernatural Literature. And our teacher said we had to read a book and write a paper, so we asked instead *"can we just shoot a half hour movie about a vampire?"* Well she agreed so we basically shot a 30 minute version of (what would become) *How To Slay a Vampire*. We showed it for our final project and it was a hit! People laughed and laughed and we got an A. So after *Hellspawn*, we thought to make a feature version of *How To Slay a Vampire*. We knew we could do comedy. And there was some really funny stuff that never made it in, but it was funny. We made fun of ourselves and other things. And it's something you can just watch and have a chuckle at and have a good time. The ending was totally improvised because the movie was running short (we were editing it as we were shooting so we knew) and that's why there's this big boxing match and why we recap what happens to all the characters.

Was a lot of *How To Slay a Vampire* improvised?

Not as much as you'd think. The whole beginning is what the short was based on; the entire beginning before the vampire leaves and they're tracking him down like Van Helsing. A lot of it was written and we might have improvised a little on the set. But when you're shooting a movie like that, you can't improvise too much because then things just don't work. But maybe there was some. I think John and I were pretty funny together and the vampire had his own little scenes, which were funny. So I'm very fond of that movie. We sent a couple copies to Tempe Video who passed, probably because it was better than the shit they make (joke). But you know, it sat around until a deal came through. It wasn't a waste because I knew this stuff would get out, but you make three or four movies and they don't get released? It does get frustrating and depressing. Our first real movie got released right away (*Splatter Farm*) but then you struggle for the next couple.

I love how *How To Slay a Vampire* breaks the fourth wall and literally goes into the video store.

Breaking the fourth wall was intentional. And video stores were big! We thought *"why not exploit that!"* Yeah, that movie's a lot of fun. You see John and I as actors but really we are not acting, we're just being ourselves. That's really us in a lot of ways.

And soon after came possibly your biggest hit - *Feeders!*

Feeders was our real big hit. We shot that and did a rough assembly which was really bad, but even that was eventually released. We met Jon McBride through our distributor dealings with *Splatter Farm* and we got together and clicked right away. We thought we'd do a movie which we shot and then re-edited later, and that's the version Blockbuster picked up. And it was a huge hit! We sold 7500 copies of that movie ourselves. We didn't go through a distributor, we did that ourselves. But it came out at the right time. *Independence Day* had come out and Blockbuster wanted alien movies. We just happened to be at the right place, at the right time. Years later, I talked to someone at Blockbuster at a high level and THEY knew *Feeders*. That movie did great! The president of Blockbuster took it on vacation with him and watched it. He was the one who decided if it was going to be in the store or not. And apparently, he liked it. They ordered 4500 copies! 6 months later, they ordered 3000 more! It was their biggest independent rental of 1996. That means it out-rented Charles Band's movies, Roger Corman's movies; all that stuff that must have cost a fortune.

Did you get a financial boost?

Yeah we did okay with that because we controlled it. We still had to deal with a sub-distributor and they took their cut, but we still did alright. For a movie that cost $500, we did okay. Is it cheap? Yes. Is it tacky? Yes. But if that movie was black and white and released in 1950, it's no worse than some of the other stuff that came out. And that's what its intent was, to be a 1950's homage to those kinds of movies. The thing that hurts it technically is that we used a couple different cameras. And you can tell in the quality. But *Feeders* is probably the turning point in our career. It was a hit! For a movie that cost that much and did as well as it did, it was a huge success. And we needed it at that time because things are looking pretty grim when you make five movies that don't go anywhere. It was supposed to be a lot more extravagant than it was, but it didn't turn out that way. We were shocked when we got the aliens, they weren't what we really wanted but we were stuck with them. We ended up redoing all the spaceships digitally. We may even be the first shot on video movie that used digital effects to the extent we did, I'm not sure. But I think we were at the forefront of digital effects in SOV movies. And I love the title sequence. When Jon McBride, John and myself sat down to watch *Feeders*, we loved it! You know, in a way it's so bad it's good.

Your wife insisted on the recuts?

Yeah, she saw the original cut and she just had this intuition. She said *"you should really re-edit this movie because it has something all your other films don't."* She thought it would be a lot better if we added to it and fixed things, maybe had some better effects. And she was right! So in 1994-1995, we picked it back up and spent time shooting new stuff, getting new effects cutting from the original footage. All from the beginning. Then we had the box work done and I love *"Earth was just an appetizer."* That's just a great tagline. So she kind of encouraged us to continue on it, like I had done with *Saurians*. She really deserves the credit in that respect. If we had left it the way it was, it would have ended up on a 10 pack. But it was the timing and the fact that people got it. It made Blockbuster a crap load of money.

Did many offers come after *Feeders?*

Oddly enough, no. We were encouraged to keep going and *Terror House* came next. And we almost got that into Blockbuster too, but they didn't like our artwork for the box so they didn't take it. But I think *Feeders* was the catalyst that kept us going. Sometimes you just need that extra jolt at the right time. And it did that. We went right into *Terror House*, based on a script we wrote in 1980 about people trapped in a house fighting a creature. Jon McBride was moving from where he lived to another place and he had this house all to himself for a week. So we thought we'd shoot something while we had access to this huge house. And that's how *Terror House* came about. Close for Blockbuster but for whatever reason, they didn't want it. But I like *Terror House*. I think it has a lot going for it.

How did your *Channel 13* anthology come about?

That's a great question. At some point, we decided to do an anthology because we had started some projects and not finished them. So we thought of this segment where some guy watches TV (to put the shorts in). We never got to shoot the wraparound but I remembered it well enough to put it together. So years later, I was looking for stuff in my house and there was this brown paper bag that had tapes in it. So I pick it up and it says *Channel 13* on it. And I'm thinking *"what is that?"* So I popped it in and started looking at it and remembered it was something we started but never finished. My favorite part is the scene where I get killed in the basement, in the "Halloween Night" segment. I think it was an excellent scene and it shows what we were capable of doing with nothing. It's well lit, it's well paced, it's well shot and with a tracking shot, it has great effects. It's just a really good example of no budget filmmaking, I think.

Another interesting connection is Bob Dennis and his film *Savage Vows*. How did you end up starring in the movie?

I got hired to shoot a gangster movie by some guy who never finished it. *3000 Bullets* and it was a really good movie; he just gave up on it. But Bob Dennis had this horror video store and the guy making this movie said *"hey you gotta check this place out!"* So we went there one day before we filmed and I didn't know Bob, but he was there. So we were walking around going *"oh look, there's our movie"* and Bob was following us around and he finally says *"you really worked on this movie?"* And then we told him what we did and he ended up in this guy's movie, but Bob and I became good friends. And Bob asked me if he made a movie, would I help and I said *"sure!"* And that's how *Savage Vows* came about. I acted in it but I also did all the editing and videography and helped him get through it. But Bob deserves the credit for that film. I just kind of held his hand through the process. We just clicked, like with Jon McBride. We became fast friends, had a lot of common interests.

You've become such an inspiration for filmmakers all over the world. And you always seem willing to help and support others too. What advise would you give to filmmakers just starting out today?

Thank you! I really appreciate that. To inspire someone from what you do, I mean what more could you want from a career? If someone says *"your hard work inspires me"* or *"that movie's so bad, we could do better,"* they're both the same thing. You're still inspiring somebody. And there's no real problems, there's only solutions. That's how you have to tackle it because the minute it's a problem, it's slowing you down. You have to overcome. We've certainly done that in so many ways; professionally, personally, financially. It takes a lot of work and effort to make movies, especially if you work a full-time job or raise kids. It's a lot of work but it's a lot of fun. Looking back, I wouldn't change a thing. It's well known that seeing *Godzilla VS The Thing* when I was 5 inspired me to get interested in filmmaking. And it's all I've ever wanted to do. We made it work, sometimes in spite of ourselves. And I hope this book will inspire people to say *"hey we can do this"* and go buy a $300 camera from Walmart that's going to look a million times better than the camera we shot *Splatter Farm* with. And they can make a movie and they can sell it themselves! You don't need distributors anymore. With a Vimeo page, you can control the cards now. For me, the concept of an idea that you can put on paper that transcends to actors that gets assembled with effects and putting music in it, that whole process still fascinates me to this very day. And that's why I keep doing it. It's not something I want to do, it's something I have to do.

Thank you so much for your time and thoughts, Mark!

AN EMMERITUS PRODUCTION

Chapter 7
EMMERITUS PRODUCTIONS

Pronounced *Emmer-ritus*, Emmeritus Productions was a Hamilton-based Canadian company specializing in feature-length movies-of-the-week throughout the 1980's. The majority of their films were shot on video and contained strong emphasis on genre storytelling. And not all were horror. There were murder mysteries, crime thrillers, horror slashers, action adventures, even fantasy features presented on television for a home viewing audience (interrupted only by commercials). Yet the bulk of their catalogue also found its way to video. Distributed on videocassette, these films enjoyed immortality as they rented and played beyond their intended timeslots. Today, they are some of SOVs most likeable lost entries; never reaching DVD or digital release.

Spearheaded by producer Lionel Shenken, Emmeritus was Shenken's attempt to take hold of the burgeoning video market and produce films he believed in. Armed with relatively basic equipment and voiced interest from filmmakers eager to make their mark, Shenken pitched his idea for cheaply produced video productions to his bosses at television station CHCH-TV. They accepted.

Some 33 titles were reportedly produced by Emmeritus (occasionally known as Visual Productions Ltd), all of which pre-sold to foreign markets before inaugural airings on CHCH and rebroadcast on the USA Network. Production costs were typically $30,000 above the line (costs specific to the movie including screenwriters, actors and director) and shot with theatre talent on non-union crews. No more than 25 days would be dedicated to a single film's production and scenes of action were required in every 6 minutes of screen time. These were the golden rules of Emmeritus, ensuring that films played steadily and could adhere to television's interruptive format. Emmeritus became a vehicle to many up and coming filmmakers wanting to make their mark throughout the 80's, producing scripts into finished features within a matter of months. But the quality of films were generally considered amateurish, likely due to their television-level violence and newcomer screen talent. Still, Shenken would successfully cultivate several noteworthy entries in SOV horror that still cheerfully entertain to this day.

But Emmeritus ended as the decade wore out. Shenken produced in the 1990's but without the Emmeritus brand or video format (which eventually seemed professionally unfashionable). Yet his films lived on as distribution carried them back into the homes of unsuspecting viewers. And like so many before him, Lionel Shenken proved that he was a visionary of video proportions; delivering shot on video movies throughout the 80's directly to a television audience.

Welcome to prime time, eh!

BODY COUNT
1986, Color, 96 min
STARRING: *Jonathan Potts, James Knapp, James Lukie*
DIRECTOR: *Lionel Shenken*

A homicidal maniac is shooting innocent people with his magnum 35. The police can't catch a break until they learn a specific red taxi had been spotted at each of the crime scenes. Soon the driver is pinned for the crime, but is he the real killer?

 *Body Count* (which is lively sung in an opening theme song) is an interesting offering from the Canadian Emmeritus company. The film essentially has two leads: the killer and the red herring. Both men are portrayed sensitively with depth to their characters. And additionally, both men progress into failed romances with question-able women. Are they each doomed? The performances are good, particularly from Potts as he scrambles for money, gleefully beds random women (his girlfriend doesn't mind) and attempts to avoid an overtly feminine bookie wanting to bust him up. But however you press it, *Body Count* has style. It lacks blood (this is television after all) but makes up for it with an overwhelming sense of fun. Great entertainment for a rainy afternoon and directed by Lionel Shenken himself!

THE BOUNTY HUNTERS
1985, Color, 60 min
STARRING: *Robin Atha, Jon Austin, Ian McPhail*
DIRECTOR: *Bruno Pischiutta*

A team of Vietnam vets are hired to kidnap an American fugitive now living in Toronto, Canada. The fugitive (a photographer hosting Satanic parties) is accused of killing three women with a meat cleaver. Once kidnapped and smuggled back to the US, the vets will collect a large sum of money.

 Also known as *Revenge of the Mercenaries* and containing a surprising amount of nudity, *The Bounty Hunters* is one of the few Emmeritus endeavors reaching beyond its television roots. Production standards are present (cameras locked down, sequences tight with television charm) but the Emmeritus logo is missing and the runtime is short. Nevertheless, this is everything you'd expect from a television production - plus breasts and a great scene of two guys phone-chatting in bed surrounded by naked ladies (each sounding like they're on the verge of orgasm). Don't they know never to call before 10am?!? Storylines remain unanswered thanks to the short runtime but the kidnapping is impressively tense. Will the fugitive get away? Will they cross the border? Who hired the kidnappers? No answers, except to say everyone makes it back to the US comfortably. But whatever happened to the fugitive's assistant who needed a gun to protect from her ex-pimp? And what's to become of all the girls who were nearly killed at the Satanic photo shoot? Oh well. A hasty television interview with a David Letterman-looking fellow pops in, saying the fugitive's been arrested and the film ends. Fade to black with no credits! Fun while it lasts.

DEADLY PURSUIT
1984, Color, 95 min
STARRING: *Doug Stone, Russell Ferrier, Laura Centeno, Craig Williams*
DIRECTOR: *Joseph A. Gaudet*

An ambush during the Vietnam war goes horribly wrong, resulting in American troops battling themselves. Years later as the survivors return home, one soldier's grudge propels him into revenge and murder. A planned getaway to a paintball game results in vengeance as the soldier tracks and kills the remaining troops.

Also known as *Commando Games* and featuring several actors who would appear in multiple Emmeritus productions, *Deadly Pursuit* is a thrilling revenge flick using the same model as most slashers. Seemingly influenced by *The Burning*, the film opens with a fiery ambush gone wrong and a scarred victim wanting justice. Obsessed with killing those who wronged him, *Deadly Pursuit* showcases its killer stalking victims in scenes eerily reminiscent of *Halloween*. The soundtrack goes one further with low-pitched beats as POV (point of view) shots ride in the killer's car. And we get the requisite sequence where all victims are warned about (and laugh off) the mysterious deaths of others. The commando-like paintball game is fun to watch and a wonderful setup for vengeance. Only the climax is hindered when violence and war descriptions are punctuated, yet feel restrained for television broadcast. But what remains is impresses enough. Highly recommended to slasher fans and featuring electric turns by Ferrier and Stone.

Doug Stone (above) in Deadly Pursuit (1984)

MARK OF THE BEAST
1986, Color, 96 min
STARRING: *James Gordon, David Smukler, Carolyn Guillet, Charlene Richards*
DIRECTOR: *Robert Stewart*

Two young students inadvertently record the assassination of a political figure while video-taping an unpublicized speech. The assassin, who's actually working for a Satanic cult with political aspirations, is then tasked with killing the boys and destroying the evidence.

Though motivated by goals of world domination (and even the resurrection of Satan), *Mark of the Beast's* Satanic cult feels more like an afterthought. This film's heart lies in political assassination and run-for-your-life chases best suited for criminal dramas. Its focus is away from horror but still enjoyable thanks to Emmeritus' panache for charming characters and plot twists. The two leads are charismatic with charming dreams of becoming great filmmakers (making this a special film for analog fans; the movie uses video within its video). Several scenes involve rewinding and fast-forwarding footage on editing decks and high-end cameras are featured fantastically with nostalgia. In addition, the dogged chase from the assassin at times resembles the quieter moments of *The Terminator* and even *The Godfather* (as bedridden Don Corleone is shuttled between hospital rooms). *Mark of the Beast* may not be great horror, but it's a nostalgic trip for fans.

 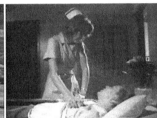  

NIAGARA STRIP
1987, Color, 96 min
STARRING: *Paul De La Rose, April Johnson, Ron Byrd, John Tench, Tracy Harvey*
DIRECTOR: *Jim Makichuk*

A man with his wife and kids smuggle drugs over the Canadian border. But the planned drop-off goes wrong when punks unexpectedly steal the drugs and kill the man. Now the police investigate.

A slow moving drawn-out bore, *Niagara Strip* is a pointless venture. The cast mopes as

Makichuk (returning from Emmeritus' excellent *The Tower*) falls asleep at the wheel. An action-less mess with apparently every character hiding a romantic past, *Niagara Strip* is a strong contender for the worst Emmeritus has to offer. Video is never used effectively, the setup isn't interesting, the proceeding is a waste and worst of all... it's boring. Horrific only in quality.

   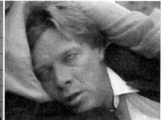

PRICE OF VENGEANCE
1985, Color, 97 min
STARRING: *Edmund James, David Sisak, Jim Walton, Ron Kashin, James Macri*
DIRECTOR: *Alastair Brown*

A businessman investigates when his younger brother is murdered. Turns out the brother was involved in an Asian snuff porn ring and a mafia takeover.

 Ah, the charms of Canadian television. More investigation than discovery, Emmeritus' *Price of Vengeance* is a zippy drama verging on future *8mm* territory. James is good as the grief stricken brother, while Walton supports as the friendly pimp (seriously, he's a pimp). Together they act like a *Lethal Weapon* pair when really they'd rather just play hockey. We learn James was "sort of raised" by a mafia family in his youth, but the Don shrugs off revenge because *"hey, this is 20th century Canada"* (whatever that means). But overall, the film's a good time waster. It never stretches beyond its premise and delivers a satisfying conclusion towards the end. Plus a couple guys get beat up, shot, and one dude is garroted for kicks. Take off, eh!

SHOCK CHAMBER

1985, Color, 94 min
STARRING: *Doug Stone, Russell Ferrier, Jacqueline Samuda, Karen Cannata, Bill Zagot*
DIRECTOR: *Steve DiMarco*

A horror anthology. A reporter interviews a widowed mother at her son's funeral. Told in flashback, the mother relates the doomed outcomes of her three surviving boys. Up first is "Symbol of Victory," in which a millionaire's love-struck son buys homemade love potions to drug the girl he wants to marry. Then in "Country Hospitality," a ransom extorter is killed by four country bumpkins hoping to steal the money for themselves. Finally with "The Injection," two brothers orchestrate a scheme where one fakes death while the other fraudulently collects life insurance. All stories end with a twist and failed outcomes.

Though more horrific in tone than anything shown, *Shock Chamber* is a pleasing television anthology that I steadily enjoy revisiting. Also known as *Greedy Terror*, the film plays it straight offering lean stories with easy to follow characters. Stone drives the three tales, giving each brother subtle differences that ultimately end in doom. But this is horror for the timid; quaint, pleasing and comfortable. *Shock Chamber* makes for an excellent introduction to Emmeritus, and easily recommended based on charm alone. But you're not likely to get nightmares here.

SURVIVAL EARTH

1985, Color, 80 min
STARRING: *Jeff Holec, Nancy Cser, Craig Williams*
DIRECTOR: *Peter McCubbin*

In post apocalyptic Canada made of ruins and wilderness, a scholar and his "mutant" girl-friend fend off attacks from vagrants. They eventually become friendly with a soldier who joins their tribe.

Also confusingly known as *Survival 1990* (though a character openly states this is 1996), *Survival Earth* is a lightweight entry in Emmeritus' television programming. A pre-credit sequence showcases newsreel footage before "the big one," and we're told that mass world bankruptcy and looting led to the explosion. Physically unharmed survivors now roam the countryside while equally normal "mutants" scavenge beside them ("mutants" because they wear rags). No one finds a moose. The film focuses on one man and one "mutant" woman, who has no memory prior to 1986. A solitary soldier eventually enters their lives, bonding with the pair and then the film becomes a tale of trust and friendship. Horror you say? Not really, but horrific elements are peppered throughout. "Mutants" are generally portrayed as frantic crazies, most of which are shot to death at first sight. And the center of the film revolves around a subplot of cloning! The late-coming revelation being that a clone is stalking one of the main characters, wanting to kill and takeover his identity. But it's totally shoehorned in and doesn't go anywhere! Still, the film is quaint and mildly entertaining... and I'm pretty sure they eat the family dog too.

THE TOWER

1985, Color, 103 min
STARRING: *Ray Paisley, Jennifer Cornish, George West, Paul Miklas, Zuzana Struss*
DIRECTOR: *Jim Makichuk*

A high-rise tower's state-of-the-art computer becomes self aware. It takes over the entire building, trapping late-night workers inside and killing them one by one (fatally zapping for their heat energy). The race to escape begins!

One of Emmeritus' best. Though made for television, *The Tower* is a suspenseful nail-biter with a surprising amount of violence and skin (stopping just shy of nudity). But like all Emmeritus productions, it's the dialogue that make it shine. A good mix of characters are gathered here, including a young security guard, his sexy girlfriend, a crook, the boss' wife and more. Together, they keep action flowing and the script plays things smart. Enjoyably, the film doesn't focus on the computer's newly developed sentience, but rather treats it as a monster-of-the-week villain. *"You're killing people! We have to stop you!"* But the cuts are tight, the action well paced and the tension moderately high. This is a solid made-for-TV film written and directed by *Ghostkeeper's* Makichuk (whose only mandatory stipulation was that he had to showcase a girl in a bikini). Highly Recommended!

Interview
DOUG STONE

Emmeritus' leading man Doug Stone is a familiar face to SOV horror fans, but you may know his voice even better. Born in Toronto, Doug parlayed his onscreen work into an incredibly successful voice acting career in Los Angeles. Known today as the voices of Matt Trakker, Bruce Sato and Hondo MacLean from the 80's animated series *"MASK,"* as Psycho Mantis from *Metal Gear Solid* video games as well as countless other characters, Doug's talents reach far beyond his onscreen television origins. In the early 1980's, Doug starred in *Shock Chamber*, *Deadly Pursuit* and *A Death In Hollywood* for Emmeritus Productions.

Doug, thank you for giving your time to this interview! What initially lead you into becoming an actor?

Sure thing! Well I had done some acting as a kid. When I was little, I was doing school plays and writing comedic material in public school. So I got the bug and was interested but at that time, there was really no venue for children in Toronto. So I would do camp plays and amateur theatre. Then I got caught up in the hippie era and was very involved in that world. Writing poetry and getting published a bit. And then I abandoned the hippie world when I got married in my 20's. But the bug was still in me so I began to do amateur theatre again. At the same time, I was working for IBM and they were doing scratch tracks for commercials. You know, they'd bring in someone (before the main star) to read the commercial in the same vein as the actor would, and they'd time it out. So I auditioned and I'm doing it for fun but after a while, they started paying me. And the fellow in charge eventually said *"you know, you're good enough to do commercials."* So I created my own voice demo, which was very amateurish because I didn't know what I was doing. But I sent it out to advertising agencies and I caught on with a studio that was doing commercials for malls. And I became the guy doing all the voice work for malls just outside of Toronto. It was like a dream come true!

How was it pronounced: Emmer-itus or Emmer-*ritus?*

I think it was Emmer-*ritus*. It's been so long, but that sounds more familiar. Visual Productions. A couple of different names it was going under.

How did you become involved with Emmeritus?

I was doing theatre and I was trying to get on-camera work, which was very difficult to come by in Toronto. I had not come up through all those legitimate acting schools and places like the CBC were very snobbish. It was very difficult to get auditions with them. So you'd look for independent productions in the trades. And I saw this ad that said *"half-hour independent film being shot, looking for actors."* So I auditioned and met the gentleman there named Steve DiMarco. He was funding and doing this film himself called "Transplant." So I got it and did the film and "Transplant" became Steve's entre into directing. "Transplant" was about this criminal (me) wanting to transplant his brain into another body. So he approached Emmeritus with that half-hour and said he was looking for directing work. And they said it was interesting and then he had this thing called *Shock Chamber*. If I remember correctly, he had conceived the idea of doing half-hour anthologies. So he had three disconnected stories which he made into one, and made it about three brothers. And coming right off of "Transplant," Steve approached me about playing the three brothers in the project. So I said *"absolutely!"* The chance to find different ways of walking, different ways of carrying my body. You know, doing that in the same film is very challenging. So we reviewed the scripts together and hence *Shock Chamber* was underway.

So *Shock Chamber* was the first?

That one was the first. Emmeritus liked my work enough, they gave me a chance to audition for other roles and I did two more films for them. The first was *Shock Chamber* and the second was *Deadly Pursuit*. The third was *A Death In Hollywood*, which I felt was too talky. The fellow who directed that was a theatre director and I think it was his first or second time directing to video. But that piece just felt too theatrical, like it belonged on-stage.

Any lasting memories about *Shock Chamber*?

In "Country Hospitality," I had a scene where I arrive in a small town and I'm flirting with this waitress. Being a chauvinistic idiot, really. And during that entire scene, I had to eat pecan pie. I still can't to this day look at pecan pie without feeling nauseous. We shot over and over and over again and I had to really eat this pie. And we ran out of pie! Steve had to send out for more pie, so I must have eaten 3 or 4 pies all by myself. So I remember how nauseous I was feeling because we only had that location for the day. And that was all we shot that day, all the different angles. And at the end of the scene, the waitress has poisoned me. So I recall I grasp at her, tear a part of her blouse, and fall backwards dead. So Steve says *"we gotta get close-ups of you hitting the floor dead."* So I do it. I take a real deep breath and lay as still as I can for close-ups. And I'm lying there. And I'm still lying there. And I'm wondering what is taking so long. And finally, I just can't take it any longer so I burst open for air and look around. Steve and the whole crew are standing over me and they're not shooting at all. All the actors and crew are just standing over me laughing. Waiting to see how long I was going to hold my breath. So in that scene where I'm lying on the floor for 3 seconds, I think about how Steve tricked me and how I actually laid there for like a minute and a half. Later, they all go to bury my body and I had to lay there while they actually threw dirt on me. And Steve says *"I gotta do this!"* So they showed the other actors with the shovels, but when you actually see me lying in the dirt getting dirt thrown on my face, that's Steve. Perversely laughing and enjoying himself while burying me alive. I haven't thought about that in years.

And then came *Deadly Pursuit*.

Now when I did *Deadly Pursuit*, I was playing a straight lead. I was the hero. And that was probably the most difficult acting gig I had ever done. After that, I had great admiration for guys like Tom Hanks. Guys who could play a straight lead, play them romantic and keep them interesting. He's not funny. He's not dangerous. He's just a guy you're going to like. Wow, that's tough to play and I found that challenging to do. There's nothing to hang it on. I mean, can't I have a gun?

***Deadly Pursuit* has some great action. How did that go?**

I got injured on *Deadly Pursuit*. In the very last scene of the film (which spoiled my close-up). Russ Ferrier was a guy I had done stage with and I got Russ involved with Emmeritus when I was helping with casting. Russ played the antagonist in *Deadly Pursuit*. So Russ and I were working on the final fight scene with no fight coordinators because they couldn't afford it. But Russ had studied boxing a bit and I had done a little martial arts. So we worked out something we thought worked pretty well. But in the very last moment, he's lying on his stomach, the gun's in front of him and I slide up his body to reach for the gun.

Well whether Russ was being perverse or mean or just forgot, as I slid up his body he raised his head. And my nose cracked into the back of his skull. And I was going full force to get the gun, to make it look real. So my nose immediately began to swell and we were putting ice on it, but I had a close-up with Laura Centeno (playing my wife). I'm supposed to embrace her and say it's all ok. But my nose was 3 sizes too big. So I didn't get the close-up, only Laura did. And that's a good memory for me too because towards the end, Laura and I began to date. We ended up seeing each other for about 3 years after that.

What was Emmeritus' audition strategy? They seemed to recast the same actors often.

Yeah. When Steve DiMarco started there, I helped him out with casting and got to know the Emmeritus people a little bit. It turned out that they did have a group of their own actors that they had been using, some of them repeatedly. And the actors I brought in for *Shock Chamber* (I was happy to see), they liked. So some of them became part of the group that did more Emmeritus films. So I think they did generally have a group that they looked to for the audition process. I don't know if they necessarily advertised. I think they had enough people in-house that they could generally call on.

Did you ever interact with Lionel Shenken?

The fellow who ran the place. Not on set, but I would see him quite often in the offices. He would come and speak to everybody. He was good about that, he would come when you had meetings with the directors or the writers. As an actor, he only interacted with me a little bit. I remember on *Shock Chamber*, he was very concerned about my character's moustache - was really worried it wasn't going to come across on camera. I had approached Steve and thought it could better differentiate one brother from the other if I had this silly little moustache. Help weaken his face a little bit and use a duck walk by spreading my feet apart a little bit. But I remember discussing that with Lionel and he wanted to see the moustache. I brought it out and showed him the glue and all that stuff. But I don't recall him ever being on set. He was very involved in the pre-production. You know, discussing the details with the directors. My impression was he'd pretty much let the directors do their thing, once he was satisfied with the pre-production details.

How were their shooting schedules?

It was pretty rushed. I never felt really pressured but I was new and wasn't used to the Hollywood style of shooting (where things are very slow). But it was a pretty fast and furious shoot. We'd go long days. It was not unusual to be shooting 12-hour days, as I recall. And as a lead actor in two of them (*Shock Chamber* and *Deadly Pursuit*), I was kept pretty busy. They were low budget and had to get them shot quick. Non-union but the crews were generally pretty good.

Did you ever think it strange you were making movies on video?

Well it was fairly new. The films that I shot may have been released in 1985 but they were shot between 1982-1984, as I recall. So it was exciting. Obviously I would have loved to be on film instead because it feels more legitimate. But it was exciting because we were shooting films low budget, giving us all a chance to get our footing in the industry and getting experience on camera. I just saw it as an opportunity. I knew it wasn't going to have that warm look that a film would have, but there's always new technology coming along. It was exciting to be at sort of the forefront of something new. This was before the government got involved and grant money became available in Canada. There was just so little on-camera work available at the time.

These movies were shot and made for television, but then they wound up on video store shelves. People still own and watch them today!

Yeah, that was amazing. I used to joke to Laura Centeno about that. She thought it was a silly concept that these films would be popular anywhere (outside of the original viewing). But to know that these things actually went out and are still being viewed is shocking. I can't speak for others, but I think our concept was that these were something almost like a play. That they would be shown, maybe rerun a few times and disappear within a year. We did not think they were going to be out there. But I've always thought that about all of my work. A cartoon series I did in 1985-1986 *"MASK: Mobile Armored Strike Command,"* has fan clubs around the world! I still sign autographs for it, can still go to conventions for it. So I guess I'm naive. I tend to think that the work that I do is just going to be seen and disappear. And I'm so surprised to hear that it's still popular and still entertaining people so many years later.

Beyond Emmeritus, have you done anything else in the horror genre?

No, I only did those ones in Canada. And I did very little on-camera down here (Los Angeles) before my career transitioned into strictly voice-over. Though I did one other horror thing down here but they didn't have the budget to finish it. And it was very reminiscent of the work I had done with Steve. I had a "loop group," a group of actors providing voices for television shows and films, and we had the *"Hercules"* and *"Xena"* series in the 1990's. And I met somebody through that who was doing sound effects for those shows. A huge horror buff. And he asked if I was interested in playing a mad professor in this half-hour thing he was going to shoot. So I did it and we had this giant bug which ends up killing me. This huge mosquito-like bug that skewers me. So there I am on the floor with blood pouring out, this huge nose of the mosquito going right through my chest, and it was a lot of fun! And that was shot on film, I believe. But that's the only other horror thing I've done on-camera.

What prompted you to move to Los Angeles?

Yeah, it was actually thanks to the on-camera work. When we were shooting *Shock Chamber*, the cinematographer took me aside and asked me who my agent was in Canada. And I was with a very small agent. Remember, there was a snobbishness at the time (if you didn't come up in all the right schools, it was difficult to get a good agent). But this cinematographer said I was a very good actor and that I should be with a bigger agent. And he recommended one to me. In the meantime, I'm shooting these Emmeritus films and on his word alone, this agency signs me. Almost sight unseen. So I started to audition for better on-camera work in Toronto. Coincidently, a French company was doing a co-production with an American company to produce a cartoon series in LA called *"MASK."* And they were going to cast only Canadians. And I had actually gotten into the union after the Emmeritus stuff. So I auditioned and they were interested in me for the lead and a couple other characters. And I was fortunate enough to be cast as the lead Matt Trakker, Bruce Sato and Hondo MacLean. But they were going to record in LA so I flew down. It grew into eventually eight characters on a 65 episode cartoon series on network television. So I thought I'll do this and then have something on my resume to go back to Toronto with. But while I was here, the director and studio owner took me and asked if I was planning on staying. And they were encouraging me to get an agent down here and getting involved in the voice-over industry. So after some back and forth, I decided to take that chance and relocate here. And I was fortunate enough again that in a couple of years, I was able to make a living and do fairly well.

Do you prefer voice-over to on-screen work?

Well, I've been away from on-screen for so long now. It's tough for me to make that comparison. I'm very comfortable in the voice-over world, particularly as I've aged. In my home office, I have a setup where I can do auditions. I can sit here in my shorts and sandals and do audio books from home. I ain't a young pup anymore! So for that aspect, the voice-over work has been wonderful. But I do miss stage work and being on-camera. I flirt with the idea of making the attempt, but to go back at this point in my life? When I first came to LA, my on-camera work in Canada meant nothing to them. My Canadian resume meant nothing to them down here, so I had to rebuild myself from the beginning. I'd go in and do monster voices for anime at 3:00am just to meet directors and casting people. Get a foothold; get established. It was like starting all over again. So the little bit of on-camera I had done didn't mean anything. But the closest I came before dropping out of on-camera all together, was for *"Seinfeld."* The role of Babu (*"You're a very bad man, Jerry Seinfeld"*). I can look like a lot of different ethnic groups and part of my specialty is doing accents. So I got down to the final two or three for that role but Brian George got it. And you don't mind losing roles to good actors, so that was fine. But that was the last real shot I had at swinging the bat on-camera. Voice work is acting, just not in front of the camera. People think that with cartoon work, it's all about funny voices. And you do need elasticity in your voice but it's an acting gig. You're an actor who can change your voice. You look at a picture they give you and say *"what would this guy sound like?"* And you have to decide, who is he? What's his core? It's just like you would for an on-camera role. What does he want? Where is he going? You're looking for hooks and the voice develops from that.

A Tim Boggs connection?

Well Tim was the ADR supervisor on *"Hercules"* and *"Xena."* I met him in the 90's and I knew he had done some directing. But he never showed it to me and we didn't discuss it a great deal. Our connection was all about the voice work. But I used to see him socially too. He was the ADR supervisor but we got along really well. Very nice guy. I was married at the time and we would go out, he and his wife. I've been to his home, met their children, go out for dinner a bit. So we hung out quite a bit during the mid 90's. And I won a few awards with Tim. We won some Golden Reel awards, sound awards which included for voice casting and mixing on *"Hercules"* and *"Xena."*

After so many roles, which ones stand out as favorites?

Wow. You know, I happened to be in LA towards the beginning of the anime world and towards the beginning of the video world. So I did an on-camera thing for something called *Zombie Dinos From Planet Zeltoid* (a video game). And I was covered in prosthetics as a monster of sorts. There's little clips of it on YouTube. I'm up in the corner of the screen, screaming out these versus in a British accent. So it's those little oddities that I remember because they were strange. There was a cartoon called *"Gigantor,"* one of the first Japanese cartoons that was ever dubbed to English. Made in the early 1960's. And it had a character they called Dr. Bob Brilliant. So flash forward many years later and they decide to do *"The New Adventures of Gigantor,"* and I ended up doing the voice of Dr. Bob Brilliant. So I got a kick out of that because it attached me to something very early in the history of cartoons and anime. It was meaningful to me. *"MASK"* is another one of course, because *"MASK"* established me here in the US. Psycho Mantis from *Metal Gear Solid* because for a lot of gamers, the character has become rather iconic. The early on-camera work and doing the *Shock Chamber* stuff, doing the "Transplant" piece. This helped my career get off and helped it get its footing. They were fun. And the *"Hercules"* and *"Xena,"* there were so many. And Jackie Chan pictures! When I formed my own company down here, I had been doing dubbing directing on a lot of anime and foreign films. One of my first clients was

Golden Harvest Pictures and they sent me the early Jackie Chan pictures which (at that point) nobody had known Jackie Chan in America. And these were the first films of Jackie Chan's that were dubbed into English. And that was a lot of fun because I would play the outtakes for the actors and say *"this stuff's great!"* We were all suddenly Jackie Chan fans. And voice matching for Joe Pesci! You know, quite often actors can't come in or don't do their own voice work. Joe Pesci hates doing voice work. So sometimes in films, they have to redub the actor from some sound issue or they want to change a line for television. So I'd come in and do Joe Pesci a couple times here and there [Doug breaks into a pitch-perfect Joe Pesci]. *"You know, for the television shows. Can I fucking swear here? How can I do Joe Pesci and not fucking swear? Just let me do Joe fucking Pesci."* So voice matching people. I recently was voice matching Sean Penn. It's so exciting and so many fun things you get to do. It's amazing the variety of things that voice acting can lead to. So when you look at my online stuff on IMDB or Wikipedia, you're not seeing half the credits. So much of it goes uncredited. We're meant to be invisible.

Are there any roles you'd like to do, but haven't yet had the chance?

Oh gosh, I haven't thought about that. The only thing I'm flirting with these days is doing some screenwriting. Like everybody in the world, I have 4 or 5 screenplay ideas that I haven't sat to put down yet. I think my dreams now are more in that regard, instead of returning to on-camera. If I can kick my lazy butt and actually write some of these screenplays. See if I can get some interest to be produced.

To the fans of your Emmeritus work...

I'd be happy to sign copies of *Shock Chamber*, but I'm sure my jaw would drop! Just as I was surprised about this interview, I couldn't believe that the topic was Emmeritus. Voice-over work is what I get asked about. I'd probably ask fans how they knew about it, where they saw it, did they watch it in its original format. And of course, happily sign it for them! That they might remember something from 35 or so years ago? And that it meant something to them after all these years? I'd be shocked. My own personal *Shock Chamber*. But it would be an incredible thing. If people can enjoy something I did 35 years ago? I mean, that's a lifetime! That gives me great satisfaction and pleasure. To think that I contributed something that has been meaningful to someone. That's just so wonderful. And I hope Steve DiMarco gets to read this because these were his beginnings too.

Thank you so much for your time and thoughts, Doug!

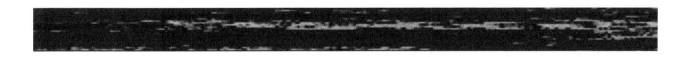

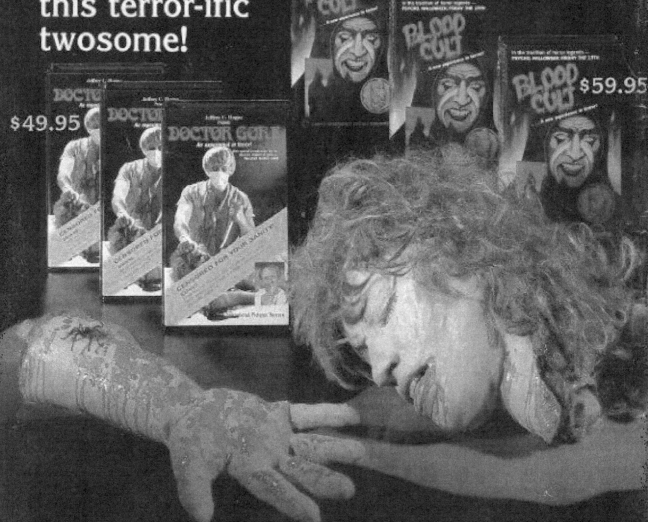

Chapter 8
THE EXPLOSION (1986)

With the format everywhere and *Blood Cult* leading the charge, more producers embraced video than ever before.

Blood Cult's advertising proved that content specifically fashioned for the video market could be successful. But its use of video also provided viewers with an easy to follow template that actually seemed obtainable. *Blood Cult* engaged. It showed "this is how you make a movie on video" and indeed, it inspired. It was a gory slasher without recognizable stars, shot on video for video release. It may have been made by industry professionals, but the line between professional and amateur was now crossed. With video, anyone could make a movie and many saw *Blood Cult* as the new standard. Paired with *The Ripper*, United's mega releases influenced several independents to pick up camcorders and start making movies. And no better example can be seen than in the Polonia brothers' earliest work: *Church of the Damned*.

Filmed in late 1985 (but shelved until 2013), teenaged twins Mark and John Polonia embarked on their first feature film while still in high school. Together with friend Todd (and after experimenting with shorts), the boys took what they could from *Blood Cult* and re-imagined it through innocent eyes. But *Church of the Damned* wasn't a one-off. Mark, John and Todd continued honing their skills with *Hallucinations* (a nightmare of paranoia and ghostly interventions) and the trio continued their home-grown productions into the 90's and beyond.

And independents weren't the only ones inspired.

Freelance Fangoria reporter Donald Farmer launched his own analog sizzler *Demon Queen* after learning distributors were so hungry, they would buy anything. And 1960's softcore skin director Nick Millard embarked on his first (of what would be many) video escapades with *Gunblast*. More celluloid-experienced filmmakers returned with video too, including Jeff Hathcock with *Night Ripper!* and Renee Harmon in *Escape From the Insane Asylum*. Nigeria's Charles Abi Enonchong crafted the zany *Witch Doctor of the Living Dead* and the legendary Donald Pleasance himself appeared in the coyly produced slasher *Into the Darkness*. Even Michigan's famed Black River Farm got into the mix, hosting and producing *Black River Monster* to help boost summertime popularity. Emmeritus was steadily pumping out movies-of-the-week, and video was used to help boost horror awareness.

Video in 1986 seemed to know no bounds, and titles became more varied than ever before.

Yet the most striking observation is the ratio between independents to professionals. This was still a time when experienced filmmakers dominated. Aside from *Hallucinations*, the majority of video ventures were embarked upon by companies and filmmakers looking to make money. Films were marketable products. Some were wonderfully inept, but many stayed close to genre and maintained expectations. A killer (or force) randomly kills until they are stopped - a simple premise easy to duplicate without major expense. And sometimes the best way to ensure profits is to do what works.

But the constant marketing of camcorders to the public was taking hold. Cameras were being used at home, at local events and for important family functions. And it was only a matter of time before movies would be made with them too.

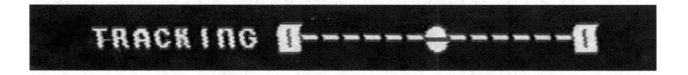

BLACK RIVER MONSTER
1986, Color, 49 min
STARRING: *Craig Martin, Bruce Phillips, James Larsen*
DIRECTOR: *John Duncan*

A heavy-set man starts a summer job at an "all-girls" ranch and campground. Trouble is, the grounds are being hunted by the legendary Bigfoot! But that's strangely the least of his worries when two transient sleazebags try to steal horses from the ranch. Will the sleazebags be stopped? Will Bigfoot keep knocking over the horse feed? Will our hero survive to work next summer too?

Black River Monster is a real hum-dinger. On one hand, it's a relatively light horror film aimed at a family audience. On the other, it's a showcase piece advertising the real Black River Farm (a ranch in Croswell, Michigan). Black River still advertises the film today and Camelot Studios still sell it, so it must have gained success! But what's eye-opening is how objectionable it is towards women, showcasing the ranch as an "all-girls" attraction. Within the first 3 minutes, Bigfoot eyes a bevy of girls riding horseback and focuses exclusively on a babe in bikini. Later as our beefy hero sleeps in a barn, we see him dreaming the gallant rescue of a tied-up woman (in skimpy clothes) before Bigfoot tries to...? And when Bigfoot appears in the grand finale, he chokes the transients into submission in what can only be described as a bizarrely hilarious climax. Was it meant to be funny? Solid entertainment for SOV connoisseurs but largely mystifying for everyone else. I wonder if *Black River Monster* actually motivated girls to go camping...

CARDS OF DEATH
1986, Color, 92 min
STARRING: *Ron Kologie, Gregg Lawrence, Chip Howe, Will MacMillan, Shamus Sherwood*
DIRECTOR: *Will MacMillan*

An underground card game run by sadists forces each winner to kill the losers within 24 hours. But when a police captain is killed, the cops investigate the deadly dealings.

Filmed, completed and shelved (except for limited release in Japan), *Cards of Death* made its legitimate North American premiere thanks to independent VHS enthusiasts from Bleeding Skull (a film review website) in 2014. Was it worth the wait? That depends on how much you love neon swastikas and Ted Danson. The film is well put together and considerably shot, almost with a *Blood Cult* class of skill. But more impressive is its conscious shift in style between scenes of sadistic card games (stable close-ups) and scenes with police (handheld pans). This not only gives the police a sense of urgency but it demonstrates planning from the filmmakers. *Cards of Death* isn't a backyard production. Yet the film's greatest strength comes from its lead detective, who sounds exactly like Ted Danson! It's a wonderful feeling to know hell or high water, Sam Malone will stop at nothing to end the perverse murders plaguing downtown LA.

Written and directed by MacMillan (who previously appeared in 1973's *The Crazies*), *Cards of Death* is an interesting and uncomfortable entry in shot on video horror that sadly never got its chance with North American audiences. It's quite sleazy and entertaining, bursting with an almost European vibe in visuals and lighting. It makes a great pairing with 1988's *555* and shares the same narrative too. Not essential SOV, but quality stuff.

CHANNEL 13
1986-2015, Color, 70 min
STARRING: *John Polonia, Mark Polonia, Matt Satterly, Dave Fife, Chris Beacom*
DIRECTOR: *Mark Polonia, John Polonia*

A man returns home from the video arcade, finding only one channel working on his television. Hosted by a green-faced ghoul, the broadcast airs three short films before zapping the man into oblivion.

 Essentially two shorts plus wraparound (the middle story is more of a quick vignette), *Channel 13* proves difficult to place in the scope of shot on video history. *"I just came across all these tapes"* says Mark Polonia, fresh from discovering and assembling the footage. Indeed *Channel 13* shows that one may never know how many SOV horror films truly exist, as so many are only seeing the light of day now. The wraparound (everything featuring Fife) is footage produced in the new millennium. But the end result would likely be the same had it been shot 30 years earlier. Like *Church of the Damned* and *Hallucinations*, *Channel 13* is an impressive piece of teenaged sophistication from the soon-to-be known Polonia brothers.

"All Hallows Eve" is the first and most interesting story. John Polonia plays an outcast who takes revenge on his tormentors via a deadly resurrected scarecrow on halloween night (the brothers actually shot this story twice and would so again several times, culminating in 2009's *Halloween Night*). Camera work, gore and lighting are all impressive; tainting the film with a heavy halloween look. John particularly impresses with his portrayal of a character split by shame and anger. And now knowing how many times they would return to this story, it's interesting to see which aspects the brothers would later expand upon and perfect.

The second entry features a man walking in the snow, followed by a large demonic bird. The bird is unintentionally silly with crude stop-animation movements, but the story is simple. This footage appears to have been shot standard digital (suggesting that it may have been filmed in the late 90's) but it fits well enough.

Things happily return to 80's analog with the final story "Slaughterhouse." Somewhat based on what the brothers thought *Motel Hell* was about (having only seen posters), "Slaughterhouse" again features John as the heavy. Here, he's serving ground-up bodies to unsuspecting motel houseguests. Dressed as a hillbilly with pillows jammed into his shirt, John hilariously licks his lips each time food, blood or bodies appear. Mmm! Mark gets more screen time too.

Ultimately *Channel 13* contains long lost pieces of Polonia history. It doesn't have the strength of *Church of the Damned* but it does fair better in technique, mood and

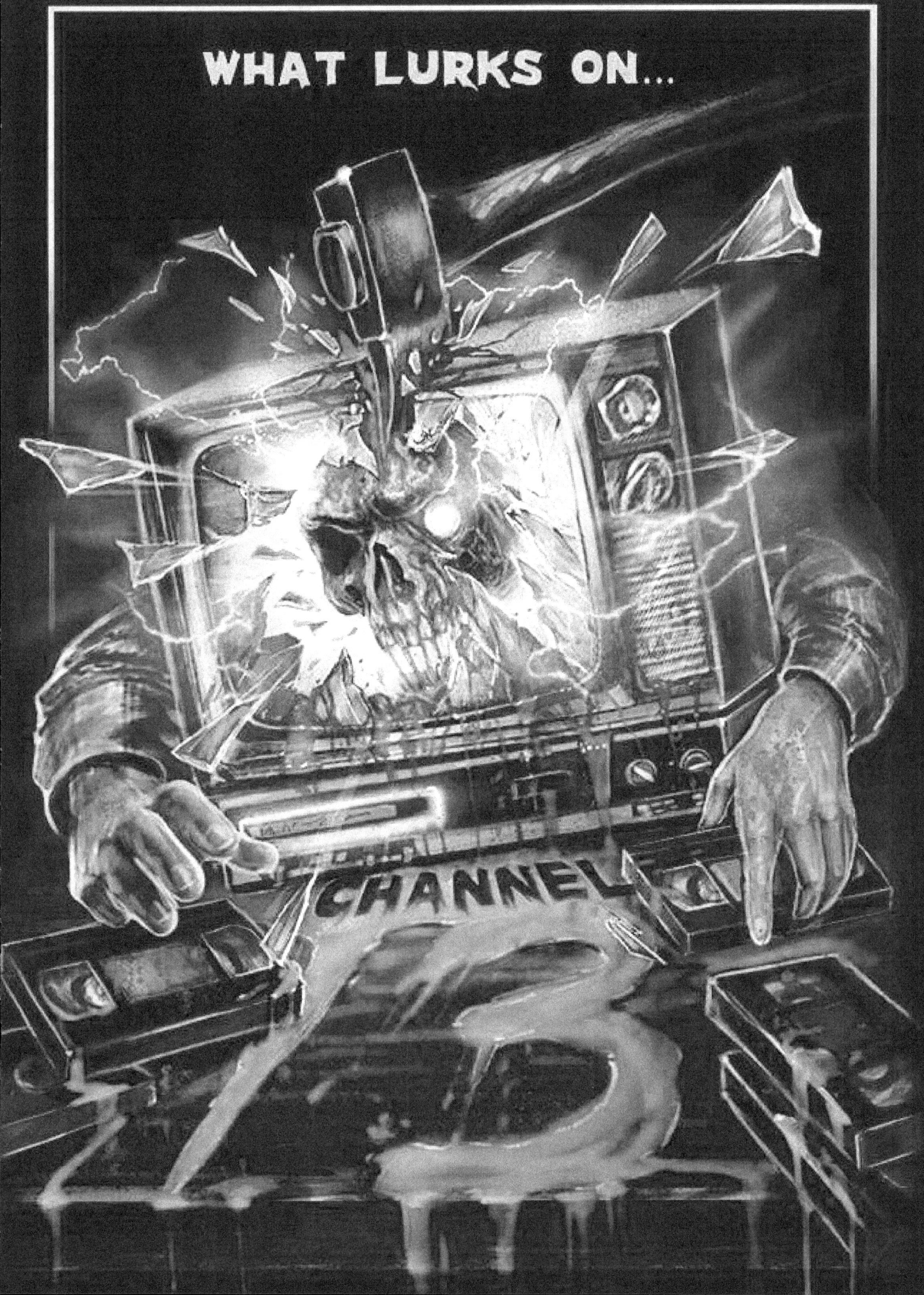
WHAT LURKS ON...
CHANNEL
3

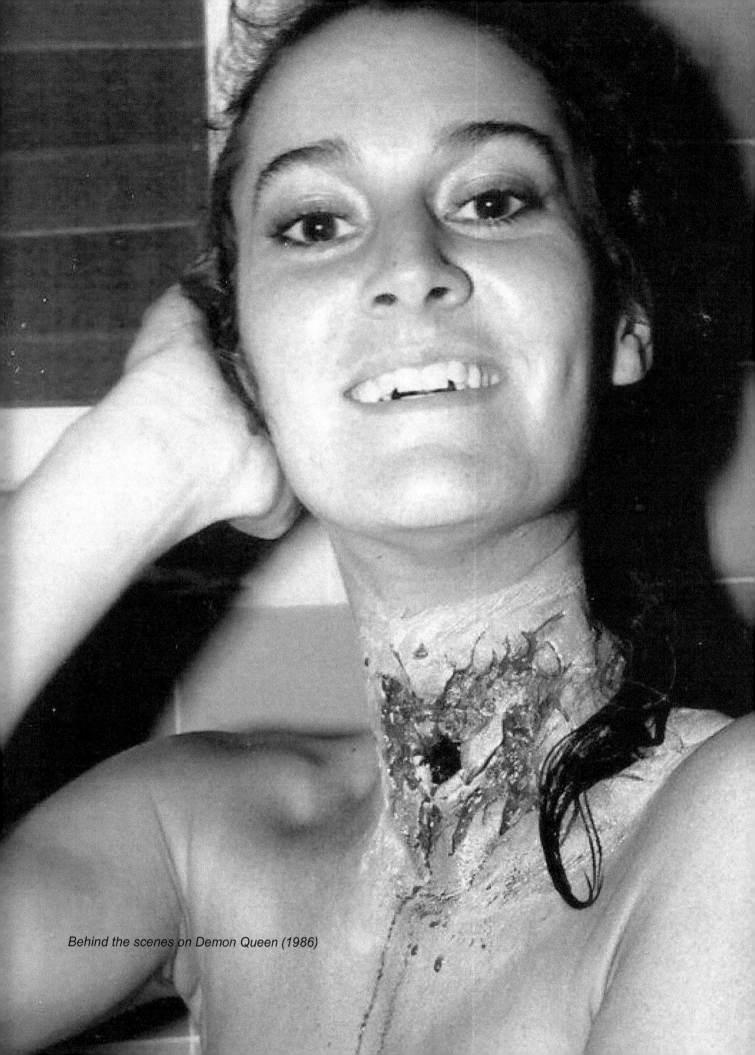

Behind the scenes on Demon Queen (1986)

consistency. Though like *Church* (and *Hallucinations*) we'll never know what impact these films might have had if released originally during their timeframes. But appreciation must be given for what we have today and indeed, they impress mightily. Highly Recommended!

DEMON QUEEN
1986, Color, 54 min
STARRING: *Mary Fanaro, Dennis Stewart, Rick Foster, Clifton Dance, Patti Valliere*
DIRECTOR: *Donald Farmer*

A beautiful, succubus-like woman is seducing and killing men in downtown Florida. She winds up staying with a kind drug dealer while her victims turn into flesh-eating zombies. Soon the dealer learns what's happening and kills the woman.

Donald Farmer has arrived.

Running less than an hour and filled with wonderful dialogue, *Demon Queen* marks a fundamental change in the approach of SOV horror. The film is lean, direct, straight to the point and gory with (at least) two fantastic money shots. *"When I found out Rick Gonzales worked on Day of the Dead, I told him the one effect he had to do was a zombie bite just like he did for Romero"* says Farmer, and it does impress. But equally impressive is Farmer's grassroots approach to filming, essentially due to a lack of time and money. But the result feels more geared towards the home video audience than anything else. The opening music (reminiscent of a Double Dragon arcade game) cracks over a live-filmed poster of Umberto Lenzi's *Nightmare City*. Then we're immediately introduced to the villain and taken on a non-stop cycle of blood and breasts. Farmer certainly knew his ingredients! *Demon Queen's* gore splatters messily, quickly paced compared to *Blood Cult's* languishing slow builds. Part of *Demon Queen's* charm is that it equates boobs and blood with the pulsing power of rock music, turning its 54 minutes into a dose of sugary adrenaline. The film even incorporates scenes filmed in an actual video store (the horror section, naturally) showing that Farmer truly knew his audience.

This is one of the earliest examples of a backyard shot, independently made SOV movie that gained wide release on videotape. It's not clean, neat or terribly professional (save for Gonzales' excellent make-up). But it has power. Highly Recommended.

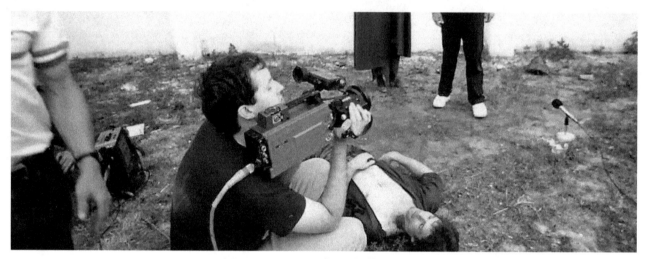

Donald Farmer (with camera) on Demon Queen (1986)

ESCAPE FROM THE INSANE ASYLUM
1986, Color, 90 min
STARRING: *Renee Harmon, Henry Lewis, Frank Neuhaus, Lynn Whitmire*
DIRECTOR: *Felix Girard*

Two psychiatrists perform experimental brain surgery on an asylum's inmates, turning them into obediently trained assassins. To fund the procedures, one doctor attempts to commit his rich wife to the asylum so he can better control her assets. Elaborate schemes of a dubious haunted house and a catatonic killer (dressed as a ninja) pursue the woman until she cracks.

Also known as *Night of Terror, Escape From the Insane Asylum* takes a fair amount of time setting up the plot. Editing and performances are tight, but the first 20 minutes drag as we spend the entire opening amongst 'crazies' in the asylum. Random scenes of people shouting at walls are intermixed with Renee Harmon convincing us she's not crazy (when she very much appears to be). Finally breaking into act two, the film becomes something of a *Boardinghouse* sequel with 80's rock; the aforementioned haunted house and a bevy of partying teens. Indeed so good are acts two and three, you almost wish the opening asylum was a different film but alas, *Escape From the Insane Asylum* would be a dreadfully misleading title. Ultimately, this is an attractive film with an endlessly rewatchable sense of fun in its later half. Camerawork is clean, framing shots with an almost Emmeritus-like charm.

But what's the deal with that catatonic assassin?

Bizarrely, scenes from Harmon's 1975 thriller *Frozen Scream* appear randomly without explanation (the *Night of Terror* version does not include them) . *Frozen Scream* does share plot similarities with doctors turning victims into killer zombies, so perhaps intention was to link the films? Regardless, this is still a fun entry.

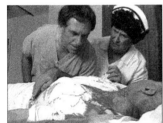   

GHOST STORIES: GRAVEYARD THRILLER
1986, Color, 56 min
STARRING: *Bob Jenkins, Ralph Lucas, Laura Kay, Sandra McLees, Maria Hayden*
DIRECTOR: *Lynn Silver*

A group of people stand and tell stories in a graveyard.

I wish I could embellish this film; rave about the savagery of its stories or describe the gore seen in flashbacks. But alas, that just isn't going to happen. We literally have an hour of actors standing in a field, delivering monologues. Is that good? Well I suppose some of the stories are a little grizzly. Is it fun? Hell no. *Ghost Stories: Graveyard Thriller* is lacking every component that might make it interesting. No flashbacks. No re-enactments. Not freeze frame pictures here and there. It's purely theatre-level delivery. No bells, whistles, meat or sizzle.

When looking at SOV films as a whole, sometimes the swindle of attractive box art becomes apparent. People paid money to rent movies occasionally based on box art alone.

I get that. But I can only fathom the amount of video renters who brought this title home, only to be bored to sleep. As evidence for the power of direct to video sales, *Ghost Stories: Graveyard Thriller* makes for an interesting relic. But as a film, this is bottom of the barrel.

THE GROUNDHOG'S DAY MASSACRE
1986, Color, 27 min
STARRING: *Brandy Slusch, Biff St. Hubbins, Buzz Sawe*
DIRECTOR: *H. J. Olminsky (Harold Olminsky)*

An absolute riot. Filmed in 1985, Olminsky's first film is a powerhouse of (lifted) rock & roll tracks and senseless violence. A man wearing a bag on his head (Baggyface) chases victims with his power saw... connected by large extension cord. When the cord unplugs, his victims hold the saw while he runs back to plug it in. The feel good movie of the year! Highly Recommended.

The film (along with its sequel) was re-released as bonus material on the limited *Attack of the Mutant Roadkill* VHS from VHShitfest in 2013.

WARNING: May cause severe laughter. do not operate heavy machinery while watching.

Approx. 207 min

GUNBLAST
1986, Color, 65 min
STARRING: *Marland Proctor, Christina Cardan, James Cunningham, Albert Eskinazi*
DIRECTOR: *Nick Millard*

A hired gunman (with a mac-10) ambushes money carriers for a cartel. Now the cartel hires an ex-cop to track and kill the gunman. Additionally, a young man learns to cheat the casino with loaded dice.

Also known as *Mac-10*, Millard's action-grinder about money and machine guns will be of high interest to SOV horror fans. Featuring several familiar faces from the director's work, Millard weaves a thriller similar in style (and look) to his later *Cemetery Sisters* and *Death Nurse* films. Clunky, abrupt, unpolished and chaotic, *Gunblast* is a joy for fans. This is also the initial entry of Millard's video outputs and many of his "cinematic traits" appear in full force: random stock footage, his mother and daughter appear in cameo, his San Francisco house doubles for locations, Las Vegas exteriors, large portions without dialogue and Millard himself playing multiple roles. The film is more erotic than his later work, featuring inserted footage from his 70's skin flicks (lots of nipple teasing). And the plot is wider in scope, allowing for independent storylines without crossover. But with great sincerity, Millard is the master of movie meandering. No one can quite make a movie as hypnotically imperfect as he can. *Gunblast* may not be his best, but it's a genuinely fun and heart-warming venture. Charmingly Recommended.

HALLUCINATIONS

1986, Color, 60 min
STARRING: *Mark Polonia, Todd Smith (Todd Rimatti), John Polonia*
DIRECTOR: *Mark Polonia, Todd Smith (Todd Rimatti), John Polonia*

Three brothers (one adopted) spend the weekend home alone while their mother works double shifts. Plagued by visions of blood and death, the brothers soon learn they're being pitted against each others' fears by a spirit in the house.

Finished in 1987 and shelved until 2008 (released as a supplement on Camp Motion Pictures' *Splatter Beach* DVD), *Hallucinations* was the first completed feature from the Polonia brothers. Teenagers at the time, it's a fascinating look at the early stages of genius as horrific passions exude from every frame. One by one, each character witnesses (or participates in) scenes of horrific violence. One scene in particular (which was later inserted into the original version of *Splatter Farm*) has a contorted John Polonia shitting a bloody butcher knife into a toilet, followed by disembowling himself through his mouth. It's over the top and beyond amazing. Later we see John naked in the shower being attacked by some sort of large worm! Highly creative stuff. On how *Hallucinations* came to be, Mark offers *"I think we dropped Church for something more attainable,"* which helps give context. That three teenagers could grow from Super8 shorts to feature length nightmares that rivaled big budget counterparts, is truly outstanding (and many scenes would later be perfected in following films). But what *Hallucinations* shows that *Church of the Damned* didn't is Todd, Mark and John's determination to complete the project. They weren't afraid of failure and created their own rules when needed, making this a sophomoric stepping stone teetering on the verge of brilliance. Recommended.

Hallucinations would eventually enjoy its own release on VHS and Blu-ray from SRS Cinema. Notably, SRS' version contains the original opening and closing credits absent from Camp's supplement (new computer text was created for Camp's release).

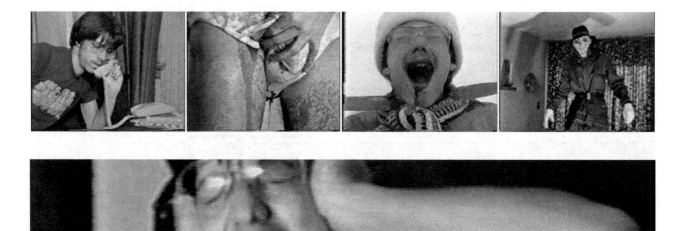

INTO THE DARKNESS

Starring
DONALD PLEASENCE

INTO THE DARKNESS
1986, Color, 92 min
STARRING: *Donald Pleasence, John Saint Ryan, Ronald Lacey, Polly Jo Pleasence*
DIRECTOR: *David Kent-Watson*

A homicidal maniac (with a strong hatred for his mother) is killing models on a tropical island fashion shoot.

Like *The Ripper, Escape From the Insane Asylum* and *Spine, Into the Darkness* top bills an established star in its cast. Surely a tremendous selling point, Donald Pleasence's credits reached far beyond *Halloween* at the time with Oscar worthy turns in *The Great Escape* and *You Only Live Twice.* What luck! Though it is slightly jarring to see him here, on video with video's cheap presentation. Pleasence worked on many smaller films throughout his career, but analog isn't film. On video, the man's mystic is completely gone. It's a fascinating experience, really. And his real-life daughter is in the film too (perhaps she's the reason why he's here). But this is an incredible moment: Donald Pleasence in a SOV horror movie. Get ready.

Filmed largely on location in Malta, this UK production impresses with lush photography and a vexing storyline. Who is the killer? Thankfully none of the red herrings draw attention, leaving the audience to guess. The final reveal and chase are well executed and several moments effectively creep. But Pleasence steals the show every time he's onscreen. Some of the camera angles feel a little too *Halloween* influenced but hey, they've already got its star so why not go for broke? Performances are generally strong and the murders (though tame) stand out. So who's complaining? Recommended.

LIPSTICK AND BLOOD
1986, Color, 84 min
STARRING: *Joseph Peters, Jane Linter, Chris Plume, Aidan James, Paul Ashe*
DIRECTOR: *Lindsay Shonteff*

A psychotic man kidnaps a stripper. Holding her captive, he rapes and berates her while confessing his love. She escapes and plans revenge.

Though featuring several murders, *Lipstick and Blood* is focused more on victimization and mind control than excessive violence. Peters as the kidnapper and Linter as the victim do wonderful jobs here, uncomfortably showcasing a "forced love" relationship. Peters demands sex at every turn; insulting and threatening her into believing it's love. And sadly, this has been a real life horror for many women stalked, raped and controlled in this manner. To his credit, Shonteff doesn't over dramatize with sensational elements. But the film still feels obsessively confined as one creep repeatedly forces himself on a woman. Linter weathers the storm and enjoys an emotional sense of justice in the end, but this isn't *I Spit On Your Grave*. Linter escapes and eventually returns to dancing, using it as the vehicle for her revenge. A recommended UK production.

MIAMI VENDETTA
1986, Color, 92 min
STARRING: *Maarten Goslins, Frank Gargani, Sandy Brooke, Barbara Pilavin*
DIRECTOR: *Stephen Seemayer*

A Los Angeles cop investigates a series of murders connected to Cubin drug runners.

Some films never get it right. Either they run too long and bore, or they come up short and don't deliver. *Miami Vendetta* gets it right. And like the dark asshole of Hell, it knows where things end. Because if you stick around long enough, Detective Malone will put a bullet in your head.

A hard-nosed thriller released to video in 1987, *Miami Vendetta* is a flick with balls.

Victims are hung with fingers cut off, chained to weights and dumped in rivers. Cops smoke 24-7 and bitch about following procedure. Cubin donut bakers only think about one thing (getting laid). And Detective Malone? He just wants his goddamn gun back. *Miami Vendetta* is the best and worst of 1986 and it's glorious. Goslins fills the screen as the overworked cop, busting ass and *"catching slime."* He gives us a character we never want to leave. Seemayer's direction is tight and gritty too, impressive as this was his only film. And *Vendetta* even visits a real life video store, documenting the 80's rental business amongst cardboard standees of *Ghostbusters*. Best of all, the film carries a real world vibe thanks to the analog visuals (feeling like a foul mouthed Emmeritus). A supremely fun, re-watchable crime drama. Recommended!

NIGHT RIPPER!
1986, Color, 89 min
STARRING: *James Hansen, April Anne, Larry Thomas, Danielle Louis, Simon de Soto*
DIRECTOR: *Jeff Hathcock*

An unknown assailant is killing models with a large butcher knife. Police investigation points to the photographers themselves, but who is the real killer?

Admittedly, *Night Ripper!* is an incredibly simplistic film (someone with a fetish for models kills) but it sadly spends an enormous amount of time meandering. Nearly the entire picture is spent on a wholesome photographer dealing with his cheating fiancé, then dumping his fiancé, then dating a model, then dealing with his vengeful fiancé again. It's supposed to offer red herrings but it only bores. We know who the killer is the moment they speak. More interesting is the photographer's business partner, played sufficiently bonkers by Larry Thomas (who would famously later portray the Soup Nazi on TV's *"Seinfeld"*). Thomas' performance is hugely deadpan, rivaling the best of Herschell Gordon Lewis. The audience wants him to be the killer. And with lines like *"I was a butcher for five years and now I'm a photographer - anything can happen"* and *"this isn't love, it's two sweaty bodies fucking under a flood lamp. And I'm sick of flood lamps,"* *Night Ripper!* comes out okay. Yet its real pizzazz is found in its murder sequences. Shots of swinging knives are intercut with freeze-frame inserts of the blade stuck in faces. It's an interesting effect I cannot recall seeing anywhere else. And when the killer lunges at the victim towards the finale, the lunge is first-person directly at camera. The killer lunges at you! This brings a style not typically found in your basic bottom-dollar slashers. As for the film's subject matter, Hathcock states *"I like stories where women are in jeopardy because you can always get a readymade audience. Women empathize with other women."* I'm not sure whether that's true, but *Night Ripper!* contains seeds of greatness within.

SPINE

1986, Color, 72 min
STARRING: *R. Eric Huxley, Janus Blythe, Lise Romanoff, John Howard, James Simonds*
DIRECTOR: *John Howard, Justin Simonds*

A deadly serial killer is stalking and stabbing nurses in downtown Los Angeles. The cops are baffled, finding the word "LINDA" painted on walls in victims' blood. Only a newly upgraded computer system and two exhausted detectives can stop this madman before it's too late. The killer's looking for Linda and that could be ANYBODY!

Originally filmed in 1984 then released in 1986 with a gorgeously gruesome "big box" video package, *Spine* became infamous for its lavish box art depicting a bloody shirt-torn victim cowering from an unknown assailant (reminiscent of 1980's *Maniac)*. But in a bizarre choice during production (due to lack of time and special effects know how), the film actually shies away from violence with quick fades to black. I always wondered if these were censored versions on video but indeed, the fade-outs were intended (nothing is missing). This is noteworthy because 4-Play Video Inc (the company who created the picture) was previously making hardcore pornography and certainly knew the importance of a money shot. So make of this what you will. Instead *Spine* tells the viewer with dialogue *"she was stabbed seventeen times in the chest and twenty-seven in the back,"* and laugh out loud zingers like *"no rape this time. He's one-in-five for the rapes."* Our killer (who looks straight out of 70's porno) sports an all-weather vest, mirror-reflective glasses and a generously healthy comb-over, calling everyone *"Linda"* as he flicks out his switchblade. But even this can't rival the lunacy of co-director Howard's portrayal as Detective Meadows: the one cop who can't show excitement, take off his baseball cap or use basic word association (especially when it counts). Add on the amateur camerawork (shaky, out of focus hand-held stuff) and *Spine* delivers in ways not possibly imagined. We never get anything as gory as the box promises, but we do get a lot of heart and an ending that really goes for the gusto.

Yet there's still one incredible factor that needs mention... *Spine* stars Janus Blythe! And she's really very good in the role, crying onscreen. Was money tight for the horror actress in the mid-80's? *Spine* enjoyed a $20,000 budget with $1200 paid to Blythe. The production originally lasted 7 days before editing began, to which everyone discovered the film only ran 45 minutes! So pick-ups were scheduled 9 months later to help flesh-out the police scenes. And thank goodness they did because with its sheer outrageous gusto, *Spine* is incredibly fun to watch.

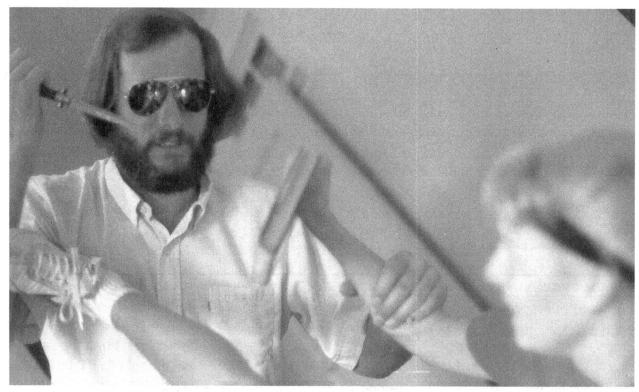

R. Eric Huxley in Spine (1986)

WITCHDOCTOR OF THE LIVING DEAD
1986, Color, 80 min
STARRING: *Joseph Layode, St. Mary Enonchong, Victor Eriabie, Larry Williams*
DIRECTOR: *Charles Abi Enonchong*

A Nigerian village is plagued by mysterious deaths and corpses coming back to life. Thought to be the work of an evil witchdoctor, a detective and local priest join forces to stop the madness.

Reportedly filmed in 1985, *Witchdoctor of the Living Dead* stands head and shoulders beyond most backyard SOV productions as the most amateur to date - and here lies its charm. Multiple scenes play as if actors are standing in front of an unmanned camera. Zombies growl and lurch directly into the screen. People mumble a barrage of dialogue only to look at the camera and then loudly repeat it again.

This is true independent filmmaking.

It's usually easy to identify the type of audience a film is geared towards, but *Witchdoctor of the Living Dead* buries assumptions under a filthy heap of straw. Was this horror film made for horror audiences? Was it a backyard joke for laughs? Was deeper meaning intended between the battle of two religions, or law enforcement's inability to intervene? Only Enonchong knows for sure (I'd wager it all has some weight here). *Witchdoctor* is a hilariously entertaining, engaging meander through a Nigerian lifestyle struggling with black magic and superstition. It's wonderfully silly with machete carrying, white powdered zombies shuffling zanily through the town. And it feels political too (though animal lovers beware: a goat is graphically killed in a protracted sequence).

Interview
DONALD FARMER

An industry professional in every sense of the word, Donald Farmer exploded onto the video scene with *Demon Queen* in 1987. Self-taught in the 70's on Super8 shorts, Farmer entered the booming video horror business by submitting articles to Fangoria magazine in 1984. While writing on-set coverage for *Day of the Dead* (and performing as a zombie), Farmer eventually learned of makeup effects wizard Rick Gonzales and subsequently hired him for his premiere video project *Demon Queen*. Successfully making and selling his own independent features, Farmer quickly became one of the most instantly recognizable SOV horror filmmakers of the decade.

Donald, thank you for giving your time to this interview! Your first SOV horror film was Demon Queen from 1986. It's highly impressive.

Thanks! Yes, produced in 1986 and released in four countries in 1987: America, France, Belgium and Korea.

Had you shot anything before that?

Yeah, I had done several Super8 short films in the 1970's. Some horror, some experimental. Two Blu-rays recently came out from SRS Cinema with them on it. But I had done this whole string of Super8 movies back then and we wouldn't really do anything with them. Just show them to ourselves or show them at parties. I had a couple of public showings but that was it. This was before the video market came along and people started buying up videotape players and recorders for home use. I didn't see many people buying videotape players and recorders until about 1979, but I did these movies between 1973 and 1976. There was no home video outlet at the time, otherwise I would have made something at least an hour long so they would have been commercial. And I'm always kicking myself that in the 1980's it never occurred to me to edit three of these together to make an anthology (I could have easily got a distribution deal for it). But in the 1980's, you could get almost anything distributed. The distributors were just so hungry. There's never been a time before or since where video distributors were so hungry for product. And they didn't care what it was. They said if they could put a good cover on it, they could sell it. And that's why I started making movies again. So after a 10 year break, I got back into making movies.

Were you aware of any SOV horror films at the time you started *Demon Queen?*

There was already a trickle of a few SOV movies I had seen were coming out. I think *Boardinghouse* was one of them; one of the ones that got the best distribution. So I started investigating distributors and finding out *"if I was to make my own movie, who would be the distributors for it?"* So I started doing heavy duty investigation. I was going to video stores and taking note of names of distributors on the back of the boxes, seeing if there was an address, trying to get a hold of these people. I did a lot of research before I did *Demon Queen*. If I made this movie, who would distribute it? How would I get my money back? So I ended up coming down between two companies. Mogul was one; I was introduced to them by my friend Jeffery Hoag. And the other company I thought would be too big of a company, but the vice president assured me that they would be interested in distributing the movie. But I found this hard to believe because they distributed movies theatrically, not so much on video. And he even offered to buy it sight unseen just based on the title (which really shocked me). But he didn't come along with this incredible offer until after I signed the contract with Mogul. So a bit of a regret that I signed the contract with Mogul.

What was *Demon Queen's* production like?

For shooting, we were very cramped for time. I brought the cameraman down from Nashville and had to drive all the way to Miami where we were shooting. And he was only able to stay there 3 days. But after shooting those 3 days, we only ended up with about 45 minutes of footage. So once he went back to Nashville, I arranged some shooting with him up there. The video store scene was part of that additional shooting. And also I had shot some additional scenes on my own with my 1/2 inch camera. He had come down with a 3/4 inch studio camera, which is what's used most in the movie. But *Demon Queen's* star

Mary Fanaro, I got her because Tim Ritter had just finished his first movie *Truth Or Dare?* with her in it. And he recommended her to me. So she was the one person that I got on my own without having to go through the casting director. Today, Mary runs a charity with Courtney Cox so she's been featured on Entertainment Tonight, Access Hollywood and all over YouTube with these charity videos. She acted for several years after *Demon Queen*, but then retired to concentrate on her charity work. But *Demon Queen* was shot in south Florida and after I wrapped, I moved to LA.

Demon Queen has this amazing trifecta of blood, boobs and nudity.

Well that's what these horror movies had, and I always liked movies that had lots of gore and lots of nudity. Those were just the elements. If I was just making a movie for me and my friends, those are the elements I'd want for myself.

Demon Queen also appears to be the first SOV feature with portions shot in a video store. How did that come about?

That video store a friend of mine ran in Nashville called Fantasy Video. Basically since we were filming scenes and we needed to film those scenes somewhere, I said *"why don't we film in your video store?"* I wanted to immortalize his store; tried to have the camera go by so you could read the labels clearly. I just wanted to capture it for posterity and his video store was better than most. He had way more horror titles than most and he went for a lot of the Italian releases. So we wanted to take advantage of that. And the guy who ran the store, he wasn't a very good actor but we had a professional actor play the clerk. The guy who actually owned the store played the customer wandering around in the background. But his store is long gone now. The building is there but it's a bakery or something.

How did you meet special makeup effects man Rick Gonzales?

Well Rick worked on *Day of the Dead* right before we hired him for *Demon Queen*. I had been on *Day of the Dead* too, sort of a coincidence that we had both been on *Day* but we had not met each other. I played a zombie during the Pittsburgh part of the shoot and Rick was involved in the makeup part of the Florida shoot. So the way I met him was through a guy in Miami named Gary Levinston (who plays Lobo in *Cannibal Hookers*). Gary was friends with Rick and used him to do makeup effects for custom videos (a mail-order company that was similar to W.A.V.E. Productions). So Gary was showing me these movies and I asked who did the effects. Told him I was thinking of doing a movie on my own and asked if he thought I could hire Rick for it. But when I found out Rick had worked on *Day of the Dead*, I told him specifically that *"the one effect you've got to do is a zombie bite."* Then Rick came up with the idea of making a zombie where his face would slide off.

So we had these really state of the art effects because of this lucky accident of me meeting Rick through Gary.

When *Demon Queen* released to video, *Nightmare City*'s poster art famously appeared as the box cover image. How did this happen?

The company that was distributing *Demon Queen* was Mogul Communications, a company staffed out by people from England. They had some sort of relationship with a British director named Dick Randal and they came to America and opened their own office in Hollywood. They put out a ton of VHS in the 1980's, all in these big clamshell boxes. And they usually had an in-house artist paint original covers for their movies. I was hoping they would do that for *Demon Queen*. So they asked me if I had any ideas for the cover and I thought they meant ideas for their artists. I looked at some old posters in press-books and I had this old press-book for *Nightmare City*. So I showed them that and I said *"it would be good if you could do something like this."* So I'm thinking they would have their artist do something with it. You know, use it for inspiration. But they just took the art I gave them and used the exact art on the cover. They didn't change a thing. They said *"oh it's perfect just like this!"* So that wasn't my original intention but that's what ended up happening.

And then we come to *Cannibal Hookers* from 1987.

Made in 1987 and released in 1988. Pretty much the formula of making a movie one year and having it come out the next (*Savage Vengeance* was made in 1988 but that didn't come out until 1992, so that one sat on the shelf a while). With *Cannibal Hookers*, I co-produced with Gary and put him in it as one of the main stars. The big lug who gets all the hookers, so we named him Lobo after the Bela Lugosi movie *Bride of the Monster*. *Cannibal Hookers* was the only movie I shot entirely in Los Angeles. The castle scenes were all filmed at this real castle in Glendale, the former home of Ted V. Mikels. It was a pretty leisurely shoot.

Donald Farmer... the actor?

Well I have two scenes in *Cannibal Hookers* as a bartender and a guy at the party. But I usually just put myself in these things because it would save me from getting another actor, not because I wanted to be in it. Just more expedient. But the first movie set I ever worked on was *Day of the Dead* were I was playing a zombie. That sort of got me a little bit interested in acting. And I did a little bit in a friend's movie *They Bite* (a horror movie starring Ron Jeremy). And in the 1970's, I did some plays in college. But for *Savage Vengeance*, I just did the lead because I didn't know another actor who was available to play such a big part. *Scream Queen* and *Savage Vengeance* were made back to back; same partners, the same co-producers. Same crew with very little breathing room between them.

Demonic women is a reoccurring theme in your films. Did you ever intent to connect your films, perhaps as an unholy trilogy?

Not really. Well we did connect *Savage Vengeance* with *Scream Dream* because they have the same night club. So the two movies are both going on in the same movie universe. But I connect the movies I do in different ways too. I like to reuse a lot of character names, reusing the name Caroline. I like a lot of female leads.

Scream Dream's opening scene is wonderfully memorable: a girl on a bed with a running chainsaw. Was that a last minute addition?

No, that was always from the very beginning. That was how the movie was intended to open. Usually it's a rule of low-budget filmmaking to try and have an opening scene that grabs people. The distributor liked that scene so much that when they did the photo shoot for the video cover, they recreated it with a different model. Back in my early movies, a very typical thing my distributors would do was use photos. They said that the cover image was the most important thing about marketing a movie. And they were right. *Scream Dream* was my favorite of all the covers. And since they wanted higher quality photos than ones that I took, that meant they weren't showing the real actors who were in the movie. They were showing models. In the case of the *Cannibal Hookers* video cover, they used models to show a scene that never even takes place in the movie!

How did you cast Camille Keaton in *Savage Vengeance?*

Well the reason she's in the movie is because in the break between *Scream Dream* and *Savage Vengeance*, I worked on Rick Martin's movie *No Justice*. And one of my jobs on *No Justice* was celebrity casting. Back when I lived in LA, I became friends with Camille. So I told Rick when he put me in charge of celebrity casting that I bet I could get her to be in this. And that I also knew Cameron Mitchell and had his home number because I interviewed him years earlier. So Rick gave me a $10,000 casting budget which I spent on those two. I got Camille in *No Justice* and right after that, I wanted to make my own movie and use her immediately. So I told her she'd be the star and I'd pay her exactly what she was paid for *No Justice*. So nothing would change for her but for *Savage Vengeance*, her salary was 90% of the budget. So I was basically making a movie where any money I could get, I was just spending on Camille. The rest of the movie would be made for absolutely nothing. And it was quite a bit of a shocker for her, when she saw how the movie was so drastically different in budget to *No Justice*. She was thinking it was going to be the same experience with lavish catering!

Is *Savage Vengeance* a sequel to *I Spit On Your Grave*?

It wasn't originally intended for Camille's character to be anything like her character in *I Spit On Your Grave*. But I brought in this other partner who was suppose to bring in some of the production money, this guy who owned Lettuce Entertain You in Toronto, Canada. He distributed *Cannibal Hookers* in Canada in 1988. He said he would put up some amount of money for a Camille Keaton movie, so I sent him my treatment for *Savage Vengeance*. It was not at all like *I Spit On Your Grave* but about a female cop avenging crimes against women. So he told me he would only give me the money if I tailored it more similar to *I Spit On Your Grave*, which I didn't want to do. But that was the only way I was going to get the money. So we made these changes to accommodate him. And it turned out to be a big regret because after all the changes, he ended up sending us a bounced check. So he was not even credited as the producer and his portion of the budget I ended up having to cover. I thought we could trust him because he had distributed *Cannibal Hookers* and paid us upfront. But I never spoke to him again after his check bounced. Otherwise we would have shot the movie to my original treatment.

"Jennifer Hills" replaced with "Jennifer."

Yeah we took that out. That was his wanting us to do that (Jennifer Hills) and once his check bounced, we wiped that all off the soundtrack. Even though it was too late to change what we had filmed, we at least wanted to get that off the soundtrack.

Rape scenes with jeans on?

Well since we had zero budget, we couldn't afford to hire actors who would do a really hardcore rape scene. You can't ever get actors with nudity for free. You always have to pay them and that includes men too. Once in a while you can get a guy to do nudity for free but almost always, you'll have to pay them. And every penny we had was going towards Camille's salary. In a perfect world, I would have liked to film it more graphically. But we were tied by the budget and our only other luxury was a few days to have Rick Gonzales do effects.

There's a rumor that Camille Keaton walked off set. True?

Yeah, well she got very upset when she found out how cheap the movie was. She said she had never worked on a movie that wasn't 35mm. But I thought as long as we were paying her the same amount of money as *No Justice*, that she would not have any concerns with what kind of cameras we were using. This was the first time she had ever been on a set shot with video, which (she told me later) gave her quite a shock. We were shooting it with video cameras. We literally had a two person crew, the camera operator and a production assistant. So she was very upset but she got over it.

How did *Savage Vengeance* get misspelled on the original release?

That was totally the fault of our initial distributor, Magnum Releasing. When we made *Savage Vengeance* and *Scream Queen* in 1988, *Scream Dream* got released right away. But we did not offer *Savage Vengeance* because at the time, we were so unhappy about how it turned out. We weren't even sure if we wanted to distribute it. Camille hadn't finished all her scenes and we had to use a body double for her. And then several years later, this company (Magnum) came to me and said they wanted to put out a film series called *"I Dance On Your Grave."* So they wanted to know how many movies could I license them for this four movie series. So I had *Cannibal Hookers* (which had been licensed to Lettuce Entertain You, but they technically only had Canadian rights) and my friend Tim Ritter had just completed *Killing Spree*, so I hooked them up with him. And I had *Savage Vengeance* which I had been sitting on. So when I gave them my 3/4 inch masters, my master of *Savage Vengeance* had the title spelled correctly. But what they did is they wiped off my title and replaced it with *I Dance On Your Grave: Savage Vengance*. And when they did that, their guy spelled *Vengeance* incorrectly. But I can never get anyone to believe it wasn't me.

You've also shot many films on 16mm and 35mm, but what are your lasting thoughts on your video output?

Well I'm just sorry video technology was not what it is now. Back then, we were shooting with 3/4 inch cameras. *Red Lips* was shot in 1994 on 3/4 inch too because that's what the producer had. I would make deals with video companies to come in as a co-producer in exchange for cameras and editing services. There was a local video production company in Tennessee and his bread and butter was taking family portraits in his photo studio. But he also had video cameras and he could edit, so I got him to provide the cameras and editing facilities. And he also had the studio. The girl in the opening of *Scream Dream*, that was shot in his studio. So when you do a deal like that, you basically have to use whatever kind of camera your partner happens to own. The whole point is to not have to go out and rent (or buy) cameras. At the time, 3/4 inch cameras were not the best but that's what he had. I was always wishing someone had Beta SP because that was better quality.

Thank you so much for your time and thoughts, Donald!

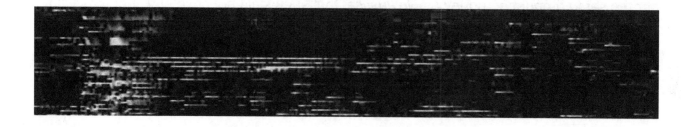

Chapter 9
THE YEAR OF PERFECTION [1987]

It was the year of excess and the year of change. But for horror, 1987 was a year of new beginnings. The classier horror films of yesterday had disappeared, replaced by neon funk and excessive pizzazz. Everything was loud and MTV had taken over. *A Nightmare on Elm Street 3: The Dream Warriors* cross-promoted a title song by Dokken, *Slumber Party Massacre 2* was about an all-girl rock band and *The Lost Boys* looked like a night-time headliner. Horror icons had already been made in Freddy and Jason (Michael would return the following year) and the genre started feeling like a fast-food commodity. Horror was weird, horror was big and horror was everywhere.

And nowhere was horror more prevalent than on videotape.

Through sales and rentals, horror titles continued to generate astounding profits for video stores across North America. Even in the face of controversy (parents often complained about excess violence and nudity), demand continued to grow. More horror! More gore! More skin! And with those demands came more product. Studios green-lit more slasher sequels, and non-horror genres started incorporating horror-like qualities. *Predator*, *RoboCop*, *The Monster Squad*; all non-horror movies using horror genre themes. And the number of shot on video productions grew too, with more titles produced in 1987 than anything before.

But after years of marketing direct to consumers, the tides were turning.

Camcorders had become commonplace. VCRs were the "must have" item in the home and *Blood Cult* was still the blueprint. In short, more people started making their own independent movies. Gary Cohen, Tim Boggs, Gary Whitson, Ricardo Islas, Pericles Lewnes; all contributing alongside returning directors Nick Millard, Chester Novell Turner, Donald Farmer, Jeff Hathcock, Todd Rimatti and the Polonia brothers. 1987 became the year when non-professionals officially joined the party.

More risks were taken, more work was varied and more bizarreness was enshrined on analog video. MTV had entered pop-culture, bringing a lifestyle with fashion and in-your-face rock to the masses. And nowhere is this better enjoyed than in SOV horror films. It's as if the video revolution, hair-metal rockers and horror all mixed together in a beautiful swill of Mountain Dew coolness with a side of fries.

This was the year when video could do no wrong, and every entry was a winner.

BLOOD LAKE

1987, Color, 82 min
STARRING: *Doug Barry, Angela Darter, Travis Krasser, Andrea Adams, Mike Kaufman*
DIRECTOR: *Tim Boggs*

A carload of teens drive to their parent's lake-house for a weekend of booze and waterskiing. But their fun is cut short when a husky, bearded, boot-wearing killer starts knocking them off one by one. A quick dip in the lake turns into a bloodbath of horror!

 *Blood Lake* is not just a movie, it's an experience. It is the greatest vacation that you didn't actually take, caught on camera. On-screen, you sit with the teens as they race down the highway. You speed in the speedboat as they jet through the lake. You're there when they eat and you're there when they drink. Half an hour later, you *feel* these people. Performances are honest and everything is totally natural. Dialogue overlaps with the inexperience of moviemaking but with the touch of real banter. And physicality never feels staged. It's just real life and it's refreshingly good.

Shot in Southwestern Oklahoma, the wonderful twang of local accents permeate the film. Outstanding dialogue like *"Wife? Susan's just a sex partner"* and *"are you going to be a butthole this weekend, or are you gonna let me drink?"* (both uttered by pre-teen Krasser) endears when it probably should offend. And the mullet-sporting 12 year old is the most sexually aggressive of the pack! Yet he's only one of the film's many highlights. Two guys threaten to *"kick your ass"* 20 times in less than 2 minutes. A drunk game of quarters plays disturbingly live onscreen. The boot-wearing bandit kills for the silliest reason imaginable. Four *completely original* heavy metal songs are featured (I dare you not to head-bang) and as for the lake itself? Let's just say *"an act of God"* will leave your jaw on the floor. *Blood Lake* is untouchable.

I've seen this film more times than I probably should have, but it's only made me a better man. It's become a staple at my house and should be in yours too, because this isn't just a film to be compared to others. It's the film which all others should be compared against.

Required Viewing!

BLOODY DYNASTY (DINASTIA SANGRIENTA)

1987, Color, 89 min
STARRING: *Sergio Goyri, Jaime Garza, Diana Ferreti, Carlos Rotzinger, Dacia Gonzalez*
DIRECTOR: *Luis Quintanilla Rico*

Some time ago, a vampire was killed in a Victorian house. Years later, a blood transfusion reawakens the fiend as he falls in love with the descendent of his old acquaintance.

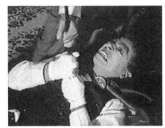 Presented in Spanish, this Mexican production wears its Hammer Horror influence proudly. Essentially a remake of 1966's *Dracula: Prince of Darkness*, *Bloody Dynasty* (also known as *Sed de Venganza*) is really a lot of fun. Cheaply made with occasional mugging for camera, the film borders between a melodramatic farce and a staged play of horrific woodiness. There are times when the vampire moves to bite the camera, then an oversized bat swings into victims' necks. A quaint breeziness zips through the film and while everything's set in modern 1987, it features a classical soundtrack of grandiose proportions. Wonderfully over the top during scenes of action too. Check it out.

  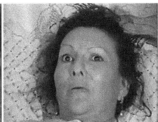 

BRAINBLAST

1987, Color, 78 min
STARRING: *Julie Mitchell, Cathy Jukes, Lisa-Jane Stockwell, Toby Zoates, Michael Salmon*
DIRECTOR: *Andy Nehl*

In 1988 Australia, a new drug is sweeping the nation with deadly results. Called 'Intensity' and delivered straight into the jugular vein, the user gets either an incredible high or instant death depending on the dosage. But a new video program is being created with subliminal imagery, allowing viewers a better high with safer results. Now a gang of thugs want to steal the program.

An energetic sci-fi/horror comedy from Australia, *Brainblast* is a punchy picture. Filled with pop-rock music and montage interludes, the film opens strong. A television reporter (Nehl) provides hilarious narrative for the audience, keeping us on point with the plot. And the creation of 'Intensity' is well developed in the film (though essentially dropped once the video program is introduced). Think 'Nuke' later seen in *RoboCop 2*. But *Videodrome* is perhaps the biggest influence here, and the film is clearly focused on its more humorous elements. Oh, and there's a bit of gore and a drugged girl making love to a frog amidst green screen foolery. Only in Australia!

BUTCHER KNIFE
1987, Color, 56 min
STARRING: *Albert Eskinazi, Irmgard Millard, Joan Simon, Leslie Simon, Frances Millard*
DIRECTOR: *Nick Millard*

A doctor performing abortions is distraught over his work. Believing his patients evil, he stabs the women to death with a large butcher knife. But his personal life complicates when his cheating wife becomes pregnant and requests his services.

Commonly known as *Doctor Bloodbath, Butcher Knife* is Millard firing on all cylinders. Shot on consumer-grade video and filled with Millard regulars, *Butcher Knife* is impressively controversial for what should be a throwaway production. One need only see the opening credits (shamelessly lifted from 1975's *Criminally Insane*) to know we're in familiar territory, but *Butcher Knife* has a bite not found in other SOV titles. Millard's use of stock footage actually works to his advantage rather than dropping the audience into a dream (and into boredom). Here, 80's video characters talk to 70's film characters; stock footage by creative editing! And since all of the director's movies were shot in his San Francisco home, locations haven't changed one bit. In addition, *Butcher Knife* features the least amount of recycled footage yet; refreshing if considering a Nick Millard marathon - which I highly recommend.

Special recognition goes to Albert Eskinazi, driving the film with an insanity that never falls into camp (where arguably, this production belongs). Irmgard Millard is also quite good as the cheating wife who, in addition to being real wife to the director, suffers the most uncomfortable death in the picture. And look for the Simon twins! Nasty and Highly Recommended.

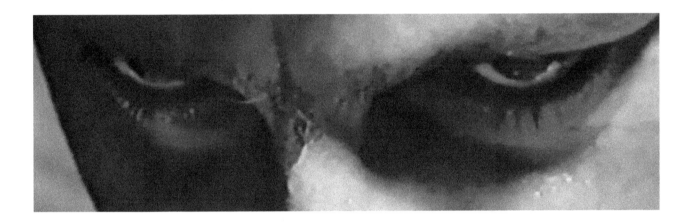

CANNIBAL HOOKERS
1987, Color, 67 min
STARRING: *Amy Waddell, Anette Munro, Shiela Best, Gary J. Levinson, Tommy Carrano*
DIRECTOR: *Donald Farmer*

Two girls pledging a sorority are forced to pose as hookers for initiation. But after visiting the local whorehouse, the girls learn that the real hookers in town are actually bloodthirsty cannibals.

Donald Farmer strikes again!

An analog return for the *Demon Queen* maestro, *Cannibal Hookers* is a smorgasbord of babes, boobs and blood as the ladies swallow more than (I'll let you finish that sentence). Resembling a porno, *Cannibal Hookers* showcases its barely dressed, neon-clad killers strutting their stuff in broad daylight. And you know it says a lot about a town when the hookers own the daylight! But strangely, all the killings and cannibalism are indoors at night. There's a life lesson here. But while bloody, this isn't Rick Gonzales bloody so focus is more on bare asses than bloody torsos.

A strong sense of technical growth comes from Farmer as time is spent developing characters. Performances are good (particularly from sorority honcho Best) and cheesy dialogue is spun with wide-eye expressions and mondo hair tossing. And while the hookers' resurrection abilities are a little muddy (most victims die after being munched, but some return as zombie slaves), the film is easy to follow. Bizarrely, *Cannibal Hookers* features a 2 minute anomaly towards the end as a scene repeats itself in an editing glitch. But this is easily recommended nonetheless.

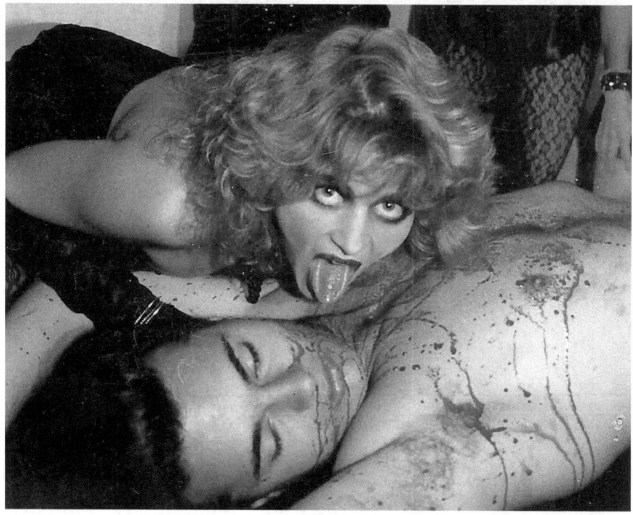

Matt Borlenghi (being licked) in Cannibal Hookers (1987)

CAPTIVES

1987, Color, 84 min
STARRING: *Lisa Cohen, Jackie Neill, Art Neill, Neil Cerbone, Linda Herman, Gary Cohen*
DIRECTOR: *Gary Cohen*

A woman and her two brothers invade the home of a wealthy businessman. Holding his wife, mother and infant son hostage, the woman reveals her connection to the family before enacting revenge.

A taught home-invasion flick played in real-time, *Captives* was Cohen's immediate return to video after his impressive *Video Violence*. But shoddy distribution (re-titled *Mama's Home* and unfairly marketed as a slasher) released the film in 1988 to little fanfare. It deserves a second look. *Captives* once again shows Cohen ahead of the curve, using video to entertain and to reflect upon itself.

Impressively acted by all involved, Cohen enlists his own wife (who had a small but memorable part in *VV*) and even their infant son Zachary. The Neill's return (also fresh from *VV*) but against type as the somewhat-incestuous villains. Cohen himself shares screentime too, playing a coke-fuelled businessman who'd rather attack hookers than spend time with his family. But video again becomes the most interesting factor within the film. Like *Video Violence*, a videotape is used to convey motive behind the invasion. The family is made to watch as video plays film-transferred footage from years past. It's quite interesting that the footage is not analog like the film itself, considering that *Video Violence* used video within video and considering that the invading-woman claims this footage to be true. In *Captives*, videotape does not contain video photography. Therefore is the video in *Captives* a lie? *Video Violence* used video to prove something was true, but *Captives* seems to use video proving the opposite. Cohen doesn't explore this idea in detail, but suggestion exists that the invaders may indeed be misguided by their insane sister's claims. Regardless, the film runs at an impressive pace without the need to look beyond face value. This is a tense hostage thriller by a master of the analog genre. Highly Recommended.

Captives is available today in its original form from Camp Motion Pictures, presented in a wonderful "big box" 5 pack called *The Basement* (named after an unreleased Super8 anthology found within).

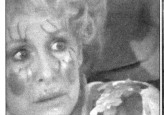   

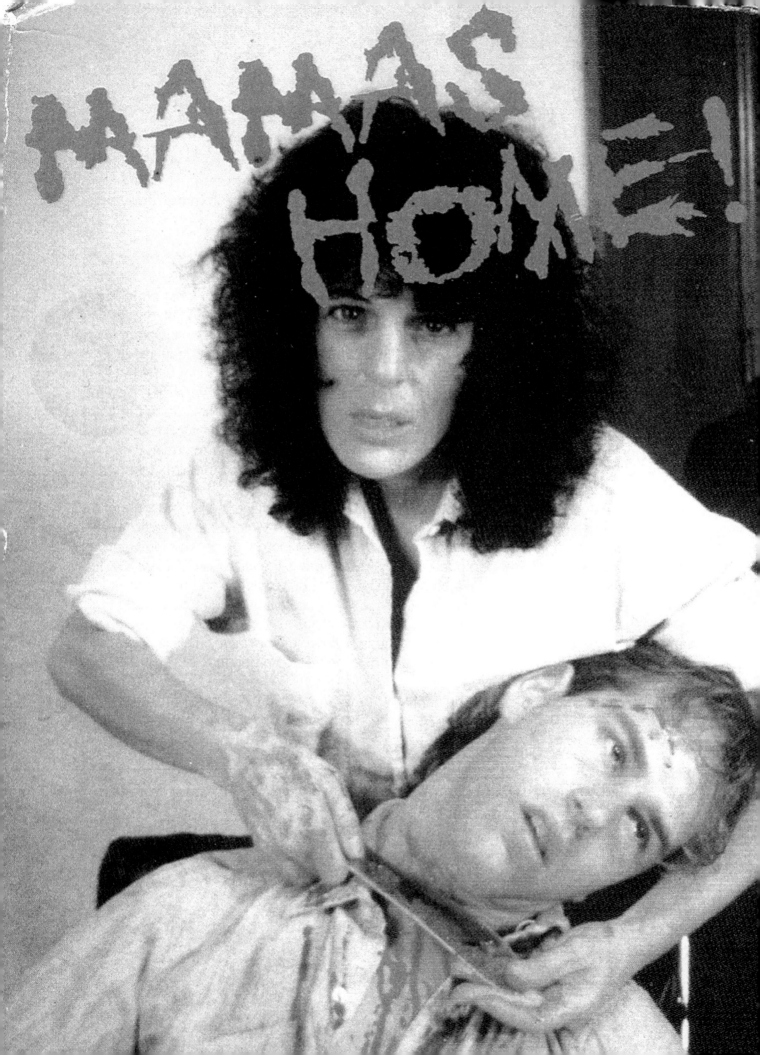

CEMETERY SISTERS

1987, Color, 58 min
STARRING: *Leslie Simon, Joan Simon, Irmgard Millard, Albert Eskinazi, Nick Millard*
DIRECTOR: *Nick Millard*

Two sisters marry and kill several men in order to inherit their assets. After a series of murders, the sisters have enough funds to buy a mortuary business.

Along with *Criminally Insane 2* (and *Death Nurse* and *Butcher Knife*), *Cemetery Sisters* is Nick Millard running with friends, a camcorder and an idea. But while *Criminally Insane 2* was a sequel to a moderately successful 70's horror film (and both *Death Nurse* and *Butcher Knife* were satirical looks at the medical profession), *Cemetery Sisters* bumps along aimlessly with its singular vision.

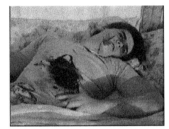 From the opening moments, we see one sister marry and the other sister kill. It's fun and their motives are immediately explained (money) but the film goes nowhere. One sister marries, the other sister kills and so on. The only diversion is the untimely arrival of an overtly-sexual aunt, outrageously played by the director's wife. And she's such a diversion that one wishes she had a larger part (suffering a fatally nasty stabbing early). But this illustrates the problem with *Cemetery Sisters*: the interesting characters are all killed off. Scene stealer (and Millard regular) Eskinazi opens the film but is hacked to death minutes later. Another character is stabbed after finishing his morning eggs and a gun-toting suitor is blown away after modeling his favorite gun. There's punch to the killings (all horribly edited with charm) but at least some of these people could have stuck around. Why not let the sisters argue? Put their plans in jeopardy a bit. They do disagree once but it's quickly resolved before returning to the marry-kill cycle. This makes for light viewing without obstacles, and the ending feels somewhat easy.

But simplicity aside, *Cemetery Sisters* is another welcomed plunge into the analog realm of Nick Millard filmmaking. It may not have the endearing greatness of *Death Nurse* or the vengeful panache of *Butcher Knife*, but it does share the ingredients that make each Millard entry something special.

CRIMINALLY INSANE 2
1987, Color, 61 min
STARRING: *Priscilla Alden, Frances Millard, Albert Eskinazi, Fred Sarra, Nick Millard*
DIRECTOR: *Nick Millard*

Still institutionalized following her multiple murders and flesh-eating, Ethel Janowski finds herself transferred to a minimal security halfway house due to a budget shortage. But with more freedom comes more murders as Ethel slays everyone coming between her and the refrigerator.

Excessively padded with scenes from the 1975 original, this is a sequel no one asked for but got anyway. Also known as *Crazy Fat Ethel 2*, this was almost certainly the vehicle Millard hoped would jumpstart his career (thanks to name recognition and a returning star). But it's definitely the worst of the director's entries as actors stare into space and lay down for naps. And somebody eats flies. *Criminally Insane 2* exists so a highlight reel can be cut into it. Newly shot footage appears only to bridge existing sequences into a cohesive whole. But does that make it all bad? Not on your life.

Knowing what this film is, Millard's brazen re-use of footage actually becomes endearing. Nick would eventually create six camcorder movies throughout the 80's, all featuring the same stock footage for inserts. *Criminally Insane 2* just has the highest amount. Yet the film still carries a certain uniqueness than cannot be denied. One character behaves like a giant spider, sipping flies from soup. Stone-faced Albert Eskinazi (a Millard regular) black-mails Ethel after witnessing her murder another inmate. And great theatricality turns deadpan performances into comedy farce (later perfected in the *Death Nurse* films).

This is the weakest of Millard's video six, but it successfully marked his return to the horror genre. And aside from *Gunblast*, Millard used video's exploding market to cash-in on his 10 year old hit (*Criminally Insane*) with innovation. *Criminally Insane 2* may ultimately be more remake than sequel, but it reintroduced Ethel Janowski to a new generation and brought Nick back where he belongs; camera in hand. And thank God it did - Extraordinary!

CROWLEY
1987, Color, 78 min
STARRING: *Fany Dertinat, Daniel Lacoste, Ricardo Islas, Juan Lazzarini, Mario Fernandez*
DIRECTOR: *Ricardo Islas*

A 300 year old vampire climbs out of his grave and attacks young lovers. Police investigate before college kids determine the culprit to be a bloodsucker. One of the college girls is a descendent of the vampire's lover, so he takes her to be his bride.

Possibly the first feature length horror film from Uruguay, *Crowley* is a fun moody take on Bram Stoker's classic. Only a teenager at the time, Islas impressively fills the screen with creepy camera angles and blood-drooling gore. Not that everything's legit, mind you. Some clearly "borrowed" music helps build the movie, tracks from *Jaws 2* and *Amityville Horror* (or was it *Exorcist II*) occurring throughout. But all's forgiven considering the inspired and energetic visuals. Favorite moments stand out, such as a gang wanting to mug Crowley in the park (only to get their asses handed to them) and the heroine's boyfriend randomly getting a swirly by the fanged one. But most impressive is Islas' direction with an almost art-house approach. Yes it's cheap, but it's bursting with heart and blood sprays of panache. Recommended.

DEATH NURSE
1987, Color, 57 min
STARRING: *Priscilla Alden, Albert Eskinazi, Frances Millard, Irmgard Millard, Nick Millard*
DIRECTOR: *Nick Millard*

Brother and sister pose as nurse and doctor at a fake medical clinic. They perform untrained surgeries (resulting in death) then bill the state for fraudulent work. But some patients aren't so lucky; Nurse Mortley has a nasty habit of stabbing people almost as soon as they come through the door.

"Get back in bed you nosey old bitch!"

DEATH NURSE

Death Nurse is, without question, quintessential Millard. Priscilla Alden wonderfully headlines, Albert Eskinazi supports and Millard's own mother (and wife) appear. Everything is shot in and around his San Francisco home, and the entire runtime is less than an hour. Welcome to the world of Nick Millard cinema! Like visiting an old friend, there's a familiarity to everything in Millard's cannon that's undeniably charming. And *Death Nurse* is no different.

The mid-80's were particularly good for the director too, bringing no less than six shot on video cheapies to camera. In 1975, Millard released *Criminally Insane* starring the incomparable Priscilla Alden. A relatively impressive entry in the frenzy-killer subgenre, it made enough impact for Millard (particularly when paired with his equally sublime *Satan's Black Wedding*) that he essentially gave up making softcore titles. Then he tried his hand at action films before finally returning to horror when budgets were at their lowest. But in the 80's with a camcorder, Nick knew movies could be made for the cost of a cassette! *Criminally Insane 2* was a surprise sequel in 87, particularly as the first film had largely been forgotten. But produced directly on video and filmed in his own house, costs were eased. And recycling footage from part 1 was not only a great way to extend runtime, but reintroduce audiences to the original film. Yet *Criminally Insane 2* did little else. *Death Nurse* makes things right.

Featuring the same cast, location and format as the others, *Death Nurse* is free from the story confinements of a sequel. Priscilla Alden plays Edith Mortley (not pre-existing Ethel Janowski) and the characters couldn't be farther apart. Edith kills purposely while Ethel kills reactively. Edith is a strong-headed smarmy character, smiling one moment before turning killer the next. Brother Gordon (hilariously deadpan by Albert Eskinazi) fancies himself a surgeon, but Edith pulls the wool over his eyes too. She tricks Gordon when she needs to. Indeed she wildy kills those who annoy her, feeding dead rats to patients and relentlessly billing MediCare in the process. Why? Because it's all about the mighty dollar! The film is a total riot; satirically looking at rehab clinics as a racket run by crooks. Camerawork (filled with zooms on faces) is pitch perfect with handheld cheapness. Actors sit on couches and stare into voids. Knives turn into foil-wrapped cardboard the moment violence strikes. And Millard himself appears; smothered and buried in the backyard, then dug-up and hosed when a social worker visits. More *Criminally Insane* stock footage appears (presented as Edith's dreams) but it's par for the course so buckle in. Am I the only one craving chocolate ice cream? Required Viewing!

  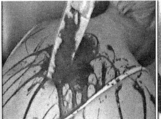 

GANJASAURUS REX

1987, Color, 89 min
STARRING: *Paul Bassis, David Fresh, Rosie Jones, Howard Phun, Rich Abernathy*
DIRECTOR: *Ursi Reynolds*

An engineer and her three friends plant softball-sized seeds which grow into immense marijuana plants. Unfortunately, the government has just launched a new anti-marijuana task force and a large pot-eating monster has mysteriously risen from the ocean floor.

An incredibly unfunny "comedy" based on a singular idea, *Ganjasaurus Rex* may be one of the worst films ever recorded. Filmed in static masters and written by the entire cast, *Ganjasaurus* is that rare release best left forgotten to time. The one positive is the stop-animated monster terribly blended into live-action locations. But that's the only thing memorable in this sleeper (and Reynolds never capitalizes on it). We want a cheesy monster! We want it crashing throughout the town! Instead we get talking heads and hard-to-understand jokes about pot trees. Random stock footage appears with "1985" superimposed, obviously footage of someone's family video. But *Ganjasaurus* just doesn't understand what it's trying to be. And just when the film builds momentum, the plot peters to its meaningless conclusion. Phew!

THE HACKERS

1987, Color, 72 min
STARRING: *Howard Coburn, Dale Caughel, Steve Pricharo, Michelle Rank*
DIRECTOR: *John Duncan*

Old Pa Hacker and his two sons (one of them reticent and wearing a mask) drive across town doing odd jobs. But they also have a habit of killing those who don't pay their bill! Assigned to re-roof a home while the owners are away, the boys take a liking to a woman staying on the property.

Essentially a replay of *The Texas Chainsaw Massacre*, one might assume *The Hackers* is an uninspired copy of the classic backwoods slasher. But from its opening scene of a hitchhiker thumbing a ride (only to have his thumb cut off), we know we're in for a treat. *The Hackers* is a fun, relatively unknown rural slasher with morals. That's right, morals! Pa Hacker may not approve of killing, but he sure knows when it's deserved. Performances are top notch from all involved (especially Caughel, bringing charisma to the family) while Rank carries the "final girl" role well. Rank's feathered bangs and athletic build are impressively unique, so it's a shame she never returned to the genre. Coburn as leader brings authenticity to the film, giving a true-to-life persona belying performance. And blood is splashed around nicely, satisfying gorehounds and providing belly laughs for the initiated (the fisherman's head in the bucket is charmingly gruesome). Part *Blood Hook*, part *Blood Lake*; *The Hackers* is one of the finest SOV horror films of the decade. Required Viewing.

THE LAST SEASON
1987, Color, 95 min
STARRING: *Christopher Gosch, David A. Cox, Mark Eric Charbonneau, Louise Dorsey*
DIRECTOR: *Raja Zahr*

Mike, a good kid vacationing with his dog, is staying with grandparents in their wooded cabin. Mike cares about others and loves nature. But when four beer-guzzling yokels go hunting and shoot Mike's dog and grandfather, all hell breaks loose. Now the men want to eliminate Mike, and Mike wants revenge.

 Taking a cue from *Deliverance*, *House By the Lake* and just about every woodsy revenge flick before it, *The Last Season* is an impressive thriller with a broadcast television persona. In what could easily be mistaken for an Emmeritus production, *The Last Season* hits the ground with a tight pace and tense moments. Zahr lets the audience know exactly what type of movie this is too, laying groundwork for the simple murder/revenge plot that never strays. But what really impresses are moments scattered throughout. The film effectively uses profanity, gunshots, blood, attempted rape and a fairly cold-blooded bit involving the death of Grandma to its advantage. This is what makes *The Last Season* stand out, giving an otherwise forgetful drama kicks of adrenaline. It's also interesting to see how Dorsey (shortly after being saved from a rapist) engages in a romance with our teenaged hero.

Dorsey gives Mike his first sexual encounter in his dead grandparents' house. Innocently portrayed, but perhaps not the best time? Yet my most favorite bits are the haphazard, slow-motion montages of Mike and Grandpa chopping wood and walking the elderly in the forest. Kodak moments, to be sure.

NIGHT OF THE LIVING BABES
1987, Color, 57 min
STARRING: *Michelle Bauer, Andy Nichols, Louie Bonanno, Forrest Witt*
DIRECTOR: *Jon Valentine (Gregory Dark)*

Lying to their wives, two guys visit a brothel and become captives. Dressed in tutu's and chained to the wall, the men are starved as the house Madame attempts to forcibly change their sex with a ray-gun. The wives become saviors as they march in and free their husbands.

From the director of *New Wave Hookers* (featuring an underage Traci Lords), *Night of the Living Babes* is a comic gem of farce, slapstick and marriage relations. So why is it in a horror book? The title is obviously a play on *Night of the Living Dead* and scenes of Romero's classic appear throughout. Kidnapping and (implied) castration are frequent themes too, but honestly? It's too damn hilarious with Scream Queen Bauer leading the cast. Everything feels like a softcore porno with bite. There's no blood but the film is laced with slasher setups and payoffs. Bauer raves about killing her husband for most of the film and while she doesn't, the build-up is fun. Plus there's a catchy theme song throughout and the film feels like it was shot on a weekend. It's not horror, but *Night of the Living Babes* is comic genius using genre trappings. And it's endlessly re-watchable. Highly Recommended.

REDNECK ZOMBIES

They're Tobacco Chewin'
Gut Chompin', Cannibal
Kinfolk from Hell!

REDNECK ZOMBIES
1987, Color, 90 min
STARRING: *Lisa DeHaven, Bucky Santini, Pericles Lewnes, Tyrone Taylor, William Decker*
DIRECTOR: *Pericles Lewnes*

A barrel of toxic waste gets lost in the backwoods of rural America. It's quickly found by a family of rednecks who slosh out the waste, turn the barrel into a swill and brew moonshine. And the radioactive drink becomes the taste of the town! Only thing is, one sip turns you into a flesh-eating zombie.

Distributed by Troma Entertainment (Lewnes and producers were huge *Toxic Avenger* fans), *Redneck Zombies* is possibly the best known SOV horror from the 80's. Troma represented the film around the globe, claiming it *"the first film distributed worldwide, made on home video."* This may be true. The film is an absolute riot. Lewnes states *"we wanted a great title"* and *"based the story off of it."* They knew they would be shooting on video with no money, so they wanted something *"really gory, funny, slapstick and silly."* *Redneck Zombies* was born. Shot on a year's worth of weekends, *Zombies* features a deadly sharp and offensive wit. Lewnes pokes fun at incestuous rednecks, African-Americans, homosexuals, the military, child neglect, rape attempts, drug use, addiction and even transsexuals. But it's all so joyous! Watery blood and guts adds to this, creating an overall schlocky glee that permeates throughout.

The uniquely original soundtrack (consisting of actual songs depicting what's happing onscreen) is amazing. The acting delivers comically, with a bone-chilling turn from E.W. Nesneb (William E. Benson) as the Tobacco Man. His head entirely wrapped in a dirty sack with a single eye staring out, Benson's garbled rants about *"dark times a'coming"* and how drugs will lead to facial deformities and cancerous sores is outright cringing! The film also spoofs several horror films (mostly *The Texas Chainsaw Massacre*) and even features someone reading Fangoria in a mental hospital. If you haven't seen *Redneck Zombies*, you haven't lived. Required Viewing.

An R-rated, 84 minute version was widely available from Trans World Entertainment throughout the 90's. Devoid of gore and completely missing the rape/pregnancy, this cut has become quite rare since Troma began their own video label circa 1996.

SEXANDROIDE

1987, Color, 57 min
STARRING: *Daniel Dubois*
DIRECTOR: *Michel Ricaud*

Three vignettes of torture, perversion and monstrous body horror. A woman is stripped, tortured and burned through use of a voodoo doll while in a public washroom. Another woman is attacked, stripped, cut, stabbed and eye-gouged by a hideous zombie monster (who eventually disembowels himself) in a filthy castle. Finally, a widow cries over an open casket as the dead man inside suddenly wakes, strips the widow and bites her on the neck. Now a vampire, she performs a 10 minute dance before climbing into the casket for some private love.

The connection between SOV horror and pornography has always been strong. Camcorders were widely adopted by porn producers throughout the 80's, mostly due to their low cost and immediate reproduction abilities (no time/money spent on film developing). It changed the porn landscape. But another advantage was video's "real-life" aesthetic. Video looked real. In contrast, film seemed artificial with orchestrated performances designed with light and makeup. Actors *performed* on film while people were *captured* on video. Therefore, pornography looks infinitely more unfiltered and unprompted on videotape as if it were captured live. *Sexandroide* benefits from this by including both sex and gore convincingly mixed on video.

Though the film really doesn't follow a narrative, the vignettes are more than simple scenes of killing. And while strong erotic perversions and female nudity override the film, no pornographic sex occurs (though some distributors reportedly inserted hardcore clips in various versions around the world). The horrific elements are disturbing (breasts punctured by needles, vaginal stabbings, face slashings), yet humor remains since the acts are performed by supernatural elements. Particularly towards the end, humor dominates as the vampire widow suddenly dances nude to Tina Turner's *"What's Love Got to Do With it?"* (I kid you not). But also used are portions of George Romero's *Creepshow* soundtrack. The "Do Not Disturb" sign left hanging on the casket while the two vampires have sex is the proverbial cherry on top. *Sexandroide* revolts, disturbs, titillates, arouses and entertains all without narrative plot. It's strong and perverse, but enjoyably recommended.

SISTERS
1987, Color, 69 min
STARRING: *Clancey McCauley, Aven Warren, Joe Siciliano, Mike Brady, Gary Whitson*
DIRECTOR: *Gary Whitson*

A jealous sister arranges the death of her twin.

Originally sold under the title *Stalked* and with more plot twists than a tornado, *Sisters* marks the beginning of Whitson's W.A.V.E. Productions in feature-length style. Soon to be familiar faces McCauley and Warren shine, both pulling double duty in multiple roles. But it's *Sisters'* quieter moments as Whitson "tests the waters" of video production that really count. Characters are wonderfully devious. Everyone's pulling the wool over each other's eyes to hilarious heights. The investigating cop suddenly cracks the case when a suspect forgets Daylight Savings Time. People seem really excited about coffee. A radio reporter uses his on-air voice at all times (even when admitting guilt at the kitchen table) and the quirks keep rolling! But *Sisters'* accessibility lies in Whitson's focused plot and tight editing, qualities that would continually bring W.A.V.E. Productions beyond standard SOV cheapies. W.A.V.E. Productions are fun; they're enjoyable to watch and surprisingly innocent considering their reputation. And here's where it all started!

SPLATTER FARM

1987, Color, 74 min
STARRING: *John Polonia, Mark Polonia, Todd Rimatti, Marion Costly*
DIRECTOR: *John Polonia, Mark Polonia, Todd Rimatti*

Twin brothers Alan and Joseph drive to their Aunt Lacey's farm for summer vacation. When they arrive, they meet a young farmhand named Jeremy who enjoys self mutilation and chopping up human bodies. Privately, he even enjoys sex acts with the body parts. But none of this seems to alarm Aunt Lacey, who's busy lusting over teenaged nephew Alan. Joseph confronts Jeremy over his weirdness, leading to a brutal night of anal fisting, pissing, oral rape, pitchfork stabbing and finally being buried alive. Alan doesn't fare much better though, getting shot in the face with a rifle the following morning. Then Aunt Lacey reveals that Jeremy is the product of incest, to which he responds by shoving a firecracker between her legs and blowing her apart.

Most films have limits. Most films have a line they won't cross.
Most films know when they've gone too far.

Splatter Farm isn't most movies.

Hungry for a hit, the Polonia brothers and friend Todd let their minds run in 1987 and never looked back. With every disgusting act they could muster, the trio created one of the most vile, unbelievable, sickening, hypnotic and perverted horror films imaginable; tempered with a charming slice of teenaged honesty. *Splatter Farm* delivers. And today, we now know that Mark, John and Todd were not really the demented degenerates they seemed to be. They were teenaged professionals with a plan.

 Impressive camera angles, homemade corpses, sly editing techniques; remind yourself that these teenagers handled every aspect of production. So what were you doing at their age? Only through steadfast determination were they able to get it done. That, and the incredible participation from Marion Costly appearing as a child-lusting corpse-keeping wacko. Costly's performance (a combination of stunted speech patterns and puckering lips) is so unassumingly bizarre, it borders on outrageous. Yet her most notorious scene (the drugging and rape of her nephew) is handled innocently. The music (in its original release version) is both insanely grating and poetically hypnotic. The editing smacks of consumer grade equipment with delayed sound clips. Zooms are prevalent and gore gets extreme close-ups. Even the opening/closing credits reveal the boys limitations; filming text off the computer screen. But with little more than a camcorder, the boys put a lot of heart and honest passion into what they were doing. In addition, special mention must be given to a totally fearless John Polonia; not only for playing victim to a lot of compromising acts but by playing them half naked in a barn! Tied to pipes, John really bared all against the dirty

floor and later, agreed to be fully buried (fully naked) in the earth. Painstakingly long without cutaways, John disappears as shovels of soil cover every inch of Polonia bod. Now that's dedication! But this is not your typical horror film. Brimming with unbridled passion, *Splatter Farm* pushes the limits of acceptable storytelling into inspirational video nirvana. Required Viewing!

In 2007, Mark and John seized the opportunity to refurbish the film; creating what they called their "intended vision" (apparently original release was a rough edit not intended for public eyes). Now running a scant 69 minutes (3 minutes of which is an incredibly slow credit scrawl), whole sequences have been removed while others re-edited and score replaced. The film still packs a punch, but the original release is the superior version.

STREETS OF DEATH
1987, Color, 94 min
STARRING: *Tommy Kirk, Larry Thomas, Guy Ecker, Lawrence Scott, Susanne Smith*
DIRECTOR: *Jeff Hathcock*

Someone is brutally killing hookers, leaving their bodies scattered throughout the city. The police are stumped until a female officer goes undercover as bait. Turns out the killers are actually two film students looking to sell snuff films to foreign buyers, and hookers were the easiest prey.

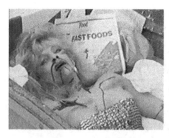 Coming off *Night Ripper!*, Hathcock makes a welcome return to analog horror in *Streets*. And where *Night* spent most of its time spinning wheels, *Streets* gains traction. The majority of the film follows two cops as they investigate the crimes; trying to resist romance and they fight hand-to-hand combat with a female pimp. But at least the police are tied directly to the crimes here (the less said about *Night's* tangled affairs, the better). As for the hookers, they barely have 3 minutes before being axed and most deaths occur off-screen. Basically a tease as each girl is introduced then dumped in the trash. Bummer. But with no emphasis on violence and gore, *Streets of Death* feels more crime drama than slasher. *"I can actually watch it. It's one of my films that I can watch,"* says Hathcock and the

murders do feel inspired. Especially one girl who, after being stripped and tied face down to a table, gets a power drill in the ass. And later, another girl is made to strip while singing to herself. Sleazy! It's also never stated if something else motivates the killings, but the villains seem strongly against sex. One even says to the other *"You do it. You know how I feel about that!"*

The theme of videotape as reality reoccurs here; killings singularly done for the purpose of being filmed (murders caught on tape). And no character asks if special effects were used, strongly echoing Gary Cohen's snuff in *Video Violence*. Videotaped murder appears totally real to characters within the story. Yet the difference between *Video Violence* and *Streets of Death* is Cohen's awareness that he was making a movie on videotape about videotape. Cohen had something to say, while Hathcock just happens to be using the format.

TALES FROM THE QUADEAD ZONE
1987, Color, 62 min
STARRING: *Shirley L. Jones, Keefe L. Turner, John Jones, Larry Jones, Lawrence R. Jones*
DIRECTOR: *Chester Novell Turner*

A mother reads two morbid stories to her dead son's ghost. When her abusive husband arrives home, she fatally stabs him before committing suicide. Now her spirit is free to be with her son again.

An anthology like no other, *Tales From The Quadead Zone* is pure gutter trash in the best way possible. After the lovingly offensive (and sexually charged) *Black Devil Doll From Hell*, one could have written the director off as a one-hit-wonder. But after this most welcome return, audiences can truly see Turner's deprived genius. Back with his consumer camcorder (and again headlined by Shirley L. Jones), *Quadead* takes *Black Devil Doll's* filth and polishes it with confidence. Camera framing is assured and stable, performances are solid and the music (again by Turner) is a riot. But even more impressive is the bargain basement special effects. Coffee cups float, chairs deflate and doors close as ghost-boy does his rounds. And Shirley Jones' performance is disturbing and positively chilling in her knife fight. As for the stories, "Food For ?" is a great idea (a large family kills its own members to match amounts of food provided) while "The Brothers" shines as a tale of twisted revenge (one brother exhumes his older brother's body, dresses him like a clown and reburies him in his basement for kicks). The wraparound becomes the third tale, officially titled "Unseen Vision."

Quadead shines a welcomed return for a distinctly subversive craftsman, demonstrating what can be achieved with consumer grade equipment and a lot of heart. And part 2 is promised in the end credits! We're still eagerly waiting, Chester... Highly Recommended.

   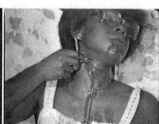

VIDEO VIOLENCE
1987, Color, 98 min
STARRING: *Art Neill, Jackie Neill, Uke, Bart Sumner, Lisa Cohen, William Toddie*
DIRECTOR: *Gary Cohen*

A video store owner happens upon a town-operated snuff ring when a ghastly videotape is mistakenly returned as a rental. Soon the town's involvement becomes clear as more murders on video appear, leading to a store takeover.

Similar to how Wes Craven's *Scream* would change the course of horror in the 90's, Gary Cohen's *Video Violence* changed the course of SOV horror in the 80's. The film is self-referential, self-aware, uniquely original and hysterically frightening.

Could this happen at your video store?

 In 1986, Donald Farmer staged a scene for *Demon Queen* in a video store. *Video Violence* places its entire story throughout one, branching outside only when necessary. 80's release posters line the walls, "big box" videocassettes pack the shelves, a night drop-box for returns, the club member account numbers, late fees - it's all documented here at the zenith of home video's popularity. But it actually plays a part in the story. The store owner (Art Neill) is a regular guy surrounded by a world he doesn't understand. Video has taken over. But he

also doesn't understand the town's appetite for bloodlust, which his patrons will soon embrace wildly over video itself. Briefly consider that in 1987, Britain's "Video Nasties" scandal was still fresh in the minds of viewers. Slasher films, though playing strong at the box office, continued to be a source of controversy amongst parents. Parents occasionally picketed films, demanding they be pulled or sanitized for general audiences. Parents felt that some films had gone too far. Now the real horror of *Video Violence* becomes clear as we journey down the rabbit hole. Could *viewers* go too far? Cohen chillingly demonstrates what could happen if consequence was abandoned and bloodlust overtakes... and it's a hell of a lot of fun.

The scariest part is undoubtedly when Neill happens upon a snuff tape and realizes that his missing employee has been killed in the store. And Cohen's direction truly shines, showing video play to the main character and to the viewers as well. The murders are quite grizzly and equally full of blood, consisting of victims tied to mattresses or white walls. Jokesters Eli (Uke) and Howard (Sumner) are the local bumpkin killers, gleefully carving, slicing and hacking their way to recorded infamy. They love what they do. And the film carries a *Village of the Damned* vibe as more participants join, eventually taking the video store over in a deadly customer mutiny. Art and Jackie Neill (a real married couple) are both fantastic here, consistently convincing as paranoia grows. And they would later return with an equally stong dynamic in *Captives.* But *Video Violence* is a game changer. It presents videotaped murders as real, just as this videotaped movie was available in real video stores. And indeed, the end of *Video Violence* portrays just that: a title available for rent within itself. This is video used as the format distinguishing reality from fiction, and analog is real life! Required Viewing.

Tim Boggs is a multiple award winning Sound Editor and ADR supervisor of countless critically acclaimed shows, including *"Breaking Bad," "The Good Wife," "The Sopranos"* and the *"Hercules"* and *"Xena"* series. He is also a noteworthy painter and photographic artist. But in 1986, Tim directed his sole motion picture on analog video: the fan favorite teenage slasher *Blood Lake*. The film has forever stayed with me; it's charms undeniable. Yet much of its production history has remained unknown for decades. Until now.

As mentioned in the Introduction, I first contacted Tim with the hopes that I could shake some of his secrets loose. I wanted to hear and share his unknown tales and to my excitement, Tim was ready to talk. Tim's *Blood Lake* memoir became the catalyst for my entire SOV journey. I had specific questions (which he graciously answered towards the end), but this is his story in his own words. This is the story of *Blood Lake*.

BLOOD LAKE RECOLLECTIONS

It's been strange, visiting a memory that's now [over 30] years old, reflecting on the "whys?" and "hows?" The most painful part is not the memories themselves, it's the things I don't remember - names of people and places, the loss of contact with those people, and the realization of how much time has now slipped by. I will do my best to be as accurate as possible, but remember, this is just my memory from my perspective. Doug Barry and the other participants may have a different recollection altogether. But one thing I have realized as I've journeyed down the memory trail: the making of *Blood Lake* would make a good story all by itself.

To accurately discuss the making of *Blood Lake* I feel compelled to trace my own history a bit, and how I got interested in movie making.

A Brief (sort of) Biography

I was born and raised in Bartlesville, Oklahoma (home of Phillips Petroleum Company where my father worked). My birthday is October 31, 1958 - Halloween! (and seems somehow appropriate). As a child, I always had an incredible imagination. I used to make up stories using my toys as characters. I think my brothers thought I was a little crazy, because I would voice the different toys and make sound effects, totally losing myself in the story I was telling. As I now look back, I can see where my love of storytelling started.

I have always been a movie buff. When I was a kid there was a TV show in the afternoons called *"Dialing for Dollars."* They played classic movies and during the commercial breaks people would call in to win prizes. I remember hating the commercial breaks because I just wanted to watch the movie. But those afternoons were the beginning of my movie education.

In October of 1972, a few weeks before I turned 14, my parents and I were transferred to London, England. This event changed my life considerably. Moving from a very small city in Oklahoma to the megalopolis of London in the early 70's was a major culture shock. I attended high school at the American School in London. Some of my classmates were the sons and daughters of film directors and actors, including Geoff Edwards (Blake Edward's son) and Suzie Landau (Martin's daughter). I lived in a very upscale neighborhood called St. John's Wood. In fact, the flat my parents and I lived in was across the street from David Astor (Waldorf-Astoria family), and next door to them were Paul and Linda McCartney. That was cool. We certainly weren't rich by the American or British standard (more like lower middle class), but the transfer to London gave my family an opportunity we could never have dreamed. I was able to travel through Europe and even parts of Africa, which broadened me in ways I still can't totally comprehend. But the most influential thing for me was the music scene. The Progressive/Art Rock movement was at its zenith, and I became a huge fan of English bands such as: Yes, Pink Floyd, Genesis, ELP, King Crimson, Jethro Tull and Led Zepplin. These bands were the Rock counterparts to the Romantic period of "Classical" music where music told a story. I would sit in my room with my eyes closed listening to this music and visualize stories and amazing images. Of course my experiments in drugs (pot, hash, opium and LSD) had an influence too. All of these influences over the four years I was in England contributed to my desire to be an artist, storyteller and eventually a filmmaker.

After graduating high school in 1976, I moved back to Oklahoma to attend The University of Oklahoma. After a rough freshman year (too many drugs and not enough focus), I finally settled into the Art school where I was turned on to experimental film and video. The Art school was anti-Hollywood. Their focus was on non-narrative filmmaking. They encouraged freedom of expression, and the visual over storytelling. To balance my artistic side with my need to tell stories, I began attending the English Department film study classes. I never enrolled in a class; I would just sneak into screenings and lectures. I bought used textbooks of those classes and would study on my own. It was in Art school that I first used a video camera. Film and the processing fees associated with it were prohibitive to me, but video…! I first started with an open reel half-inch tape machine, then the portable unit. During my senior year, the Art school acquired a 3/4 inch portable rig, and later an editing console. I loved to play and experiment using these different formats. A friend and I got keys to the studio so we could go in at all hours and work on ideas. I remember waking up at 2am and feeling compelled to go to the Art school to work on a video idea. I guess you'd say I "caught the bug."

After graduating OU, I tried to find work at TV stations, commercial/advertising agencies, and corporate video departments, but had no luck finding a proper video job. I didn't have the experience or proper resume reel to be considered for one of those highly competitive jobs. I ended up going back to Norman to attend graduate school, focusing on video. I got a job at Dorset Educational Systems, a small educational software company that made little digital programs for the budding personal computer market. It was also around this time that the Home Video revolution took off. A friend who worked with me at Dorset, John Schulte, and who was also interested in making movies agreed to go halves with me on a portable VHS rig. This was before camcorders, so the camera was separate from the deck (like the 3/4" and open reel 1/2" machines I had used in college). We would make little short videos and either transfer them to 3/4" and edit them using the Art school's facilities, or in a couple of occasions, rent a VHS editing system. For me, these early shorts were the bridge between my non-narrative videos of undergraduate years and the narrative films I wanted to do. A lot of it was just video and music (no dialog) to tell a story. Music was always SO important.

We eventually ventured into wedding video production. That was a great education because you are essentially telling a story (a wedding) shooting and editing in the camera. I had to learn how to anticipate a shot, frame it, shoot it, find a transition to another shot and then know when to cut. I've shot well over a hundred weddings over the years. It is a great exercise. If I were teaching a video production class, I would probably begin with this lesson.

In 1984, John moved to Los Angeles. I followed shortly after and tried to get a job in the film industry. Ironically, I encountered the same problems as after graduating from OU - not enough experience, etc. John and I used our wedding video experience to land a job with a company that specialized in weddings and industrial videos: Mattern Video owned by Howard Mattern. In our spare time, we managed to make another short video using our consumer VHS equipment. "Ashes" was quite imaginative. Since the camera was so small, we could put it in unusual places including under a bed. We edited at night on the company's editing system. We de-saturated the color so the video had a black & white film feel to it. I still like the look of "Ashes" but after a viewing a few years back, I realized it needs a better edit job.

Two of the video shorts I worked on with John eventually won awards at the CAN (Cable Access of Norman) Festival. I remember in my acceptance speech for "Ashes" in the Entertainment category I ended by saying *"It's amazing what you can do in half inch."* That caused quite a stir as at that time there was a distinction between professional equipment (U-matic and higher) vs. consumer grade (Beta, VHS and lower). Half inch was considered below broadcast standards and was usually pooh-poohed by the "Professionals." So for me to tell a group of industry professionals that they had just been beat by a consumer grade user surprised a lot of people. Forgive the clichés, but throughout my life I've tended to go against the grain as I tried to think/work/live "outside the box." The decision to shoot *Blood Lake* on U-matic was the result of this experience. I try to not let certain limitations or expectations hold me back. One of my personal mantras is "Do your best with what you have to work with."

I had left my girlfriend and her son in Oklahoma while attempting the move to LA, and was missing them badly. So after 3 months I decided to move back to Norman and marry my sweetheart. But I vowed I would someday move back to Los Angeles.

In the spring of 1985, I got a job in Oklahoma City at Ford Audio Video as a salesman (YUCK!!!!). I had hoped that by selling video equipment, that I would have access to it and possibly meet other users that could help me get a job in a more creative occupation. I hated that job. I was too honest to be a good salesman. I didn't like the owners much either. I don't mean to vent, but..... They made me work the Saturday morning of MY WEDDING DAY!!! *"Company rules are company rules..."* and jeeze how I hate rules that are either arbitrary or make no sense at all. By that fall I was moonlighting shooting weddings for another guy, Roger Gower, but this time using his portable U-matic deck. This at least kept a camera in my hand from time to time.

By the following spring I was getting very frustrated. I was barely scraping by, living in a small two-room apartment in the country with my wife and stepson. I hated my sales job, and was working 6-7 days a week including shooting weddings. I felt I was getting no closer to my goals. In fact, it seemed like the ship had sailed and I was watching it disappear over the horizon. Then one afternoon a young man entered Ford Audio Video looking for pricing on buying or renting video equipment. His name was Doug Barry.

The Making of *Blood Lake* (as best as I can remember)

With my history out of the way, I figure I should just tell the story of how this thing got made.

By writing it all out, this will help me to remember details you'd be interested in that just answering questions might not include. (Sorry for the length, but once I got started I found it hard to stop.)

Unlike me, Doug was a born salesman. He was slick; had that sparkling smile that was immediately engaging. Doug originally wanted to be an actor. He had the good looks and the attitude required. The thing he mainly lacked was opportunity. In 1982, Doug traveled to Tulsa to audition for Francis Ford Coppola's film *The Outsiders*. He got beat out by the likes of Tom Cruise, Rob Lowe, Patrick Swayze, Emilio Estevez, Matt Dillon, C. Thomas Howell, and Ralph Macchio. Undeterred, he and his brother moved briefly to Los Angeles to pursue acting careers. I don't remember the details, but only know that their first attempt was much like mine, and soon returned to the safety of friends and family in the bosom of the heartland - Oklahoma.

Doug decided the best way to achieve his goal was to do it himself. So he bought books on Producing and Screen Writing and studied his butt off learning what he needed to know to make a movie. He knew that funding would be very limited, so the movie had to be simple to make. The key to that simplicity was using only a handful of actors in a handful of locations - the fewer the better. And because he didn't think he could hire professional actors, he decided to write a story using characters based on people he already knew (and might need as actors basically playing themselves). Very simple. Very smart.

When Doug entered Ford Audio, he told me he was looking to make a movie and wanted some advice. He asked me about the difference between film and video. I told him about my experiences using video because of the prohibitive cost of film. I explained the differences between consumer 1/2" video vs. the higher (but not high) quality of 3/4" U-matic. And, while I was at it, I mentioned my desire to direct a movie. If my memory serves me correctly, within just a few minutes we were already talking about making the movie together - Doug, writing, producing and starring, and me directing. That movie was *Blood Lake*.

Doug was still writing the script. He had the story down, but was still molding the characters to fit his friend's personalities. Even most the names of the characters are names of his friends - just not necessarily attributed to the corresponding person/character. "Mike" (Doug Barry) was based on Mike Kaufman - who played "Bryan," based on Doug's best friend Bryan Barker (who was credited as assistant director and who played two roles in the movie - the Sheriff and the Man with the boy). "Becky" was the name of Doug's fiancé. "Kim" (I think) was Becky's sister and Bryan Barker's girlfriend/fiancé (confused yet?). Yes, it was Oklahoma!

We planned to shoot in the summer. We needed to secure a location, cast the movie, rent equipment and supplies, and most important - find the money to pay for it all.

At that time, Doug was working for his future father-in-law as a driver for his limousine service. He had driven for VIPs and rock stars including Eddie Van Halen. He wanted desperately to break out on his own and to make it in the movie business. But from what I saw, he was virtually alone in that sentiment. My impression was that his family and Becky's family were merely tolerating Doug's quest for independence. Subtly (and sometimes not so) Becky and her family [seemed] to undermine Doug and *Blood Lake*. Again, this is my impression and I don't mean to point fingers. But this what I remember and what I felt at the time.

Doug's dad was a Doctor or a Dentist. He made good money. But from what I remember, he wouldn't invest in the movie. I don't know their history. Maybe he'd already given Doug money that was squandered and didn't want to do it again. Doug eventually had to borrow several thousand dollars from Becky's older brother. This would turn out to be problematic.

I remember when Doug told me he had found the location, a lake house on a small lake in Southwestern Oklahoma, Cedar Lake, near Hinton (not to be confused with the Cedar Lake in Southeastern Oklahoma near the Arkansas border). But there was a catch. The owners were friends of his family and to make sure we didn't destroy the place they wanted their daughter Angela Darter to be involved. Angela was bright and attractive, so Doug did what any good producer would do - he offered her the female lead.

Doug had cast most of the major characters with his close friends or their family members. There were just a few left. Tiny Frazier was an acquaintance of Doug, and had made an impression because of his size and his sort of crazy menacing look. He made the perfect killer (or as perfect as we could expect at the time). The role of Kim, the best friend of the character Becky went to the only person who had any real acting experience. Andrea Adams had previously acted in another low budget horror movie *The Ripper* (also a United Home Video release). The final actor to be cast was The Gardner. A friend of mine seemed perfect for the part. Thom Renbarger not only had the look I was going for, but he just happened to be the father of my oldest son. Yes, Thom was my wife's ex-husband. And so I got to do something many men have only dreamed about - to kill their wife's ex-husband! (The irony there is, Thom and I were/are very good friends. I consider him more of a brother-in-law than my (now ex-) wife's ex.)

As we approached summer, I knew I wouldn't be able to leave Ford Audio for the week or so required for our initial shoot schedule. I talked to Roger Gower and he agreed to try to work me full time - shooting 1-3 weddings on the weekends, then editing them during the week. It usually took a day to properly edit each wedding video. Roger told me that he'd hire me, but that he expected *"complete loyalty."* I agreed, not really understanding what he considered that to mean. But with the assurance that I could actually work full time making videos instead of just trying to sell the equipment, I gave my notice to Claire Ford, the co-owner for Ford Audio Video. I timed my announcement to coincide with completing a major sale that I had been working on for months. I figured I could use the commission as a sort of severance pay. But Claire had another idea. She informed me I would not receive the commission until after the equipment had been completely installed and full payment received. And if I were no longer working for them at that time, there would be no commission paid. Whatever…. Commission or no commission, I was just glad to leaving that place. (Assholes!)

The first time I visited the location with Doug was in June. It was during a week when Roger was on vacation and I had the video rig. I met Doug behind his Limo office and we transferred the video equipment into his Trans Am. The area was sort of seedy - a warehouse district. I was a little worried about leaving my car, but Doug assured me it would be fine.

It was an hour or so drive out to Cedar Lake. There were several locations we needed to find. The house itself, a dock with another dock nearby where the killer could watch the kids, a cove where Bryan and Kim would be killed, the tree where a friend of theirs would be tortured and killed, and finally a house or shack where the killer stored the Gardener and where the final scene would occur. The house was great. Better than perfect because it was two stories - downstairs had the living room, dining area and kitchen. The upstairs had one large communal bedroom with several beds + one small bedroom. Since we were going to have to live at the lake house the ten days or so we were going to be shooting, the upstairs would be our main living quarters while we shot downstairs (and vice-versa).

I shot a lot of test video around the area so I could better visualize the scenes. We easily found the two docks, and a nearby tree. The cove presented a problem because there really wasn't one that we had access to. We found a reed-covered area about 200 feet from the house. Doug's character was suppose to swim across the lake to find the boat and discover the dead bodies, but I figured we could shoot him swimming out, then switch angles and shoot him swimming into the reed bank. But the greatest discovery was the little storage house next to the main house. I realized this would be where the killer lived, and stored his victims - the dead gardener and later Becky and the two kids. There was no way we could shoot the interior scene there, but I knew where we could - at MY house. Or more correctly, at the other end of the garage apartment I was renting from Dorsett Educational Systems. There was storage space there that wasn't being used. The locations turned out to be fortuitous.

That night when Doug and I returned to my car behind the Limousine Service, we had just transferred the video equipment into my car. At that moment colored lights flashed with the quick burst of a police siren. A cop emerged, hand on holster, flashlight in our faces. *"Don't tell me, you guys just found this equipment."* That pissed me off. Now, I'm not a hot head. In fact, I'm usually the calm, cool and controlled person in a group. But this cop was accusing me of stealing and I wasn't going to stand for it. I raised my voice - *"What?!"* and was just about to lose it. Doug grabbed my arm and pulled me back. He flashed that smile of his and calmly explained who we were and what we were doing. He showed he had the keys to the limo service and offered references if there was any doubt. The cop seemed a bit disappointed as he got back into his cruiser and drove away. I swear, we really could have stolen that equipment and Doug would have still talked our way out of it.

As the summer wore on, we began the "on again, off again" part of the story. We had to coordinate everyone's schedule so we could all be there for 10-11 days. But Angela Darter's parents started having second thoughts. They had decided to sell the lake house property and didn't want to risk having anything broken. I actually don't know if they ever intended to sell the place, or if that was just a story to sound like a good excuse not to let us shoot there. But again, credit Doug for smoothing things over and convincing them to let us use the place.

My final hurdle was when I told Roger Gower that I was going to need to take 10 days off to shoot this movie. I had been up front with him from the beginning about what I was planning, but I don't think he ever really took it seriously. So when I told him I needed the time off to work on another project, he pulled the *"complete loyalty"* clause in our agreement. He gave me an ultimatum - my job with him, or the movie. I told him that just the fact he was giving me an ultimatum was all I needed to decide. I quit on the spot. I literally quit two jobs to make *Blood Lake*.

With my help, Doug rented the video equipment. A Sony camera and portable U-matic (ENG) unit. Two lighting kits - one Lowell kit containing two spots complete with barn doors and reflector umbrellas, and a Lowell Soft-Light kit with two double halogen lights with reflector tents. I had a sennheiser shotgun mic and mic stand, and a tripod. And other than a few other things - extension cords, duct tape, a few gels and clips and several cases of videotape, that was it. There would be no crew to help me other than Bryan Barker and the other actors. I was the only one that had any camera or lighting experience.

I knew it was going to be tough. I knew it was probably going to turn out looking and sounding like shit. I even realized it probably would never be finished and even if it did, few people would ever see it. But I also knew I had to try.

After reading the script for the first time, I remember thinking that it stunk. For one thing, it was only about 75 pages. We needed to make it at least 80 minutes long to be considered a "feature." I tried to smooth out some of the dialog and wrote some extra scenes. I wrote the dock scene where they see the body floating only to find it's Bryan playing a trick. The other thing I knew early on was that it really didn't matter how bad the movie turned out, as long as it had a dynamite cover. That doesn't mean I didn't care how it turned out, only that I knew people chose a movie mostly based on the cover. I also rationalized that the movie was geared toward pre-teens. That was my rationale anyway. It helped get me through a very tough shoot and an incredibly long post.

I don't remember the exact date we all drove out to begin shooting the movie. I think it was August 15th, 1986. I know it was middle to late August and that the Edmond Oklahoma Post Office was attacked by a disgruntled worker (one of the earliest examples of "Going Postal"). It happened either just before we arrived or while we were there. I looked it up and it occurred on Wednesday, August 20th, so I believe we were already there. Also, we had pushed the shoot about as late as we could. Another week and the two kids would be back in school. And then at the very last minute the kid's parents got cold feet and decided they didn't want their children to be involved. Doug and I convinced them that they would be safe and that we would not get crazy around them.

It seems to me there were problems all the way up to the day we left. I know Doug was sort of caught in the middle of a tightrope - needing to shoot this movie and at the same time keep his fiancé and her family happy and secure. After all, he was going to be at a lake house with a bunch of guys and two attractive women that Becky and her family didn't know. Doug did his best to walk that tightrope, but I could tell it weighed heavily on him. Of course, he did manage to make the movie, but I know it put a strain on his relationship with Becky and his future in-laws.

The first day (Friday) was a complete waste. We were getting organized and settling in. I think we tried to plan out the driving shots but nothing much else. Most of the time was spent just scoping the place out and deciding who was going to sleep where. The next day the shooting was going to commence, and so were the problems.

I remember picking something easy to shoot that first morning - something just to get started. Doug had come equipped with a production board. We had the entire shoot planned out in advance, but of course those plans were quickly tossed out once we began. In the beginning it was hard to get everyone motivated. The kids were hard to rouse in the mornings. There seemed to be a vacation attitude starting to creep in. Doug and I had to get them and keep them motivated. We started by shooting the driving scenes. Those were fun and actually helped bond the actors. Most of that stuff was just ad-lib. Since most of them weren't actors, I figured it best to let them be themselves and just shoot what they did. Of course, that's where some of the real gems of dialog came from. Much better than what was on the page.

By the afternoon we started to get visitors. The kids' moms had shown up to chaperone. Becky and her brother and sister also arrived. They were all demanding attention and distracting us from what we were there to do. I could sense Doug's tightrope getting more and more frayed. More people showed up on Sunday. The word had gotten out that we were shooting a movie at a lake house and people just wanted to come out and party. I had a talk with Doug. Precious time was being wasted. These friends and family members just wanted a vacation. They didn't seem to understand that we were there to work. Doug knew he had to ask them all to leave. It was tough on him, but I admire that he did it. I actually didn't mind the mothers being there. They were great at fixing us meals and cleaning up after us so we could concentrate on shooting. But in the end everyone had to go. By Monday we were on our own.

Once we were alone to do the work, we all felt a renewed bond. Everyone pitched in to help me between takes. I found I didn't need a crew - I already had a crew - they were just doubling as my actors. And I don't remember any tension between any of us. It was only when outsiders would visit that tension would mount. As the week progressed so did the amount of shooting. Because we squandered so much time in the beginning, I was trying desperately to catch up. I got less and less sleep each night, and by the end I was getting only 1-2 hours of sleep. I remember thinking at the time that there was nothing else in the world that I would work this hard on, for this many hours and with so little sleep. And if nothing else came of my time spent directing this movie, at least I knew I had what it takes to do it. The confidence I built that week I carry with me to this moment.

Since none of these people were actors, I found it better to let them improv the scenes. The more they were able to play themselves the more real their performance became. You'll notice that the first scenes arriving at the house how stiff the performances are. That's because we were sticking to the script and it was the first stuff shot. But later, the cast became more comfortable and were able to loosen up their performances a bit. Travis was a cool kid. I liked him a lot. He was naturally funny and wanted to keep up with "the guys." We encouraged him to be himself, and Doug often set him up with good opportunities to say some really funny stuff. I don't know what happened to him. The scene of Christie Willoughby's first time skiing was real. That truly was her first time and we got it on tape.

The beer was real. No such thing as "near beer" back then. The quarters game was only slightly longer than what you see. During editing, Doug was pushing every scene as long as they could go. The empty chair in the foreground was to symbolize the one person missing - the killer. Seems silly now, but there were a lot of visual symbols I was trying to get into the movie. Most never worked out for one reason or another. But at least I was trying.

The one thing I was trying to do that didn't make it into the movie was shots of the ducks that hung around the lake house. I wanted the ducks to quack and go crazy after each killing. I thought it would be eerie. I shot a lot of footage of them. The problem was that when we returned on the weekends in September to do the last killing scenes, the ducks were gone. I guess they flew south for the winter. I never got the footage I needed, so I had to scrap the idea.

We had a number of problems during the shoot. One was lighting the exterior at night with only four lights (and two of them were soft-lights and not meant to be used as floods). And trying to get power to those lights at a fair distance without blowing fuses. I think on one night we actually tapped into one of the neighbor's outlets. They weren't there to ask or complain. I wonder what they thought about their electric bill that month. (Sorry...)

The night we shot the dock scene with Tiny Frazier, we weren't sure if he was going to make it. He was running a high fever. The steam coming off his head was because of that. I think we just got the silhouette shot we needed and then sent him home. I still needed to get the shot of him stabbing at the water and didn't now what to do. Bryan ended up doubling for Tiny. Those are Bryan's hands, as well as the waist down walk up shot. Bryan also doubled for the killer's hands on the tree torture scene and the shadow in the window.

The night of the ambulance arriving and taking the survivors away, Doug had arranged for a paramedic friend of his to come out to the lake. He didn't arrive until well after dark. This was before cell phones so it was hard to coordinate with him how to find the place. He made a wrong turn at the entrance of the lake and got lost. But we could see him on the other side of the lake, as he would turn on the flashing red & blue ambulance lights. I think we sent out a search party in one of our cars to find him.

During one of the afternoon dock shoots, the video camera's eye monitor magnifying lens (about the size of a half dollar) popped out and rolled off the end of the dock. Doug and I tried to feel for it with our bare feet, but that was in about 5 feet of water in an area covered with weeds. We knew we would never see it again (unless somehow miraculously all the water of the lake would disappear!)

By the end of the week we had shot the majority of the movie, but there were still key elements to shoot. We managed to return to the lake house for two more weekends to finish that location. The opening scene where the gardener is killed was actually one of the last things we shot. You can tell that autumn was starting to set in. After that, we completed the climactic scene (if you can call it that) where Becky and the kids are tied up and Mike rescues them.

About a month after we had wrapped, some sort of seismic event happened that ripped a hole in the bottom of the lake and under the dam. For several days the water flowed out creating a giant whirlpool like a bathtub draining. Doug and I read about it in the newspaper and wanted to get out there with a video rig to shoot it. By the time we could arrange things, most of the water was gone. But we came up with an idea to shoot one last coda. We got the rig and Tiny and drove out to the lake. Since the killer had mysteriously disappeared at the end of the climax, we thought it would be cool to take advantage of this amazing natural special effect and have Tiny appear in this sort of nether world. It was late autumn, a dreary overcast day and all the water in the lake was gone. It seemed like divine providence. Thank you God!

After shooting those scenes, there was one last thing I had to check out. I walked to the end of the dock, now lying flat on the muddy lake bottom. I looked down, and what do you think I spied with my little eye - yes indeed - the video camera eyepiece lens. I carried it back to the house where Doug was. I looked at him and smiled. *"You'll never guess what I just found."* and revealed the little lens. He looked at me with a disbelieving expression. *"No!"* he said. *"No way. You bought that, didn't you?"* I just shook my head. *"Can you believe it?"* All he could say was *"No fucking way!"* and laugh. Simply amazing!

Other Memories...

The day we shot the skiing sequence we were all feeling good. This was to be the fun day.

It was early in the shoot (either Sunday or Monday) but it was a day where all of the cast and I would be together and away from the distractions of any visitors.

I set up the tripod in the center of the boat with the widest spread I could get, and with one leg pointing toward the back of the boat. I didn't want any mishaps, so I tested the tripod balance and stability the best I could. I attached the camera and pushed and pulled at the rig. With the weight of the rig and one leg pointing toward the rear of the boat, everything seemed safe and secure. We loaded everyone in the boat and took off toward the playground area located on a small peninsula near the main entrance, where we would drop off the kids. As we sped across the lake, I continued to test the camera and my positioning to ensure the best control. I found the best position standing on the left side of the tripod where I could lean on one of the rear seats. After dropping off the kids, we made our way out to the center of the lake to begin our first shot - the opening of the sequence where Tony and Bryan rise out of the water to the rock music of Voyager. Doug and Mike took their skis and got into position. We took up the slack and I stood up, framed and focused the shot and the guys gave me the thumbs up sign. We were all ready to shoot.

If memory serves, it was Bryan Barker piloting the boat while Angela Darter slated the shot. I yelled *"Hit it!"* and Bryan gunned the engines.... Now, with all my preparations, I never performed an actual dry run-through with the engines gunned. We did some short bursts, but not a full-fledged pedal to the metal full throttle take off. So when Bryan gunned the engines, we took off with a power I was completely unprepared for. I'm sure there is some physics equation that would properly explain what happened. All I know is the force sent the tripod and me with camera and recorder attached flying toward the end of the boat.

If you look at the shot in the movie, as Doug is trying to rise up to ski, he is met with a face full of water. So from his point of view, as the boat starts to pull, he sees the camera and I starting to fall toward the rear of the boat and the water. He is then temporarily blinded with water, and when Bryan cuts the engines and his vision clears, all he sees is the boat - no Tim and, more importantly, NO CAMERA! Doug told me later that in that moment, he knew the movie was over and that he was going to be liable for the camera, recorder and tripod as it had all gone down to the bottom of the lake. As panic was about to engulf him, he saw me start to rise from the back of the boat, and then pull the tripod and camera up with me. He had never been so happy to see me.

What I remember is feeling the force throw the tripod and me to the back of the boat. I was NOT going to let the camera fall - either in the water, or even to smash on the floor of the boat. So as I'm falling, I grabbed the camera and tripod and cradled it as I spun my body so my back hit the floor with the camera held firmly against my chest. Afterward I checked everything. Nothing was broken, neither the camera, tripod or me.

After that, I learned that I could not stand while shooting the initial rise out of the water, and that I had to prep the shot so everyone would stay in frame while I sat next to the tripod firmly holding it down. Then after we got to full speed, I could stand up to operate the camera while one of our cast/crew held on to tripod (just in case). We continued shooting as planned and finished the sequence without incident. But we all knew just how close we were for the whole endeavor to be over.

Another memory was when we shot the murder scene of Bryan and Kim in the boat. It was probably 1 or 2 am by the time we got to Kim's scream. I set up the shot so that as Bryan's throat is cut, a stream of blood would hit Kim in the face. Bryan Barker served as my FX guy, and had filled a syringe with our fake blood concoction - Karo syrup and red food coloring. Just before we started to roll, Andrea Adams asked me if she could rehearse her scream to warm up her vocal cords. I didn't have a problem, so I said sure. She belts out the most extreme blood-curdling scream, and every dog in the lake begins to bark. I remember thinking that someone was going to call the cops. We had warned the lake residents that we would be doing some screams that night, but I hadn't counted on the volume of her scream. After several minutes the dogs settled down and we began the shot. Andrea again belts out another intense scream, but Bryan missed the mark hitting Andrea on the side of her head. Again, the dogs bark and I thought *"I gotta get this shot soon before the cops arrive."* I think it took two more tries before Bryan hit his mark. The winner hit Andrea right in the eye. And though Andrea sounded like she was being savagely murdered, the police never showed. Doug had already called the Police Station and warned them what we were doing.

Post Production

After everything was shot, we began the time consuming work of logging each tape. The first thing we did was transfer the masters to 1" timecoded tape, then had those copied to VHS. Doug and I would take each VHS tape and write down what was on them. The plan was to hopefully edit the movie on paper so we would be more efficient when it came time to do the actual physical editing. It took nearly a year before we were ready. Also, Doug had to raise another $3000 to pay for it all.

In the interim, I kept busy with my new job. I was hired by Oklahoma City Community College to be a "Media Technician." Some would call it a glorified AV guy. But to me, it was an opportunity to do what I loved to do - make movies. Actually, they were instructional and promotional videos for the college, but it allowed me to write, light, shoot, direct, edit, and even in a few of them - act. My skills as a director/video photographer/editor increased significantly with this experience. I remember thinking that the one thing missing in my movie-making development was the opportunity to work with good experienced actors. The irony of this thought would hit me years later.

During the spring of 1987, my wife Shan and I came up with an interesting idea. Since I had shot photos of the dry lake bed, we thought we would create a spooky semi-true story about the making of *Blood Lake* and the eerie disappearance of the lake water, then send the story and before and after pictures to "The Weekly World News" (a supermarket tabloid that specialized on the very weird). To our surprise, they accepted the submission, though they rewrote the story to spice it up even more than we did. Unfortunately Shan was not paid for her work, but I was compensated for the photos. The story ran and it was the first time I had a photo published. I was thrilled, though Shan was a bit disappointed.

In July of 1987, I took my now pregnant wife to Los Angeles for a vacation and to prepare her for a possible move to the area. While we were gone our dog Chris, a full-blooded golden retriever, was attacked by ticks. Upon our return he was sick and weak. We got him to a vet for a blood transfusion, but he still remained weak from the ordeal. The following night we began editing. We spent about two weeks editing only at night (for a discounted rate) while I worked during the day at my regular job. It was a grueling schedule. Chris wasn't getting better. I kept in touch with my wife Shan on how he was doing. The night before we finished editing I got a call from Shan. Chris was in a bad way. She had called a vet who was preparing for another blood transfusion for him, but it would have to wait till the morning. When I got home around 2am, Chris was lying on the floor of the living room/kitchen in our two-room apartment in the country. I cradled him in my arms and stroked his fur telling him it was okay, that I was home. After about 30 seconds, he stiffened up, shuttered and exhaled a long breath. He was gone. He died in my arms.

This memory will always haunt me and will always be connected to *Blood Lake*. I've had to ask myself if I was paying too much to the finishing of this stupid movie and not enough on the ones I loved. I swore I would never again put my career over my family (that includes my pets).

As far as the editing itself, all I can say is that I was pretty disappointed. I wanted a tighter cut, but Doug was overly concerned about the length. Because we felt the movie needed to be at least 80 minutes long, he drained every frame out of each shot. I finally got tired of arguing with him. After all, it was his investment. But I cringed when he would leave flaws in - extra camera movements and so forth - and privately wondered what I was expecting. Bad script, bad acting, bad quality video, bad sound, and yes bad directing - why should I think the editing would be any better.

Once editing was completed we found a composer, Russell Allen, who jumped at the chance to score a movie. And best of all, he did it for free. Once the music was composed, we went back to the editing studio to lay it all in. I remember getting a copy of the finished movie and just holding it. I thought about all my time and effort, all the struggles, the highs of accomplishment and the very lows of losing my beloved Chris. I took the video home and that night Shan and I watched it from start to finish. When it was over I turned to her and said, *"I never want to see this again."*

It took me 20 years before I would watch it again, and even then I wasn't really trying to. My family had gathered at my brother Steve's house in Granbury, Texas. My two sons, Sam and Aaron (who was still in the womb during post) along with my two older brothers wanted to watch *Blood Lake*. Steve had a copy I had sent him years before. My two boys had never seen it. So while they watched, I tried to stay busy in the kitchen. But I could not escape the sound - the dialog and the music. I'd hear my family laugh, or groan or make a comment and I found myself being pulled back 20 years in time and all the memories of the shoot. Soon I was in the living room giving a running commentary to each scene.

The movie was still as bad as I remembered - maybe even worse. And though for years I have read commentary of other viewers on IMDB and the complete trashing of the movie, I don't regret a thing. It's because it didn't matter that the movie was a piece of crap - I did the best I could with what I had to work with. Didn't really know what I was doing in the beginning, but by the end I had learned. I was able to do something that I'm sure few if any of those commentators have done. I made a movie. I've learned that most people are too afraid of failure to even attempt to chase a dream. I am not afraid to fail, because each failure is one more step closer to success.

The cover design was the last item on the menu of things to do. Being an artist, it was easy for me to visualize the front cover. I sketched out an image of the killer standing on the dock, his knife raised, silhouetted by the moon. I think it was Doug who suggested putting a beautiful woman, dead at the foot of the killer. Doug found a photographer who specialized in nude photography. He was an overweight guy with stringy hair - not attractive at all. His studio was covered with pictures of beautiful women (some more than others, obviously) in all manner of dress and undress. Some were in very provocative poses. I realized I had gone into the wrong business! This was a perfect way for an unattractive man to be surrounded by beautiful naked women. He told me that one of his specialties was to photograph the wives of rich men - in bondage. Certain rich people it seems LOVE to have their fetishes immortalized. We constructed the dock using some old warehouse pallets that were painted yellow. Tiny Frazier took his position, knife in hand, with a beautiful model sprawled at his feet. The whole shoot probably only lasted 30 minutes.

Doug found an advertising agency to complete the cover art. I was blown away by the finished artwork. It turned out better than I ever imagined. I knew we had something we could sell.

Selling *Blood Lake*

Doug contacted a number of video distribution companies, but no one seemed interested in our shot on video production. But there was one company that was interested - United Home Entertainment. Located in Tulsa, it was the only in-state distribution company and was one we were familiar with. Doug and I met with them. We were hoping to actually make some money and possibly get some royalties. To our disappointment, they offered us around $6000 to buy us out. I say us, but it was really just Doug. We told them we would think about it and left. ($6000 is what I remember, though it might have been more. This number comes from what I remember the production costing Doug, which was about equal to what he was offered. It might have been $8000 or even $10,000, but I still think it was more like 6.)

On the way home, I tried to convince Doug to hold out for more, or to at least keep looking. He agreed with me, but after a few days he called me to tell me he had accepted the deal. I think Doug was under a lot of financial pressure. The movie cost him around $6000 and with this deal he would break even. To this day, I'm not sure if what Doug told me was even true. It's possible he got more out of them. I actually hope he did. I didn't do the film just to make money. Sure, I would have liked to, but the money was always a secondary issue with me. I got what I wanted - a chance to direct a movie. I did that. I'm happy I did that. And I have no regrets or feel any ill will that I didn't make money in the process. To me, the act of doing is more important than financial rewards (but I certainly would not refuse them if offered). After we sold *Blood Lake* and we all went our separate ways, I pretty much lost touch with everybody but Doug. And even then, Doug and I talked only occasionally. There was no discussion of a sequel. I haven't directed any features since, just a few shorts. I continue to write and have not given up on the idea of directing again, I just want to have more control (and money) when I do.

Post Answers

The one thing *Blood Lake* did for me was to prove to myself that I really wanted to be involved in motion picture making. I LOVE the creative process. I'm happiest when I have a camera in my hand (still or movie). I can work very long hours under tremendous pressure and deadlines and still be happy. It gave me the confidence to move my family (my wife, two young boys and a dog) to California in pursuit of my dream to work in the entertainment industry. In the summer of 1990, I did just that. I quit OKCCC in June of 1990. I then began work on Chris Reynolds' 2nd film, a cop drama called *Lethal Justice* as his Associate Producer. That gave me a lot of experience dealing with many different aspects of producing a film. For the next 18 months I did a lot of odd jobs - videotaping weddings, industrial videos, city council meetings, sporting events and horse races at Santa Anita Racetrack. I even shot an infomercial with Judge Wapner.

I worked part time as a PA on a few movies - *"Harley Davidson an the Marlboro Man,"* *"Mistress,"* and *"Grand Canyon."* It was a real thrill for me to be on the set of a Real feature film, talking to actors that I had been watching for years (Robert DeNiro, Martin Landau, and Steve Martin). But this work was very competitive and very hard to come by. In the winter of 1991 everything seemed to dry up. By February of 1992, things were looking bleak. I answered an ad in the LA Times for "Sound Editor Wanted." A few days later I received a call back from the headhunter doing the search. She told me there were over 500 applicants - and that I was their #1 candidate. A few weeks later Sound Trax (a post-production studio in Burbank) hired me.

During my first interview, I was waiting in the lobby. I remember preparing myself for the interview when from down the hall I heard a blood-curdling SCREAM! It startled me. It then dawned on me that this was what they do here. They were cutting sound effects on (one of) the *Amityville Horror* films. Every 20 seconds or so the SCREAM would repeat. I chuckled remembering Andrea's screams in *Blood Lake*.

One of my projects was to cut some of the sound effects for the movie *Maniac Cop 3*. I was to cut the fire effects of the maniac cop during the climax of the movie. The cop is on fire and swings his arms around during a high speed chase. To accomplish this, I went to my boss' house to record "fire foley." We soaked a tennis ball in gasoline, lit it and recorded the sound of the flame as we swung the ball around using a barbecue fork. We produced a lot of smoke that made the neighbors concerned. You see, this happened to be the night Rodney Kings' Police abusers were exonerated - the first night of the L.A. Riots! The other thing I was asked to do for the movie was to create the sound of the car crashing and sliding on pavement (at the end of that same chase sequence). I wanted to listen to a scene that was similar, so I went down the street to Blockbuster Video to rent *Terminator 2*. The store was located at the corner of Burbank Blvd. and Buena Vista in Burbank - just down the street from Walt Disney Studios. After finding the movie, I decided to check one last thing. I went to the Horror section of the store, and there it was - *Blood Lake*. I picked it up and held it, realizing where I was. It was a great feeling to know it had made it to "Hollywood" (even though technically we were still just in Burbank). That was a great moment for me. I knew I hadn't "made it" yet, but felt confident I was on my way.

A message to my fans? I didn't know I had any. But if I do indeed have any real fans out there, I would merely say this - Dream. Work hard. Never give up on your dreams if you really REALLY want them to come true. Be realistic, but not so much that you never try. There is nothing to fear. Fear and worry are obstacles one must overcome in order to achieve great things. And why worry about things you can't control? Life is not a race. It is a journey to be savored. Take time for the little things, and a lot of time for the important things - family, friends, the people and things you love. Meditate. Listen to the quiet voice deep within yourself. It will tell you what you need to do. Now, go out and LIVE! Okay, that's the story the best I can remember. I'm sure I probably got some of the particulars wrong, or that someone else may remember certain events differently. But this is the best I can do after not thinking about it for (over 30) years.

Thank you Tim, from the bottom of my heart.

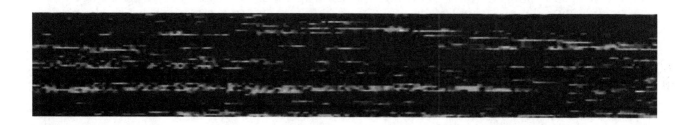

Interview
ANDREA ADAMS

An Oklahoma native, Andrea landed her first onscreen acting role in 1985's *The Ripper* while still a sophomore at Oklahoma State. Andrea portrayed "Cindy," one of the leads who is tragically disemboweled in the final act. Building a relationship with the film's director, Andrea was quickly asked to appear in his next film - the 1986 *Blood Cult* sequel, *Revenge*. Finally (and after dying onscreen for the second time), Andrea would return to the world of SOV horror with the slasher classic *Blood Lake*. Now married and living in LA (known as Andrea DeLesDernier), Andrea will forever be recognized as one of the orignal SOV horror Scream Queens.

Andrea, thank you for giving your time to this interview!

Thank you so much for the opportunity! I am honored that you enjoyed my deaths.

Was *The Ripper* your first starring role? Had you done any acting before?

The Ripper was the beginning of my many demises. I was a sophomore at Oklahoma State majoring in Theatre. It was my first movie role.

The Ripper was (almost) totally cast with local actors. What was the audition process like? Were you given much time to rehearse before shooting?

Since *The Ripper* was my first movie role, I was not too familiar with the movie making process before hand. I learned a lot on *The Ripper* set though. I paid close attention behind-the-scenes to learn all I could. The audition I went to was in Oklahoma City. If my memory serves me correctly the call back and final decision on my role was all in the same day.

I felt that we had ample time for rehearsal. They locked me in a hotel room with my co-star Wade Tower in hopes of sparking some chemistry. I knew early on I did not appreciate such tactics. If you're a good actor you don't need that motivational trickery. Other than that, I enjoyed the few days we rehearsed and never felt rushed. It was a 14 day shoot and I think I filmed less than 5 days; great experience.

And you got disemboweled! What was it like working with the special effects?

It was a blast! I was thrilled to die so horribly. I loved working with the FX guys. Pretty sure their names were Robert Brewer and David Powell.

Were you aware that Tom Savini would eventually be cast as the Ripper towards the end?

I knew who Savini was because I was a fan of *Friday the 13th* and *Creepshow*. But I worked more closely with his stand-in [Robert Brewer], who was one of the FX guys so he knew how to kill someone. And by that I mean he knew the best angles to hold the knife and rip someone's guts out.

In *The Ripper*, there's a scene where you and Wade Tower are playing Trivial Pursuit. There's an in-joke as you both debate one of the answers - *Emmanuelle 2* or *The Joys of a Woman* (they're both the same movie). Do you recall shooting this scene?

I have no idea what the joke was. I don't remember if Chris Lewis explained it or not. It was a fun scene to shoot thought. We filmed it at the Tulsa Rose Garden. I remember I went to the mall to buy a new outfit for the scene. I told the sales clerk I needed an outfit in which to die!

The film was a great experience. The professional lessons I learned while working on *The Ripper* helped shape all the other acting, producing, and PR work I've done. I understood early not to sit in my trailer on a break, but to watch others work and learn everything I could about other actors, the crew, direction, producing, the camera, and makeup.

What are your memories of director Christopher Lewis?

I was treated so nicely on the movie by Chris and Linda and everyone for that matter. I was spoiled early on. I remember thinking it was so cool that they would give me straw to drink with my soft drink so I wouldn't mess up my lipstick. I thought I had 'arrived.'

So after *The Ripper*, you came back for *Revenge*.

I didn't have to audition for *Revenge*. Chris and Linda called me in for that role; another great experience. I liked it because even though it was only one scene, the dialog ran longer than with Cindy in *The Ripper*. It was a lot of continual 'up the stairs and out the door' takes.

And you got to die again!

Revenge (*Blood Cult 2*) was my favorite death scene of all. I decided to play it so: After being gorged and my chest cavity ripped upward with a tire iron it was a slow death as she bled out. I made Karen aware she was dying. She had time to think about it which I think would be a really sad way to go; being aware you are dying. You can see that she is crying as she floats to the ground and ruins a pair of $200 shoes.

Doing the body casting for this scene was another fun experience.

Chris Lewis has stated that almost the entire opening sequence in *Revenge* needed to be looped (ADR) due to a noisy generator and the use of a Steadycam. Was this your first experience looping dialogue or doing voice over?

Is that why? LOL! I looped my scene in one evening at Rod Slane's studio in Tulsa and fell in love with acting all over again. To this day I pride myself on my looping talent. At the entertainment company [I worked with years later], if they needed a substitute line they'd call me in. I match the voice and hit it right at the insertion point. It's like sinking a basket, or making the perfect putt.

Any wild stories from your experience on *Revenge?*

Taping the scene where Josef Hanet (Peter Hart, who played Dr. White) and I were riding in the car was memorable because the camera-man was rigged on the hood of the auto. Josef was actually driving on a real street and his view was obstructed by the camera man. We literally almost drove off of a bridge. We can laugh about now right?

It was just such a cool experience overall. To be able to do that as young as I was and in Oklahoma was fantastic.

Finally after *Revenge,* you returned to video - starring in the most amazing SOV vacation movie turned slasher, *Blood Lake.* What was that production like?

A true sense of realism… Now you're just being kind. I believe it's secured its place in horror history as one of the best of the worst.

The set was a lot more casual than *The Ripper.* Tim Boggs, the director, had his act together. If it hadn't been for him I might have bolted. I was high school friends with Angela Darter, one of the actresses in the movie and her parents owned the lake house. She called me one day and said that the producer was looking for someone to play Kim. I remember speaking to her on a pay phone outside Git 'n' Gallup in Stillwater, across from the Seratean Theatre Center at Oklahoma State where I was attending school. The only thing I regret about the *Blood Lake* was never being paid. The producer did not honor the deal. But I loved working with Tim and spending two weeks with Angela at the lake house.

We all lived in the lake house together for two weeks while shooting. If anything, that helped the intimacy of the characters. The partying scene was fun. I showed them oregano would substitute for pot. My throat burned for a month. The beer was fake too, but can't remember how we made it. I do remember this evil old lady clock on the wall in the kitchen.

One of the great things about *Blood Lake* is its sense of realism. Dialogue overlaps, live sounds (like the fridge or boat motor) are heard, and lighting seems limited to general room atmosphere. Was there any talk/concern about these aspects while shooting?

No. It was all because there was no budget. Tim made it work though. I remember showing them how to make better fake blood.

What did you think about waterskiing on camera?

I look back on the water skiing scene and realize how awkward I looked. You would have never guessed I'd been water skiing since I was kid. Angela Darter's skiing was gorgeous! And umm, I guess gaffers tape won't hold a camera still against the propulsion of a boat engine. LOL. Ask Tim about the camera rig for the boating scenes. We almost lost the camera in the water several times. For some reason one of my favorite scenes to film was pulling the boat up to the dock and walking to the shore. I have no idea why, it must have fulfilled some fantasy. I remember what bathing suit I was wearing.

Blood Lake features some amazing music by Voyager. Do you know what happened to the band after the film was released?

I don't know. I never met the band. My cousin's cousin was in the band though.

And you die again in Blood Lake! Did it bother you dying three times in a row?

No way I love dying. The death scenes were the best part! You can imagine the jokes we made about the blood squirting.

After Blood Lake wrapped (now your third horror feature), did you continue acting? Did you decide at some point to change careers?

I did continue to act. My husband, Paul DeLesDernier (a musician, author, and actor whom I met at OSU) and I co-produced two films with our college buddy Todd Wade in which we starred or had a role. *Slaughterville* was one of the first feature length horror films shot on Super8 and even made it into the Cannes Film Festival. Not too many copies of it exist today. The movie is awesome. A rich, creepy, texturized film, great music (from our band The AnAesthetics), and the FX created by David Friend were superb. The producer of the movie Jerry Crow, finished all the post on a pizza delivery salary. Jerry cut that film by hand, white gloves and all. My husband was a brilliant sound producer and it was fun creating running footsteps, slams, cuts, explosions and gushing brains. We worked on ADR for so long. But it paid off; I've never heard better sounding vomit hitting the pavement. The three of us also made a black and white noir thriller on 16mm called "The Appointment." I had some good roles in other films other than horror. I got to work with Bud Yorkin and Jeff Daniels on *Love Hurts*. I've done a several commercials and continued to act in theatre.

My biggest love turned out to be music, I am a singer. My husband and I formed The AnAesthetics so we could work together and not spend too much time apart. So we traveled together.

I also did a lot of improv comedy and handle publicity for a lot of comedians and bands now. I parlayed the experience I gained promoting into a career in entertainment publicity. I was Director of Communications at New Wave Entertainment in Burbank, CA. and before that I was at Priority Records home of NWA and Ice Cube.

It's been a good life and there's more to come.

Thank you so much for your time and thoughts, Andrea!

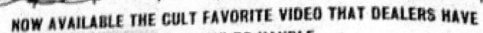

NOW AVAILABLE THE CULT FAVORITE VIDEO THAT DEALERS HAVE FEARED TO HANDLE

555

BLOOD, GORE, SEX, NUDITY AND OTHER THINGS WE CAN'T MENTION. SEE IT & BELIEVE IT!

KING VIDEO PRODUCTION

SHOT IN BLOOD-VIVID VIDEO FOR YOUR VIEWING PLEASURE

UNEDITED VERSION

1988/Color/1 Hr. 20 Min.
VHS Hi-Fi

CAUTION:
Viewing may cause severe damage to your brain cells.

NOTHING HAS BEEN CUT!

Available to Deep Red Gore Hounds at only $34.95. VHS only.

SPECIAL EFFECTS BY JEFF SEGAL OF RE-ANIMATOR FAME

17" x 22" Poster Available With Every Order

"Callers have raved about 555," Buzz Kilman, WLUP, AM 1000, Chicago

"Has a story line and a plot," Chuck Shubert, Lerner Papers Chicago

"Very well done," Steven Kerr, Ankor Productions, Ft. Worth, Texas

Aunt Mary says, "How could you? This is DISGUSTING." Chicago, Illinois

TO ORDER SPECIFY *DR 555 ONLY $34.95 + $2.00 HANDLING FEE.

KING VIDEO DISTRIBUTORS, 2034 W. RICE STREET, CHICAGO, IL. 60622.

*YOU MUST ATTEST THAT YOU ARE 18 YEARS OLD TO ORDER. YES.

Chapter 10
MAY CAUSE SEVERE DAMAGE TO BRAIN CELLS (1988)

The powerful hits of independence continued in 1988. Newfound producers entered the market with a proven business model and an eye on profits, and they quickly took over through attrition. More and more people were attempting video production with incredible success.

Though business had been good, larger producers and more reputable companies had moved beyond video's capability. Amidst vast complaints of cheapness, companies such as United (*Blood Cult's* originators) abandoned video in favor of film. They had lead the charge a few years earlier, but United chose to produced *Terror At Tenkiller* and *Revenge* (*Blood Cult's* sequel) on celluloid. Independent horror was still the big draw, but now seemingly without video's detracting status. Returning to film was United's attempt to reclaim viewers annoyed by analog's shoddiness (and note the abundance of movies shot on film, yet released direct-to-video in this timeframe).

But consumer independents remained.

Armed with the only format feasibly available (and still managing to find distribution), amateur productions thrived. More impressive and innovative titles came forth from untested filmmakers and others who continued to stay in the video game. Some films were greatly inspired by major Hollywood releases, while some were imaginatively based on true-life crimes. But they all continued in the spirit of dedication and love for the genre. SOV continually found a way.

Amongst them, gold prospector Wally Koz famously produced *555* after witnessing several horror films turning profits *"with little or no redeeming qualities."* Jon McBride and Tom Fisher came onto the scene with fan-favorite *Cannibal Campout*. Charles Pinion practically burned the screen down with his teen revenge flick *Twisted Issues*. And Nick Millard, Donald Farmer, Gary Cohen, Gary Whitson and Ricardo Islas all returned with new nightmares. 1987 was the takeover but 1988 proved to be the dominance. Shot on video became the sign of true independence; lovingly executed by talented individuals devoid of training but full of heart. Profits were there and these people pushed as hard as they could to get them. But most importantly, video stores continued to stock SOV, though not as rampantly as the *Blood Cult* days. Therefore new forms of advertising were needed. Films were starting to be marketed directly to the audience now, listed in horror magazines for interested readers. And by in large, it worked.

With consumer support, shot on video continued to thrive into the early 1990's and beyond...

555
1988, Color, 80 min
STARRING: *Greg Kerouac, Mara Lynn Bastian, Greg Neilson, Charles Fuller, Bob Grabill*
DIRECTOR: *Wally Koz*

A series of gruesome murders in a beachside town leave authorities desperate for answers. The lone eyewitness describes the killer as a 1960's hippie. With the aid of a persistent reporter, the police connect the murders to a similar case five years prior and five years before that.

Packed with splashy gore, rapid profanities and more cheese than any SOV before it, *555* wears its heart on its sleeve. Essentially a passion project by director Koz (who sadly passed away before its recent resurgence in popularity), *555* stands as one of the most recognizable shot on video horror films around. It's title alone has become a statement of low-budget quality (though the film is quite impressive). But before its pop-culture resurgence, *555* was nearly unknown to all but the most hardcore of fans.

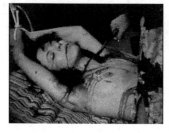 Made with friends and family, Koz successfully created a feature film with zero training. A career miner and gold prospector, Koz reportedly crafted *555* after witnessing several horror films turning profits *"with little or no redeeming qualities."* Blood Cult was reportedly one such title. Figuring that his film would be better than most, Koz wrote a fast paced slasher with extremely memorable dialogue. The female reporter jabs *"You're a prick"* while the police chief responds *"and you're a cunt,"* surprising the audience while giving blunt introductions to the lead characters. Indeed with the entire picture on their shoulders, Kerouac and Bastian drive the narrative with valiant performances and fevered deliveries. The killer (dressed hilariously in huge fake beard, wig and Hawaiian shirt) gleefully slashes victims before raping their dead bodies - while still wearing his pants. It's a kaleidoscope of bad dreams! And more humorous than horrific, the killer yells a prolonged *"Noooooooo!"* as he finishes dry-humping the dead. But more interesting was the marketing campaign, bathing the poster and box art in unforgettable pink neon. *555* was a sight to behold. The goriest scenes punctuated the advertising with the infamous machete-beheading as its front cover image. One can only imagine customers coming across this beauty, nestled between respectable Hollywood titles at the video store.

As for the movie? It's shocking how well it plays to younger audiences, since there's nary a character under 40 within it. *555* is about middle-aged cops trying to stop a middle-aged killer, with the help of a middle-aged reporter (who enjoys seducing suspects for a scoop). But what makes *555* so breezy is that Koz knew what he was doing. For better or worse, Koz was aware of low-budget SOV horror and that awareness shows. He made a good movie. He reuses shots, actors say lines direct to camera and he essentially remakes 1986's *Spine*. Could that have been another film he wanted to best?

As an insider joke, crewmembers' initials were spray-painted on walls behind the decapitation scene. Outrageous and Highly Recommended.

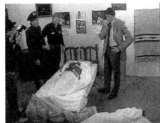   

BLIND FAITH
1988, Color, 87 min
STARRING: *Eric Gunn, Kevin Yon, Lynne Brown, David Winick, Kirk Swenk, Doris Quest*
DIRECTOR: *Dean Wilson*

An overworked detective (and alcoholic psychiatrist) interrogate a pseudo-cult leader and his accomplices, hoping to find four women captive in a basement.

Based on the real case of Philadelphia sex-killer Gary Heidnik (who tortured and killed in his suburban basement), *Blind Faith* is a disturbing thriller *Silence of the Lambs*-style without Hollywood panache. The film smartly follows two investigators as they sift through horrific testimony of victims and participants. Yet both suffer from their own problems at home. Each character is flawed and supportive to one another, allowing the audience to invest emotionally. The psychiatrist's daughter has run away, but he stifles his concern with booze. The detective is repeatedly berated by his masochistic girlfriend for not hitting her, then is tempted by the abuse shown to the tortured women. Both men are put to the test here, resulting in one succumbing to his demons when separated. But the film accomplishes more, thanks to Wilson's excellent direction and editing. The pseudo-cult killer doesn't appear for the first hour, leaving other characters to describe his horrific acts. This builds the character faceless, evil before introducing him, bringing real terror to the film. Quick inserts of violence are effective but the detailed descriptions of rape present an ugliness not found in most SOV horror films. *Blind Faith* easily stands next to *Confessions of a Serial Killer* in this respect; powerful, painful and just as good. Highly Recommended.

  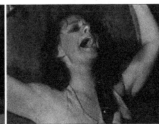 

THE BRAINSUCKER

1988, Color, 81 min
STARRING: *Jonathan Mittleman, Herb Robins, Marjorie Morris, Bob Carlisle, Paul Cuffee*
DIRECTOR: *Herb Robins*

A mad scientist experiments on a 20 year old delinquent, attempting to create the most "good" person imaginable. But his assistant flips the "good/evil" switch, turning the delinquent into a brain-sucking menace.

Horror fans stay clear... *The Brainsucker* is one of the most ridiculous, taxing, grueling parodies out there. Direction from Robins (who also helmed *The Worm Eaters*) is atrocious. Actors scream lines and mug faces while the plot goes nowhere. And I'm pretty sure it's intended. Robins (who also "acts") can often be heard directing from behind camera (*"Get out of my shot! Zoom! Zoom!"*). Mittleman as the brainsucker does his best, carrying a large corkscrew for impromptu mealtimes, but there's nary a drop of blood and the corkscrew never drills. It just spins near heads! Brains magically "appear" through jarring jump-cuts and the film fails to embrace the slimy mess that should be onscreen. A missed opportunity. Independent legend Ted V. Mikels appears in cameo.

CANNIBAL CAMPOUT

1988, Color, 88 min
STARRING: *Jon McBride, Amy Chludzinski, Richard Marcus, Christopher Granger*
DIRECTOR: *Jon McBride, Tom Fisher*

A pack of teenagers drive into the woods for weekend camping. But they've been followed by a trio of deadly cannibalistic brothers who've made the woods their hunting ground.

Fully aware of the slasher genre, *Cannibal Campout* is a solid "campers attacked in the woods" entry that pokes fun at itself while still generating thrills. Not that anything should be taken seriously. The lead star/director openly sings about all the ways to die as he drives his (soon to be dead) friends deep into the unknown. And *Cannibal* keeps hitting the

 mark. This is the fast food version of *Friday the 13th.* But where McBride could have resorted to a single masked killer, he gives us three rape-hungry cannibals gutting whomever is within reach. The trio are most offensive when dealing with women, offering to *"staple a girl's tits to the roof"* when she turns down their sexual advances. Another sequence (feeling slightly out of place) is a black & white memory shared by the three of a recent rape. Unusually heavy considering McBride's later films (the family friendly *Woodchipper Massacre* and Polonia entries), the rape is the strongest scene in the movie. But note there were two directors involved, so be warned. The gore is gruesome and sloppy, splashing across the camera at every chance. Flies buzz into frame and actors run into real, dilapidated houses that were likely abandoned decades earlier. And several performances stand out, particularly Marcus' as the leader of the cannibals and Chludzinski as the final girl. And McBride? Well even if he didn't move into video nirvana with such later hits as *Feeders* and *Terror House,* his whimsical smile and care-free attitude burst forth the moment he's onscreen. A star is born! Highly Recommended.

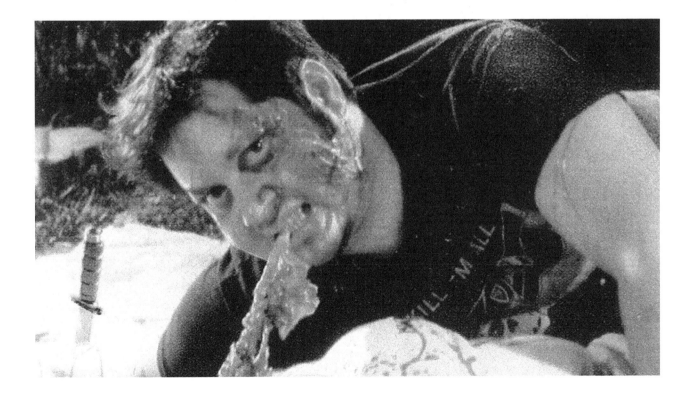

DEATH NURSE 2
1988, Color, 60 min
STARRING: *Priscilla Alden, Albert Eskinazi, Frances Millard, Irmgard Millard, Nick Millard*
DIRECTOR: *Nick Millard*

Beginning exactly where *Death Nurse* ended, Nurse Mortley kills the detective before he can arrest her. Then it's back to normal at Shady Palms clinic as another social worker brings patients in one by one.

Nick Millard is back.

Death Nurse 2 is infinitely more entertaining when played back to back with part 1. This is a must. It's the same deadpan delivery, the same blank stares into voids and the same actors playing different roles (with the same deadly fates). A hilarious crescendo that only Nick Millard could pull off. Irmgard (Nick's wife) returns showing exceptional range as a vicious drunk, while Priscilla Alden joyously brings Nurse Mortley back with wit. The lack of Eskinazi becomes apparent (his character is attacked early and bedridden) but he's still around when it counts. And an abundance of dream sequences remind us exactly who's in charge. *Death Nurse 2* is more of the same but tonally different; exactly how sequels should be. A revelation in acceptable entertainment. Required Viewing.

DEATH ROW DINER
1988, Color, 69 min
STARRING: *Jay Richardson, Michelle Bauer, John Content, Salvatore Richichi*
DIRECTOR: *B. Dennis Wood*

In 1948, the head of a popular movie studio is sent to the electric chair without his final meal. During a film shoot at the same prison 40 years later, the dead producer is reanimated into a hideously deformed creature bent on bloody revenge. And he wants his meal.

Made to showcase (and spoof) themselves, Camp Motion Pictures' *Death Row Diner* is excessively played for laughs. Scream Queen Bauer stars as an actress famous for her looks, using real life credits (*Hollywood Chainsaw Hookers*) to portray her comedic doppelganger. Deaths are few and occasionally off-screen, though some bloody moments have weight: the ping-pong paddle and decapitation scenes are truly outrageous. Yet the film never builds enough to keep momentum. The ending (reanimated producer is back running his studio) is very tongue in cheek with Bauer suddenly turning cannibal. There's a wink-wink to camera and the audience wonders what the hell they just watched. Bloopers run over the closing credits.

Why wasn't this played straight?

 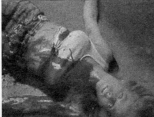  

THE EYE OF SATAN
1988, Color, 79 min
STARRING: *Cliff Twemlow, Ginette Gray, Brett Paul, Maxton G. Beesley, John Ryan*
DIRECTOR: *David Kent-Watson*

An assassin with the power of darkness pursues a crystal known as the Eye of Satan. He is hired by various factions.

A UK production, *The Eye of Satan* plays like a mafia crime thriller. $400,000 in exchange for guns, guns aren't delivered, hit-men collect the debt; all interesting stuff but lacking horror. Enter the immortal assassin with glowing green eyes and pet panther. *The Eye of Satan* wants to bring spooky elements into a British teleplay but doesn't commit. Nothing is explained! Why does the demonic assassin work for money? Why do cops eat so many sandwiches? Why does one dude look like Sean Connery? The pacing is great but *The Eye of Satan* brings little to the table.

EYEWITNESS MURDERS
1988, Color, 88 min
STARRING: *Jason Holt, Suzzane Delaurentis, Gail-Ann Brittany, Margaret Howell*
DIRECTOR: *Jason Holt*

Vietnam vet Tyler Bowie seeks to make a documentary about the seedy side of LA's under-belly with hookers, phone sex girls and drug pushers. Fuelled on cocaine, Tyler soon loses touch with reality and succumbs to Satanic prostitutes and extreme violence.

More docudrama than horror, *Eyewitness Murders* still impresses with a first-person presentation most viewers today will recognize as "found footage." The movie documents Tyler and his team as they shoot, while portions are rewound and replayed as investors (supposedly) view the footage. But taking its time, no real violence occurs until an hour in when Tyler's madness overcomes his desires. He rides with a junkie to document a drug sale, then interjects himself as the buyer. He then fights the dealer, fatally stabbing him with a kitchen knife. Then he revisits one of the hookers and realizing he knew her in Vietnam, strangles her before ripping her heart out.

There's a lot going on here, though the violence isn't as sensational as it sounds. Characters are flawed and performances (several convincingly authentic) are raw enough to convey the loneliness of street life. Tyler's descent is a little hard to swallow, given that he's a coked-up actor and supposedly a Vietnam vet. But the final scene tries to trick the audience that everything was faked, dramatized for the sake of Tyler's own film. Then a bloody heart is discovered in a forehead slapping moment of recognition. Whoops! Guess he forgot.

FEATHER PILLOW (ALMOHADON DE PLUMAS)
1988, Color, 76 min
STARRING: *Ricardo Islas, Norma Morgan, Julio Lopez, Alberto Laguna, Beatriz Rossi*
DIRECTOR: *Ricardo Islas*

A businessman's wife starts sleeping on a handcrafted feather pillow... of death! Turns out the pillow is housing large bird lice, which increasingly grows stronger as it feeds while she sleeps. Now the man must battle the full-grown lice in a fight to the bloody death.

Feather Pillow misdirects early. With an opening straight out of *The Exorcist*, Islas' creature sleeper fools audiences by appearing as a demonic shocker. Morgan hallucinates ghostly images throughout the house and is hypnotically tied to her pillow in deep sleep sessions. Her energy drains (baffling doctors) and medical tests are ordered. But her unexpected death shifts the film, learning of the vampire beasties and their intentions soon after. The final act is a one-man show with Islas "battling" the creature in a royal rumble. There are great moments that demonstrate the passion and talent of Islas' team (as with *Crowley*). Yet even with its short runtime, boredom occasionally overtakes. Repeated scenes of Islas racing around town occur, as do requisite "slowly sneak throughout the house" segments. Necessary for suspense but tedious in real time. Definitely worth a look though.

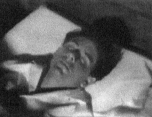

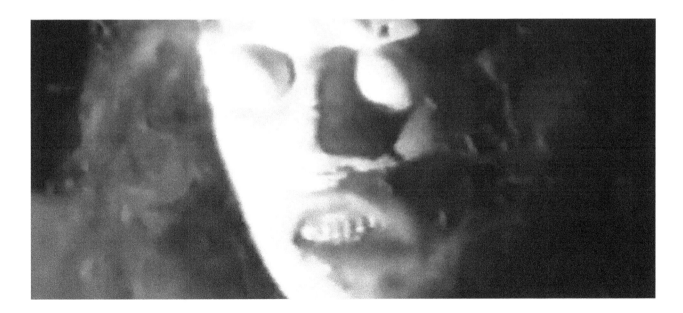

THE HEAPING BOUNCY BREASTS THAT SMOTHERED A MIDGET
1988, Color, 80 min
STARRING: *Jared Buchansky, Zachary Winston Snygg (John Bacchus), Spencer Snygg*
DIRECTOR: *Zachary Winston Snygg (John Bacchus)*

Frustrated by his students, a high school teacher buys an arsenal of weapons and turns vigilante. Killing his students for littering and being tardy, the film ends with a warning not to push teachers too far.

The premiere film from Snygg (who would return with *The Bloody Video Horror That Made Me Puke On My Aunt Gertrude*), *Bouncy Breasts* is unapologetic in its unprofessionalism; heightening absurdity by casting teens in every role. Made for laughs, *Bouncy Breasts* is no more serious than something from the files of *"Police Squad."* Yet youth must be taken into account. Teens made this movie and it's extraordinary! There are quick cuts and interesting angles. Everyone plays a stereotype but with unique innocence. Murders are humorous with guns that don't fire ("bang-bang" sounds only) and knifes that don't cut, lending a lighter tone than imaginable. It's fun entertainment but weak on horror (mass shootings aside). Yet *Bouncy Breasts* demonstrates video used by storytellers who might otherwise have stayed silent. Could the same movie have been made on any other format? Recommended.

THE HOOK OF WOODLAND HEIGHTS
1988, Color, 40 min
STARRING: *Robert W. Allen, Christine McNamara, Michael Elyanow, Justin Ballard*
DIRECTOR: *Michael Savino*

A deranged serial killer escapes from an insane asylum. Missing his right hand, the killer attaches a pitchfork to his stub and terrorizes a small town.

Paired with another short *Attack of the Killer Refridgerator*, *Hook* is the second of two tales directed by Savino and presented on the Donna Michelle label. But unlike *Refridgerator*, *Hook* is near feature-length. Impressively shot, Savino's woodland slasher embodies 1988 better than most. The killer's identity is never secret, characters purposely isolate themselves, victims constantly scream (even when hiding) and heroes always assume they've beaten the bad guy. Wonderful touches that appear almost as spoof. Slasher's golden age had passed by 1988 and Savino seems aware. But *Hook* plays as a celebration in this respect; people see the killer, the killer strikes, people die. Standout moments are sparse, but a clipboard to the head and a family barbeque divert nicely from the routine. Worth seeking out.

Director Mike Savino, Bob Allen and Producer Mark Veau on The Hook of Woodland Heights (1988)

NIGHT FEEDER
1988, Color, 95 min
STARRING: *Kate Alexander, Jonathan Zeichner, Cintra Wilson*
DIRECTOR: *Jim Whiteaker*

Bodies start appearing on the streets of San Francisco, but the manner of death is baffling. All the victims' brains have been sucked out through the eye sockets. A nosy reporter and a cop investigate, connecting the murders to a punk-rock band in the area.

Without American distribution in the 80's, *Night Feeder* only received overseas release before fading into obscurity. Yet incredibly, the film was rescued by rarity reviewers (and part time distributors) Bleeding Skull; finally hitting western shores in 2015. This may be the most exciting thing I'll say about *Night Feeder*.

Predictable, standard and slow, *Night Feeder* attempts little beyond most "deaths being investigated" crime-dramas. The reporter and detective argue before succumbing to their sexual tension. The murders (mostly off-screen) are showcased with convincing makeup that never impresses. The punk band performs with necessary attitude but comes off like rejects from *Howling II*. Yet the film does have an incredibly tense autopsy scene. The killer is later revealed to be a deranged baby, mutated under the influence of an experimental street drug.

Night Feeder is very uneven with a ludicrous twist, housed in a straightforward crime mystery. The mutated puppet is surprisingly good (illustrating that it should have been seen earlier and more frequently) but the film doesn't resonate. Forgettable.

PIECES OF DARKNESS
1988, Color, 76 min
STARRING: *Steve Lobertini, John Mayer, Earl N. Black, Daniel Reams, Robert Joe Carr*
DIRECTOR: *George Bonilla, J. Johnson Jr. III*

An anthology of three tales. "The Bootmaker" about a Vietnam veteran haunted by the deaths of his comrades. "Choice Cuts" about sibling butchers where one brother kills the other, serving his body as fresh meat. And "That's Showbiz" about an actor getting his comeuppance from people he screwed over in the past.

Simple stories with simple twists, *Pieces of Darkness* could easily be mistaken for an Emmeritus property. Except where Emmeritus generally played to television standards (no nudity or excessive gore), *Pieces of Darkness* contains a few extra touches. Racial slurs and profanity is heavily used in "Choice Cuts," including nudity. Blood is sparse throughout "The Bootmaker," though zombies appear towards the end of "That's Showbiz." But the best *Pieces of Darkness* quality comes from Bonilla and Johnson's directorial flare.

Characters deliver lines straight to camera during dramatic moments. This is particularly hilarious in "The Bootmaker," as the murderous vet stares blankly at the kid (the audience) who just dug up his victim's boots. Whoops! Yet the most entertaining tale is "Choice Cuts" with its constant butcher whacks and outrageous profanity. A great performance from Mayer too, turning polite serviceman into a crazed murderous psychopath. Recommended.

SATAN PLACE: A SOAP OPERA FROM HELL
1988, Color, 67 min
STARRING: *Warren Andrews, Nora Miller, Hollis Wood, Lisa Hatter, Stephanie Spencer*
DIRECTOR: *Alfred Ramirez, Scott Aschbrenner*

An anthology of four tales. "Disposable Love" about a loathing married couple returning from the grave. "Say Goodnight, Sophie" about a beer-guzzling slob who repeatedly hits an old man with his truck. "Too Much TV" about a television program that convinces a mother and daughter to snuff each other out. And "Sally Satan" involving erotic play with the dark lord.

Written, produced and directed by Ramirez and Aschbrenner, *Satan Place* is a fun collection strung together by a girl having car trouble (the same girl who seduces Satan later on). Characters perform normal activities bizarrely. Everyone overacts. People constantly say what they're thinking. Belches are forced and boogers are flicked. Dramatic action is satire and we love it. Everyone killed winds up returning from the grave too, so the party never ends. Special makeup gorily impresses with bloody slashes, frozen zombies and boiled skulls. And a commercial for disposable dildos pops out of nowhere. Spice for the pie, I say! This is one of the most enjoyable lower-end entries from the abyss of analog greatness. Highly Recommended.

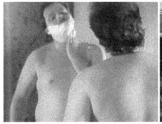  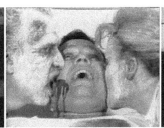 

Donald Farmer and Camille Keaton in Savage Vengeance (1988)

SAVAGE VENGEANCE

1988, Color, 65 min
STARRING: *Vickie Lehl (Camille Keaton), Donald Farmer, Phil Newman (Gene Amonette)*
DIRECTOR: *Donald Farmer*

A woman named Jennifer is gang raped in the woods. Five years later, she vacations with a friend where she (once again) runs into rapists. Her friend is killed and Jennifer is left for dead. But after recovering from her ordeal, Jennifer arms herself with a chainsaw and shotgun; ready for revenge.

An unofficial sequel to 1978's *I Spit On Your Grave*. In both films, Keaton plays a rape victim turned vigilante in a wooded setting. But unlike *I Spit* (originally titled *Day of the Woman*), *Savage Vengeance* contains none of the protracted extreme brutality displayed in the original. Instead, Donald Farmer lenses a cheap shot on video entry that tries everything it can to be trashy. Not a bad idea. *Savage Vengeance* has proven to be one of Farmer's most popular titles over the years, no doubt due to its rape-happy gusto and lead star. The return of Camille Keaton as Jennifer Hills is the most impressive aspect of *Savage Vengeance*. As before, Keaton brings an incredible fragility to the character and really knows how to put herself into jeopardy (when she screams, we feel her helplessness). Then she ramps it up for committed revenge. It's nowhere near as graphic as *I Spit*, but several moments are difficult to watch. Scenes of gang rape occur and vaginal violence by knife is heavily implied. But it's also impressive to see Farmer take on a larger acting role, appearing as the most violent rapist (well, everyone's pretty violent but Farmer has the knife). Yet as strong as the film may be, an underlying hilarity remains thanks to the miniscule budget and consumer-level video. Shots are sleazy, but everyone rapes (or gets raped) while still wearing their jeans. Dead bodies blink (they've been dead for days) and spilled blood magically disappears between scenes. Topping it off, everyone calls the character Jennifer Hills but the last name has been dubbed out of final release. So the audio just blanks the last name or is sloppily dubbed over with a different actor's voice saying *"Jennifer."* It's as if the producers filmed an *I Spit* sequel, then got cold feet when they couldn't clear the rights (be sure to read Donald Farmer's interview for the real story). And though filmed in 1988, release didn't actually come until 1993 when the distributor erroneously titled *Savage Vengance* on the opening credit. But these are gifts from a higher power. Required Viewing!

TWISTED ISSUES
1988, Color, 84 min
STARRING: *Paul Soto, Steve Antczak, Lisa Soto, Chuck Speta, Pam Gauthier, Paige Kelly*
DIRECTOR: *Charles Pinion*

A young skateboarder is run over by a group of kids in a car. Resurrected by a mad scientist, the skateboarder drills his foot to his board, dons a fencing mask and exacts revenge.

Equal part slasher, revenge and teenage propaganda, *Twisted Issues* is a trip through late 80's America. Cigarettes, acid-washed jeans and skateboards are life. Television, with its never-ending feed of war, politics and commercialism, is God. And the film mixes these concepts indiscriminately into the noise of underground teen culture. As a film, the narrative is surreal-horror/comedy (a man kills his girlfriend because she doesn't like sprouts) with the resurrected skateboarder a highly inspired touch. That he drills his foot

permanently to his board is both a hilarious and bold statement. But the film feels more like a document of pre-Nirvana punk, constantly interrupting the narrative with band footage and partying. Music dominates while montages of dead animals, war bombs and head-bangers flip by like a television changing channels. *Twisted Issues* is best left for the inebriated in some respects, as audience participation key to its understanding. But it's an entertaining trip for the stiffs too. Shot on bottom-of-the-barrel camcorders at night with flashlights, this is what independent SOV films are all about. Highly Recommended.

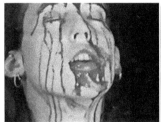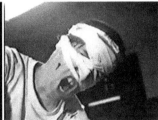

VENUS FLYTRAP
1988, Color, 63 min
STARRING: *Steve Malis, Kevin M. Glover, Kimberley Labelle, Michael Capellupo*
DIRECTOR: *T Michael*

Tough guy Turk and his gang crash a party held by posh yuppie snobs. After a tense game of Russian Roulette, Turk abuses the hosts with beatings and rape. But the tables eventually turn as the snobs reveal themselves to be even more sadistic, killing their guests while recording everything on videotape.

A remake of Ruggero Deodato's *House On The Edge Of The Park* (though producers claim they never saw it), *Venus Flytrap* accomplishes the unthinkable by actually improving on Deodato's video nasty. Tighter paced and packed with tension, *Venus* succeeds *House's* twist in only a fraction of the runtime.

After a relatively light opening (involving a wonderfully nostalgic record store), the film buckles in with its "us versus them" mentality; pitting uneducated thugs against upper-class rivals. It's standard fare, but Michael reveals deeper characters the moment Russian Roulette begins. Labelle in particular (a privileged beauty) chillingly brings her fractured persona to light during the game. *"Life's a bitch,"* she blankly states before kissing the rifle and pulling the trigger. But she appears disappointed when it doesn't fire. Later as she teases Capellupo (believing he rejected her), she again seems sincerely disappointed that she wasn't raped. These are the twisted attributes found in *Venus* that seemed missing from *House*, and it heightens the tension tenfold.

The film's direction is impressive, presenting the entire film in wide and medium shots. Close-ups are saved for Turk's vocal insults (effectively shouted direct to camera), which is apparently the result of clever editing due to a rushed production and Michael's unfamiliarity with coverage. The use of video is intriguing as we again see murders committed on camera for the purpose of viewing later (a la *Video Violence*). Yet it's only after cameras are destroyed that the audience goes from viewer to participant (we are literally beaten to death by an angry yuppie). Incredibly, the film was originally shot over 8 days in 1984 but remained unfinished for 4 years. But powerfully assembled, you'd never know it today. Highly Recommended.

VIDEO VIOLENCE 2
1988, Color, 75 min
STARRING: *Uke, Bart Sumner, Elizabeth Lee Miller, David Christopher, Art Neill*
DIRECTOR: *Gary Cohen*

Operating an underground cable access show, Howard and Eli return for more onscreen torment and killing of innocent victims.

Presented as the show itself (charmingly breaking into live television signals), the program Howard and Eli host in *Video Violence 2* is an extension of the ideas put forth in the original. So where does one go when renting is not enough? Live television, apparently.

 Turning video on its head, Cohen presents one of the most interesting SOV films of the 80's with *Video Violence 2*. The movie is literally "The Howard and Eli Show," which ends by revealing itself as fake before continuing with murders. So, is it real? Howard and Eli are presented as psychopathic killers who are also production charlatans, leaving the audience guessing. Indeed if the opening broadcast is to be believed, "The Howard and Eli Show" features real uninterrupted killings on camera. But the audience gets to witness the reveals (one victim complains about the quality of make-up) so *Video Violence 2* is more than just Snuff TV. The film also suggests that killing on camera is better faked because

glamorization for entertainment is all that really matters (and indeed, we're watching this for entertainment ourselves). But as a motion picture, *Video Violence 2* grows tedious with constant interruptions of spoof commercials that (while funny) dispel the seriousness its murders should contain. Still, a smart movie.

WITCHFINDER
1988/2008, Color, 60 min
STARRING: *Clancey McCauley, Gary Whitson, Aven Warren, Mike Brady, Chris Stonage*
DIRECTOR: *Gary Whitson*

A would-be author leads a coven of witches with faked human sacrifices. But thou shall not suffer a witch to live! An unknown killer drowns, electrocutes and hangs the coven's women one by one.

Extremely entertaining with laugh out loud moments, *Witchfinder* is one of W.A.V.E.'s earliest and best titles. Presented today in a slightly re-edited form (featuring new bookended segments with Laura Giglio and Pamela Sutch), this is one you won't want to miss. Characters explicitly state what they're about to do. Actors flub lines then restart them in the same take. And Whitson himself bursts into a hilarious fit while trying to put on pants. McCauley is wonderfully attractive here, showcasing real duplicity as the scheming manipulator and ultimate victim. But what really drives the film is its tight story and dependable camera work. Yes, the film has been re-worked slightly in recent years, but the story never meanders or feels rebuilt. Highly Recommended!

Interview

TIM RITTER

Well known throughout the genre, Tim Ritter built a name for himself after directing and releasing his own feature length films: the Super8 *Day of the Reaper* in 1984 and the 16mm *Truth Or Dare?* in 1986. *Truth Or Dare?* became an instant success, selling 30,000 copies during the first 18 months (US alone!) and later praised on national television by Elijah Wood as *"one of my all-time favorite horror movies."* The 16mm *Killing Spree* followed in 1987 and a video shot *Truth Or Dare?* sequel *Wicked Games* came in 1993. Often teaming with childhood friend Joel D. Wynkoop, the pair impressively topped themselves in 1995 with their SOV opus *Creep*. Tim's work has inspired almost every independent filmmaker throughout the 80's and 90's, and is still one of the most instantly recognizable horror directors working today.

Tim, thank you for giving your time to this interview! What initially lead you into becoming a filmmaker?

I've been making movies since 1977, 1978. I feel like I was born with a camera in my hand! My dad was an avid "film the family events with Super8 film" guy and when I saw the family camera, I knew I had to film things. Our little Kodak camera broke and my mom eventually got me an S&H Green Stamp Chinon Super8 camera, and I wore that thing out! At a very early age, I was writing stories, doing terrible drawings to go with them, but reading and writing all the same. I loved comedies, like the *Pink Panther* movies, and all things sci-fi, monster, and horror. I collected those Aurora model kits of Frankenstein and Dracula, read books on the Hammer and Universal Horror Films from the library, and just completely obsessed over movies and books. So I guess you might say I was "wired to create!" My earliest influences were *"Star Trek"* and *"Dark Shadows,"* which I watched with my mom. Then *The Six Million Dollar Man,* I was totally obsessed with that movie. *JAWS*...got my parents to take me to that one in 1975 and could not get the imagery, the music, the characters, the monster shark, out of my mind. The poster, with the naked girl swimming and the monster coming up to get her from below, was just a HUGE influence on me, that simple concept (it could be a bear, a shark, an alligator...or a crazy with a razor blade or knife, as *Halloween* and other Giallo movies later showed me...). So I think that's how everything came together for me. All these things in the late 60's and in the 70's, which were pop culture of that era. I recall *The Incredible Melting Man* trailer being a huge influence on me - I was too young to be allowed to see the movie, but the trailers that ran on TV, the books about them, sparked my imagination so much. And the grainy black and white newspaper ads. I'd cut those out, put them in a photo album shrine, and just...obsess over them. Back in those days, we didn't even have cable TV, so there was no way to SEE a lot of the movies I was reading about. So my imagination filled in the blanks on what they were, that and the books, and later getting the SOUNDTRACKS, which also helped me to "see" the movies in my mind... kind of creating my own versions before I eventually saw them. Have to say *Star Wars* and *The Empire Strikes Back* were also huge early influences, those two. I obsessed endlessly over them from 1977-1982 or so! So that was the beginning of it all. I've always had a dark, sarcastic sense of humor about myself and others, so I guess that filters into my little movies easily. *Reaper* was an attempt to emulate everything I loved in movies at that time, from *The Hills Have Eyes* to Giallo movies to *Halloween* and *Friday the 13th*. It fails miserably but the fan passion shines through, I think.

Masked killers and personal betrayals are common themes in your films. Was your work influenced by other films you admired?

Absolutely! I had always obsessed over horror films, and stuff like 1976's *King Kong* was GOLD to me. I wasn't allowed to see that in the theater, sadly (because my mom read that Jessica Lange went topless in the movie! I was so devastated) but I'd watch TV to see the trailer and I think I went to see *The Shaggy D.A.* and they had like a TWELVE MINUTE PREVIEW of *Kong* before the movie! It was so awesome to see it on the big screen, I couldn't get enough! Of course, this was long before it ran on television as a two night event, and I was more than entranced - still love that movie today! And then came the slasher movies, starting with *Halloween*. By that point, I had made probably about thirty Super8 movies, learning how to cut things together emulating the movies I loved as best as I could (especially the sci-fi stuff). Even made a James Bond movie called *License To Kill!* But when I saw *Halloween* on the Network TV Broadcast in 1981, not only did it scare me to death (that Michael Myers breathing and the music), I saw firsthand what an effect the movie had on EVERYONE that saw it. Classmates were talking about it on the bus ride to school, saying how their mom's were suddenly locking the doors... something they'd never done before! So that whole "scare" aspect of *Halloween* got me, along with the notion that I could apply its simplicity to my Super8 movies. I didn't have to emulate *Star Wars* or *Jaws*, which was nearly impossible to do with no money... but with *Halloween*... all I needed was a mask, a girl, and a POV shot with a rubber knife in the frame. Instinctively, I knew it, and applied it immediately to my movies - I was on fire with the passion to do this stuff! And of course the MUSIC, I immediately became a John Carpenter soundtrack fanatic. And what a time to "come of age," when slasher movies were just amping up in the golden era of the late 70's and early 80's! So immediately my Super8 films took a turn from stuff like *It From Saturn*, *The Born Loser*, *Superpanther* and morphed into *Bits and Pieces*, *Dead and Gone*, *The Sanguinary*, and many more crazy titles! I would score my Super8 movies with *Halloween*, *Friday the 13th*, *Maniac* and all the classic vinyl releases of the era. I was reading Famous Monsters at the time and I discovered Fangoria #1, and was a diehard reader from the beginning to the end - EVERY issue, read them ALL cover-to-cover until, what, 2016? But immediately after *Halloween*, there was *Halloween II*, *Friday the 13th Part 2*, *Maniac*, an obsession with George Romero and *Dawn of the Dead* and all of his work, and all that stuff coming down the pike in theatrical re-releases. So I was HUGELY influenced by this stuff, and at first it was REALLY difficult to see all this stuff, but I would read about all these movies obsessively in Fangoria, where Romero, Savini, Carpenter, Cronenberg and Wes Craven were Kings. And I'd listen to the soundtracks and see the pictures in the magazines, and make my own movies based on what I was indulging in. Again, I READ about it all more than seeing it until the VCR explosion, which didn't begin for me until 1983 or so, when I got a Beta VCR as a bribe for passing Geometry from my parents! *"You pass the course, you get a Beta machine!"* And it was hard for me, I hated Math and Geometry and Algebra, made NO sense to me, but I squeaked by enough to get that Beta machine and it wasn't long before I ended up in the video stores, finally seeing everything I had read about - as it hit video for the first time! So yes, all that affected my moviemaking impulses.

When I made my first feature-length horror movie while still in high school called *Day of the Reaper*, I'd have to say *Pieces*, *Friday the 13th*, early Dario Argento movies, and *Halloween* were my biggest influences. And of course, by then I was discovering the worlds of H.G. Lewis and John Waters, so those guys (with production values in their movies that were like my own) I could REALLY relate to. Their influences became pretty heavy. I remember one of the first tapes I rented called *Filmgore*, and it was just like clips of all the greatest scenes from a zillion B-movies I had never seen (they weren't released on tape yet at the time, only the "best of clips") and I wore that thing out. *Blood Feast*, *Snuff*, *The Texas Chainsaw Massacre*, *Drive-In Massacre*, *Astro Zombies*, I mean...it was incredible! I still have a dub of that tape somewhere, and that was one of the biggest coups of my life back then! And of course back then (even if you were 14, 15 years old) at the mom and pop stores, you could slip into that back adult room and take your pick of pleasure, so that was pretty much the way I came of age learning what sex was all about! As long as you had the rental fee, the proprietors didn't care about ID'ing you... As a matter of fact, I knew most of the video store owners well, I'd stay in the stores, perusing the aisles and the colorful boxes, for hours and hours, yammering it up. They were all just movie fans like me. And *Basket Case* (another huge influence, that movie was so awesome!) inspired me to sculpt the "Argento" character head at the end of *Reaper* when he gets all chopped up and is REVEALED! *Halloween* and *Jaws* probably remain my all-time favorite horror films, but other flicks of the age also influenced me, like the *Dirty Harry* and *Death Wish* franchises...which I obsessed over. So I think...all these influences...really fed into being obsessed with masked killers, vengeance, and betrayal. I'd love to mention every movie that inspired me, but that would take an entire review book! *The Exorcist* is another one I don't want to forget, I used to watch that on TV over and over, and when I finally saw it uncut on video... I was blown away. Such a powerful film, with good vs. evil themes of Biblical proportion, a little girl's soul in the battle... and that one has stayed with me throughout the ages!

In some of your films, women are portrayed as sexually promiscuous or having extramarital affairs. Were your movies a creative outlet to deal with real life experiences?

I was a pretty geeky, immature and sheltered kid - and my whole "reality" was movies. I mean, I was just a horror, sci-fi, and action movie nerd. So as I got older, let's just say I wasn't doing too well dating; that didn't happen seriously until later. While we were filming *Day of the Reaper*, I fell head-over-heels over the lead actress we cast. Just a severe, obsessive crush... and she did not feel the same. She was nice about it but man, her power over me... the strange, alien emotions I felt. Stunned me like a moth being zapped. I had never felt that before and didn't know how to deal with it. Anyway, she eventually let me down easy (nicely, she was cool about it) but you know...young males, hormones raging, all confused, it's hard to deal with that. And I went into a deep depression over that rejection. And it happened AGAIN with a waitress I fell for the following year. Even though she was interested in me, I must've been really immature or unappealing in some way, because I was let down nicely. And both ladies told me *"We should just remain friends"* and *"Find yourself some good friends"* and *"Start living"* and on and on, and all those early experiences from when I was 15-17 years old, being rejected, absolutely fed into my early movies, especially *Truth Or Dare?* and *Killing Spree*. Writing down those emotions and how the characters in the script reacted (violently, which I never thought of being violent about but reading a lot of Stephen King at the time), I was like... *"What IF someone reacted violently to being rejected? After being MARRIED for a few years?"* And that was the evolution of the thought process behind my early movies: rejection, depression, and dealing with it. And of course with *Truth Or Dare?*, the character is so depressed he creates a hallucinatory world all of his own to hurt himself because of his wife's rejection. I could feel that. I really wanted to hurt myself more than anyone every time I got rejected as a teen heading into an adult. I think..it's a tough time for both males and females, those ages from like 14-19, it's very rough and confusing, and it's probably hard for people to say *"No, you're not what I'm looking for as far as romantic interests"* as much as it is for the person being told. And today, with social media and all...people are a lot nastier.

So this kind of thing happened to me a few times, and I had one girl I was seeing end up with someone else, and felt the dejection of that (all so confusing at that age) and I did integrate those emotions and experiences into my early scripts as motivation for my madmen! But again, personally, I never felt the urge to hurt anyone but myself when I got rejected. And that's where *Truth Or Dare?* came from. As a matter of fact, I did go through the whole suicidal tendency thing, which was awful, at that age... I don't know how my parents got through it or got me through it, but they did. Everything worked out fine. I think those hormones can make people crazy, and even later in life, if they get unbalanced. It can make people do crazy things. So when I was creating, I made the stakes a little higher for my characters and had wives leave them as opposed to just girlfriends.

From your earliest releases, you also provided candid "making of" segments. Though very common today with DVD, you seemed ahead of the curve by showing audiences how to make a movie in the late 80's. What inspired you to create these segments?

While we were making *Killing Spree*, we had a bunch of cool cats working on the movie that had just graduated from the New York School Of Visual Arts and wouldn't you know, their professor was Roy Frumkes! At the time, I think he was working on *Street Trash* with Jim Muro. But these guys got Roy to send me a copy of the Holy Grail of "making of" segments: *Document of the Dead*, in the form he had it in back then. Of course, it was a legendary item back in 1986, 1987... I mean, it had not gotten any sort of video release then. It was shown here and there in 16mm in schools or on bootleg video tapes, and I finally scored a copy! I still have that VHS tape today, but seeing Romero being inter-viewed in that shopping mall and all those behind-the-scenes antics of *Dawn*, wow, that just...blew me away. It was SO EXCITING! So that made me want to share the making of my movies in the same way, providing anyone was interested (which they were back then). Now, it seems everyone you meet has a movie in them or is filming one with their HD Phone, but back then in the 80's... if you said you were making movies people were intrigued. *"Porn?"* they'd ask immediately. And I'd always say... *"Kind of...porn and horror mix!"* And horror they were fascinated by. Before I saw *Document of the Dead*, I got invited to a Palm Beach County Film Liaison meeting where they wanted to hear from local film-makers (there were very few in Florida at the time) and I got invited immediately after we filmed *Truth Or Dare? A Critical Madness*. They wanted me to speak, but I thought SHOW-ING them a "making of" video of *Truth Or Dare?* might be better, then fielding questions. I had paid a friend of mine to shoot all this behind the scenes stuff while we filmed, so I put together *The Making of Truth Or Dare*. After seeing *Document of the Dead*, I refined my approach to imitate that style more, and made *The Making of Killing Spree* followed by *Wicked Games* and then *Creep*. They evolved into the *Blinded By the Blood* video series, where the making of all these early analog video movies were covered. So that's how it all happened, me with the urge to show how I was doing this stuff in my own back yard without the backing of Hollywood; Romero style and seeing *Document of the Dead*.

When DVDs came into play as the preferred medium, of course I had all this stuff ready for extras! I think others also had the same experience back then, I remember J.R. Bookwalter doing the same thing for his releases, and Full Moon was doing it. And when DVDs hit, EVERYONE was doing it. Sadly now, it's routine for about everything but back then... Wow....it was exciting and new! The Criterion Laserdisc release of *Alien,* for me, was so eye opening. It was like going to Film School! Took me MONTHS to get through all the extra footage, "making of" segments, behind-the-scenes stuff, EVERYTHING - you could read the script on your TV, the whole nine yards! Of course, all that was ported over to the DVD and Blu Special Editions, but back in like 1992, it was so groundbreaking to see and experience as a wannabe moviemaker. Inspiring! So that was a big influence on keeping at the behind the scenes documentation as we went forward. By 1996 or so, it had gotten pretty routine and I kind of stopped the detailed video accounting since the notoriety really wore off. But I'm glad I did it for those early video movies, fans surely appreciate those to this day. It's a great documentation of that era.

Your first video produced feature was the horror anthology *Twisted Illusions*, co-directed with Joel D. Wynkoop. How did that project come about? When did you and Joel first meet?

Joel Wynkoop lived across the street from me when I was growing up in the 1970's, down in South Florida. Joel drew comic books, which I bought off of him with my allowance, and he was my babysitter when my parents would go out (he's like 5 or 6 years older than me). Joel also had the film bug and was shooting Super8 movies at the time, which also inspired my love for wanting to go out and make movies. My dad and I appeared in one of his movies called "The Bionic Boy," so I was making little movies with Joel when I was seven years old. Joel and his family moved away and years later in 1984, I took an ad out to sell *Day of the Reaper* in my high school newspaper. Trying to sell copies to fellow students. Joel's nephew was in the same school as I was, saw the ad, and showed it to Joel who immediately called me and we re-connected! I remember talking to him again for the first time in many years, I had just come back from viewing *The Terminator* in the theater and was so jazzed and inspired, and we connected so well. Had similar goals and movie likes, and Joel wanted to ACT, ACT, ACT for the most part and I wanted to write and direct, so Joel jumped in immediately with what I was doing and together, we went around and sold copies of *Day of the Reaper* to video stores. Joel was so enthusiastic and a great salesman, so he was just what I needed at the time; a true friend and collaborator.

As we were selling *Reaper*, we connected with other like-minded people working in video stores, like Al Nicolosi who had TV station connections and ran a video production company, where I got a job. Also we met Vincent Miranda, who ghost wrote tons of the books I read growing up on horror movies in the library, so that was awesome, and Vince had worked on *Shock Waves* and knew George Romero and Stephen King. So I was feeling I was making the proper connections, Tony Montana style! Joel and I wrote a couple of different scripts, including one called *Inner Forces* that was like a mixture of *Scanners* and other movies, but ultimately seeing we had no budget at all, we decided for simplicity: make a no-budget anthology in the traditions of say, *Twilight Zone* and *Creepshow* and get it out there the same way as *Reaper*. Only this movie would hopefully be a little more polished and have sync sound. Joel was a moviemaker as well, and this was a way to give him directing opportunities along with me. So we each wrote and directed three segments, Joel starred in my biggest one called "Truth Or Dare?" which, yes, is the short movie version of the feature. It was so cool coming up with that concept, channeling my feelings of rejection into a script with a self-destructive character. Mike Strauber's wife dumps him, so he picks up an imaginary hitchhiker, this beautiful girl, he tells her his problems, he thinks he's going to get some sexual action through the childhood game "truth or dare." And from there, things spiral down with her "daring" Mike to chop off body parts and rip out his tongue, and at the end, it's revealed she is not there. Joel did a fantastic job in the part, going all out at the end, and Joel, Al, and I had a blast shooting it along with Colleen Foley, the hottest cheerleader in high school. She was so fun to work with and had acting ambitions, and had appeared in *Day of the Reaper* so...it was just a great time. "Truth Or Dare?" and another segment we did "The Clean-Up Job" proved to be fan favorites when the movie was finished. So naturally, as we progressed on to what was next, the idea became using the short version of "Truth Or Dare?" and expanding it into a feature length script and making it into a movie direct for the videotape market, as VHS ruled the day! The idea was to raise a budget for it, shoot it locally, and sell it ourselves again with Joel in the lead, Al taping and producing, and me writing and directing. We had shot *Twisted Illusions* on 1/2" VHS and 3/4" Umatic video, and wanted to upgrade "Truth Or Dare?" to being shot on Beta SP, that was our goal at the time.

Why was *Truth Or Dare? A Critical Madness* shot on 16mm? Did shooting on film carry more legitimacy than shooting on video?

No, *Truth Or Dare?* would've had the same success even if we had shot it on video (which was the way I had planned it all along). The VHS market was an open maw for material at that point, hungry for anything packaged well. Beta SP was what I had my sights on, and we were ready to do it (we had already cast Joel in the lead, Al Nicolosi was going to shoot the movie with equipment rented from the TV station where he worked, I had met a local casting director that worked with the producers of *"Miami Vice"*- it was insane). All this had happened when I was still a senior in high school, believe it or not, and I just couldn't WAIT to get out of high school to start my movie career! [laughs] I saw school as a huge interruption of my goals, and the opportunity to get my little movies seen in video stores like they were the new drive-ins was not lost on me. In the process of selling *Reaper* and *Twisted Illusions*, we had connected with rackjobbers in other states, wholesalers that sold the movies in vans to other mom and pop stores in Georgia, New York, California, (all over the place) so the plan was to really roll something out and try to get it distributed with a bigger company, like Vestron.

In was a mad dash to get one of the first made-for-video, shot on video movies out there, which of course we got beat to the punch by *Blood Cult,* which really disturbed me at the time! I didn't know about movies like *Sledgehammer* and a few others that had been shot on video and I guess, released in theaters. It was many years before I realized other folks around the country had the same idea but honestly, not as many as you would've thought, considering the opportunities that mom and pop video stores presented early on! But I always thought we should've shot *Truth Or Dare?* and *Killing Spree* on Beta SP. They would've made a lot more money without incurring the costs of film, negative transfers to tape, and all that because both movies were edited directly on tape and to me, the end results looked like how Beta SP would've looked anyway. There were eventually dozens of pretty successful movies shot on Beta SP that saved tens of thousands of dollars shooting directly on video. But as we went along, our movie grew and through distributing *Twisted Illusions* to this Chicago outfit, VSI International, they saw potential in what we were doing and in my first summer out of high school, Al Nicolosi and myself went up to visit them and somehow talked them into investing over $250,000 in the project! I'll tell you, from the humble beginnings of the amateur *Day of the Reaper*, which I was shooting one summer prior on a $1,500 budget (financed by my dishwashing job) to suddenly being involved with a fully funded quarter of a million dollar flick...that's an underdog story! And I was reading everything I could on film, highly influenced by Sylvester Stallone and holding out to direct, so it was an experience I'll never forget. As we went along, though, the investors thought (probably wisely) that someone with more practical experience should produce the movie and oversee it, but this is also where a lot of problems started, eventually resulting in creative differences, egos clashing, things not being done the way I wanted. And who was I, kind of learning as I went along? Well, turns out I was right on most things. Not all, but it was decided to shoot on film and by then, being highly inspired by *Last House On the Left* (which hit VHS the day before I flew to Chicago to pitch the movie to VSI), *Evil Dead* and *Texas Chainsaw Massacre*, of course I wanted to shoot on film, like all my icons! So I was on cloud nine at the time with the change, fully on board, and got wrapped up in the "prestige" of shooting on film which is what we did. And it was fun, an interesting experiment and I'm glad to have worked in the format but personally, I always preferred video. Never had a problem with the "look" of it, whether 1", Beta SP, or even VHS! And the "instant" dailies, the ease of shooting, the low cost...I always did prefer video but got caught up in the tail end of shooting on film.

I don't think b-movies (going directly to the VHS market in 1985-1990 or so) were seen as bigger or better because they were shot on film or video. No one really knew. It was all in the fancy big box packaging really, at least for a spell. By 1990 though, customers became more discriminating and the video stigma of being "like porn" seemed to come back. I've personally never understood that (people can accept adult movies shot on video, perhaps their favorite sitcom, reality shows like *"COPS"* were big back then and even bigger now) but at the time, there was this discrimination against movies shot on video after 1990, unless it was very slick in production value. But for me as a fan and viewer, it was the movie that counted. It didn't matter to me that *Dreamaniac* was shot on 16mm and *Redneck*

Zombies Beta SP...it all came down to the material. I do know that by the time we did *Wicked Games* released in 1994, anything shot on video, and this was "pro-sumer" Hi-8 in origination, was a very difficult sell for mainstream markets. That's when my stuff started to go more underground. That one and *Creep* eventually got out quite well for what they were though. I recall dealing with Rentrak (we had done well by them with *Killing Spree*) and they were very mean-spirited about *Wicked Games*. *"If you and your friends got together with a camcorder and made a little movie, we're not going to take that!"* It was infuriating at the time because I put so much time, effort, passion, blood, sweat, and tears into every project and every extra cent I had. Not good to be treated like that. But *Truth Or Dare?* being shot on 16mm and going directly to a negative transfer on 3/4" tape for editing, and directly to VHS, had a PRISTINE picture for that time period, just great. I wouldn't say it was better than competently lit Beta SP, but...it was good. And the movie looked worlds better than *Day of the Reaper*, which I had transferred by projecting the Super8 image from a shoebox! So...by all means, I had moved up in the film world from 1984-1986 at lightning speed. What's really cool about it and probably inspiring to others, is that I was just a kid from Nowhere Florida, with a boat load of passion and a love for all things movies. I had no connections in the film business, no family to help me out or give me a break, and some-how, I was just able to push along and make my dream happen. I mean, we were DOING *Truth Or Dare?* no matter what. My mind was made up. Whether it was a $6,000 VHS movie, a $60,000 Beta SP movie, or a $250,000 dollar 16mm film with $150,000 for advertising...it was going to happen no matter what, that much was a certainty. I was young, insane, and it was just one of those things. By the time VSI came on board and formed Peerless Films to make the movie (and involved Gaff Productions) we had already done most of the casting...found the locations, so many to choose from...locked in special effects people and so many other things, there was little to do except UNDO what we had done, which was part of the problem as we went along. But in the end, it did get finished. *Truth Or Dare?* came out and was a big success. Made $1.5 million in the first 18 months internationally, and sold 30,000 VHS tapes in the U.S. alone, was at the top of the rental charts for many months! So I couldn't have asked for a better success and I knew it was all about timing, which was why I was in such a rush to get the thing done and out there. I knew there was a time limit on how long video stores would accept indie product and would eventually eschew it in favor of studio material. And of course, all that happened pretty fast! But anyone who grew up as a horror fan in that 80's era, or had parents that did, knows *Truth Or Dare?* and remembers it. Most folks very fondly, I'm pleased to say!

The fan favorite *Killing Spree* soon followed in 1987. Also shot on 16mm, did *Killing Spree* enjoy the same success as *Truth Or Dare?*

Killing Spree was my follow-up to *Truth Or Dare?* using many of the same talented cast and crew. But the market dropped out when we finished it (I believe it was Black Friday in 1988) and Vestron nearly went out of business. And eventually did. And Blockbuster began buying all the mom and pop stores out in the early 90's, so things were changing fast and *Spree* got caught up in all that. The days of getting a nice $75,000 advance for a small movie like *Killing Spree* were largely over, even though we had shot on 16mm film with a very cool director of photography, Mark Pederson, from the NY School of Visual Arts. *Spree* was basically a lot of ideas leftover from *Truth Or Dare?* and the simple concept of MANIAC MEETS *Night/Return of the Living Dead*. That was the whole concept, put together in the style of John Waters' black humor and H.G. Lewis' gore. That was the intent and it was FX man Joel Harlow's first film as special effects guru (he would go on to do the *Basket Case* and *Toxic Avenger* sequels, climbing his way to the top of the Hollywood game, winning an Academy Award for his work in *Star Trek* in 2009). It was awesome to see Joel over the years really making his mark, working with Coppola, Spielberg, and all the greats! He's a super nice guy and I can't think of anyone cooler that deserved the success.

Killing Spree entered what I call the DISTRIBUTION ABYSS phase, and that was from like 1987-1990 or so, while I tried to figure out how to get it out. The offers we were getting from all the companies back in that era were so low compared to what the investors expected so eventually, I decided to raise more money and distribute the movie myself. Made the boxes, poster, artwork, got a job at a video rental store and read up on all the inside "secrets" on how to get movies out there, and really just...lived it. Became a distributor and sold the heck out of that movie, connected with wholesalers, chains, theaters, anywhere I could that would show or buy the movie. This took me forever- a one man show, really, YEARS! All the way through 1992, so it was like 5 years where I was not only not making anything, but I was trying to sell something. Joel and I did the car thing again, getting in cars and taking the tapes around. It got more difficult each time, because chains bought out the mom and pops, so you'd have to send the movie screener to a committee and it would take them months...or years...to get back to you with a vague answer and a lowball price per unit. So it was not fun and I learned quickly, you can't really go out there and sell just your own movie, one movie, everyone wants PACKAGES of movies to choose from, and they want them each month. So what I did was unheard of, just a clown out there trying to sell his movie, and eventually, I got copies of *Truth Or Dare?* and through that into the mix, and *Day of the Reaper* and *Twisted Illusions* but still, the goal was to get *Killing Spree* out. Eventually I did okay, but not phenomenal.

We then sub-licensed the movie to Magnum Entertainment, and they made new VHS box art for it, for this series called *I Dance On Your Grave*. It had a hot looking chick on the box dressed like Demi Moore on the cover of the *I Spit On Your Grave* box, and that sold real well. They had this oddball program where you'd buy two or three copies and they gave you a certificate you could make your own copies [!] with a bunch of empty video boxes thrown into the mix, so it was weird. So suddenly all the retailers were making copies of the movie legally and renting and selling those. The picture quality, of course, suffered during that situation, and *Spree* was one we mastered on 1" video and made our VHS copies from the highest quality master, but soon that was lost in the legal piracy stuff going on. Another company bought all the sleeves off of our Duplicator, who had printed the boxes backwards and I had to have them redone, and THEY made their own VHS dubs, one at a time, so...it got to be a mess. So while the movie enjoyed a nice success in the marketplace, it definitely wasn't as big, all at once as *Truth Or Dare?* and I'd say it sold about 10,000 units at a much lower wholesale price. And beyond that, there was all these dubs being made.

Once the Magnum deal ended, we signed up with Salt City Home Video who did well with it, and they became SRS Cinema, and there's been numerous releases of the movie over the years, including an awesome Camp Video DVD release with all the bells and whistles, made directly from the 1" Master (the best release, in my opinion). And interesting to note that the original incarnation of Camp was one of the first distributors that almost got the movie, but they only offered us $10k up front, so the investors didn't want to go with them. I had Troma interested for a while, and talked to Lloyd Kaufman about releasing *Spree* and he loved the movie, but ultimately they wanted to spend more money on blowing it up to 35mm and charge us on the back end for that, so we would've never made a dime back. But eventually, yes, the movie really got out there. It was in all the mom and pop shops, Blockbuster Video had it, National Video had it, so...I'm happy to say, even though financially it wasn't a win, getting the movie out there over a period of six years or so, I did make it happen, even though the odds were against me. Making one movie and trying to sell it...just...doesn't happen. We did use Films Around The World for initial foreign sales, and they did okay, the movie played in Cannes and all the buyers got up and walked out during the opening "big lips" scene....so it was seriously a difficult sale and off to a really rocky start. But again, when you're young and full of passion and fire, I refused to let it die. I don't think I'd have the energy to push something like that nowadays! Wild memories, so many adventures making and selling *Killing Spree*. But it's lived on and there was a recent Blu Ray release that mirrored the longform, rough cut of the movie I originally did that has done real well.

So again, I can't complain with so many releases and so much interest in a movie that was made in 1987. Also, Terror Vision just had a vinyl soundtrack released of the movie, and I got to do the liner notes. I mean, what an honor! That fans and other companies have kept it alive so long now is just such a reward to me. I have been truly blessed, and I'm glad I really pushed it the way I did and others have picked it up and run with it, keeping it alive.

You eventually returned to video with *Wicked Games*, the *Truth Or Dare?* sequel. It's an absolute riot, a real crowd pleaser! Was your decision to use video purely financial?

It took time, but so many people have finally discovered this one, and I'm really happy about that. I think the German SNUFF edition that came out in 2005 really helped it get more notoriety, and that cut has barely been released in the States as of yet. It's definitely the cut I prefer, and more of what I wanted to deliver back in 1993 but couldn't put my finger on and didn't have the knowledge or experience. The SNUFF edition is one of the few movies I made that I can actually put in, watch, and enjoy! And most of the footage added was from that era, alternate takes, things that were cut, that sort of thing. So there was nothing really "reshot." It was one of the funnest features I ever shot, yet one of the most brutal and frustrating with equipment and actor problems. Constant recasting and having to shoot scenes over and over added to the dilemma. This was the official sequel to *Truth Or Dare? A Critical Madness* and it was years in the making!

Originally when we made the first movie, we were scheduled to go right into the sequel, so a follow-up was written by me before *Truth Or Dare?* filmed, believe it or not! Well, for various reasons, the sequel did NOT happen. There were lawsuits and rights issues and all kinds of things, and as time stretched out, the original cast and crew went their separate ways. I think it was 1988 or 1989... I was clear for doing the sequel, got the rights back, and I had what I consider an EXCELLENT script. Funding was set to come through (another $300,000 plus budget) and I had lined up David A. Hess, Camille Keaton, and Linnea Quigley in the lead parts, along with John Brace returning as Mike Strauber. And wouldn't you know it, funding fell through! I was just devastated, this was...like the dream cast! I just can't help to think how cool that movie might've been, and talking with Hess, Keaton, and Linnea about the project was so exciting. But sadly, it did not happen. Then I got wrapped up in selling *Killing Spree* on VHS.

But I really wanted to make a follow-up to *Truth Or Dare?* and eventually, it morphed into *Wicked Games*. A lot of the ideas in that 1988 script ended up being cannibalized for *Wicked Games*, *Creep* and *Screaming For Sanity* as I went along, so that was a lot of fun, not stopping or giving up on those concepts even as the budgets got smaller. With *Wicked Games*, we had gotten funding from this venture capital group, and it also started out as a much bigger project to be shot on film, but after receiving only like the first $5k of the budget, the company went out of business! Fortunately, we were able to use this money to start the project but as what became per usual, I had to downsize everything accordingly. I was working at a video store at the time, and one guy that always came in renting movies was Kermit Christman (who grew up with Monte Markham and William Katt), and he had his foot in the acting world in Palm Beach, running the Palm Beach Shakespeare Festival. So I hooked up with him for producing and casting needs and we couldn't raise any more money for the project, so I decided to go the "charge it on a credit card" route - a HUGE mistake for anyone! [laughs] So I got all these credit cards, got check advances for the rest of the budget, and ended up racking up another $12k in bills to make it happen.

Back then it was expensive to edit on video at a real production studio (about $25-$35 an hour), so there was that, plus the latest Hi-8 prosumer equipment I chose, and the special effects by LA based Dan Rebert and Brad Krisco ran about $3k right off the bat, so the money went FAST paying the actors, catering, the whole nine yards. Joel Harlow made the new copper mask and that was cool, but pricey, so...yeah, there was no choice but to shoot it on video! It took my wife and I until 2000 to finally pay off those credit cards! The interest kills you and I sure wouldn't recommend going into debt like that for a movie. But at the time, you know, I've tried about every way invented to get my movies funded. Video was much cheaper than shooting on film and again, something that really wasn't necessary for the previous movies I made, in my opinion. So even though the movie was a smaller budget, it took forever to pay and decades before the movie made it into the black! But I really do love the movie, it's one of the favorites that I've made, and that SNUFF cut works well for me, hiding all the flaws of the original cut that were so obvious. Some people prefer the original cut but for me, the Snuff Edition is just so much more...original and wild!

Wicked Games does not feature the Truth Or Dare? namesake. Why wasn't it called Truth Or Dare 2?

Oh yeah, it is subtitled very small on the artwork *Truth Or Dare II* but at the time, there were lawsuits going over that. I think Madonna was the first to recycle the title in 1992 with her concert film, so there was a big lawsuit on that (on whether the title was patented or fell under some sort of copyright) and she ended up calling her movie *Madonna: Truth Or Dare*. But most people just knew it as *Truth Or Dare* so...she kind of borrowed the title, and rather than confuse people, I opted to kind of just downplay that *Wicked Games* was *Truth Or Dare II* (especially since, for the most part, it was an all new cast, all new crew, and all new story loosely connected to the original, since everyone in the original had moved on and was so scattered). By then John Brace had moved to California, was touring with a play, and eventually became a big casting director out there doing *"Grey's Anatomy"* among other shows. So at the time, I didn't see the value in *Truth Or Dare II* though in retrospect, the way people are with titles these days and how small it was, I should've just called it *Truth Or Dare II*.

Writer's Block (a film by Chris LaMont) claims to be a Truth Or Dare? sequel. Did you have any involvement with this film?

Absolutely! At least in the very early stages. When *Wicked Games* caught on and was selling well, one of our biggest distributors was this outfit out of Arizona called Dead-Alive, run by Yvette Hoffman. Well, she sold the heck out of *Truth Or Dare?*, *Killing Spree* and *Wicked Games* and wanted another movie to sell. This is terrible, but I was on a conference call with her and some other person high up in the company, and she said, *"Your movies suck, but they sell well."* Sooooo... I was like...well, whatever! *"Thanks for being so candid, lady!"* [laughs] So she wanted to make *Truth Or Dare 2*. I told her look, *Wicked Games* is the follow-up to *Truth Or Dare?* but she said, *"No, a Part 2 will sell better!"* So who knows. Anyway, I Fed-Exed her script ideas for a Part 3, copies of the original movie again, and all this stuff. Compiled a budget for her and everything and suddenly, once we got to me being PAID to do all this, she balked! I was like, *"Well, I can't do all this for free!"* So long story short, I got cut out of the project due to budgetary concerns and somehow they hooked up with another group with a completely different story and went ahead and did it so she'd have something to sell!

In the opening scenes, there's flashbacks to *Wicked Games*, even though their movie is called *Writer's Block: Truth Or Dare 2*. So very confusing! Basically, she just wanted something, anything, that said *Truth Or Dare 2* on a box to hawk. So...a *Truth Or Dare 2* with flashbacks to *Truth Or Dare 2*! I never even signed a release for them to use that footage, and I was pretty upset about everything at the time, but it inspired me to go out and make *Truth Or Dare 3: Screaming For Sanity*, where we raised the font on the box art a little bigger with the *Truth Or Dare 3*, which Dead-Alive also sold the heck out of eventually. At some point, they started to stiff me on overdue bills (as always) and later, they screwed a bunch of people over, I heard. Pretty unscrupulous to begin with! But overall, I had little to do with *Writer's Block* and it wasn't a bad little movie. I did finally see it, I thought the moviemakers did the best the could under the circumstances. I'd bet they didn't have much of a budget since my original $10k budget was nixed so fast! In addition to the flashbacks from *Wicked Games* and title, I also provided them with the FX guys; had set them up with the same dudes that did *Wicked Games* for that movie, and they ended up using them. So...one of those very bizarre movie experiences. Fun to read about, awful to endure! [laughs]

Fast forward to 2013 and beyond, and now it seems everyone and their dog is making horror themed *Truth Or Dare?* movies. It's like everyone discovered that mixing this childhood game with horror is like, the best idea ever! There's a Blumhouse supernatural *Truth Or Dare*, a Sy-Fy Channel original knock-off of that one, and even the lead actress in *Deadly Dares: Truth Or Dare 4* (my movie) went out and made her own *Truth Or Dare* movie. I think there's an anthology movie as well, and a British movie called *Truth Or Dare* that we asked to change the title for the U.S. (I think it was called *Truth Or Die* over here). So the *Truth Or Dare* theme is kind of like zombies: something you really can't control with a copyright, but it seems to be making everyone money! I mean, at the end of the day, it is a game that everyone probably played as kids, and everyone has the right to do something with it if they want. Kind of like using zombies, that's the way I look at it now. We're up to *Part 5* in our franchise, called *I Dared You!*, made with Scott Tepperman of *"Ghost Hunters International."* And beyond that, we've already got producers and distributors interested in *Part 6*, so...we're definitely in an age where sequels, remakes, and all that are what sells the best. We had a remake at Lion's Gate, but that fell apart...

Finally we come to the all-mighty *Creep* starring Joel Wynkoop and the controversial Kathy Willets. The film is a masterpiece with a great *Natural Born Killers* vibe. What were the circumstances surrounding Willets' casting? Did her notoriety help the film?

Glad you picked up on the *Natural Born Killers* vibe! Definitely an inspiration, along with *Henry: Portrait of a Serial Killer*. And most definitely, Kathy Willets helped sell *Creep* and took our publicity to a whole new level! I'm not sure if many horror movies shot on S-VHS tape were covered on *"Geraldo,"* *"A Current Affair,"* or all the other crazy national shows that we got mileage out of on that movie. Making it was a whirlwind, just nonstop. It's difficult to even describe now just how HUGE the media scrutiny of that movie was back then in the pre-Internet days. We had magazines, newspapers, and national TV shows covering us the entire time, it was such a wild ride!

I was basically selling *Wicked Games* on VHS and doing a publicity run for it in South Florida (including a radio show with Herschell Gordon Lewis and a big newspaper article for the FORT LAUDERDALE SUN SENTINEL) and Jeff Willets, Kathy's husband, called me up and asked if I wanted to have a "huge celebrity" in my next movie, and eventually he revealed that it was his wife Kathy who was interested in appearing in my movie! Kathy was a scandalous celebrity who had paid sex with men while her husband videotaped the action from a closet, and one of those clients later turned out to be a big politician in Miami or something...and Jeff was a cop! So of course, there was this huge scandal, a court trial where Kathy's defense said her *"Prozac prescription caused her to be a nymphomaniac"* and all this crazy stuff that went national for a few years. When the legalities were ending, Kathy was doing an adult nightclub act and preparing to star in a bunch of pornographic movies, but she also wanted to dabble in something a little more mainstream if possible, which is why she asked to appear in one of my movies, I suppose! At that point most of my movies had been about nymphomaniac housewives of some sort, so it kind of made sense to team up with America's Most Famous Nymphomaniac from South Florida, right? I mean, I saw it as an opportunity that Roger Corman wouldn't have passed up, since he did something similar with Traci Lords and re-made *Not of This Earth* in 1988. And of course, H.G. Lewis used Connie Mason in *Blood Feast*, so I figured it was the right thing to do from a marketing standpoint.

I had just finished a script for my next movie and it was called *Creep*. Joel Wynkoop was set to star along with most of the cast of *Wicked Games*, and we were planning to shoot it sometime in the next year or so...but there was no huge rush. Of course, when Kathy Willets asked to be involved, this accelerated everything. Obviously, she was very big in the news and riding a wave of huge publicity at that time, and we knew it wouldn't last forever, so we had to jump on things while they were hot! Once we got through an audition with Kathy, then we had to go through the legalities of everything - how much she'd be paid, when she was available, and all that sort of thing. Fortunately, I had met Michael Ornelas on the set of *Creep* (another guy who called me based on a newspaper article) and he was set to produce the movie and was VERY enthusiastic when the Kathy Willets opportunity happened! So he helped set up the money end of things as we went along, and that was great. It was very stressful as we started out, because I had to rewrite the script in a certain amount of time and create a role for directly for Kathy and her part had to be shot in like three or four days, if I remember correctly. So that was kind of difficult for me at first, figuring all that out. I remember I had writer's block for a spell, and it was very frustrating! But eventually, after seeing *Natural Born Kilers* and thinking about *Henry: Portrait of a Serial Killer*, I was able to come up with something about brother and sister deviants in a very twisted storyline. But it's a completely different script than the original draft, which was more like Eric Stanze's *Scrapbook* (which he made years later) but my original *Creep* script was very close to that in style and substance before Kathy Willets got involved. Kind of in one location with a female cop kidnapped and a serial killer torturing her and playing games until she turns the tables on him. With Kathy Willets involved, I opened the story up more and added more locations, action, that kind of thing... plus, I wrote it in a way so it seemed like she was in the entire movie, from beginning to end, as opposed to just a disappointing cameo in one scene.

So delivering something cool for the viewer was on my mind, and it... just all came together so fast! Before we knew it, within a few months, we were location scouting, locking in a crew, and casting more and more people. It just became this huge circus with all the press involved! There was outrage from people, death threats because we were using such a scandalous celebrity who brought down a politician, and enraged newspaper and magazine readers because our original preliminary poster art had Joel behind Kathy with a knife to her throat - right when the murder of Nicole Brown Simpson happened. And of course, we had no control over that, it was just bad timing. We had a photo session with Joel and Kathy way before that tragic event happened, and the timing was just one of those bad things. Eventually, we changed the artwork and used a picture where he was just kind of loosely strangling her on the cover in a more lighthearted, b-movie manner. The things we ran into while making that movie, it would probably take a whole book to cover! But as we went along, the whole thing just grew and grew and I think that was the biggest crew I ever worked with, even bigger than *Truth Or Dare? A Critical Madness*. And the shoot stretched out for a few months, mainly on the weekends, with some of those national TV shows coming to the set while we filmed. It was honestly such a wild, exciting, chaotic, and uncharted adventure, shooting, editing, and distributing *Creep*. Every time you turned around, something new and crazy would happen. And we ended up getting to use original Tom Savini props from the 1974 movie *Deranged* when producer Tom Karr joined the action as an associate producer and actor, and we had 74-year-old punk rocker Dika Newlin in a part, and some of the Palm Beach Shakespeare actors from *Wicked Games* like Patricia Paul... it was just a wild mix-mash of personalities and craziness! And absolutely, there was so much interest in the movie when it came out, we decided once again to self-distribute, and we had orders for thousands of VHS tapes right out of the gate. I recall a semi truck backing up to deliver pallets full of tapes when we first started selling that thing... and of course, naturally, we ended up getting ripped off by unscrupulous rack-jobbers and middlemen on that deal. So once again... it was another distribution abyss!

But looking back on it, I'm glad we gave it a shot and it's an interesting footnote in 90's scandalous celebrities and shot on video horror! It was completely uncharted territory for me from beginning to end, a great learning experience and a whirlwind! And working with Kathy was great (by the way, she was so nice, cooperative, and professional that I was bowled over). She really gave the acting thing all of her attention and tried so hard, she was really into the part! And her husband Jeff was great to deal with too, never an issue from either of them, they were amazingly fun and down to earth, considering all they had gone through and all they were going through (trying to pick up the pieces of a big mess, capitalize on it, and make money off it). It was all just...wild, man, wild!

Creep was also shot on video, not film. Was this an aesthetic choice?

Absolutely. By then, I had no intent to shoot anything on film because I frankly couldn't justify the costs. It was much quicker, easier, and way more affordable to shoot on tape. Plus, Kathy Willets' life had been captured on video since she first got into trouble, and she was about to jump into the adult world where everything was shot on video for the most part (although one of her movies may have been 35mm, I believe. The one that told her story in two parts called _Naked Scandal_ or something like that). But to me, video was the perfect medium to shoot _Creep_ on, and I also was inspired by _Natural Born Killers_ using a variety of formats to tell the story.

We shot the bulk of the movie on 3-chip Super VHS cameras, which were huge at that time and cost about $12,000 a piece to buy, so these weren't consumer models, more what the news was using... and also Hi-8 footage, VHS, 16mm bolex, and a few other formats as we could just for b-rolls and insert shots. But by then, I really couldn't afford to shoot anything on film. It was too expensive and most of _Creep's_ budget went to catering, locations, transportation, and paying Kathy Willets, of course. I even wrote most of the gore effects around props we used from _Wicked Games_ to save money; a practice of recycling which I continue today.

In today's world of internet videos and Youtube, what advice would you give young filmmakers hoping to follow in your footsteps?

I definitely always try to help and encourage others to live their dreams! I guess my biggest piece of advice is still the same: just get out there and create. Write your script, make your movie. Push forward and don't worry about having the latest 10K camera to make your epic. If what you have at your disposal is an old mini-dv camera that works, use that to make your movie! Write your dream screenplay, try to hook up with like-minded people on social media, make a connection somewhere. It usually happens if you're persistent enough, and if you can't make a dent, do it yourself. The tools are there.

Now making a dent and being seen these days, despite all the technology, is difficult. Especially in the crowded Streaming market. But look at the successes out there, the guys who made _Clown_. It all started with a fake trailer they made and posted on the Internet, attaching the words ELI ROTH presents... and when he saw it, not only was he not mad... he was flattered enough to actually help them get that movie made for real! So there's some amazing success stories out there even today. In the world of entertainment, there's no clear, cookie cutter path. Success is unpredictable and the way it happens always differs. I think the key is just doing what you love and putting it out there, whether it's painting, writing, effects artist, or making movies. Use the resources you have, get stuff out there, one step at a time, and eventually, someone will notice. Now, will we all be resounding successes? Sadly, no...but hopefully we get to a place where we're making money off what we do or get into a job we love doing something we like... or have it as at least this awesome sideline hobby thing where we're having a blast! So the cliff notes version is create your art and network on social media! Sadly, the whole streaming thing has become very studio oriented these days, and so fast. When Netflix started back in 2007 or whenever (with their FREE Streaming service) it was all largely independent movies, including *Truth Or Dare?* and *Killing Spree*, and there was a huge resurgence of interest in my titles on there for a while. That's what made *Deadly Dares: Truth Or Dare 4* happen, all this interest in my older movies on Netflix. But now it's harder than ever to get stuff on these platforms, because they produce and hawk their own in-house material now more than anything. So for the indie moviemaker, I'd recommend Vimeo more for streaming attention and don't forget the VHS-DVD-Blu world. Selling directly at horror shows, conventions, and in Specialty Groups dedicated to those mediums on social media can reap you many rewards and keep the next projects financed!

Thank you so much for your time and thoughts, Tim!

Interview
JOEL D. WYNKOOP

Widly known today as "The King of B Movies," multi-talented Joel D. Wynkoop has appeared in numerous horror, action and fantasy films and is instantly recognizable worldwide. Also a filmmaker, Joel has steadily built an impressive career with over 150 credits and still acts today. A Florida native (who frequently babysat young Tim Ritter while still in his youth), Joel's award winning skills and charming persona often belies the bone-chilling psychos he's known for portraying onscreen.

Joel, thank you for giving your time to this interview! At what age did you realize you wanted to work in movies?

I think it was meant to be. As a kid, I was always running around with a towel around my neck pretending to be Batman. In the 70's my Dad bought me a Super8 camera when I showed and interest in *King Kong* and *Godzilla*. Finding out Kong was an armature 13 inches tall and was animated, and then finding out Godzilla was a guy in a costume? I wanted to make a movie. I was shooting with my camera that very same day. I made a movie for one of my classes in the 9th grade. It was an animated cyclops, my first shot at animation, then I used the same animated creature to attack my train board and caught my hand on fire in the process. Never throw gas on a lit object. Then my neighbor Steve Campbell and I made "The EIGHT Million Dollar Boy Meets The Invisible Transport Boy" with the help of then 8 year old Tim Ritter. I knew Tim from watching him while his parents were away over the summer. At one point the Super8 footage was lost by Sears and all my filming dreams were dead. I gave it up, I had no more interest in filming... until a year later when Sears found the footage and I finished "The Bionic Boy" and started filming again. I took filmmaking in high school in Ms Harper's class and made the movie "Escape from Banyoull VI" with classmates. I continued making Super8 movies and then getting a sound camera and started making sound movies interviewing people in the mall and making stupid skits with friends. I went to college for awhile in Tampa and was still shooting on my Super8 camera. But when I returned to West Palm Beach and finally ending up in Port St Lucia, I started shooting stuff on video. I rented a camera from a video store (yeah remember those?) and my nephews and I went out and shot a lot of *Monty Python* type stuff just for fun and then played it back in the video store with the clerk's permission. Some woman stood there and watched it and loved it and said she would rent it, so I got to thinking... maybe I should try and make something on video and sell it.

It was around the time I wound up back in West Palm Beach that my nephew Terry pointed out to me that this kid was selling a Super8 movie called *Day of the Reaper*. And it was by Tim Ritter and I thought *"is that the same Tim Ritter I knew as a kid?"* It was. We got together that night (or very close to that) and shot a little movie on video, a cop thing, I wish we still had it. I think Tim said he recorded *"Hill Street Blues"* over it. Anyway it was that night *Twisted Illusions* was born. Within days, we marketed *Day of the Reaper* and then planned to collaborate on something of our own...together. We came up with *Twisted Illusions* not only as our company name but it would also be the name of the movie. I came up with three stories and Tim did the same and added a wraparound story Tim had written early. We casted, we walked around The Palm Beach Mall and handed out flyers for auditions and canvassed the parking lots with flyers. When it came to the ORIGINAL "Truth or Dare," Tim said he needed an actor to really go crazy screaming *"Truth or Dare! Truth or Dare!"* and I said *"LIKE THIS?"* and I screamed it out. He said *"You gotta do the part man, that was cool!"* and that is how it all started. I mean I did the Super8 stuff, I was the notorious leader of the skateboard gang that fought the Bionic Boy but we were doing it now for real. We were off and running. I was hooked. But I never imagined then that some day I would be looking at over 158 movies to my name as an actor.

Have you always desired to both act and direct? Do you prefer one over the other?

At first well I guess I was directing, you know Super8 movies just yelling at friends *"Okay now you do this!"* and *"You do that."* When Tim and I did *Twisted Illusions,* I wrote three stories and I wasn't in any of mine so I did direct those. That was fun. I think I liked the acting more and still do BUT I really like directing too. I'd like to say I think I have an eye for it. AND a lot of times, I see something when we are shooting and it is like last second and I'll change something and tell the actor *"Oh this would be great, do this instead."* So I directed my Super8 movies, then I directed in *Twisted Illusions* along with Tim, then "Truth or Dare" happened BUT that was all Tim directing, I just acted, did some stunt work, props and P.A. but no directing. I acted in *Killing Spree* BUT as I was shooting *Killing Spree,*

I was writing *Lost Faith* and going on TV advertising I was making a movie. At nights I was with Tim making *Killing Spree*. I wrote directed and starred in *Lost Faith*, Tim taught me how to do a production board, a shooting schedule on index cards. I guess I really like them both. A lot of time on sets, I see the director struggling with something and I can't help but say *"Hey would you like some advice?"* Of course a lot of my projects (well let's see, ALL of projects) I direct as well as take a role. Maybe I like the acting a bit more but I love them both.

You've worked quite a lot with Tim Ritter, both as an actor and co-director. How did you and Tim first meet?

I was living in Lake Park Florida at the time. Our neighbors were The Ritter's who lived across the street from us. Tim's Mom had actually been my substitute teacher at one point in the sixth grade. One day she got locked out of their house and I used a credit card to get her in, that was pretty cool, I felt like a spy, I was 15. Anyway at one point one of our neighbors had me watching her kids and then Mrs. Ritter asked me to watch Wendy and Tim. I started going over there everyday from around 8am till 5pm and would just be there with them so they weren't alone. It was more of a friendship with Tim and I from the very beginning, we loved the same things. "The Six Million Dollar Man," Batman and Superman and if I may be so bold, I think I started him on his filmmaking career. As time went on, I was making "Robin" with my nephew Terry and I put Tim in that and of course "The Bionic Boy." It was later that Tim started making his own movies on Super8. Coincidence?.... I think not.

You seem to relish playing characters who either turn crazy, or meet their demise in hilarious situations. Extreme roles with a wide range to play. Do you enjoy larger than life characters over subtle ones?

Yes! I love going over the top. I thought I had it made when Hershell Gordon Lewis told me *"Mr. Wynkoop I need you to go way over the top for this role, do you think you can do that?"* *"Finally!"* I thought. Although I did it in *Creep* too, I remember Tim telling me after we shot a scene, he was like *"I was goanna pull you back but you were having so much fun with it I let you go."* And I think people like that. People have told me *"We keep waiting to see you explode."* I mean, I can do serious laid back roles too, it is just most directors want me flying off the wall and being intense. I can do both. But it is fun to just go nuts with the role. John Lewis pegged it by calling it... well, let me start by saying I was doing a role and my wife said *"Maybe you should do it the way they want instead of the way you want."* So I said *"Okay."* I was doing a scene for John Lewis and I finished the whole scene and he said *"What was that?"* I said *"Did I miss a line?"* and he said *"No you were perfect on the lines but what happened, I need you to go Wynkoop."* And that is where the expression came from and I have heard other actors and directors say it *"Hey I need you to go Wynkoop in this role."* Too funny. One time, I played the role of a father and I asked the director *"No killing, raping, yelling, screaming, running?"* He said *"No your just a Dad."* If I had one or the other, I'd do the over the top guy but again I love them both.

Though many of your roles have been in horror, *Lost Faith* demonstrated your affinity for kicking ass and martial arts. What inspirations did you have while making it? Did you always intent to write, direct and star?

Well I had done *Twisted Illusions*, "Truth or Dare" and was about to begin *Killing Spree* when I started writing *Lost Faith* (untitled at that time). Before this, I was also introduced to Chuck Norris in *Good Guys Wear Black* and this is what got me into Martial Arts for real. At this time I was already a black belt, I was kickboxing in the ring with other fighters so it seemed like movies would be the next step. There were like seven versions of *Lost Faith* and I finally settled on the white slavery ring story. I would write it, direct it star in it and produce it. Inspiration of the Martial Arts was all Chuck Norris and James Ryan, *Kill and Kill Again* was a big movie then too. My Dad was a minister and I thought if I could put the word of GOD into a movie, that would be pretty cool too. My Dad never got to see any of my work, but I've always wondered what he would have thought of it.

What are some of your favorite films?

Faves of mine *RoboCop*, *Dawn of the Dead* original, *Batman* (Michael Keaton), *Back to the Future*, *Evil Dead* (Raimi), *Independence Day,* oh man so many... action, horror, comedies, dramas, indie movies BIG movies... too many to name. I could do a book on them.

You've also impressively performed your own stunts. Was there ever a stunt you got hurt on, or regretted doing?

Not really. I think I pulled something on *Creep*. *Lost Faith* I took a lot of hits but nothing that knocked me out. I have done a lot of fighting in movies but the most I do is wear myself out. I have hurt myself when taking falls in fight scenes but not enough to stop me from continuing the movie. I've been kicked and punched several times and I have done a lot. But nothing like Jackie Chan or Tom Cruise.

***Wicked Games* provided you with a large role early in your career. Did you have any reservations about playing a bondage-loving cop, or the killer himself?**

I wasn't too excited about Tim telling me to put on the collar, but it was okay. Whatever to make the movie. It was cool doing both roles, well it was Hess only BUT he was also putting on the copper mask and killing people (but each of the characters had good reasons for killing who they did... as far as they were concerned). I hate being in a suit and the only time you'll see me in one is in a movie. Dan Hess is always in a suit and I have played Dan Hess in five *Truth or Dare?* movies, and seven or eight other movies who had Dan Hess guest star (and always in a suit). It's these cop roles that always get me in a suit. I think *Wicked Games* was a lot of fun, it was cool to kind of play that *Dirty Harry* kind of role. Tim tried to kill us running up and down the beach in the end, but other then that it was great!!!

You have been fortunate enough to work with different recording formats. Have you notice any technical differences between shooting productions on film rather than video?

Twisted Illusions was on 1/2 inch video, *Truth or Dare?* was 16mm but you had to send the film away and wait for dailies, *Killing Spree* was 16mm also and you had to wait on dailies with that as well (and they were not coming back when they were supposed to, Tim hated that because we couldn't see what we shot till it was almost too late to shoot it again). I think film is just kind of a pain now and I almost think video formats Red, 5K all that crap is more accepted anyway. Personally I wouldn't even know how to shoot on film besides Super8, I'd have to learn all that crap. Blleeeeeccchhhh! I'll let someone else do the technical stuff with the cameras and I'll just direct and act. I have no desire to learn all aspects of the camera and reading manuals, I had enough of that in high school. Hey, at least I'm honest!

Chris LaMont's film *Writer's Block* claims to be a sequel to *Truth Or Dare?*. Do you know the circumstances surrounding this?

It is NOT a sequel!!!! We were supposed to be paid for those scenes from *Wicked Games* and the boxed copy but we never were. Tim didn't want to make a big deal about it and neither did I, we just chalked it for *"Well it's kind of cool to see it in a movie other then our own."* BUT yeah it is not a sequel at all. I think they just tagged that onto it after it was completed. It's still a pretty cool little movie though.

Finally we come to the all-mighty *Creep* and your award winning turn as serial killer Angus Lynch. Was the character always written with you in mind?

Originally it was *Old Gus Finklestein*, but Tim changed it into the *Creep* it is now. The other one was more *Deranged* like, and was supposed to be kind of a sequel to that BUT again NOT REALLY. The first version was much darker and Gus was doing things I was like *"I don't want to do that."* Yes, I was always supposed to do it we did have one actor, he said *"I'll give you this great location but I want to be the star"* and Tim told him *"Well Joel here is playing the starring role."* And the guy was like *"Then you can't have this location."* But Tim put him in a cameo scene, as well as my friend Frank Eberling (who my Science class high school teacher introduced me too). The one thing I still don't like about *Creep* was I wasn't prepared for it like I am for roles now. You can clearly see me in *Creep* mode thru most of the movie but when I meet my sister at the strip club, I was just Joel Wynkoop and I still apologize for that today!! I hate it! I love the movie but I hate I wasn't prepared to take on that role that day. It was all better after that but I look back and say *"Man I can never do that again, I should have had that character down from the very beginning."* I had a BLAST doing it... everytime I got to go nuts like beating the roof of my car and just going nuts in the driver's seat, the pawn shop scene with my head in the counter yelling *"WE'RE FUCKIN CLOSED!"* and eatin' that gross burger and spitting it out on the counter, the blow torch scene, the whole thing was a BLAST!!!!!!!

Creep also stars the controversial Kathy Willets. Did you know the circumstances surrounding her casting?

Tim and I thought about contacting her but we thought *"Nah why would she want to work with us?"* Well I guess she did because a year or so, Jeff her husband called Tim and asked if he would like to have someone of notoriety in his flicks. And through a number of back and forth conversations between Jeff and Tim, a deal was made: Kathy would be written into a script. At first the guy said his name was "BEN" or whatever, it wasn't revealed to Tim it was Jeff Willets until a later phone call. I met her at the photo shoot and I think we hit it off right away, she and Jeff were cool. I think it helped. I mean if we did it without her, I think it still would have sold but I don't think as good, so yeah. But even still we were selling this store to store, we would drive all over and go in and sell it to the owner. One guy was like *"The actor on the cover is so filled with rage that we cannot sell this, his rage is too much for our store."* One guy got really mad at Tim and I, started yelling at us saying *"How do I know she's in this, she could just be in it for just one minute, get out of my store, get out, get out!"* A friend of mine told me he went to an appearance she was having for one of her X rated movies and he asked her to sign *Creep*. And she said *"Oh I'm so embarrassed by this."* Really? She was cool and so was Jeff. We only had one incident... when Kathy and I were in the grave. She decided her character should not die and she spun around in the grave and karate kicked me in the chest. To which I said to Tim *"Well are you gonna call cut or what?"* and I was like *"What in the hell are you doing?"* which she replied *"I didn't think my character should die."* Anyway I thought she cracked my ribs, she kicked me so hard but other then that, all was forgiven and everything else was a cool shoot.

Billed as "America's Naughty Nympho," do you have any lasting memories performing with Willets in the film? Was Creep produced shortly before she entered pornography?

I think she was billed "America's Favorite Nymphomaniac." I think *Naughty Nymphos* was one of the titles of her porno movies, and I'm not saying that as a bad thing it is just what it is, a porno. I believe after she appeared on *"A Current Affair"* (a tabloid TV show from the 90's) with us. She was seen by Seymoore Butts (a producer of pornographic movies) and he contacted her after seeing her on the tabloid show and she was off on her X rated career, I believe. It would be fun to see her again and catch up we had a good time making *Creep!!*

30 years and still going strong, Joel D. Wynkoop continues to direct and star in films to this day. What is the secret to your longevity? Are there any roles out there that you'd love to play, but haven't had the chance?

35...but who's counting? I will be playing "Hawk" in Todd Sheets movie *Clownado*, which will put me in the cockpit of an airplane so that will be interesting to see how we pull this off (*"I'm NOT a pilot....but I play one in the movies"*). I've played the common man, the psycho, the space captain, the mad scientist, several cops crazed and diplomatic with a bit of "CRAZED" in them. I have played a superhero in my TV show *"The Other Side,"* I have played several Anti-Heroes: Hammer, Hazzard, Ransom... No real secret just keep doing things... I do turn down parts but most I take. You know how Randy Quaid goes out in *Independence Day* or Bruce Willis in *Armageddon?* The hero that sacrifices his life for the world or a friend or family, that would be cool. *Lost Faith 2* has that, if I ever get around to making it. Oh and if no one is asking you to take a part in there movie, make something on your own. Don't sit around and wait...make your own future. I hear from people all the time that tell me they loved me in *Creep* or *Dirty Cop No Donut* or playing Dan Hess in movies, Cope Ransom, Nick Hazzard. So as long as I hear these nice things people are saying about me, I will keep making movies and trying to take on new characters whether they come from another moviemaker or myself. I just want to entertain people and this is the format I choose.

What advice might you offer young actors looking to break into the business today?

Just start doing something. Get involved with someone in the same mind set... get with them and tell them you want to get involved. Don't sit around and wait on your agent because they have another 3,000 clients they have to get jobs for. And if no one else is doing anything, create something on your own and just do it.

Thank you so much for your time and thoughts, Joel!

Chapter 11
DAYTIME WHORES (1989)

BLACK PAST
1989, Color, 83 min
STARRING: *Olaf Ittenbach, Andrea Arbter, Andre Stryl, Susanne Nebbe, Alfons Sigllechner*
DIRECTOR: *Olaf Ittenbach*

A young man and family move into a house, finding an old mirror boxed and chained in the attic. Within the box is a diary, stating that the mirror is cursed. The man retrieves the mirror and hangs it in his bedroom anyway. Soon enough, his girlfriend is possessed by a spirit and hit by a car in the street. Now haunted by nightmares of her return, the man eventually transforms into a demon and kills his entire family.

A mix of *The Evil Dead* and *A Nightmare On Elm Street 2*, *Black Past* was Germany's answer to horror censorship in the 1980's. Though popular when they arrived, most American productions suffered heavy edits (or were outright banned) for German audiences. Enter Ittenbach, a 20 year old dental technician looking to bring extreme gore to the masses. And after a few short films later, *Black Past* was born. Written and directed by star Ittenbach, the film teases a comedic love story before revealing its bloody intentions. Ittenbach pushes the boundaries of acceptable horror, even appearing nude with an innocent yet sinister performance. He memorably suffers penis torture via board and nail in one of the film's most famous sequences. But the movie is essentially a one man show in some respects (with everyone knifed, chainsawed or boulder-bashed onscreen). And as for the gore? Quite a few showstoppers stand out, particularly the full torso chainsaw and the abovementioned penis scene. But extreme as the violence sounds, one can't help but snicker at the dummy heads and rubbery appliances. *Black Past* is a wonderful throwback to the latex heavy days of the decade. And Ittenbach certainly deserves praise because not only is this an infinitely entertaining picture, but he turned it into a political one as well. Recommended.

THE BLOODY VIDEO HORROR THAT MADE ME PUKE ON MY AUNT GERTRUDE
1989, Color, 75 min
STARRING: *Jared Buchansky, Zachary Winston Snygg (John Bacchus), Spencer Snygg*
DIRECTOR: *Zachary Winston Snygg (John Bacchus)*

An eccentric killer rents a camcorder from the local video store. He records himself killing a naked woman, attempting to make a snuff film for foreign markets. Unfortunately, he returns the camera to the store with the tape still inside and now must kill to get it back.

Wonderful in concept, *Bloody Video* is the sophomore return for young Buchansky and the Snygg brothers. But unlike *The Heaping Bouncy Breasts That Smothered a Midget*, *Bloody Video* is a tedious sketch comedy extended forever and going nowhere. Sloppily edited, the entire production feels like a big joke missing its punchline. The idea of a snuff film returned to a video store is nothing new (*Video Violence*) but Snygg promises a different take on the material. Too bad it never materializes. *Bouncy Breasts* proved ingenuity, but ingenuity seems missing here. There are inspired moments but very few and far between.

DARK ROMANCES VOLUME 1
1989, Color, 109 min
STARRING: *Elizabeth Morehead, Julie Carlson, Brinke Stevens, Robert Rothman,*
DIRECTOR: *Mark Shepard*

An anthology of two stories. "The Black Veil" takes place during Victorian times, dealing with a drugged actress performing in the Grand Guignol. "Listen to Midnight" is told first-person in present day 1989 about a photographer and the circumstances of his death.

Overlong and highly stylized, *Dark Romances Vol 1* exists for a specific audience. With "The Black Veil" taking up much of the runtime, the film is a bit of a slog. Extreme close-ups dominate with Dutch-angles and colored lights everywhere. It's style over substance, though things (thankfully) pick up once the plot is introduced. Morehead and Carlson give commendable performances, but Shepard doesn't know when to wrap it up. "Listen to

Midnight" is greatly affected by this, as I was not persuaded to stick around for more. And "Listen to Midnight" features a more straightforward approach with great nudity. Perhaps if they were reordered? Scream Queen Stevens appears throughout.

DARK ROMANCES VOLUME 2
1989, Color, 100 min
STARRING: *Brinke Stevens, Ruth Waytz, Therese Pare, Scott Wyler, Elle Rio, Jeff Watkins*
DIRECTOR: *Mark Shepard, Samuel Oldham, Rodd Matsui, John Strysik, Patricia Miller*

Another anthology of stories. A genetically engineered monster kills a young couple in "She's Bad, She's Blonde, She's Lunch." A boy masturbates behind his mother's back in "Cardinal Sin." A man kills his wife with a unique creature in "Pet Shop of Death." A psychiatrist continues her affair with a long dead lover in "Last Love." A widowed composer makes music thanks to a devilish temptress in "What Goes Around..."

Though originally sold together (both volumes in one gigantic 210 minute release),

Dark Romances Vol 2 is the hands-down winner in terms of pacing and quality. What a difference! Opening with the sexy, gory and hilarious "She's Bad, She's Blonde, She's Lunch," *Volume 2* immediately sheds the soft-focus slog of *Volume 1*. Setting stories in present day helps too, but the real star of "She's Bad" is Waytz and her incredible breasts. Though relatively brief, Waytz delivers a sexually aggressive performance like no other. "Cardinal Sin" keeps the sleaze coming but as before, *Volume 2* semi-outstays its welcome. The stories are fantastic but the runtime just can't take a breath. *Creepshow* mastered five tales. *Creepshow 2* offered three and with good reason: *Creepshow 2* is of cheaper quality. Don't get me wrong, I love *Creepshow 2* but it gives three tales because it's quick, cheap and dirty. *Dark Romances* is shot on video and wants to be more. I'm comfortable with that, but it really should have been split over another volume. *Volume 1* was nearly 1 hour and 50 minutes. *Volume 2* is 1 hour and 40 minutes. Couldn't we have three volumes that all run 70 minutes each?

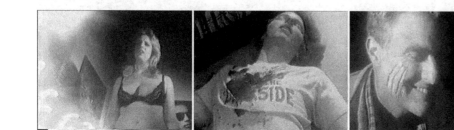 

DEAD SILENCE

1989, Color, 62 min
STARRING: *Cindy Weichbroot, Kevin Patterson, Ron Scroggins, Brad Foltz*
DIRECTOR: *Hugh Gallagher*

A serial killer is fried in the electric chair. Across town, a woman records possible ghost sounds in a graveyard. She captures the killer's spirit on tape. A grave robber finds the tape and plays it, becoming possessed with the spirit.

 A simple premise convoluted with character interactions that go nowhere, Gallagher's first is a primer for what's to come. *Dead Silence* is Gallagher testing the waters. And though light on story, the film impresses with its willful misuse of a car and joyriding tomfoolery. Actors perform their own stunts as they hang on car rooftops. Cars swerve and crash into motorcycles. Trees are smashed and rusty abandoned trucks are slammed into. Gallagher sure didn't care about insurance! But this carefree approach to an otherwise poverty-row picture is commendable. It shows a filmmaker willing to go to the wall for his film. *Dead*

Silence is fairly tame with otherwise loose references between Weichbroot and the killer, but this is really a chase movie at heart. And with one hell of a battle.

DISGUSTING SPACEWORMS EAT EVERYONE!!
1989, Color, 73 min
STARRING: *Lisa Everett Hillman, Bill Brady, Dukey Flyswater (Michael Sonye)*
DIRECTOR: *George Keller*

Intergalactic mealworms have invaded Earth. A lady drug dealer and the guy who hit her with his car, fight back.

This is not a normal movie.

Like 1988's *The Brainsucker*, *Spaceworms* is a spoof-thriller about incredible events and unbelievable characters. But unlike *The Brainsucker*, *Spaceworms* generally plays it straight. Loaded with creative special effects, dime-store filters, kickass rock tunes and enough worms for wiggly night terrors, Keller's alien invasion epic is an analog showstopper. People eat worms! Worms eat people! It's the yin and yang to life, shared through galactic genocide. Sadly we're never given a wormy backstory. But Keller reaches for lofty heights, complete with a bloody bathtub sequence reminiscent of Cronenberg's *Shivers* and some dubious cap-gun gun fights. The whole thing's a little hard to follow, particularly since two of the leads are identical. But Hillman gives it her all in assless jeans. And believe it or not, cocaine becomes Earth's great savior. Victory in the form of drugs thrown into a worm's face. Hooray! The film is a remake of the 1984 short "Terror of Disgusting Worms From Outer Space," directed by George Hampton. Enjoyable.

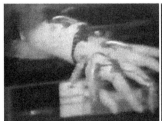   

DUNGEON OF DEATH
1989, Color, 81 min
STARRING: *Clancey McCauley, Chris Stonage, Mike Brady, Aven Warren, Terri Cavalier*
DIRECTOR: *Gary Whitson*

A woman and her sister suffer identical nightmares about being tortured and killed in a basement. Turns out the woman's husband is drugging the pair, hoping that they'll go insane as their mother did years earlier.

Though much of the film consists of McCauley and Stonage tied up and killed repeatedly, *Dungeon of Death* actually has more going for it than meets the eye. Multiple twists enter the narrative, particularly during its final moments. And the film is terribly mean spirited. Several bits involve the women being called *"bitches."* Punches are thrown into faces and knives are gleefully pushed into bodies. One girl is choked while the other is tied and whipped. And the motive? Money in the form of their father's inheritance. The film feels slightly repetitive at times, mostly due to the same victims repeatedly killed in the same environment. But the deaths have edge and the story works. A noteworthy entry from W.A.V.E. productions (and one of their first custom videos).

FATAL IMAGES
1989, Color, 96 min
STARRING: *Lane Coyle, Kay Schaber, Angela Eads, David Williams, Brian Burr Chin*
DIRECTOR: *Dennis Devine*

A serial killer traps his soul into a specially made camera. A photographer buys and uses it years later, but everyone photographed winds up dead. Turns out the killer's spirit can leave the camera, killing anyone whose picture it takes.

Wonderfully entertaining, *Fatal Images* is a favorite among SOV horror fans. When the killer first appears (stalking his victims before striking), the cinematography comes alive with low angles and point of view images. Williams as the killer gives a truly menacing performance and Devine's direction brings the scares. The script is well written with an opening sequence filled with tension (Williams thwarts police and traps his soul). *Fatal Images* runs a tad longer than it should, losing that tension during a drawn out conclusion. But this is Devine's first feature and pacing is quite good for the most part. My only real complaint is that the most enjoyable character is killed far too soon. Tall and frizzy haired, Eads' policewoman is stereotypically funny and extremely beautiful onscreen. We want her to stick around and stop the bad guy. But she dies just after speaking to the pressures women face on the policeforce. Tragic! Nitpicking aside, *Fatal Images* is generally regarded as one of the last great SOVs of the 80's. Highly Recommended.

HEAVY METAL MASSACRE
1989, Color, 84 min
STARRING: *Bobbi Young (David DeFalco), Michele De Santis, Nick Hasomeris*
DIRECTOR: *Steven DeFalco, Ron Ottaviano*

Metal jammin' cocaine sniffin' Bobbi Young is a killer. Enticing women to his warehouse apartment, handcuffing and smashing them with a sledgehammer. Bobbi doesn't mess around. And he doesn't have time for dudes harassing him about his looks either (as one guy learns with the business end of a chainsaw). Bobbi just wants to listen to music and play games with his black studded gloves and jacket. The cops are determined to stop him but they finger the wrong guy, so Bobbi's free to kill and kill again.

Featuring the greatest heavy metal soundtrack next to *Blood Lake*, *Heavy Metal Massacre* is a SOV dream. With video mosaics, filters, saturated colors and David DeFalco's reassuring stare (straight into camera), *Heavy Metal* is wall to wall joy. Shot in the hair-band rocker scene of '89, teased hairdos, black leathers and spandex never seemed more appealing. And with its multiple fist-pumping dance tracks, *Heavy Metal* becomes the ride you never want to end. But it's not all fun in the sun. The sledgehammer kills (like Bobbi) are hard hitting and easy going. At first you wonder why he takes so long handcuffing since he blasts the girls right away. But after repeat viewings, one gets to understand Bobbi's "take it or leave it" persona. This guy ties up girls for the tease. He drugs and strips one girl of her pants, only to let her wake before handcuffing & hammering away. Does he enjoy their pain? Not really. The man just has a routine and wants to play. And sex won't sway him, he's just here for the tunes and the bashing. A couple red herrings get tossed to the cops, so Bobbi's free to do his stuff with the most deserving of endings. And who wouldn't want to see Bobbi win? He's so damn charismatic. *"Check this out babe, take it or leave it!"* Required Viewing.

HOUSEBOAT HORROR
1989, Color, 82 min
STARRING: *Alan Dale, Christine Jeston, Craig Alexander, Des McKenna, Gavin Wood*
DIRECTOR: *Kendall Flannigan, Ollie Martin*

A film crew rents houseboats on a lake to shoot a music video. But the lake has a tragic history. 20 years ago, a fire interrupted a previous film's production and burned a child. Now grown and scarred, the child returns for bloody revenge.

An Australian slasher, *Houseboat Horror* feels very American. Co-directed by Flannigan and Martin (who also wrote), *Houseboat* could easily be mistaken for countless others in the genre. But SOV and set on a lake, *Houseboat Horror* differentiates itself as something more than a *Blood Tracks* riff. Crafted with wonderful shots and tight edits, *Houseboat* sails beyond most horrors of the time. Aware of what it is, the film adheres to expectations while providing new twists thanks to its unique location. And to its credit, a sense of isolation permeates the houseboats beyond the typical summer camp or sorority house. Houseboats can move into danger! This presents uncertainty as to where (or when) the killer will strike. And the killer is wonderfully identifiable; vengeful and scarred. Sort of a "Cropsy Legend" recalling *The Burning* or *Madman* before it. *Houseboat Horror* may not be the pinnacle slasher for the ages, but it is a wonderful SOV import. Recommended.

  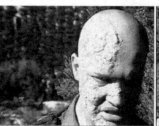 

LAS VEGAS BLOODBATH

1989, Color, 78 min
STARRING: *Ari Levin, Barbara Bell, Rebecca Gandara, Tiffany Heisler, Jennifer Quinn*
DIRECTOR: *David Schwartz*

After landing a successful deal, businessman Sam returns home to find his wife in bed with another man. Shooting them both and decapitating his wife, Sam embarks on a killing spree along the Las Vegas strip.

Filled with misogyny, *Las Vegas Bloodbath* seems to hate women at face value. The entire runtime shows women catty and chatty, making fun of one another behind backs or as helpless victims to Sam's vengeance. And at face value, this may put off a great many viewers. But the joys of this film come from its extreme heavy handedness. *Las Vegas Bloodbath* may indeed be over-the-top in misogyny, but it's extremely over-the-top in hilarity too. Actors deliver lines in stunted one-take masters. Dialogue is mumbled while insults are yelled into camera. Victims enter rooms with walls covered in protective paper. An actually pregnant woman has a bloody doll cut out of her belly, then thrown at the wall. Our killer screams about *"daytime whores"* and looks exactly like Nicholas Cage. These are only some of the memorable moments that make *Las Vegas* the SOV jewel that it is. And Sam asks questions of his victims, replying to everything with *"Ruth loved that!"* before killing; it's the bloody cherry on top. *"Ruth loved Oil Wrestling!"* and *"Ruth was a Jehovah's Witness!"* Truly laugh out loud moments.

Shot in six days (with apparently no script), the film manages an interesting editing technique in that we lose our killer/hero for much of the middle act. After 20 minutes (and some outstanding murders), the film switches gears and spends 20 more minutes with a group of female oil wrestlers. The girls sit around, play cards, drink beer and generally make fun of their pregnant friend. The pregnant girl doesn't mind though, because they all then watch a television broadcast of their recent oil fight. Finally, Sam busts in and kills them one by one. But in a normal film, such a loss of our main character could leave the audience stranded. Do we care about these girls? Are we waiting for them to die? What does oil wrestling mean to the plot? Director Schwartz takes a gamble here, which frankly works thanks to the nature of video itself.

This is real life caught on camera.

The loss of Sam does feel strange though, as the tone suddenly shifts. We're introduced to the girls candidly and made to watch as they whisper, eat and change into bathing suits. Obviously they're intended victims (Sam patiently watches from the living room window), but after 20 minutes of donuts and pizza munching, gabbing about who knocked up the pregnant girl and trying on bikinis, the audience identifies with them. We like these girls.

So when Sam ties them up and torments them, an element of horror becomes present that otherwise wouldn't be there. Schwartz's gamble works and Sam's return brings the gleeful anticipation for more gore. But not many films could lose their star for almost an entire act and keep going. *Las Vegas Bloodbath* is the exception. Add in an insanely wild ending (complete with a self-titled song) and this is one of the most enjoyable misogynistic films around. Required Viewing!

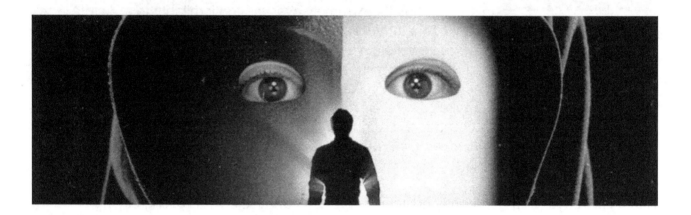

PHANTOM BROTHER
1989, Color, 87 min
STARRING: *John Gigante, Mary Beth Pelshaw, Patrick Molloy, Jon Hammer*
DIRECTOR: *William Szarka*

Abel Evans, an orphan whose family died in a car accident, spent his adolescence in a mental institution before being adopted by a family of hicks. But Abel is very much insane, hallucinating that a trio of murderers will kill anyone who enters his childhood home. His adopted family doesn't believe this though, as their only interested in the rumored money stashed in Abel's house. But when the hicks move in, people start dying.

Common to most slashers towards the end of the 80's, *Phantom Brother* plays for laughs. The film squanders what little tension it builds by being very self-aware, littering the production with wink-wink performances and terrible one-liners. It doesn't actually spoof, but even post-production editing gets in on the act (dubbing lines into scenes like *"I was running late, I had to buy some condoms because you never know"*). It's fairly disappointing because the opening minutes show promise. This could have been a haunted house flick about a killer wearing a half black, half white mask. Could have been about a guy who rarely speaks and has a penchant for big breasts and stabbing home invaders. But then the killer tries on a women's brazier. *Phantom Brother* wants laughs that it doesn't deserve. And the film ends with (perhaps) the most unsatisfying twist imaginable. The budding romance between two characters is stopped short when they're revealed to be brother and sister - and the sister knew all along!

Okay, maybe it's a little funny.

 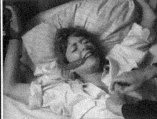  

SATAN'S STORYBOOK
1989, Color, 84 min
STARRING: *Ginger Lynn Allen, Gary Brandner, Steven K. Arthur, Leslie Deutsch*
DIRECTOR: *Michael Rider*

An anthology with medieval framework supporting two modern tales of curses and the afterlife.

A great deal of effort was put into *Satan's Storyboard*. Actors spit blood directly at camera. Dolly shots were used. Intense color-gels appear more often than *Suspiria*. But the efforts tend to work against the film, distracting from the simpler approach shown in its stories.

The film opens as an extremely over-the-top swords and sandals melodrama. The Devil appears (muscle man in a wobbly horned goat mask) sitting and listening to a Jester tell two tales of supposed horror. The first concerns a serial killer invading a suburban home and killing a young girl's parents. The killer is then sentenced to death and the young girl condemns his soul to purgatory with a spell. The second involves a drunk clown hanging himself after being fired, then has a lengthy conversation about Hell with another dead clown. By themselves, the stories are interesting. But choosing to wrap them in a medieval framework is puzzling. Did Rider want to make a sorcery film? The two stories seem made for a different project and the pacing is off. *Satan's Storybook* is fun in a "what were they thinking" kind of way and porn star Ginger Lynn Allen is a hoot, but there's little here to strongly recommend.

Horrorama's Scarlet Fry (Walter Ruether) appears as a Devil's minion.

SCARLET FRY'S HORRORAMA
1989, Color, 30 min
STARRING: *Scarlet Fry (Walter Ruether), Llana Lloyd, Dianne Nelson, Michael Rider*
DIRECTOR: *Scarlet Fry (Walter Ruether)*

An undead ghoul named Scarlet Fry hosts six tales of horror and death.

A micro-anthology originally started in 1987, *Scarlet Fry's Horrorama* is a love letter to shot on video films. Written and directed by its star Walter Ruether (who was between 19 and 21 at the time), *Horrorama* is the passion project of a true fan. In his own words, *"I was working at a video store at the time and I had seen all the horror releases. And I said I could do that."* And Ruether did. With his idea to make each story centered around a special effect and by keeping things short, *Horrorama* feels like a best-of hit list. A man chainsaws his friend's leg when he doesn't get enough to eat. A woman castrates after a man forces her to give him a blowjob. A man bludgeons his wife for ranting about wanting lunch. 10 minutes in, and we're already on the third tale! Best viewed with drinks and friends, no story outstays its welcome; breezing by with comedic flair and gut-busting gore.

Ruether's Scarlet Fry character is impressive also, particularly as no backstory is offered. Yet the film hangs on him; ending with a mock protest of signs stating *"Down with Scarlet!"* Was the character intended to become a reoccurring boogeyman in future sequels? The overall production also displays a strong confidence not found in most backyard entries, lending assuredness to the viewer. When you start this film, you know you're in for a good time. You know that you will be horrified and entertained. And indeed, I was.

SCREAM DREAM
1989, Color, 68 min
STARRING: *Melissa Moore, Carol Carr, Nikki Riggins, Gene Amonette, Michelle Uber*
DIRECTOR: *Donald Farmer*

When a heavy metal rock band gets too much attention for their demonic sounds and rumored Satanic rituals, the lead singer is fired and replaced. But unfortunately, the rumors were true! Now the demonic possession of one singer enters another, turning her into a bloodthirsty creature hungry for human flesh.

Packed with electric guitars and electrifying cheese, *Scream Dream* is a welcome return for video favorite Donald Farmer. Fully articulating his love of babes, blood and rock & roll, Farmer strikes again with (what could be considered) his third in a unholy trilogy. Like *Demon Queen* and *Cannibal Hookers* before it, *Scream Dream* revolves around demonic women victimizing men until one has the strength to resist.

Casting and original music help *Scream Dream* stand apart from other "killer band" films too. Moore (soon to reach iconic status in Jim Wynorski's *Sorority House Massacre II* and *Hard To Die*), is eye candy as the bombshell singer turned man-hungry demon. And though not asked to do much beyond lip-sync and undress, Moore makes an impression. But body double Jackey Little growls and snarls fangs with the best of them, wonderfully bringing the demonic character to the forefront. Farmer gets in on the act too, posing as a reporter's boss who asks for a Coke and gets his throat ripped-out. But Amonette as the band's manager steals the show. Also appearing in *Savage Vengeance*, Amonette's intense persona as a cussing hothead is a gift from B-movie Heaven. Flipping out on everyone about anything, Amonette dominates the screen with gut-bursting insults and memorable one-liners. Top it all off with an opening chainsaw-to-the-crotch and *Scream Dream* delivers something worth falling behind on a car payment for. Recommended!

 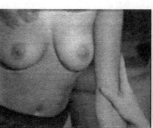  

SLEEPOVER MASSACRE
1989, Color, 95 min
STARRING: *Clancey McCauley, Chris Stonage, Carol Livingston, Terri Cavalier*
DIRECTOR: *Gary Whitson*

A group of middle-aged women reunite after many years. Planning a boozy sleepover, the women discover a coffin in the house's basement that suddenly turns one of them into a vampire. Neck bites and hangovers ensue.

Written and directed by W.A.V.E. founder Whitson, *Sleepover Massacre* is entertaining if not confounded. It's setup is simple but looses itself once the booze gets flowing. Almost 20 minutes are spent in flashback for the coffin's history which, while interesting, has nothing to do with the women. And an hour passes before the vampire strikes. But pacing issues aside, *Sleepover Massacre* delivers with impressive torn-out throats and grisly gore (courtesy of W.A.V.E regular Aven Warren). The story feels epic and there's nice interplay between the stars. I wish it had a pillow fight, but pleasantly recommended.

Donald Farmer and Jackey Little in Scream Dream (1989)

A TASTE FOR FLESH AND BLOOD
1989, Color, 88 min
STARRING: *Greg Scott, Kathy Monks, Lena Hunter, Ruben Santiago, Warren Disbrow Sr.*
DIRECTOR: *Warren F. Disbrow*

When an alien spacecraft enters Earth's atmosphere, NASA sends Captain Riggs of the shuttlecraft Enterprise to intercept. NASA loses communication but soon notes the Enterprise returning to Earth on radar. Aboard is a large deadly alien, a comatose Riggs and the torn apart bodies of the crew. Now the alien roams New Jersey in search of humans for food. Riggs awakes and is armed with high-tech weaponry to track and kill. And along the way, he teams with a single mother possessing telepathic abilities.

Epic in scope (and commonly known as *Flesh Eaters From Outer Space*), Disbrow's space opera is wonderfully gory and incredibly entertaining. Riggs, who pursues the alien with a Rambo/Terminator-like determination, is fantastic (though would an astronaut really be the best choice for alien combat?) And the dynamic between Riggs and the telepathic mother is the heart of the film. Disbrow (who also wrote, produced and edited) carefully weaves the story with impressive results. Hair metal bands scream ballads as girls wax about boyfriends *"only wanting one thing."* And then of course, everyone gets wasted. The ending involves an underwater alien nest and the ultimate sacrifice, which registers because we really care about the characters. Outstanding! Disbrow would return for a sequel in 1991. Highly Recommended.

TWISTED TEENS
1989, Color, 83 min
STARRING: *Clancey McCauley, Christine Cavalier, Beth Carlton, Silvia Blake, Terri Cavalier*
DIRECTOR: *Gary Whitson*

A teenage girls' club gets their kicks by killing unsuspecting victims. A hopeful member attempts to join, killing randomly as she goes through initiation.

Presented mostly in vignettes, this early W.A.V.E. Production is a satisfying tale of unchecked teenage rebellion. Opening with the most hilariously staged "girl luring boy" sequence of all time, *Twisted Teens* gets to the action early. We know why the girls are killing and it's all for kicks. Death is a game. A few nice twists unwind and the film essentially concludes 60 minutes in. But an unnecessary (though fun) epilogue remains as we're treated to the killers' final outcomes. Several performers appear in multiple roles and nudity punctuates a bathtub electrocution. People are stabbed, choked, hung and Sal Longo turns up in (perhaps) his first W.A.V.E. appearance. Pretty good!

UFO ABDUCTION
1989, Color, 66 min
STARRING: *Tommy Giavocchini, Patrick Kelley, Shirly McCalla, Stacey Shulman*
DIRECTOR: *Dean Alioto*

Presented as first person camcorder footage, a family documents the birthday celebration for their young niece when the power shuts off. Searching outside, they find a large spaceship on their property while aliens try to invade their home.

10 years before *The Blair Witch Project* (and nearly as long after *Cannibal Holocaust*), director Alioto pre-dates the "caught on camera" craze with this fairly memorable entry in alien hysteria. Opening with text stating the proceedings to be real, *UFO Abduction* likely had audiences questioning what was fact from fiction. And when viewed today with familiarity for the gimmick, it's impressive to see how effective Alioto was. Both elderly and child actors appear. The camera shows just enough to spook and truly, *UFO* could easily have been made today. Indeed its only misstep is providing a grandiose opening and closing credits. A noteworthy addition to the shot on video universe (remade in 1998 as *Alien Abduction: Incident at Lake County*).

TO AVOID FAINTING

KEEP REPEATING IT'S NOT A SNUFF MOVIE

VIOLENT SHIT — A REEL GORE PRODUCTION. DIRECTED BY ANDREAS SCHNAAS
RUNNING TIME 75 MINS. COLOUR. GERMAN LANGUAGE. PAL/NTSC/SECAM
ALL RIGHTS RESERVED. © 1989 BLOOD PICTURES HAMBURG WEST GERMANY.

VIOLENT SHIT
1989, Color, 72 min
STARRING: *Andreas Schnaas, Gabi Bazner, Wolfgang Hinz, Volker Mechter*
DIRECTOR: *Andreas Schnaas*

A deranged psychopath (who killed his mother 20 years earlier), escapes during a prisoner transport. Loose in the woods, the killer butchers everyone he meets.

Film in Germany over 4 weekends with friends, Schnaas' *Violent Shit* is exactly what it claims to be. With little to no reason, much of *Violent Shit's* runtime is spent on nameless victims hacked to death in the woods. Blood sprays everywhere. Limbs are torn apart. And nothing else really happens. Hints to the killer's story are sprinkled in (he was locked in the cellar by his mother, he fantasizes that a demon tells him to kill) but characterization isn't the emphasis. Hapless victims show up and die. There's impressive gore, but *Violent Shit* may have benefitted from a tighter narrative structure. Nothing beyond death motivates the film. Though Schnaas (20 at the time) should be commended for picking up a camera and starting a franchise smorgasbord. He certainly delivers some violent shit, complete with a show-stopping female death via vaginal dissection. But death is easy when no one cares about your characters. Thankfully, things would improve for the 1992 sequel.

WOODCHIPPER MASSACRE
1989, Color, 81 min
STARRING: *Jon McBride, Denice Edeal, Tom Casiello, Patricia McBride, Kim Bailey*
DIRECTOR: *Jon McBride*

A father rents a woodchipper before being called away on business. He requests his sister stay home with the kids, but she's a nagging pill. And after a misunderstanding and struggle over a mail order Rambo knife, the kids' aunt is dead on the floor. What's a middle-class family to do? Chop up the body and feed it into the woodchipper!

Hot off the heels of *Cannibal Campout*, Jon McBride strikes again with the positively hilarious *Woodchipper Massacre*. Billed as horror, McBride's sophomore entry feels more *"The Brady Bunch"* meets *Texas Chainsaw Massacre* as kids debate whether they should mulch the grounds with dead aunt's remains. Tightly directed, *Woodchipper's* horrific elements don't come into play until 30 minutes in. But thrills and gore aren't the emphasis. Well staged with over-the-top performances, this is wholesome McBride through and through. McBride also leads the *Woodchipper* cast, allowing every actor's performance to shine uniquely. The script allows for just enough danger and the *"Benny Hill"* ending (everyone racing to clean the yard) becomes the laugh out loud climax. Yes, most actors scream their lines but that's part of the charm. *Woodchipper Massacre* is a wholesome slice of American cheese presented on analog foil. Highly Recommended.

ZOMBIE RAMPAGE
1989, Color, 76 min
STARRING: *Dave Byerly, Erin Kehr, Stanna Bippus, Beth Bellanti, Brian Everad*
DIRECTOR: *Todd Sheets*

After a late night gang fight, a rival leader tries to resurrect his lost members with a book sold to him at a pawnshop. Unfortunately it reanimates walking zombies, hungry for living flesh.

A *Night of the Living Dead* riff punctuated with long hair, mullets and extreme language, *Zombie Rampage* is a youth-fuelled take on dead material. Sheets (already cranking out multiple shorts) appears tireless with stamina and determination. Reportedly, this was his first feature. Large in cast and low on budget, Sheets enlisted the help of everyone he knew and with great effect. Characters are barricaded in bars and homes, fighting one another while puss-oozing zombies crawl at the doors. Filmed exclusively at night, set-light never "shines" beyond flashlights while sound is basically an onboard mic. But gore excels with extreme close-ups and splattery squirts. Basically a horror fan's dream. Though as fun as the proceedings are, *Rampage* rubs the wrong way. Foul language and aggressive characters litter the screen like an anti-social statement of Peace on Earth. Sheets peppers the carnage with onscreen talk of armageddon and *"being judged by the Creator,"* attempting to give the bloodshed meaning (charmingly, all of Sheet's films contain some sort of special thanks to Jesus in the end credits too). Today, the most commonly available version is Sheet's self-billed "Director's Cut" which still runs longer than it should. But the original release by Video Outlaw is rumored to contain an additional 15 minutes. Heaven help us!

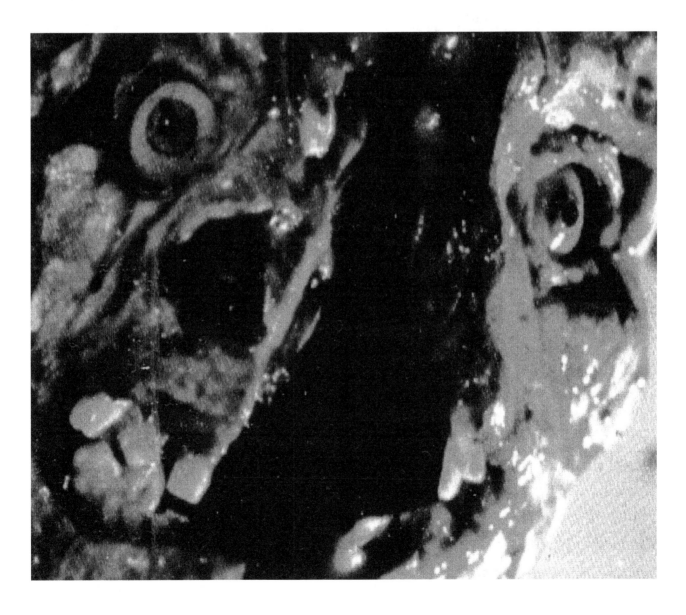

Interview
"SCARLET FRY" WALTER RUETHER

Hugely influenced by horror and rock music, Walter Ruether created his Scarlet Fry persona while still in his youth. Working on a number of short films with childhood friend Michael Rider (who went on to direct *Satan's Storybook*), Walter launched *Horrorama* as a way to solidify his Scarlet Fry creation. A combination of Alice Cooper and other famous horror icons, Walter used Scarlet to host his *Horrorama* anthology - which he self-distributed into video stores throughout 1989-1991. Today, Walter is a working actor and director of such horror titles as *Junkfood Horrorfest*, *Nightmare Alley*, *Death By VHS* and *Scream Machine*.

Walter, thank you for giving your time to this interview! You are credited as directing your first feature *Scarlet Fry's Horrorama* in 1989. How did that project come about?

I always wanted to make horror movies since I was a kid reading Fangoria. My friends were just like me and one day my best friend Mike decided to make a movie (known today as *Satan's Storybook*). *Horrorama* was another anthology we were working on at the time. It was to establish the name Scarlet Fry.

Was *Horrorama* your first time directing?

Yes it was my first film that I did for distribution. Before that I had done tons of short films with Michael Rider who unfortunately passed away in 2006. *Horrorama* was never finished, so I decided to call it when it was just six shorts and host it. It was too short in duration for any distribution in the 80's, so I self marketed and got it into a handful of video stores in 1989-91 before it's re-release decades later. There is even an ad for it in Fangoria #119.

Who (or what) was Scarlet Fry?

An alias I created that was similar to Alice Cooper. First I wanted to start a band but I couldn't sing. I created the character as my alias from my life-long desire to be a famous Horror icon. I knew i'd need a name, and I really liked Alice Cooper as a kid so I came up with something I thought would be similar and also sinister sounding. I think Scarlet & Alice could be evil sisters haha.

Why did you shoot *Horrorama* on video?

I loved the SOV stuff I was seeing. It also inspired me, I would rent SOV films (the worst the better) and that's when I realized I can do this too. So I did. I just wish I'd done more of it then instead of waiting so long to make a follow up film, which wasn't until 2005.

Were you inspired by any prior SOV horror films? Which ones?

Yes! I was inspired by every single one I got my hands on, *Splatter Farm*, *Video Violence*, *Boardinghouse*, all that stuff.

There's a rumor that Christina Applegate was approached to star in *Horrorama*. Can you elaborate on this?

I was in production and working in a video store at the time, and Christina Applegate was a member there. She had come in to rent movies and so I naturally asked her and offered her a hundred bucks. She rolled her eyes and told me she was making $1,500 a show with *"Married With Children"* and was too busy. I got it, I was just out of my league. But never the less, gave it the ol'college try.

The structure of *Horrorama* is very lean. Stories last mere minutes before characters meet their grisly (and gory) ends. Did you always intend to have short vignettes?

Yes the idea was to host six shorts and have it be a full-length feature when we were done. But we realized we were gonna need more to make time. Life must have got in the way because we finished it at the six shorts and I then proceeded to get on the phone to all the video stores I could and worked my magic. I got it into at least 100 in the first 2 weeks.

Was trying distribution on your own difficult, as the film is only 30 minutes long?

I had to sorta self distribute with the folks over at Even Steven helping me along the way. They paid for some advertising and some promo materials.

Your name also appears in Michael Rider's *Satan's Storybook* (and Michael is credited in *Horrorama*). What were your experiences being on the *Satan's Storybook* set?

Yes, me and Mike grew up together. That movie was a blast to work on, I remember I was told by Ginger Lynn I couldn't sit in the directors chair. She had no idea he was my best friend LOL so I thought *"oh what the heck."* So when I got up to move, I tripped on all this wiring and knocked all the monitors over. Needless to say the crew yelled at me. Then they did some sword fighting scenes with Ginger & the Evil queen. Accidently clocked Ginger in the forehead with the prop sword, it was so loud the whole set went dead silent until someone roared with laughter (that was me). Yes *Satan's Storybook* was great. I'm actually the first one to be killed in the film with a crossbow, then I played the leader of the Servants, and also a servant in some pick-ups.

Are there any other horror films you participated in between 1982-1995?

Yes I was in a film *Gross Out* with Carl Crew and most of the people from *Blood Diner* (which came out in theaters but it was more an homage to John Waters then a Horror film). I did other films that were not horror but had some ties, like *"Sunset Beat"* a TV show only aired overseas and I did a scene with Tuesday Night (I still have yet to see this film).

What were SOV horror films like for you as a fan? Did you have any favorites?

I loved them because I always knew I was in for a treat. Do I see them as an easy approach to filmmaking? Yes but once I rolled the camera I realized this was work and it takes dedication and even if your doing something SOV and fun, it has to be treated as professional (as you would treat anything you do).

Any favorite titles? *Video Violence, 555, Redneck Zombies.*

Thank you so much for your time and thoughts, Walter!

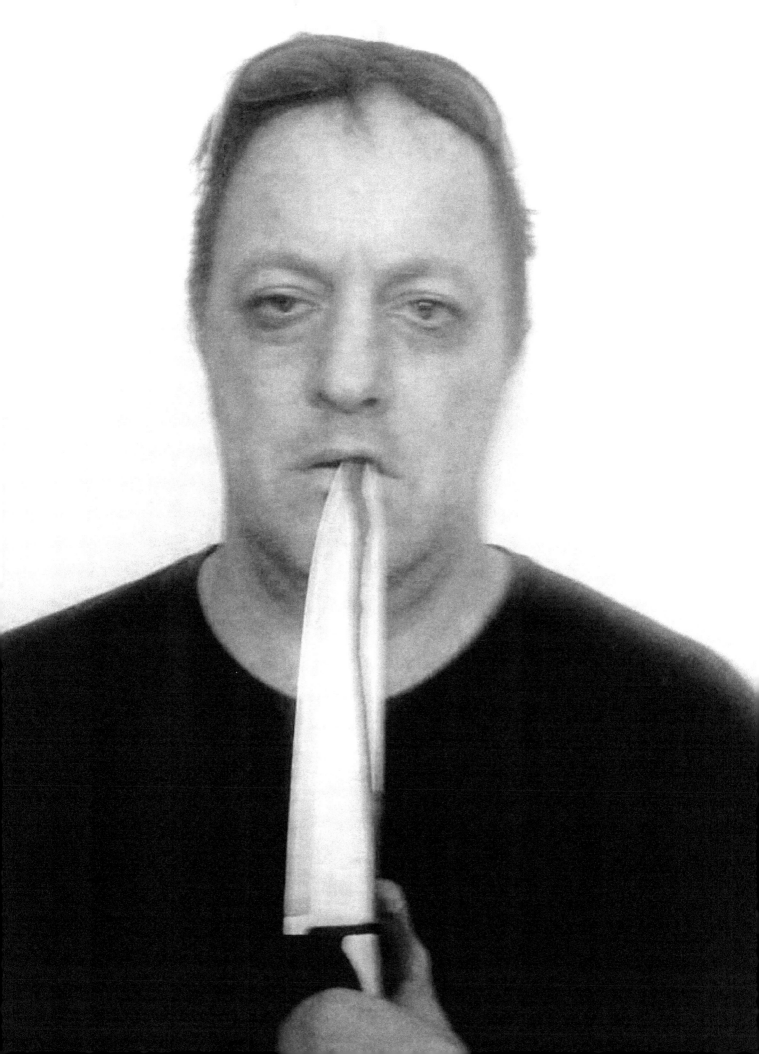

Chapter 12
THE NINETIES (1990)

BIMBOS B.C.
1990, Color, 68 min
STARRING: *Jenny Admire, Deric Bernier, Tonia Monahan, Holly Starr, Todd Sheets*
DIRECTOR: *Todd Sheets*

In post-apocalyptic New York, a rebellious tribe of women fight against corrupt mayor Salacious Thatch and his team of warriors. But when the women's leader is poisoned by a mutated bird, the tribe must enter Thatch's layer to find the antidote.

Another cheapie from prolific Sheets, *Bimbos B.C.* is one of his best films to date. There's comedy, action, gore, babes and even a few zombies because hey, Sheets loves zombies. But what *Bimbos* gets right is heart. Wonderfully leading the pack is Admire; hot tempered and beautiful. She leads with gusto, making rash decisions and somehow saving the day. The only thing missing is a love interest (but we all can dream). Bernier is sufficiently greasy as the evil cannibalistic mayor, though it's Sheets who steals the show. Cast as Thatch's right-arm man, Sheets is duplicitous in loyalty and ends up fighting for both sides. He wears his trademark leather jacket throughout too (which appears about two sizes too small). One should understand the poverty-row aspect going in, but half the fun is spotting the dime-store props along the way. Is Bernier wearing a hubcap?!? Ultimately more fantasy/comedy than horror, but a few scenes of flesh-eating and bodies being hacked apart remain. Recommended!

THE BUTCHER
1990, Color, 59 min
STARRING: *Boris Klemkow, Arnold Duda, Knut Riechmann, Maik Ude, Tino Weege*
DIRECTOR: *Maik Ude*

Three boys accidently kill another, who returns from the grave hungry for vengeance.

A German splatter flick (without English dubbing or subtitles), *The Butcher* was obviously a labor of love. Like the Polonia brothers indulging in their goriest fantasies, teenaged Ude and friends hit the ground running with excessive blood and minimal story. Several impressive deaths appear, notably an electric screwdriver to the head and a boy thrown from a very high tower. But it's the headstrong angst that makes it fun. The killer is a hooded crazy using any weapon he can grab, and the music is illegally lifted from a *Friday the 13th* sequel. Nobody cares and it's damn fun! We even get live heavy metal from three dudes needing a haircut because hey, why not? And there's definitely another subplot here as zombies start coming out of the ground (but since I don't speak German, I'm guessing). Reminiscent of *Violent Shit*, *The Butcher* is a hardcore joy ride from the youth of today. Smoke a cigarette and relax. Two sequels followed in 2001 and 2005.

The version reviewed here is the 2006 Director's Cut. Some additional filters have been added with a new song playing over the credits. The film may also have enjoyed some additional editing, though I cannot fully confirm this.

CROWLEY'S ASHES (LAS CENIZAS DE CROWLEY)
1990, Color, 84 min
STARRING: *Mario Fernandez, Julio Morante, Patricia Diaz, Yanaina Sanchez, Ricardo Islas*
DIRECTOR: *Ricardo Islas*

The sister of one of Crowley's victims wants to resurrect her dead brother. Unfortunately, she ends up resurrecting Crowley too... and they're both vampires! Police investigate and put an end to the madness.

Continuing the *Crowley* story with an unexpected twist, *Crowley's Ashes* shines backstory on the deadly vamp rather than push him forward. Newly filmed flashbacks allow Crowley (Islas) to appear sans makeup, building a tranquil romantic doom for present day. Yet *Ashes* suffers from the same predictability as most sequels: the audience knows what's going to happen before the characters do. Gore is noticeably in short supply (even though two vampires control the story) and Islas limits his camerawork to standard close-ups. Why? The film's highlight is surely the midway vampire battle, but it ends too soon. *Crowley's Ashes* is a nice extension to the impressive original, but it's clearly the weaker film. Recommended to fans only.

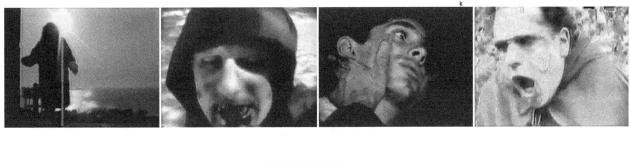

DARK HARVEST
1990, Color, 89 min
STARRING: *David Kramer (David Zyler), Jamee Natella, Debbie O'Der, Patti Negri*
DIRECTOR: *James I. Nicholson*

Young adults plan vacation riding horseback and camping in the desert. But their van fails along the way and hiking gets them lost. So setting camp near an old abandoned scarecrow, the group tell stories and settle down for the night. Soon the scarecrow is missing and people start dying.

Also known as *Bloody Harvest*, Nicholson's *Dark Harvest* is a fun entry in the scarecrow thriller/horror genre. Though light on blood, isolated locations and the diverse cast keep things moving. Atmosphere is everything (desperately needed for a film like this) but

emphasis is on adult relations rather than the scarecrow himself. We spend an hour listening to intimate thoughts; characters talk about marriage and (no lie) the thrill of hunting beaver. Then things culminate with a nice fireside spook story - with actors reportedly enjoying real booze. *Dark Harvest* unapologetically takes its time developing characters. With only 20 minutes left, the scarecrow finally gets moving and pitchforks a guy mid-shag. Then things unravel with mostly off-screen kills and scarecrows who talk, drive and (incredibly) fly helicopters. It all boils down to an Indian curse and a land dispute, with the most hilarious end-credit of "Gay Scarecrow played by." Say what?!?
Lightly recommended for a Sunday afternoon.

DEATH BY LOVE
1990, Color, 85 min
STARRING: *Allan Grant, Frank McGill, Yvonne Aric, Brad Bishop, Donald Hendrix*
DIRECTOR: *Allan Grant*

A sculptor has affairs with lots of ladies. One by one, they die at the hands of a killer.

A slow-burner, *Death By Love* features a few off-screen kills with a lot of softcore shagging. And after 40 minutes, our hero suddenly turns vampire! Written, produced and directed by Grant (a three-fingered actor later appearing in *Dark Harvest*), *Death By Love* has all the hallmarks of a memorable slasher but none of the drive. Basically the film exists for Grant to bed as many women as he could, nakedly rolling on the floor with them at every chance. All ladies are portrayed intelligent, but none possess the power to resist Grant's magnetism. Yet the real interest is behind the scenes, as Grant apparently wrote the film after reading a "How-To" book on screenplays. But this is more vanity than horror. Best left forgotten.

GORGASM
1990, Color, 76 min
STARRING: *Gabriela, Rik Billock, Paula Hendricks, Paula Gallagher, Flint Mitchell*
DIRECTOR: *Hugh Gallagher*

A cop investigates a murder where the victim was bound to a chair and slashed to death. Finding S&M mail order pamphlets at the scene, the cop looks further into the world of sexual perversions. He eventually finds Tara, a voluptuous dominatrix responsible for the murder.

Though not Gallagher's first shot on video entry, *Gorgasm* exploded onto the video market with instant notoriety. Like an actual S&M video, *Gorgasm's* box art teased something between sexual-thriller and violent-porno. Thankfully, it's just a good old slasher. Shot in 5 days on SVHS, the film is fun, innovative and chocked full of nudity. Breasts are all over *Gorgasm* as Gabriela bares all in almost every scene. Gore is surprisingly minimal (save for a garage decapitation and hand chopping) but a standout weed-wacker bit must be seen to be believed. Yet the biggest surprise is that the film isn't as sleazy as you might think. I was initially hesitant going into *Gorgasm*, expecting a porno in horror's disguise. But I was impressed with how accessible the investigation and murder scenes actually were. Plus there's great bits of comedy, helping things along the way. Recommended. The original version is 10 minutes longer and *"filled with useless padding,"* says Gallagher.

  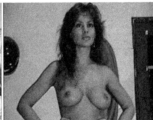 

THE GROUNDHOG'S DAY MASSACRE 2
1990, Color, 57 min
STARRING: *Lorraine Lash, John Dulles, Biff St. Hubbins, Buzz Sawe*
DIRECTOR: *Harold Olminsky*

Unavailable for review. As with the first, Olminsky's *Groundhog's Day Massacre 2* is more of the silly "Baggyface" killer. The front of the box states: *"The Violence! The Brutality! The Stupidity!"*

The film (along with the original) was re-released as bonus material on the limited *Attack of the Mutant Roadkill* VHS from VHShitfest in 2013.

HUNG JURY

1990/1994, Color, 119 min
STARRING: *Shelly Deuber, Tom Beschler, Judy Pasternak, Dave Castiglione*
DIRECTOR: *Gary Whitson*

A deadbeat father murders a woman while trying to steal her purse and is hung for the crime. 20 years later, the man's offspring enact revenge on the jury members' relatives.

 Though originally filmed in 1990, *Hung Jury* took a few years before eventual release. Multiple sequences were added during this time, including a Clancey McCauley car murder and a Tina Krause bit (originally recorded for *Love is a Stranger*). Nevertheless, the film works. Ingeniously set during a mock "murder-mystery weekend" island adventure, *Hung Jury* smartly keeps the audience guessing while the body count builds. The cast is wonderful (including Castiglione's first official appearance in a W.A.V.E. production) and the blood flows nicely. Indeed, the ending is especially gruesome as one girl is crucified and shot against a wall! Others are wrestled and stabbed without mercy. And unlike most revenge thrillers, pretty much everyone dies here; a nice mean streak that should please slasher and b-movie fans alike. Recommended!

JUNGLE TRAP

1990/2016, Color, 72 min
STARRING: *Renee Harmon, Frank Neuhaus, Heidi Ahn, Valerie Smith, Rhonda Collier*
DIRECTOR: *James Bryan*

A team of archaeologists journey into the jungles of a long-dead tribe, spending their nights in the rickety remains of an old hotel. Unfortunately, the hotel is filled with dead tribal ghosts, hungry for revenge over a stolen idol.

Gleefully campy and over-the-top, *Jungle Trap* exists thanks to the efforts of the Bleeding Skull web founders. Originally produced in 1990, this Bryan/Harmon entry was roughly assembled and plum forgotten about for over a quarter century. Enter Bleeding Skull's Zack Carlson and Joseph A. Ziemba, who (somehow) got hold of things in 2015, completing the film with soundtrack and final editing. And thank Betamax they did! *Jungle Trap* is a uniquely entertaining analog outing in the jungles of cheese, unparalleled by anything else in this book.

True to its jungle/cannibal roots, our crackpot team of explorers are lead into the jungles amidst numerous omens. Large snakes slither in trees. Their pilot is drunk. Wild cats roam the land and severed heads appear in cabins. But no omen deters! So when the dilapidated hotel reveals it's operated by ghosts, all Hell breaks loose like *The Shining* on crack. Guests are found decapitated. Ghosts sit for dinner then vanish from sight. And an adulterous researcher thinks he's in love, but he really just loves sex. This is a Renee Harmon film and like *Run Coyote Run* and *Escape From the Insane Asylum*, Harmon's analog wonders are built around healthy supplies of 16mm inserts. Helicopters, monkeys, explosions, all sorts of jungle action is supplied when necessary (cut from other films into this). There's not much blood or violence, but damn if people don't scream silly after each decapitation. And look for the most unlikely character to save the day. Highly Recommended!

 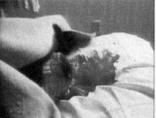  

LAST DAY AT THE BEACH

1990, Color, 41 min
STARRING: *Peter Preston, Lorraine Tyrer, Brian Davies, Chris Williams, Paul Roberts*
DIRECTOR: *Brian Davies*

A British beachside hotel is secretly sold to American investors. Overhearing the news, the staff gossip about losing their jobs when suddenly a prison-released psychotic killer pays them a visit.

Though short, *Last Day at the Beach* is filled with subplots. A maid is jealous of another and bickers constantly, the manager woes over getting sacked (fired) and an agency's representative gets lost. All personal relations appropriate to daytime television. Some nice pacing with tight edits between scenes, but nothing horror. And the biggest thrill is watching two middle-aged tarts pillow wrestle over a bed.

Then the killer shows up.

Barely telegraphed, *Beach's* deranged loony stalks and kills indiscriminately like a *Final Exam* reject. His backstory is zilch. His weapons are whatever he can find (including a seatbelt). But damn if he isn't determined! After impressively chasing our heroine, he holds her down and VOMITS in her face! Just for kicks! And a nice bloodbath occurs too, particularly after a brutal face-beating with a beachside rock. *Last Day at the Beach* may meander, but it sure is fun in the end.

 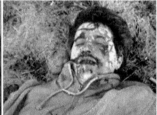  

MOUNTAIN FURY
1990, Color, 76 min
STARRING: *James Bell, Anita Wong, Bob Chomyn, Phil Baker, Judy Hanes*
DIRECTOR: *William Dever*

When a lawyer tries to serve an injunction on a tree-cutting operation, a group of radicals armed with crossbows kill the loggers.

Filmed with the clean photography of a made-for-television movie, *Mountain Fury* is another title easily mistaken for an Emmeritus production. Shot in the mountains of Alberta, Canada (with some impressive aerial footage via helicopter), Dever mixes romance and comedy into a slasher-drama with political underpinnings. The crossbow killings (though only featured in the first act) are bloody and unexpected. They wonderfully hook the audience before characters are introduced. But *Mountain Fury's* goal is to side audiences with wanting to save trees - and it hilariously subverts this by hanging signs on hacked stumps stating *"Future site of 24 Hour Video."* We're video fans! I used to rent from 24 Hour Video (*Mountain Fury* posed a fun dilemma as it rested on store shelves) but I doubt anyone was swayed into becoming a tree-hugging hippie. And the film meanders as two rangers bicker about women, a lawyer's daughter sleeps with the opposition's boss and a 20 year old lackey has an affair with the 60 year old typist (seriously, watch them going at it). But there's enough charm to keep it going.

THE SCARE GAME
1990, Color, 70 min
STARRING: *DJ Vivona, Michael Bradley, Don Shaffer, Jennifer Sweeney, Eric Stanze*
DIRECTOR: *Eric Stanze*

Six friends play a mysterious game that transports them into an alternate dimension. Battling against a demonic adversary, each must overcome their fears or die trying.

Shot in 1990 when Stanze was just 18, *The Scare Game* is surprisingly effective. Strong in style and confident in execution, Stanze and his team impress with an unusually steady hand. Gore is prevalent though never without context as mystery surrounds the game. Indeed parts of the film feel more experimental than narrative, like a waking nightmare. One of the faced fears involve a girl chased by a chainsaw wielding maniac. Another involves a man (Stanze) chained to a bloody mattress and beheaded. And the goal of besting the demonic adversary becomes clear midway through. *The Scare Game* feels somewhat reminiscent of *Hellraiser* at times, with a style wonderfully its own. Stanze (quite obviously) poured his blood and tears into this and it shows. Recommended!

SHRECK

1990, Color, 73 min
STARRING: *William Lantry, Anthony Vandeuren, T.K. Malone, Big Joe Mueller*
DIRECTOR: *Carl Denham, Anthony Vandeuren (uncredited)*

Three men obsessed with Max Shreck (a dead Nazi) pretend to resurrect the merciless killer's ghost. Unfortunately the resurrection works; bringing Shreck into 1990 before transporting the men back to 1958. Wearing a gas mask and armed with homemade implements, Shreck kills them one by one.

This is not a Disney film.

Though light on gore and filmed entirely in one location, *Shreck* brews a deadly game of moody séance and home invasion. Wonderfully cheap, *Shreck* gains points for its

*DJ Vivona in
The Scare Game (1990)*

innovative death scenes (reminiscent of today's *Saw* films). A swastika-shaped ceiling fan made of blades and garden-stomping spiked shoes are only two of the methods of death here. And they're nicely bloody. Our killer (army fatigues, hockey gloves and gas mask) resembles the iconic look of *My Bloody Valentine* while enslaved victims appear as minions (eerily rising from the ground into ghost-like sheets). The film also builds a great atmosphere, setting scenes around abandoned trains and isolated fields. Indeed, *Shreck* pulls no punches for a film that essentially takes place in one house with only four actors. The effort put forth by Denham and crew is impressive and commendable (though it also contains real war and Nazi propaganda footage, so be warned). Recommended.

SPACE ZOMBIES
1990, Color, 73 min
STARRING: *Carl J. Sukenick*
DIRECTOR: *Carl J. Sukenick*

A masked alien chokes humans into submission, creating a race of slaves. Nunchuck-wielding Carl Sukenick fights back.

Though most references state a 1990 production date, this is more likely somewhere mid-late 90's (and Sukenick himself may not know for sure at this point). But considering *Alien Beasts* was 1991, *Space Zombies* definitely feels a few years removed. Carl looks older, his hair is lighter and camerawork is (arguably) more improved. Nevertheless, the film features an even less structured framework.

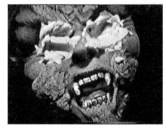 Opening with the bizarre notion that a dream has just ended, the real dream is just beginning. Cue movie. In an attic, a naked girl lays on a mattress while the camera repeatedly zooms on her breasts. A masked "alien" enters and chokes her. Another woman walks in, strips and is choked by the same alien. A man now walks in and is choked. There's still an hour to go. The film feels like five or six setups, replayed at nausea. Carl walks in a forest three times before attacking a zombie with a machete. Later, he tells his friend about slow motion lenses and we get to watch playback in slow motion. Finally Carl brings a nunchuck

outside for some single-handed swinging and an old man states *"the aliens have been defeated."* Hard cut to black.

I genuinely like Sukenick's work. *Alien Beasts* was a hypnotic trip that left me puzzled for days. But I don't find the same wonder in *Space Zombies*. Perhaps there just weren't enough people available at the time, or perhaps the never-ending synth rock played one too many times. But so much of *Space Zombies* felt like time wasting. And I myself became the zombie.

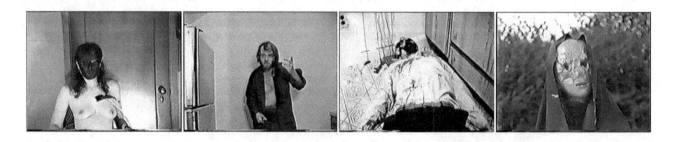

VAMPIRES AND OTHER STEREOTYPES
1990, B&W/Color, 87 min
STARRING: *William White, Ed Hubbard, Wendy Bednarz, Anna Dipace, Mick McCleery*
DIRECTOR: *Kevin J. Lindenmuth*

A gateway between our world and Hell has opened in a deserted New York building. Two "agents" are sent to close the breach, while a group of party-hungry teens get trapped inside.

Originally titled *Hell's Belles*, *Vampires and Other Stereotypes* is not the clips-heavy anthology its title suggests. This is a full-length feature of great design and Lindenmuth's premiere entry in video productions. Camerawork is impressive, lighting is superb and makeup effects (while occasionally silly) help carry the tale. Yet above it all is Lindenmuth's writing. This is a well thought-out tale of demonic creatures breaching from one dimension into another, with Lindenmuth firing every creative muscle he has. Performances are mostly strong and plot twists aren't telegraphed. *Vampires'* second half is not as much fun as its first (characters succumb to clichéd actions and hasty plot devices) but the setup is fantastic. This is really an impressive picture that deserves attention as a high-class production. The *Vampires* title may be a throwaway, but everything else stands the test of time.

Featuring a 1992 copyright date (though Lindenmuth states a 1990 production date on his YouTube account), the film was eventually released to video in 1994.

ZOMBIE RAMPAGE 2
1990-1991, Color, ? min
STARRING: *Tonia Monahan, Jenny Admire, Durville Sweet, Dilynn Fawn Harvey*
DIRECTOR: *Todd Sheets, Alexander Bourne*

"The film was started in 1990, had more shooting in 1991 and then was lost. We found the footage, what survived, and Wild Eye Releasing asked us to finish the film. Alexander Bourne ended up directing pretty much 85 or 90% of the new footage and even edited the first cut of the film. Just like the original Zombie Rampage, the sequel was also cursed. So many setbacks, technical issues, people not showing up and even editing nightmares. But it's finally done" says Sheets (in a 2018 Facebook post).

"The reason the original ZR2 was never finished was basically schedule issues, money issues and the we had to make another film that we had signed a contract for. By the time we were able to get back to ZR2, half the people involved had moved away or moved on to other projects. So we never finished it."

Zombie Rampage 2 is slated for DVD release 2018/2019 from Wild Eye Releasing.

Interview
ERIC STANZE

A native of St. Lewis, Eric started making 8mm movies in his teens. At 18, he finished his first feature length film *The Scare Game*, which gained national distribution along with his second feature *The Fine Art*. *Savage Harvest* (which Eric desribes as his "real" first movie) was shot when he was only 21. Together with his production company Wicked Pixel Cinema, Eric has continued making impressive and thought provoking films such as *Ice From the Sun*, *Ratline* and *Scrapbook* (named *"Best Independent Film Of The Year"* by Rue Morgue Magazine). Now a critically acclaimed award winning director/writer/producer, Eric is one of the leading forces in independent pictures today.

Eric, thank you for giving your time to this interview! At what age did you first start making movies? What initially lead you into becoming a filmmaker?

In my mid teens I started making 8mm film shorts, inspired mostly by *The Evil Dead* (1981), *The Toxic Avenger* (1984), slasher films, and the George Romero living dead films. I don't think there was one specific event that lead me to becoming a filmmaker. I just loved movies, I wanted to make them, so I started doing so. And I just never stopped.

In grade school I was into science fiction, especially *Star Wars*. On TV, it was *"Space: 1999,"* *"Buck Rogers,"* and *"Battlestar Galactica."* I continued to be a sci-fi fan, and I am to this day, but at nine or ten years old, the horror bug bit me when I saw *The Blob* (1958) and

Invasion of the Body Snatchers (1956) broadcast back-to-back on late-night TV. Many of the filmmakers and films I discovered during my teens, in the mom-n-pop video stores or on TV, would influence my work when I later started making films. George Romero's original living dead trilogy, Sam Raimi's *The Evil Dead* (1981), Peter Medak's *The Changeling* (1980), S.F. Brownrigg's *Don't Look In the Basement* (1973), and Tobe Hooper's *The Texas Chain Saw Massacre* (1974) had a major impact on me when I was a kid.

The Scare Game appears to be your first feature as a director. What was that production like, being so young?

We shot *The Scare Game* in 1990, when I was 18 years old. It was feature length, and we put our all into it, taking the production seriously, working very long hours in both pre-production and production, sacrificing a lot of sleep. Especially for a bunch of teenagers, the drive, passion, and work ethic were through the roof. But I don't consider it my debut film, because we were really just making it for ourselves.

We had no plans to release it to the public. It was always intended to be a learning experience and a great way to have a memorable summer adventure. We assumed nobody would ever see the finished movie beyond cast, crew, family, and friends. We were teens with camcorders, experimenting.

A couple of years after it was done, I was offered a home video distribution deal for *The Scare Game*, and I signed the contract, but that was never part of the plan. It was a very surprising deviation from our intentions.

In terms of shooting it, I did have an above average amount of production experience for an 18 year old - enough production experience to have my head around the process. I understood the basic building blocks of making a movie, so I did not feel like I was diving in to learn how to swim - and just hoping I'd learn before I drowned. *The Scare Game* proved I could make a feature length movie, and I could do it at an uncommonly young age. But I understood that next, instead of just making movies, I had to learn how to make movies that were good. That process would take much longer!

So was making The Scare Game the ultimate learning experience?

It was a huge learning experience, of course. However, I'd describe all my films as the ones I make my mistakes on. If a filmmaker is to continue growing, evolving... expanding one's skill set, and sharpening one's instincts, that's the way it should be. No matter how advanced you are, you're still going to make mistakes, and you should always continue learning from your errors. I think my first few movies are around 95 percent mistakes! And I can still note the flaws in my more recent films. I can see the flaws in the film I just finished, *In Memory Of*. But that's okay. I think I'm a pretty good filmmaker today - and that is because I've made so many mistakes... and learned from them. I'll continue to make mistakes, and learn from them. I'd much rather continue to explore, take risks, and expand - and never get it completely right - than settle into making the same kind of movie over and over so I can perfect the procedure. I'd rather be flawed and continue growing than be perfect and stagnant.

The Scare Game does not appear on your IMDB credit list. Is there a reason why?

The Scare Game is not on IMDB because it was a student film, never intended for public release, just like my moviemaking endeavours that came before it. While its eventual release on VHS had a significant impact on my mindset - it was my rounding the corner from hobbyist to professional - the movie's release was a fluke. As to why there is very little information about the movie online, I'm assuming it's because its audience is so limited. It's a clunky movie made by teenagers, and it's not good. Very few people are going to rush out to find such a movie and then spend time discussing it, me thinks.

The Fine Art was your next feature, yet it's also missing from your IMDB credits. Would you mind discussing it?

The Fine Art was produced and edited at a small TV station where I worked at the time. I knew the station would broadcast the movie as many times as they wanted... and in return, I got the whole boat - cameras, lights, post-production... everything - for free. Again, other than being broadcast by a small cable channel to what I assume was a very small audience of St. Louis viewers, *The Fine Art* was never intended for public release.

The Scare Game was my big high school student project, and *The Fine Art* was my big college student project. *The Fine Art* distribution deal was part of the deal for *The Scare Game* - kind of tacked on in the contract. Another fluke, another surprising turn of events. Another clunky student film popping up in home video stores across the US and in several foreign territories. It feels more weird than embarrassing.

I'm more embarrassed that I made crappy student films than I am embarrassed about them being released to home video. But that's how it's supposed to go down. You're supposed to be embarrassed by your student films! If you're in your 40s, and you still think two movies you made when you were 18 and 20 are amazing cinematic achievements, you've got issues.

The talented Lisa Morrison appeared in several of your earliest films, most notably as the lead in *The Fine Art*. How did you first meet Lisa?

We were classmates in high school. We're still friends, and we still cross filmmaking paths from time to time. She was my assistant director for a couple of the bigger days of shooting on my recently-completed feature *In Memory Of*.

You then did *Savage Harvest*, with an impressive mix of special effects and makeup on a rural location. It also notably appears as your first official credit on IMDB. Do you regard *Savage Harvest* as your first "real" feature?

Savage Harvest is indeed my first "real" feature, primarily because it was the first movie I made knowing it would be released to the public.

Based on the *Savage Harvest* script and the reasonable profits *The Scare Game* and *The Fine Art* had generated, I had a distribution deal in place before we started shooting. So I was building upon a budding track record, I was thinking about contracts and distribution, and for the first time, I was going into production knowing in advance that the movie would be seen by a lot of people.

I knew the movie would be in release throughout North America and in a lot of other places around the globe. It was the first time I experienced that kind of pressure, as well as what seemed like genuine progress as a filmmaker. The budget was low, and I knew the market saturation would be a small fraction of the numbers a major studio release would reach. But it was still a first for me - a big step up. I was 21 when I directed *Savage Harvest*. I was still very inexperienced, but for the first time I was approaching filmmaking more like an adult, less like a kid. More like a professional, less like a hobbyist.

Your company Wicked Pixel Cinema was also founded during this time, with *Savage Harvest* its first release. Did you enjoy a larger success with *Savage Harvest* beyond the prior films?

Yes, *Savage Harvest* made a much bigger splash than the student works. But upon release, *Savage Harvest* got mostly bad reviews. And I was very unhappy with the finished movie - which just motivated me to make something better next. Oddly, in recent years, *Savage Harvest* has been revisited by critics and given pretty favorable reviews. I'm not sure why that is.

Your bigger successes (and perhaps the films you're best known for) *Ice From the Sun* and *Scrapbook* came out only a few short years after Wicked Pixel's creation. Did your earlier work help your grow as a filmmaker? Did your use of video (over film) ever hinder your success?

Without a doubt, the student works and *Savage Harvest* helped me grow as a filmmaker, and I believe that growth shows in both *Ice From the Sun* and *Scrapbook*. Experience is everything. It sharpens one's instincts and helps you make better decisions. You learn how to identify and solve more problems on set instead of figuring out how you should have fixed things after the film is released.

Shooting on video, I think, did little to hinder me. *Ice From the Sun* was shot on Super 8mm film, mostly Kodachrome 40. I am glad I shot *Ice* on film, but I don't think the acquisition format had any impact on *Ice* being a better-received movie compared to the shot on video *Savage Harvest*.

I've always found your films to contain great character dialogue. Do you enjoy writing as much as directing?

I've always enjoyed directing more than any other hat I wear on a production. Writing is a skill I learned much more slowly than the others. Directing, producing, and editing skills came much easier to me, comparatively. Because learning how to write was a much slower process, a much longer learning curve, it was one of the most frustrating phases of making a movie in the early years. Today it is a much more pleasurable experience.

Can we hope to see re-releases of *The Scare Game* or *The Fine Art* in the future?

I doubt it. Those movies served their purpose and did what they could for me back in the day. In fact, they did so much more for me than they should have. But they were never intended to be part of a filmography. They were war games, not combat.

Lastly, your background of training and working your way up in the industry is impressive. Particularly since you are still a working director. What advice might you offer a young person looking to break into the industry today?

The path I've been on for nearly three decades is not for everybody, but if it is for you, I recommend you start building your skill set by working on other people's films, which you will do for free, and then making your own films. Try to get on bigger and bigger productions as an intern. Be relentless about gaining that experience. Make it a priority, not a pastime.

Unless you have the mega-bucks to go to a film school that offers tremendous networking opportunities, don't go to film school. I've seen far more success and progress result from on-set experience than I've seen result from film school. I did not go to film school, and I've never regretted that.

When you start making your own movies, make them to learn, to get your head around the process. Then start making them to experience the entire course - including the release and promotion of them after they are complete. Even if you are breaking even or losing money, move your films all the way through to a professional release. Don't just upload them and offer them for free. Don't just let them sit on the shelf. Execute a proper self-release or sign a distribution contract for each movie you make. Establish a track record, then start selling yourself as someone who can be paid to work in the industry.

Be proud of the progress you make, even if it happens very slowly. I am happy with and proud of what I've built over the past 25 years - even though the general public tells us that not winning an Oscar or getting interviewed by major publications at Sundance means I should have accepted my failure and quit the biz a long time ago. I consider myself extremely lucky to have never had to work outside of the film / video / television industry to make money - and I'm even more lucky that earning an income to pay my bills has always intertwined with, instead of hindered, the making of my own films. I did not come from a family with money or industry connections. So, if I can do it, you can too... if you are truly interested in being an actual filmmaker, and not fixated on becoming famous or being The Next Quentin Tarantino or whatever.

And when it comes time to make your own movies, if you don't get the budget you think you need, if you don't get The Name Actor you think you need, if you are going to put your own money into it instead of getting paid to do it, don't complain... do not quit... embrace your situation and the resources you do have - and make the movie anyway. Branding yourself as a filmmaker, establishing relevancy and viability in the industry, growing your fan base... none of that happens when you don't make your movie because you didn't get everything you want. Make the movie - and be passionate about it. Obsess over it. Make your film. Then make another. And another.

Thank you so much for your time and thoughts, Eric!

Thank YOU for your interest in the movies I've made!

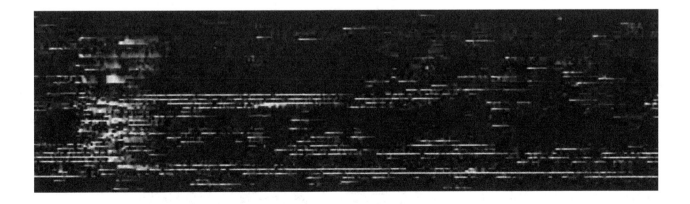

Chapter 13
SECURITY CAMERA INOPERABLE (1991)

THE 13TH FLOOR
1991, Color, ? min
STARRING: ?
DIRECTOR: *Todd Sheets*

An unfinished anthology.

"The reason The 13th Floor (like Zombie Rampage 2) was never finished was basically schedule issues, money issues and the we had to make another film that we had signed a contract for. We were making the film basically just to stay active until the next contracted film came along" says Sheets (in a 2018 Facebook post).

ALIEN BEASTS
1991, Color, 74 min
STARRING: *Carl J. Sukenick, Sara Victor, Neal Dealosi, Joe LaPenna, Abe Sukenick*
DIRECTOR: *Carl J. Sukenick*

Commander Carl J. Sukenick leads a special CIA team, fighting to stop enemy agents from space. In addition, alien radiation is turning humans into mutated beasts while massive exposure levels have opened a parallel universe.

And the security camera is inoperable.

 Few films can test a viewer's patients, imagination or sanity more than a work of Carl J. Sukenick. Habitually smoking, constantly screaming and hypnotically repeating himself, the films of Sukenick are therapeutic outlets of a chaotic mind held together in narrative form. In other words, they're phenomenal. Sukenick's camera (often abandoned in singular wide-masters) is the canvas of imagination brought to life with endless sequences of pretend fighting and people staring into voids. Story is told first-person by Sukenick who repeats himself constantly. Then the security camera is inoperable and we see a black screen for 2 minutes. Incessant claustrophobia permeates due to static camerawork (never panning or zooming from lengthy takes) while several sequences repeat throughout. Sukenick's

voice alternates between screaming and mumbling dialogue, while his thick New England accent charms. A masked woman changes clothes for 15 minutes before a man busts in, says he has to *"punish her"* and fondles her breasts. A mutated beast gets shot in the chest with a cake sparkler. Conversations occur while the video is paused and Sukenick narrates. And everything climaxes into a stop-animation fiasco with Play-Doh and ninja stars. Truly, a film like no other!

Interestingly, multiple versions of the film exist under different titles. *Mutant Massacre* (running 72 minutes) is an amalgamation of footage reordered to convey a slightly different story. Certain scenes run longer while others are missing entirely (no stop animation is present). Sukenick achieves this thanks to *Alien Beasts'* narrative structure, largely told via text screens and voice over. By changing the details, he has shifted emphasis. *Mutant Massacre 2* (running 76 minutes) is another variation that presents *Alien Beasts'* animation climax as the opening segment. All three versions were released by Massacre Video in 2015 as a limited edition DVD package. Required Viewing.

AMERICA'S DEADLIEST HOME VIDEO
1991, Color, 85 min
STARRING: *Danny Bonaduce, Michael L. Wynhoff, Melora Walters, Mollena Williams*
DIRECTOR: *Jack Perez*

A married man learns of his wife's infidelity and leaves for a cross-country trip. Documenting himself with a camcorder, he's quickly captured and held by a trio of fugitives when he accidently records them ditching their car. Now forced to film as they rob convenient stores, the man is slowly adopted into the gang as a participant.

Released in 1993 and presented entirely as first-person footage, *America's Deadliest Home Video* is one of the earliest "caught on camera" video thrillers. It continued the blur between staged action and real horror perpetuated by Gary Cohen, but with a zippy *"Cops"* presentation. Indeed, what'cha gonna do? But *America's Deadliest* pushes further by turning the viewer into a participant. By the 1990's, camera technology had evolved so considerably that handheld devices were commonplace. People could record what they were seeing live. So the possibility of putting a camera into the hands of a killer was terrifying. Killers could record their murders or crimes. *America's Deadliest* capitalizes on this idea, structuring itself as a videophile's worst nightmare. But the film's most important (and impressive) feat is the introduction of the villains themselves. Our hero happens upon them in their most dramatic moment: pushing a car down a rock quarry. An incredible sight, the production actually uses a full-sized car falling hundreds of feet to the ground below. It's a real act that throws the narrative and shocks the viewer into submission. (Note that for "found footage" to work, the audience has to believe what they are seeing is real). The crash occurs and we're immediately confronted with guns pointed direct at camera (at the audience). It shocks us because we too are now taken prisoner. And this is why the film works.

We also already identify with the main character because he is a familiar face. Danny Bonaduce, the instantly recognizable child star of television's *"The Partridge Family,"* is boldly cast as our hero (and by extension, ourselves). And allowing a celebrity to mix with film's faux-reality pushes boundaries even further. Bonaduce is an actor, so seeing him should remind us that he is acting. But instead, the actor's persona is broken because he is forced to do things he wouldn't normally do. Bonaduce is smacked around at gunpoint. Later he becomes wounded and starts to identify with his captures. It's a fascinating performance that allows real vulnerability on his part. Other performances are equally good, but Bonaduce's celebrity works to the film's favor.

Though not the first SOV presented as "found footage" (see 1989's *UFO Abduction*), *America's Deadliest* is certainly the most accomplished. Excellent in structure and wonderfully presented, the film was years ahead of its time. Required Viewing.

BEAUTY QUEEN BUTCHER
1991, Color, 119 min
STARRING: *Rhona Brody, Kathryn A. Mensik, Tammy Pescatelli, Laura Schutter*
DIRECTOR: *Jill Rae Zurborg*

Four mean girls trick overweight Phyllis Loden into entering a Beauty Queen pageant. And after being ruthlessly insulted, Phyllis places last. But things get worse when the girls kill Phyllis' cat three days later. Now Phyllis is out for revenge.

Less is more, go in late, get out early - alien concepts to Jill Rae Zurborg.

Bloated, overlong and uneven, *Beauty Queen Butcher* is a chore. In what should be a simple tale of teenage revenge (ala *Carrie*), *Beauty Queen* fumbles into a film so unending, it's a challenge to endure. A 5 minute setup extended by 115 minutes! I literally fell asleep and woke in the same spot. And after a whopping 25 minutes of pageant competitions, the established outcome arrives: Phyllis loses. Three days later, revenge comes after the death of a cat (which tells you how misguided the title is).

Beauty Queen's only saving grace is the dastardly cat killing (which is pretty damn dastardly). Without warning, the girls microwave the cat live. Ballsy and cruel, the microwaved feline almost saves the film. And if Phyllis used this as her cause for revenge, we'd have a stronger movie. *Kitty Kat Killer* would get my recommendation! But instead, it's a drop in the bucket as revenge is centered around bumping-off Queens to rank higher in the pageant. The film also (inexplicably) casts a man in drag as the pageant's host. Why? For absolutely no reason. But make no mistake, I am thankful the film was made. People put effort into this. Only *Beauty Queen* doesn't feel like a finished movie.

It's a workprint waiting to have 45 minutes of filler removed.

DEAD NORTH
1991, Color, 111 min
STARRING: *Tom Beschler, Theresa Hoyt, Gary Whitson, Clancy McCauley, Aven Warren*
DIRECTOR: *Gary Whitson, Sal Longo*

A trio of couples plan a group camping trip in the woods. But one spouse believes the other is cheating, so a private investigator is hired to tag along. Turns out everyone is cheating and one has turned killer too.

Co-directed by W.A.V.E. founder Whitson and character actor Longo, *Dead North* is a fantastic look at mixed affairs with deadly results. Parts of the film are quite funny, parts are sexy and a lot of it is just plain entertaining. Except that it's way too long. At nearly 2 hours, *Dead North* turns from bedroom antics to forest foreplay at a very slow pace. The film opens with a poisoning, then takes a whopping 40 minutes arranging its second murder. But believe it or not, horror is not everything. *Dead North* charmingly plays because characters are fun (particularly Whitson in a deadpan role). The first half works to establish its vixens, hilariously leaping from one bed to the next. A game of erotic misdirection. Then everyone drops their sneaky ways once tent is pitched. Death and strangulations take it from there, leaving a final twist at the end. There's no nudity across the board (which hampers the pay off slightly) but *Dead North* entertains like a forbidden tease. Recommended.

DREAM STALKER
1991, Color, 85 min
STARRING: *Valerie Williams, Mark Dias, Jan Stearman, Pamela Hong, John Tyler*
DIRECTOR: *Christopher Mills*

A young woman's boyfriend (a motocross racer) dies. Haunted by visions, the woman vacations in an isolated house deep in the woods. But soon her lover returns from the grave, hoping to be reunited in the afterlife.

Sloppily executed, an easy mix of *Friday the 13th* and *A Nightmare On Elm Street* becomes a drawn-out bore in *Dream Stalker*. Rather than develop characters, scenes are thrown together without care. Racing, a proposal, saying goodbye, murder, a dream, on a plane, he's dead; meaningless sequences randomly butted into an opening montage. And none of it matters because it doesn't resonate. The film wants to begin but it already feels over. Excessive padding is the cause, as several other scenes were cut (due to technical issues) leaving the film short. So character development had to be stuffed into the opening minutes. Not a good idea.

Some sequences do resonate later (cheesy jokes that weren't in the script) but they feel out of place. During an early vision, the half-mangled boyfriend slides on a condom before raping his girlfriend (*"Better be safe than sorry!"*) then stops as it tears open (*"Oops!"*). But he's a ghost so why the condom? A more interesting addition is having a camp of "violent teens" reside next to the isolated house. A nice way to introduce a body count. But questionable moments occur here too when the adult-leader starts bedding the teenage girls. And the male teens try raping Williams later! So the only characters we can root for are the woman and the ghost-boyfriend. The make-up effects are excellent with exposed brains, torn flesh and stabbings onscreen. But is that all I can say? The film was originally titled *Kinetic Nightmare* but it turned out far different than the script promised. Many additions were made (some good and many bad) and its story was build out of sync with the premise. Is *Dream Stalker* about dream stalking? Is it about the dangers of sex before marriage? Is it Freddy on motocross? You decide.

HOLY MOLY
1991, Color, 41 min
STARRING: *Lance Ozanix, Chris Schott, Rafael Robletto, Tom Schott*
DIRECTOR: *Lance Ozanix*

A priest named Holy meets an evil preacher who possesses him with a demon. Holy starts to hallucinate, drink booze and puke before having a fatal battle with the preacher.

Ozanix, known for puking live on-stage with his metal band Skitzo (previously called Venom), directs and stars in this vanity vehicle for his noteworthy talent. But thankfully, there isn't a lot of puking here. What *Holy Moly* does contain is a slow burning madness that climaxes in a balls-to-the-wall "fight" between Good and Evil. And refreshingly, Evil gets to win by pulling Holy's spine out of his ass. Makeup ranges from halloween masks to complex zombie appliances. And in addition to the ass ripping, there's a wonderful bit of finger violence against someone wearing a bald cap. *Holy Moly* won't be winning awards anytime soon, but there is some fun here.

KILLER NERD
1991, Color, 91 min
STARRING: *Toby Radloff, Heidi Lohr, Tony Zanoni, Niko DePofi, Richard Zaynor*
DIRECTOR: *Mark Steven Bosko, Wayne Alan Harold*

After years of torment, a middle-aged man embarks on a total makeover to help shed his nerdish ways. It backfires. Now fed up with being the butt of jokes, the man kills all who wronged him.

More comedic than horror, *Killer Nerd* is a hilarious character study with deadly results.

Documentary-like, *Nerd* follows the antics of antisocialism personified in Toby Radloff's performance. Perfectly cast, Radloff dominates the film with his unique line-delivery, costume and mannerisms. He is the embodiment of nerd. And after an attempted stretch of trying to fit in, Radloff flies off the rails with murderous glee.

This is the film *Napoleon Dynamite* wanted to be.

Shot on SVHS, director Bosko admits he was influenced by past SOV titles like *Blood Cult* during *Nerd's* production. Not that *Nerd* is terribly gory, but in the way that video productions were able to achieve mass distribution. Later released by Troma, *Nerd* accomplished just that. But its longevity as an entertaining comedy/thriller is due solely to the charms within. Radloff excels at attempts to be cool (wearing his heart on his sleeve) and his murderous outbursts are filled with hilarious zingers like *"Roses are red, violets are placid, now here's a face full of acid!"* Supporting roles are fine, but this is Radloff's rollercoaster all the way. Camera work is impressive and blood (though fleeting) makes an impact when needed. Look for *Chickboxer's* Shawna Baer during a nightclub dance scene. Highly Recommended!

KINGDOM OF THE VAMPIRE
1991, Color, 70 min
STARRING: *Matthew Jason Walsh, Cherie Patry, Shannon Doyle, Tom Stephan, Jo Norcia*
DIRECTOR: *J.R. Bookwalter*

A teenaged introvert and his overbearing mother are the last of a centuries-old tribe of vampires. Reluctant to kill, the mother commands and abuses her son into becoming the night stalker he should be. But torn between love and death, the young man struggles with his killer instinct.

Equal parts *Martin* and *Psycho*, Bookwalter's *Kingdom of the Vampire* is a wonderful yarn of chills and dread. Inexpensively shot, the film exceeds limitations with innovative writing and impressive performances. Walsh particularly delivers as the meek yet deadly outcast teen. Patry commands as the fanged mother from Hell, beautifully sparring with Walsh's inability to vamp. Nature versus nurture is at the heart of the film, lending *Kingdom* an authenticity not typically found in low budget productions. Here, everyone involved was striving for greatness and it shows. Music is impressively creepy and composed by Walsh himself. And the film occurs over a halloween weekend with enhanced production atmosphere.

Humorously, *Kingdom* merchandise (sweatshirts, music, film clips) would often appear in later Bookwalter productions. In-jokes from the director working at breakneck speed throughout the 90's. But this was the first of six films funded and produced by David DeCoteau for Cinema Home Video (which Bookwalter later dubbed "The Six Pack"). DeCoteau provided the titles and Bookwalter produced the films. 6 films in 7 months. Unbelievable. Yet unlike some of the later entries, *Kingdom of the Vampire* is an excellent thriller with brains, blood and fangs. Highly Recommended.

MADHOUSE
1991, Color, 62 min
STARRING: *Bobby Westrick, Jenny Admire, Mike Hellman, Chuck Cannon, Dave Byerly*
DIRECTOR: *Todd Sheets*

An anthology of several stories, all (supposedly) inspired by Edgar Allen Poe. Two detectives are attacked by female vampires. Girls in the woods are attacked by a werewolf. A hillbilly and his son terrorize hikers in the woods. Zombies attack unsuspecting visitors.

More accurately titled *Todd Sheet's Edgar Allen Poe's Madhouse*, this is yet another camcorder excursion by prolific Sheets in anthology form. Hosted by its director, *Madhouse* begins a framework most beneficial to Sheet's video style. Here Sheet's sets up stories, telling us what to expect as the film unfolds. The introduction is mildly effective, as it initiates the viewer into the mindless fun of a Sheets production. But the effort falls somewhat flat as we're then lost with random drunks turning their backs to camera. It's the trying that counts. Sexless-seduction, gore and halloween masks follow. A cop (who just heard his partner scream bloody murder) walks around with his hands in his pockets. And then someone licks a sweaty neck.

At their best, Sheets' films are fun when they're focused and paced. At their worst, Sheets' loses the audience in a tangent of nameless faces and darkness. *Madhouse* places somewhere inbetween. Missing the insanity of *Goblin* and the cheery excitement of *Bimbos B.C.*, this still earns recommendation for a tough Thursday night.

NEIGHBORHOODZ
1991, Color, 95 min
STARRING: *Julie Chavez, Kevin Cooper, Darlene Harris, Lemy Hassan, Mindy Meyers*
DIRECTOR: *Lemy Hassan, James Tucker*

An inner-city black community is overrun by drugs. When a young girl becomes hooked on crack cocaine, she turns into a murderous green-faced crack monster.

 Also known as *Devil Snow*, *Neighborhoodz* is a sordid tale of addiction gone wrong. It's heart lies in the true horrors of drug abuse as main character Chavez turns from honor student into pipe-smoking prostitute. There's a strong *Lethal Weapon* vibe too, as two cops try to clean up the streets. But Hassan and Tucker scratch all that with inexplicable transformation scenes and demonic possession. And several characters smoke crack, but only Chavez is affected into a raging garbage face. Poor girl. She grows fangs and turns green, yet her preferred method of murder is still by butcher knife. Hilariously, the film features about 20 minutes of Chavez randomly killing off men in a prolonged montage of crack and death! And as for the possession? Well, it's never explained. But the film climaxes when our crack monster attacks an undercover cop, who arrests and walks her out the front door green-faced. Grrr!

SOUL OF THE DEMON
1991, Color, 78 min
STARRING: *Sky Daniel, Garry Godfrey, Harold Allen, John Bonito, Kirk King*
DIRECTOR: *Charles T. Lang*

Two boys discover a gargoyle statue buried by an old lake. Later that night, another boy holds a séance with some friends. The séance awakens a demon held in the gargoyle, possessing one boy and sending him to kill the others.

Soul of the Demon operates in *Night of the Demons* territory. Not that there's anything wrong with that (surely the world could use more halloween demon flicks). But where *Night* knew how to party, *Soul* falls asleep. Almost nothing happens in the entire first hour. Then suddenly a guy's head explodes and a girl's body is ripped in two. Someone else's head is twisted 180 degrees and a girl meets a rusty saw while tied to a bed (reminiscent of *Scream Dream*). Basically the film wakes up and kills everyone. The possessed kid is forever destined as the gargoyle's keeper and we call it a day. *Soul of the Demon*, we hardly knew you.

A TASTE FOR FLESH AND BLOOD 2: RAISING HELL
1991, Color, 87 min
STARRING: *Kathy Monks, Warren Disbrow Sr., Gary Hoffman, Jim Cironella*
DIRECTOR: *Warren F. Disbrow*

Beginning immediately where the original ended, the nuclear blast killed everyone except the alien and telepathic-widow Sandra Lynn. Miraculously recovering, Sandra is armed and asked to hunt down the creature yet again. But after learning that she is a robot under synthetic skin, Sandra teams with a loudmouth slacker looking for revenge.

Commonly known as *Invasion For Flesh and Blood*, Disbrow's bizarre sequel is all over the place. Things start with the great promise of Sandra Lynn's story continuing, but then everything gets thrown aside. A mean-spirited rape comes out of nowhere (featuring pre-*Clerks* star Marilyn Ghigliotti) and the alien never interrupts, so why is it there? Then Sandra's telepathic abilities are all but forgotten as she incredibly discovers that she's actually a robot. What?!? Then she demands her robot self to be rebuilt into the drawing her deceased husband did years prior. And after her cosmic makeover, she joins forces with a guy who should have been killed the minute he comes onscreen. And the pair banter terribly throughout the remainder of the picture. As for the aliens, they're an after-thought; slow to react and relegated to the background. One of them inexplicably talks at the end too, saying that they're eating humans *"so they don't pollute the world anymore."*

A Taste For Flesh and Blood was a fun, serious attempt at a *Terminator* meets *Alien* splatter film. A Don Dohler-like epic on analog video. But *Raising Hell* is all over the map with terrible humor and misplaced focus. Forgettable.

TWISTED TALES
1991, Color, 81 min
STARRING: *Freddie Ganno, Mick McCleery, Laura McLauchlin, John Collins, Brett Heniss*
DIRECTOR: *Kevin J. Lindenmuth, Rita Klus, Mick McCleery*

An anthology of three tales introduced by a singing comic. "Nothing But the Truth" features a guy lying about how many thugs beat him up, "The Shooting" involves a man killing his brother and "Hungry Like a...Bat?" showcases a werewolf meeting a succubus.

Short on horror, *Twisted Tales* feels more like random shorts put together for runtime. Two thirds of the film deal with muggings and hold-ups, while "Hungry Like a...Bat?" suddenly remembers the genre. This is surprising because Lindenmuth was involved throughout and his intention to anthologize was always in the cards, so what happened? My suspicion is either the filmmakers weren't concerned or Klus and McCleery were allowed to direct as they wanted. Regardless, *Twisted Tales* is quite uneven. Performances are fine, but the film flows aimlessly from drama to silliness before settling into comical horror. And the tales themselves have issues. "Nothing But the Truth" lacks resolution or even explanation. "The Shooting" is deeply poetic but also lacks the same. "Hungry Like a...Bat?" is the most developed (and Lindenmuth directed) but ends with a comic tie-in to "The Shooting" instead of relating to its story. An unfortunate series of missed opportunities.

ZOMBIE '90: EXTREME PESTILENCE
1991, Color, 75 min
STARRING: *Matthias Kerl, Ralf Hess, Mathias Abbes, Marc Trinkhaus, Christian Biallas*
DIRECTOR: *Andreas Schnaas*

A plane carrying a secret nuclear chemical crashes, beginning a zombie epidemic. Two doctors try to contain the outbreak as they travel throughout the town.

Fresh from his directorial debut, Andreas Schnaas returns to video with an insanely gory and overly hilarious zombie epic. With more gore than Romero and Fulci combined, *Zombie '90* goes for the throat, guts and groin more times than I could count. Heads are gleefully lopped off (or split open), fingers chain-sawed, limbs hacked into pieces and a dick is severed and thrown clear across a field. But it's the infamous English language dub that makes *Zombie '90* so memorable. Sounding like a bunch of foolish 15 year-olds, incredible lines like *"what is it about the woods that makes me want to take a shit outside?"* and *"now I'm going to drive over your dick, motherfucker!"* will have you rolling on the floor. Schnaas even perfects a few sequences from *Violent Shit* as he (again) gives vaginal-violence a whole new meaning. And a zombie hooker bites off a man's dick! But as disgusting as the effects are, they never lose their "homemade" quality. This film wants to entertain, culminating into an impressive homage to Fulci's 1979 classic. Required Viewing.

THE ZOMBIE ARMY
1991, Color, 80 min
STARRING: *Cindie Lou Acker, Jody Amato, Michelle Anderson, Jack Armstrong*
DIRECTOR: *Betty Stapleford*

Two deranged inmates (one with knowledge for brain lobotomies) hide in an asylum's basement. Soon after, the asylum is shut down and control is handed to the US army. Cadets mistakenly free the inmates, who strap soldiers to an electrical machine and zap them into zombies.

In the wake of George Romero's *Dead* trilogy, zombies went from boogeyman to pop-culture explosion. And due in large part to the enormously successful *Return of the Living Dead*, zombies quickly became one of the most loved horror villains by teenagers and adults alike. But in terms of independent cinema, many newcomers started making zombie horrors in their backyards. Todd Sheets may be the most famous, repeatedly hosting zombie invasions throughout his hometown. But *The Video Dead, Flesh Eater, Ghoul School* and countless others also rode the undead wave to great success. Yet only one film dedicated its production to *"the brave men and women of the United States Army, the Army Reserve, and the National Guard."* And that film with *The Zombie Army.*

Combining a "training video" vibe with the same poverty-row corniness found in *Splatter University*, *The Zombie Army* is a trip into madness. Here, an operating asylum is closed and abandoned for no reason. Cadets are given 5 minute breaks that last for hours. Abandoned drugs of any kind are highly sought after. Zombies are sad about losing their limbs. Horny couples love to shag in abandoned buildings. Zombie menaces can be controlled with battery acid. Oh, and misuse of an electrical blanket will bring back the dead. But can cheese alone make a good movie? You decide. Recommended.

ZOMBIE COP
1991, Color, 61 min
STARRING: *Michael Kemper, James Black, Ken Jarosz, Bill Morrison, James L. Edwards*
DIRECTOR: *Lance Randas (J.R. Bookwalter)*

A cop is killed while in pursuit of a voodoo-practicing fugitive known as Doctor Death. Though both are believed dead, Death cursed the cop into becoming a zombie. Now fresh from the grave and out for revenge, the pursuit continues.

Already making a name for himself with low budget wonders *The Dead Next Door* and *Robot Ninja*, 1991 would be an important year for director Bookwalter. Shooting both *Zombie Cop, Kingdom of the Vampire* and two full-length documentaries on low budget filmmaking, Bookwalter began a longstanding career which still thrives today. *Zombie Cop*, a movie that both director and writer state was *"a bad home video that should never have been released,"* is a throwaway that impresses with comedy and action; undeserving of its negative reputation. Though light on horror, inspired references shine such as the zombie cop's look (*The Invisible Man*), his recovery after being gunned down (*The Terminator*), his adhering to police procedures at all costs (*RoboCop*) and even that he was buried at Mourningside Cemetery (*Phantasm*). Performances also impress, particularly from Black as the Jamaican doctor of death. Note this was the second of Bookwalter's six pack, with a nice production appearance thanks to the SVHS quality. In 2007, the film was remastered complete with a new sound mix, new opening and closing credits and some new digital effects. But fans should seek the original VHS for that less polished, true to video feeling. Recommended.

Interview
JAMES L. EDWARDS

Known for appearing in numerous productions by J.R. Bookwalter, James first started acting at age 12 when he answered a zombie casting call for *The Dead Next Door*. Roles in *Chickboxer* and *Galaxy of the Dinosaurs* soon followed, along with his memorable turn in *Humanoids From Atlantis* (lovingly regarded as one of the worst movies ever made). But James' charming abilities and heartfelt performances continued to mature in *Polymorph* and the critically acclaimed thriller *Bloodletting*. Finally in 2017, James announced his directorial debut with the romantic horror feature *Her Name Was Christa*.

James, thank you for giving your time to this interview! In 1991 you appeared in your first SOV horror film *Zombie Cop*, though it wasn't your first time in horror. What was your first experience acting professionally?

I don't know if you could call it "professionally," but although I had a few bit parts in *The Dead Next Door*, my first speaking role came in the Tempe follow-up *Robot Ninja*, a gory low-budget super hero flick. When I started out, I actually had no interest in acting. It was the 80's and I was a Fangoria and Savini kid so I wanted to be a special effects make-up artist. I was devastated to discover that I had no artistic talent whatsoever. Luckily, director J.R. Bookwalter and company liked my commitment to the project, so they kept me aboard as a production assistant. The further the production went, the more I realized I had an interest in acting. After that, I was fortunate to have been involved in all but two of the Ohio lensed Tempe movies. *Kingdom of the Vampire* and *Midnight 2: Sex, Death and Videotape*. *Kingdom* I was asked to play the lead but I missed out on because I was out of town at the time. It would have actually been my first lead acting role. I always regretted not being in that one. *Midnight 2* I was offered the role of Abraham which I turned down. I'm fascinated with serial killers, but I felt the script was really bland and I didn't want to take on a role that really should have gone to John Amplas, the actor from the original *Midnight*. I always hate sequels that recast the original actors. I'm not even sure if he was ever contacted about the part, but I felt that the few fans of the original would have been disappointment with another actor taking over the role and I didn't want to be part of a potential backlash.

In *Zombie Cop* you had a short (but memorable) role as the sidekick in a convenience store hold-up. You also got wonderfully blown away by a shotgun blast. Do you have any lasting memories over this production?

That was a weird time. We had just come off of *Robot Ninja* and *Skinned Alive*, two movies that weren't fantastic by any stretch of the imagination, but at least they had a bit of a budget behind them and were shot on film. Now we were entering into much lower budgets and shooting on video, which at the time not a lot of people were doing. The way those movies were made, the executive producer David Decoteau of *Creepozoids* and *Sorority Babes at the Slimeball Bowl-O-Rama* fame would send us a movie title and a budget and we would set out to make a movie. We would shoot them two at a time and with each batch the budgets would get smaller and smaller. By the time we made *Humanoids From Atlantis* and *Galaxy of the Dinosaurs*, I think the budgets were under $1K each. There were actually supposed to be two more Cinema Home Video titles that Decoteau wanted us to do, a blaxploitation movie and a western. From what I heard, J.R. passed on them because we wanted to do *Ozone*.

As far as a lasting memory about the making of *Zombie Cop*, for me the movie was only a one day shoot. J.R. had asked me to come in to reprise my Scully role from *Robot Ninja*. We were shooting at a Mom and Pop's convenience store that J.R.'s father owned. It was late at night and I was sitting near the street smoking a cigarette waiting for the crew to set up lights. All of the sudden, I hear something zip past my ear. I look behind me and standing by the store holding a handgun is the weapons expert that they brought on to handle the guns for the scene. This crazy asshole shot the fucking thing into the woods right past my head. I turned over and yelled *"What the fuck, man?!?!?"* and this lunatic looks at me and quietly says *"You would have never known it hit you."* I was furious but this guy was the only one we knew that had guns so we had to deal with him.

Late 1991 also saw production on the infamous *Chickboxer*. This time you had a notably larger role as Billy Anderson - a cop's son and romantic interest of lead character Kathy Sherwood. Your performance is smooth and assured, yet

innocent. What are your thoughts on the finished film?

Well, thank you. That was an interesting shoot. Scott Plummer, who was a producer on *The Dead Next Door*, had his directorial debut with that one. He was a really great guy and a phenomenal producer, but he really wasn't that much of an actor's director in my opinion. I remember being really frustrated on the set due to lack of communication. In particular, the scene in the diner where Ken Jarosz has to grab me and slam me on the ground. We must have done that scene like 15 times because either Scott couldn't convey what he wanted or I just couldn't understand it. Again, I'm not trying to piss on the guy. He was a really incredible producer. I just think that either he had trouble working with actors or he and I just didn't mesh well. As far as the finished project goes, it met my expectations because they were zero. I mean, come on. I'm playing the male lead in a movie called *Chickboxer*. We weren't making *The Godfather* here. The completely unrelated and out of left field sex scene with Michelle Bauer was a nice addition to an otherwise forgettable film though.

***Chickboxer's* main character Kathy Sherwood was played by actress Julie Suscinski. Do you know whatever happened to her?**

Sadly, I haven't spoken to Julie since our final day of shooting on *Chickboxer*. She seemed like a really nice person, but we weren't in any way close and I think she was doing the role as a favor to director Scott Plummer. If she had any prior acting experience, I wasn't aware of it.

My personal favorite - *Humanoids From Atlantis!* Sometimes cited as the worst film ever made (which I don't agree with). How did this film come to be? Was there ever an original ending planned?

That was one of our final films for the Cinema Home Video deal. Again, by that point, the budgets had become almost non-existent. It was bittersweet because on one hand it was the first true lead role that I had gotten, with *Chickboxer* being more of a male lead in a supporting role. On the other hand, it truly is one of the worst movies ever made. Considering it clocks in at under an hour, I don't even think you can truly call it a movie. If I'm not mistaken, J.R. wrote the screenplay with me in mine. I have to imagine so - over excited movie geek. That was pretty much me. Our intentions were good. It just didn't work out. There were supposed to be cameos from other characters from previous Tempe movies like Dr. Death from *Zombie Cop* and the Sheriff from *Kingdom of the Vampire*. It didn't happen. The humanoid was supposed to be a full body suit. It didn't happen. We were supposed to have a fight scene in the water. It was 40 degrees outside so that didn't happen. What did happen is poor Arvin Clay running around in that ridiculous costume at Springfield Lake, my love interest delivering dialogue with English as her second language and Christine Morrison, who was an absolute sweetheart but a really, really bad actress.

The last 15 minutes of the movie is completely ad-libbed. The exact original ending I'm afraid I don't recall, but I seem to remember a fight in the water and an award ceremony for Ken for the finished Tempe Lake documentary. Again, just didn't happen. I really think that was the straw that broke the camel's back for J.R. and his future with doing the Cinema Home Video movies.

Would you ever consider returning for a possible *Humanoids* sequel?

Of course I would. I'm a whore. If the price was right, count me in! Hell, you could probably pay me in Blu-Rays and Pop! figures. I'm pretty sure with the original, I was paid with *Cannibal Holocaust* soundtrack CDs and Scream Queens Illustrated trading cards, items that J.R. was shilling through Tempe Video at the time.

We next see you in 1994's *Ozone* as three separate characters, all with various levels of makeup. Your stand out role as the main villain cast you under full head-to-toe appliances! What challenges did you face performing under such extreme makeup?

I really loved working on *Ozone*. I always joke that it was my Eddie Murphy movie because I got to play multiple characters. I was cast as the Drug Lord because it was known that I was comfortable performing under make-up appliances. I had actually started out as an effects model for David Barton, the effects artist from *The Dead Next Door* who went on to work on *Phantasm 2*, *Deep Star Six* and *Freaked*. I got to play Sam D'Bartolo at the beginning, his mutant incarnation, the Drug Lord plus I got to play Spikes, the gay Chinese cenobite rip-off. Complete blast.

The thing that was cool about that one is that we were finally doing a movie that was all ours. Don't get me wrong, I was incredibly thankful that David Decoteau was financing the Cinema Home Video titles because it was keeping us working. It was just nice to finally get back to telling stories that we wanted to tell. David Wagner's script was a fun action ride and a fantastic vehicle to really show off actor James Black's talents, who later went on to have sizable roles in *Soldier* with Kurt Russell, *Out of Sight* with George Clooney and a reoccurring character on *"Anger Management"* with Charlie Sheen. It felt like we were really heading in the right direction.

With *Ozone*, everything just fell into place perfectly. The cast was fantastic, the effects were slick, the locations had production value. It in no way feels like a $2K movie. Just really a fantastic time.

1995's *The Sandman* is a wonderfully creepy film, though seemingly plagued with issues during production (referenced in the DVD liner notes). I wonder if you could elaborate on what issues, if any, arose during production.

That movie was a clusterfuck. It was a runaway movie. Complete excess. A ton of mistakes were made with that movie. J.R. was going through a divorce. I was broken up over a relationship. Neither of us were in the proper mindset to be making a movie. J.R. got it in his head that he only wanted to work with professional actors instead of the stable actors we had always worked with. The problem with that was that most working actors in Ohio at the time mostly did only stage or extra work, so the performances come off ridiculously larger than life. Mark that with the fact that midway through pre-production, he decided to hire the head of the talent agency we were casting out of to co-produce with me and considering she got a percentage of any actor that was cast, she had a secret agenda. The budget ballooned up way past what it should have. We were shooting in a trailer park in Niles, OH, literally the armpit of America. J.R and I actually got into such a screaming match off-set that I was banned from the set for three days. To this day it's the worst movie experience I've ever had. I produced the fucking thing and I actually refused to watch the finished film until I was forced to when we recorded the DVD audio commentary years later. I didn't even go to the premiere

What's funny about that one is that I'm not even sure how it came about. At the time, J.R., David Wagner and myself were all listed as producers for Tempe Video. J.R. had held a meeting for us to talk about what the next project was going to be. I was really fighting for it to be a really amazing screenplay that J.R. had written called *Seven Body Parts, Six Feet Under*. Dave Wagner was pushing for an *Ozone* sequel. I could be wrong, but I think J.R wanted to do a *Wizard of Gore* inspired horror movie called *Abra Cadabra*. At the end of the meeting, J.R said *"OK, I'm going to sleep on it and I'll let you guys know which one I decide on tomorrow."* The next day, I get a call from him and he tells me we're doing *The Sandman*. Completely out of left field.

Right off the bat, I wasn't a huge fan of the screenplay. I subscribe to the David Wagner theory of filmmaking where "there has to be an exploding head in the first 10 minutes to grab the audience." Nothing happens in this thing but talking heads for the first 45 minutes. There originally was an opening scene with a kid trying to convince his dad there was a boogeyman in his room and the dad blowing him off as we see the Sandman's glowing eyes under his bed. As slight as that was, even that would have helped. It didn't help that one of the cast members was given free reign to insert his stand up comedy routine into every piece of dialogue that the character had, which I believe made the script even more unbearable. Mark that with the entire ending being changed due to uncooperative effects and it was a complete recipe for disaster.

Did you enjoy being a producer? If you could choose to work in any capacity, what would it be?

It really depends on the project. On "I've Killed Before," the short we made in order to get financing for *Bloodletting*, pre-production was a blast as was most of of the shoot as far as my producing duties go. It wasn't until post-production that everything went sour due to in fighting and too many cooks. On *The Sandman*, the entire experience of making the movie was a horrible one. We were out of our element. We had no business making that movie. On the flip side of that, I produced a movie a few years later for *Killer Nerd* effects man T. Michael Conway called *June 9* that was an extremely rewarding experience. So again, I think it really depends on the people that you are working with. Also, keep in mind that I typically only work as a producer out of necessity. It always helps to branch off from what you are know for in order to make yourself more in demand. If I had to choose, my true passions remain with writing and acting.

Your next film *Polymorph* saw you again starring as the lead, but also credited as the film's writer. What was it like seeing your words come alive? Was *Polymorph* something you had been working on for years, or freshly written?

I had actually started writing because I felt that I wasn't getting cast in the type of roles I wanted to play. My hope was that if I could not only master screenwriting but write those type of characters, I would entice J.R or another director to take notice and cast me in that role. To prove myself, I wrote two screenplays, a Bonnie & Clyde style drama called *Fugitives: A Love Story* and a horror anthology called *The Returners* - neither produced. Shortly after that, I was approached by New Jersey filmmaker Pete Jacelone. At the time I was the head review writer for Tempe's Alternative Cinema and I had written a scathing review of Pete's film *Psycho Sisters*. Instead of getting pissed and angry about the review, Pete contacted me and said *"You think you can do better? Prove it."* He handed me his screenplay to the remake of *Psycho Sisters* that he was planning on and gave me free reign to do what I wanted. It was one of the classiest things I've even seen a filmmaker do and it really put the heat on from me to show results. I had actually written in roles for both Ariauna Albright and I to play, but my big mouth ruined that. The lead actresses that they had cast as the new psycho sisters didn't realize that I was the writer of the film until after they agreed to be in the movie. Just a few months earlier, I had written some mean spirited but pretty funny things about one of them in the magazine, even going as far as asking readers to donate money so we could get her acting lessons. They were livid and demanded I not be permitted on the set. Huge bummer, but the story was well worth it.

JR took notice with my new found interest in writing and offered me a chance to write a screenplay for a treatment that he had written for *Polymorph*. I took the treatment, locked myself in a room with coffee and cigarettes for two weeks and cranked out the screenplay, sticking exact to the treatment. Originally in JR's treatment, there were no alien sci-fi elements in the film, instead the creature is the result of a chemical spill. Also, there are no gangsters, the kids were just campers and Tarper (in the final film portrayed by Sasha Graham) was a male redneck killer in the woods type. I turned the screenplay in and Ariauna Albright, who was JR's producer at the time, just ripped it to shreds. I then asked to take another crack at it, but this time be allowed to put my own spin on it, straying from the treatment. JR agreed and two weeks later, we had the script that ended up being made. Once the script was agreed on and the casting process began, JR and company assumed that I had written the part of Carlos for myself. All were shocked when I said I wanted to play Ted, the shy hero. It took a bit to convince them because everyone was used to me playing loudmouth scumbags and villains but after a screen test, I was able to get them to agree. J.R. actually gave me one of the nicest compliments years later after doing that one. He had mentioned that although most people site *Bloodletting* as my best performance, his favorite had always been my take on Ted in *Polymorph* because it actually showcased me playing a role rather than just being myself and that I had completely sold the performance. That really meant a lot to me.

I truly love writing. Again, it was originally only to attempt to get parts I wanted, but it turned into something that I really enjoy.

Your final role for Tempe was also the one your most known for - serial killer Butch Harlow in *Bloodletting*. You've often stated that it's your favorite role. Why?

It's been well documented that this was another production that was plagued with problems so I won't bore you with the details of that. Look no further than the "making of" documentary that I really, really hate on the DVD special features. The important thing is that with all it's problems, *Bloodletting* as a finished film turned out exactly the way that I had envisioned it when I read the screenplay, which is a rarity. There are three main reasons that I love that movie more than anything else I've ever done in my "career." Number One: As I mentioned before, I'm fascinated by serial killers so to have the opportunity to not only play one, but to play such a well written one was a huge incentive in taking the role. Number Two: The character was written as "What if James L. Edwards was a serial killer?" which was incredibly flattering. I can't speak for every actor, but for me part of the allure of acting was getting the chance to play another person. To get into their mindset. More actors than not suffer from depression, low self esteem and anxiety. They want to become other people because they have a shitload of demons surrounding their own personalities. Myself, I'm an incredibly high strung person and my own worst critic. As much as I talk shit about other people, which I'm very guilty of, the person that will typically get it the worst from me is me. The idea that someone thought so highly of me to write my personality traits into a lead character was the highest compliment. For years, I was fighting to play roles that were nothing like me. Now I'm getting the chance to play myself. Number Three: I love working with Ariauna Albright. We have had our ups and downs and been at each others throats on many, many occasions, but at the end of the day we have an incredible onscreen chemistry together. I always wanted us to become the no budget Paul Bartel and Mary Woronov. Here's hoping there is still time to do that.

After the Tempe split, you disappeared from 1998 until 2005 when you reemerged with *The Red Skulls*. Why the long hiatus?

After the falling out with Tempe, I was a bit disgruntled. On one hand, I was so pissed that

I wasn't even sure if I ever wanted to do another movie again. On the other, I think a part of me had something to prove. I wanted to show that I didn't need Tempe in order to continue to attain my dream of being a no-budget Bruce Campbell. Another problem during that time was that my second wife was incredibly discouraging with me accepting film roles because she felt that it took too much time away from the family, which was ironic because the only reason she was interested in me in the first place was because I was an actor. I was still fortunate to do several productions during that time.

First off was a three picture stint with Andy and Luke Campbell at Compound Pictures, the directors of *Midnight Skater*. During that time, I worked on *The Red Skulls*, *Poison Sweethearts* and *Cordoba Nights*, in which I was lucky enough to work with Duane Whitaker of *Pulp Fiction* and *Eddie Presley*. That was an absolute honor. What was funny about working with the Campbell brothers was that with the exception of *The Red Skulls*, every time they contacted me to do a movie, the character that they wanted me to play had no written lines. They would pretty much contact me and say *"Come up with some dialogue that this person would say. We need about 1-3 minutes."* Now, I'm a huge fan of ab-lib, but I don't recall ever discussing that with them. It's like somehow they just knew, which was very liberating.

Next, I was asked produce and act in the caught-on-camera horror film *June 9* for T. Michael Conway. Conway and I have been friends for decades and it was a blast to work with him. Extremely talented and easy going, that gig was possibly the most relaxed set I've ever worked on and I was so glad to be a part of it.

After that, I was approached on Facebook by Cleveland filmmaker Joe Ostrica of Old School Sinema to play an aging grunge rocker in *The Spookshow*. The film featured *Night of the Livind Dead* lead ghoul Bill Hinzman and a bunch of extremely beautiful goth girls who were known as Sinema Sirens. Joe's sets are more of a party than a production and I think that's why his crew gives 110%. Definitely a fun group to be with.

Most recently, I've been fortunate enough to work with Brad Twigg of Fuzzy Monkey films. Brad was a huge supporter of my work when he was a kid and it's really amazing to watch him grow up to become a fantastic director. I've done three films for Brad, *Fiendish Fables*: a horror anthology that I wrote the wraparound for, *MILFS VS Zombies*: which I got to play a TV evangelist in, and *Killer Campout*: an 80's throwback slasher movie that I co-wrote with Matt Hill and played a bounty hunter. Currently, Brad is working on *Wrestlemassacre* with WWF stars Nikolai Volkov and Jimmy Valiant. There's word that I may reprise my TV evangelist role from *MILFS* in a cameo in that one. I also did a cameo as a mugger for Ohio filmmaker Tim Novitny in his vampire movie *Pharisee*. It's been refreshing to continue to find roles even though I had taken off so much time.

You recently announced that you are venturing into the director's seat with the romantic horror *Her Name Was Christa*, which you also wrote and are starring in.

What made you transition into directing?

Christa was originally something that I was working on with the intent of hiring a director and just acting in. Once the script was completed, I had fallen in love with it and didn't want anyone else touching it, hence the decision to direct. We're currently about a third of the way done with principle photography and it's been an absolute blast. [It's given me] the chance to work with several performers that I was dying to work with such as Drew Fortier, the guitarist from the band BANG TANGO, who is making is acting debut, Rick Jermain, who I was fortunate enough to work with on *Killer Campout* and had such a great chemistry with that I knew I had to include him in this, and Kaylee Williams who I was a fan of from her roles in *Model Hunger* and *Slices of Life*. Plus we have surprise cameos from a few SOV veterans. It's been an incredible time.

What are you lasting memories of shooting so many movies quickly on low-budget videotape? From an actor's perspective, did you notice any difference between shooting on video from shooting on film?

If you had asked me when I first started, I would have definitely been pro-film. In the early days of SOV, 50% of the battle was convincing an audience to sit through your production even though most of the time it either looked like someone's home movies or a bad soap opera due to the limitations of the format. I know for a lot of fans, that was a selling point, but to the casual movie goer, they just weren't having it. Even if you had an amazing script, mind blowing effects or an insanely talented cast, there was a huge prejudice against that videotape look. As technology has advanced and more filmmakers are working digital, it's becoming more and more accepted. Another thing that's nice about the format now versus 30 years ago is that because there are so many people shooting on video, it forces filmmakers to up their game. It's not the like old days when only a handful of people were doing this. With the advent of better equipment, stellar film-look processes and YouTube, anyone can make a movie. If you want to stand out from the crowd, you have to have an angle. I'm mean, film is incredible, but it's really no longer cost effective. Plus shooting on film is extremely time consuming. I can't even imagine shooting on film now. From an actor's perspective, the only real difference I saw between shooting on film versus shooting on video was set up time and scheduling. The amount of downtime is astounding with shooting on film where with video and the right lighting, you can pretty much point and shoot. Not to mention the instant gratification of shooting on video versus having to wait for a processing lab to develop when you are working with film. It just makes far more sense.

Thank you so much for your time and thoughts, James!

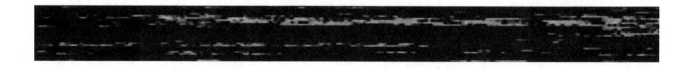

Chapter 14
THINGS ARE GETTING SILLY (1992)

THE BLUE ANGEL
1992, Color, 93 min
STARRING: *Nick Millard, Raine O'Connor, Scott Cannon, Bill Buch, Darrel Joyce*
DIRECTOR: *Nick Millard*

A college professor discovers a video produced by his students. Enchanted by the girl seen in the video, the professor tracks her down and seduces her. A sordid romance follows. But the girl's desire to dance and sleep with other men corrupts the relationship, leaving him for a job in Hollywood.

Adapted from Heinrich Mann's novel "Professor Unrat" (or so the film claims), *The Blue Angel* is an interesting entry for Millard fans. Though clearly far from the horror genre, Millard builds another mesmerizing tale of analog entertainment here. Cast as the lead, Millard shuffles around waxing about the finer things in life. Art by true artists! All good films have good themes! Paintings, wine and Tchaikovsky! And with a stern look and turtlenecks, Millard carries himself well. Then a sleazy dancer opens the door to temptation and Millard embraces lust too.

Previously the director of softcore nudies, Millard's roots show strongly in *The Blue Angel*. Not that anything explicit is displayed; lots of butt cheeks and cunnilingus over panties. But there's a racy element totally missing from his horror titles. Performances are notably more dramatic and conflicted beyond anything seen from Millard before, lending authenticity to the story. And yes, we do have momentary cameos from Millard's wife and mother with the same San Francisco house featured. But they somehow feel new since a few years have passed. Ultimately, the film hangs on the doomed romance between professor and stripper and the viewer is invested for its outcome. Well done, Nick. Recommended.

 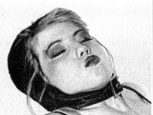  

BRIDE OF KILLER NERD

1992, Color, 72 min
STARRING: *Heidi Lohr, Toby Radloff, Lewis DeJulius, Mimsel Dendak, Kathleen Hogan*
DIRECTOR: *Mark Steven Bosko, Wayne Alan Harold*

Haunted by ghosts of the original, Harold meets a high school girl as equally tormented as he was. Together they find solstice and romance. But when bullies humiliate the couple at a party, Harold and his love exact revenge upon the masses.

A predictable sequel lacking much of the original's heart, *Bride* zips characters into conflict without characterization. Returning "nerd" Radloff is the production's strongest asset, promisingly opening the film with the ghosts of his murdered tormentors. But things turn quickly as we're stuck in school with jocks and a bookworm. Where's Radloff? Doesn't matter, because we're now asked to care about Lohr's desire to fit in - and here lies the problem. Lohr plays a completely new character in *Bride* but in the original, she was Radloff's beloved. Lohr and Radloff are both quirky here and it feels disingenuous. Lohr is a wonderful actress but the audience knows it's an act. And *Bride* is Lohr's film which strangely changes Radloff into a sidekick. Vengeance has less impact too because Lohr and Radloff participate in the killings, yet only Lohr has the emotional investment. Plus, the bullies are mere teenagers. And no one thinks it strange 30 year old Radloff is suddenly dating a high school teenager? Forgettable.

THE BURNING MOON

1992, Color, 99 min
STARRING: *Olaf Ittenbach, Beate Neumeyer, Bernd Muggenthaler, Ellen Fischer*
DIRECTOR: *Olaf Ittenbach*

A teenage drug-addicted rebel is forced to babysit his kid sister. High on heroin, the brother tells two ghastly stories to the girl. One about a blind date with a serial killer, and the other about a priest who's wrongly killed and returns as a zombie (with graphic dismemberments in Hell). Finally the brother kills the sister.

Returning to the genre after his impressive *Black Past*, Ittenbach directs and stars in this anthology that really delivers the gory goods. Infamous for unbelievable levels of violence, the film is surprisingly clean and welcoming in its first act. Resembling a television miniseries, I was actually bewildered by the professional lighting and camerawork throughout. This is not a gritty gore film. Instead, Ittenbach carefully showcases gruesomeness with a bright, clean, homogenized clarity. And while this allows the audience to appreciate its craftsmanship, it also eliminates the scares. Gore is mostly kept to the latter half and presented so damn cleanly. Compare *The Burning Moon* to *Violent Shit;* a ropey grunge permeates *Violent Shit's* visuals that seem needed here. But Ittenbach goes for gusto as he kills the kid and has the main character committing suicide. The dismemberments in Hell are incredibly impressive too, making *The Burning Moon* extremely popular around the world (though banned in its native Germany since 1993).

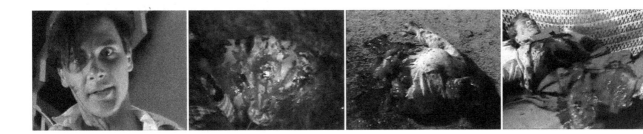

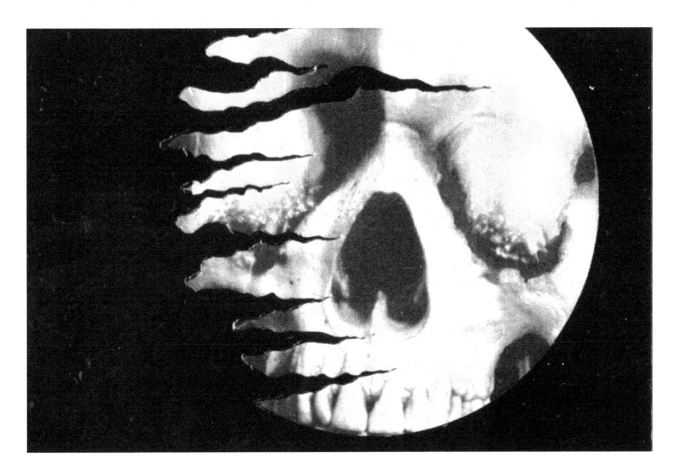

CHICKBOXER
1992, Color, 62 min
STARRING: *Julie Suscinski, Shawna Baer, James L. Edwards, James Black, Tom Hoover*
DIRECTOR: *Yolonda Squatpump (Scott Plummer)*

Kathy Sherwood is a huge fan of the television program *"Chickboxer."* Idolizing its star, Kathy joins a local kickboxing karate class. But the class is run by a nefarious gang aiming to replace the mayor with a corrupt politician! Now Kathy must arm herself like *"Chickboxer"* and fight back.

Told through first-person narration, *Chickboxer* is more talk than action, more action than comedy and more comedy than horror. It's a silly twist on superhero fandom, existing for no other reason than to make money at the video store. You see, *Chickboxer* (like *Galaxy of the Dinosaurs* and *Humanoids From Atlantis*) was a film made to satisfy box art; a production deal between J.R. Bookwalter and Cinema Home Video. Cinema provided the title and budget while Bookwalter manufactured content. Yet Bookwalter was given almost no turnaround time, producing six features in a matter of months. And there's no denying it, the only thing horrifying about *Chickboxer* is that the film manages to entertain. Suscinski is exceedingly perky as the *"Chickboxer"* fan, while Edwards (finally getting more screen time) is charismatic in a bashfully innocent way. Black stands out as the heavy (though I'm sure he'd rather be somewhere else) and while there are no deaths, *Chickboxer* almost achieves a sordid crime-thriller mentality. Even Scream Queen Michelle Bauer appears in an extremely out of left field nude sequence. A fun throwaway. Recommended.

DEAD IS DEAD
1992, Color, 73 min
STARRING: *Mike Stanley, Connie Cocquyt, Rob Binge, Dave Hildwein*
DIRECTOR: *Mike Stanley*

A drifter finds a concoction that can re-grow severed limbs and bring the dead back to life. Called "Doxitol," the drug was created in a hospital that an assassin burned down. Indebted to the assassin for a prior loan, the drifter is now targeted for assassination.

A passion project for writer, director and star Stanley, *Dead Is Dead* is not without its problems. Pacing is the big issue, stumbling its action and delivering lines frustratingly slow. Stanley makes a meal of everything, pausing for dramatic effect throughout his monologues. And the film opens with a confession that becomes a little hard to follow... The drifter's brother was in a mental hospital. The drifter borrowed money from a man who later burned down the hospital. The drifter still owes the man so he offers the man the drug. The debt is repaid but the man wants the drifter dead. Am I getting this right? Visually, the film impresses with locations from Michigan to New York City. Wonderful shots of Times Square remind us how rough the city was (even in the 1990's). Yet the editing also works against itself, flashing scenes of gore without the necessary coverage to show what happened. Were the drifter's intestines just pulled out? No, he's still walking around so... drug effect? Shitty editing? Then there's the romantic subplot that comes out of nowhere. Confusingly, the film was re-released in 2008 (containing footage from its 1993 sequel) and another sequel came in 2014. But that's the thing about passion projects...

DOMINION

1992, Color, 78 min
STARRING: *Carol Barta, Frank Dunlay, Stefan Hilt, Jenny Admire, Todd Sheets*
DIRECTOR: *Todd Sheets*

A swarm of vampires (lead by a child) attempt to resurrect the original bloodsucker.

A rather tame and pedestrian entry, *Dominion* is largely forgettable. Sheets presents a villain in young Hilt but forgets to give a hero. Police investigate the murders (which don't include much bloodsucking) and the film centers around an elderly couple rekindling their romance. No fangs, little blood but strangely a lot of flesh-eating.

EVIL NIGHT

1992, Color, 55 min
STARRING: *Holly Aeck, Spencer Trask, Joseph Fautinos, Todd Jason Cook*
DIRECTOR: *Todd Jason Cook*

Teenaged outcast Jimmy Fisher is constantly bullied by his classmates. Entering summer break, the kids plan one last prank as they invite Jimmy to a house party. But when he gets there, they strip and leave him unconscious on the front lawn. Later that night, Jimmy plans revenge by drinking a telekinesis cocktail, donning a clown mask and returning to kill.

The first feature from skateboarder (and future Screamtime Films distributor) Todd Jason Cook, *Evil Night* is a charming combination of ideas. The main story of a teased misfit taking revenge is the strongest element, wonderfully personified by the killer's bizarre clown mask. But a few too many ideas get in the way. We accept that Jimmy creates a telekinesis serum because it's important to the story, but not because it makes any sense. Now Jimmy has the ability to kill when not present, allowing for imaginative deaths like exploding cigarettes and fingers in eye-sockets. But telekinesis is a cheat. If Jimmy can kill by thought, why does he kill with weapons too? What are his limitations? Revenge is a personal act so it's easy to see why he's in the house, but deaths happen when he's not around. And then *Evil Night* introduces zombies! A surviving girl mixes a reanimating agent literally on the spot by pouring unknown liquids into the mouths of dead teenagers. Flesh-hungry ghouls rise and rip Jimmy apart. And Jimmy never uses telekinesis against them. Huh?

But regardless, *Evil Night* works. Shot handheld with a consumer camcorder, Cook's video captures early 90's middle-America like a documentary. People park at the mall, sit in trucks and chat. *Wayne's World* jokes run wild. Fashion lives through acid-washed jeans and neon shirts. And the safest house party gets interrupted when a decapitated head tosses on the dance floor. All props look like they were ordered from Fangoria magazine (which indeed, they may have been) and Cook opens the film with slow-motion skateboard tricks. Bam! *Evil Night* feels like a horror valentine to the genre. Recommended.

Not satisfied with his original version, Cook has since re-edited the film into a longer final cut. The film was also remade in 2014 by Chris Seaver.

THE FINE ART
1992, Color, 52 min
STARRING: *Lisa Morrison, Jeremy Wallace, Beth Pollock, Pat Coffey, Eric Stanze*
DIRECTOR: *Eric Stanze*

A young girl goes on a blind date. Unbeknownst to her, the man is a serial killer who paints his victims before murdering them.

Stanze's follow-up to *The Scare Game*. Only 21 at the time, *The Fine Art* reflects Stanze's natural ability to convey drama and suspense simultaneously. Dedicating much of the runtime to a budding romance, Stanze allows actors to build rapport before pitting them against each other. And it works. Genuine chemistry comes early, largely thanks to Morrison and Wallace's performances. But things turn as the couple prematurely pleads love. It's no surprise that Wallace is actually a serial killer, but his reveal is suspenseful. And as Morrison rejects and then invites Wallace to pursue her, the audience is primed for confrontation. Things do resolve a tad easily, but a nice twist provides the peppy climax. Recommended.

GALAXY OF THE DINOSAURS
1992, Color, 63 min
STARRING: *James Black, Christine Morrison, Tom Hoover, Bill Morrison, James L. Edwards*
DIRECTOR: *Lance Randas (J.R. Bookwalter)*

A team of astronauts crash on a planet filled with dinosaurs.

Featuring dino-scenes from 1977's *Planet of the Dinosaurs* ($500 stock footage provided by DeCoteau), Bookwalter's *Galaxy* spends most of its time searching for the plot. The crew (laughably dressed in suburban outfits) crash on a "planet" that looks a lot like backyard forests. For nearly an hour they wander, hiding from faded inserts of stop-animation monsters, only to be confronted with the bloated monologue of a lost crewmember. In short? I loved it.

To imagine *Galaxy* as a horror film would be unrealistic, yet so many trappings of the genre exist. Characters are torn apart and eaten (at least through editing) and the fate of humanity hangs in the balance. And though designed as science fiction, comedy plays the heaviest part. Bookwalter fills the film with bad puns and wacky faces. It's all in jest as the film was produced on an incredibly small budget (with an incredibly short timeframe). But three twists occur towards the end which really make things memorable: Edwards' incredible explanation, a reveal of the planet's origin (stolen from *Planets of the Apes*) and Black's sexual orientation. Solid laughs throughout! The fifth in the six pack.

HELL ON EARTH 2: ARENA OF DEATH
1992, Color, 119 min
STARRING: *Phil "Chip" Herman, Bryant Sohl, Matt O'Connor, Barry Gaines*
DIRECTOR: *Matt O'Connor, Phil "Chip" Herman*

In the post-apocalyptic future, a serial killer is drugged and recruited by mutants to help kill human survivors. But after a double-cross, he turns tables against them during an arena-brawl royal rumble.

Taking six years to make under the most grueling circumstances, *Arena of Death* stands as one of the most entertaining SOV titles around. The movie shines as the best example of independent film with heart, and deserves to be watched by every person reading this book. It's that good.

Epic in story (yet fixed on character), one wonders how O'Connor and Herman stayed

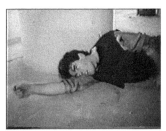

focused as everything else stacked against them. Real fires were set, fights staged, stunts executed and people got hurt. Locations were stolen and masked actors ran wild with prop-guns. Yet through it all, a good movie prevailed. Highlighting the film are its moments of unintended hilarity, such as the changing hairstyles and aging actors between scenes (results of the prolonged production). But my personal favorite is when main characters are jailed, then appearing a decade older as they start talking. And only a minute has passed! The film also lets characters explain events already seen, eliminating plot confusion for the audience. And while gore is present (including several beheadings), emphasis is on physical brawling commando style. Yet *Arena's* most impressive aspect is its camerawork with tilts, pans, wide angles and point-of-view shots.

Like early Polonia brothers films, Herman's team is a marvel of analog enthusiasm and creativity at its best. This is the film for everyone who has ever dreamed of making their own movie. Against all odds, these guys showed that it can be done and done well. As for part 1? It was Herman's original upon which *Arena* was based. Required Viewing.

HELLROLLER
1992, Color, 72 min
STARRING: *Ron Litman, Gary J. Levinson, Michelle Bauer, Penny Arcade (Mary Woronov)*
DIRECTOR: *Gary J. Levinson*

After learning that his mother was raped and killed by conjoined twins (before he was also raped and crippled as a baby), handicapped psychopath Eugene goes on a killing spree with a slow-minded friend.

Ineptly filmed, *Hellroller* may be the most irritatingly terrible film contained in this book. Directed by Lobo the flesh-eating beast from *Cannibal Hookers*, *Hellroller* is an exercise in excruciating bad taste. Live footage of people walking Hollywood Boulevard cuts to sequences shot on rooftops. Talented thespian Mary Woronov(!) inexplicably appears with lines like *"your mother was raped and killed in a back alley before they got from you what she couldn't give."* And tangents run wild as stripteases and bad jokes overtake the narrative. Scream Queen Bauer appears (as an obvious favor to the director) stripping, dancing and bathing but it's all filmed so poorly. Death scenes don't actually occur but "appear" as bloody inserts after the fact. Everything is filmed in extreme close-up. Actors speak direct to camera. And Levinson casts himself as the slow-witted friend claiming to be a filmmaker; an obvious dig/nod at Donald Farmer (*"the Fellini of horror pictures in Tennessee"*). Need I go on?

I commend Levinson for making his own movie. I am impressed at the star-power he managed to involve. But *Hellroller* is a terrible excuse for entertainment that misfires its own premise. Interestingly, a photograph taken on-set of Bauer's death was illegitimately used as cover art for the 1992 documentary *Invasion of the Scream Queens*, directed by Donald Farmer. A lawsuit followed, famously handled on the television program *"The People's Court"* with Judge Wapner. Levinson lost.

HOW TO SLAY A VAMPIRE
1992, Color, 82 min
STARRING: *John Polonia, Mark Polonia, Todd Rimatti, Gary LeBlanc, Marion Costly*
DIRECTOR: *John Polonia, Todd Rimatti, Mark Polonia*

Twin brothers are forced to clean their basement... and find a vampire! Comatose and rolled in an old carpet, the brothers attempt to kill the vampire but only piss him off. Now awake and roaming the town, the brothers must find and destroy him before it's too late.

 Though unreleased until 1995, *How to Slay a Vampire* is a unique film for the Polonia brothers as they outright attempt comedy. Horrific themes appear but only in small doses. Here, slapstick meets bad puns with repeated breaks against the forth wall. John, Mark and Todd seem to be having the time of their lives spoofing themselves (and low-budget cinema in general) and for the most part, it works. The brothers hilariously discover the vampire in the opening sequence and try to kill him. But he won't die! So the vamp gets up and runs away, spending the next 10 minutes dancing and having sex with a blow-up doll. It's funny,

but not 10 minutes funny. Yet superb moments occur too: Mark's visit to a video store and John delivering a bitter monologue about girls screwing him over. You actually sense that this is Mark and John just being Mark and John.

How to Slay a Vampire is a fascinating watch, particularly for Polonia fans. It feels like a fairy tale as Mark and John journey further down the cinematic rabbit hole. Highly Entertaining. Recommended!

HUMANOIDS FROM ATLANTIS
1992, Color, 47 min
STARRING: *James L. Edwards, Sandra Wurzer, Christine Morrison, Arvin Clay*
DIRECTOR: *J.R. Bookwalter*

When young Ken Adams gets his first big break as a documentary filmmaker, doom strikes as he's drawn into the mutated depths of the monstrous gill-man from Atlantis (well, so the box claims). But Ken does capture the lost sea creature on videotape! Only the footage can't be watched because the sheriff plays VHS and Ken shot Betamax. And now a beautiful scientist wants him dead so he doesn't risk her forthcoming Nobel prize.

 Exhausted on no-money productions for David DeCoteau's Cinema Home Video, *Humanoids From Atlantis* is the epitome of Bookwalter's "desperate to finish" pictures. But like *Galaxy of the Dinosaurs* and *Chickboxer*, there's something more to *Humanoids* that prevents it from being forgettable. Bookwalter charmingly spins expectations. *Galaxy* is a stranded space movie with dinosaurs. *Chickboxer* is a television show's fan fighting back. *Humanoids* (for 30 minutes) is a low-budget yarn about a low-budget movie. So one shouldn't take these films at face value. Even in their sloppiness, the people involved poured their hearts into making them. And particularly Edwards here.

Though he wouldn't find true leading-man material until 1997's *Bloodletting*, Edwards impresses as *Humanoids'* loveable Ken Adams. The man brings a wonderful innocence to his performance and the film benefits from his talents. Wurzer aids as the plucky girlfriend, comically rushing her lines with inexperience. But the misstep comes in the final 15 minutes when everything falls apart (actors talk to camera, the creature pulls off his mask and everyone breaks character). It's an ending the film doesn't deserve. Suddenly we're asked not to care but *Humanoids* built enough steam to warrant a pay-off.

This would ultimately be the sixth and final film in the DeCoteau produced six pack, though I wish there were still six more. Recommended!

INTO DARKNESS (RUMBO A LA OSCURIDAD)
1992, Color, 67 min
STARRING: *Ricardo Islas, Virginia Moar, Fernando Gomes, Alberto Laguna*
DIRECTOR: *Ricardo Islas*

As warned through a child's telekinesis, Earth will suffer three days "dark" while aliens purify the planet. The claim is to restore our ozone layer. But aliens are actually invading the planet, taking control of government to enslave humanity as livestock.

Fantastically written, Islas' *Into Darkness* is a low-budget *Invasion of the Body Snatchers* meets *The Terminator*. Quickly paced, Islas moves the plot effortlessly. The film opens with a biblical quote before the world turns completely dark, then backtracks 2 months prior to build story. This allows audiences to see what's coming, putting the viewer on edge as the countdown begins. And terror truly builds as the aliens' intentions are revealed. This isn't a gory film but tension develops solely from action and tight editing. Impressive stuff! The film ends where it begins too (which may frustrate viewers as no further conclusion is offered) but the fight for humanity continues. *Into Darkness* is an excellent thriller for a lazy afternoon. Highly Recommended.

LADY IN DANGER
1992, Color, 33 min
STARRING: *Lorraine Tyrer, Brian Davies, Peter Preston, Chris Williams, Ken Tryer*
DIRECTOR: *Brian Davies*

A cheating wife's boyfriend hires an assassin to kill the husband. Only the assassin is the husband himself!

Returning from his surprising *Last Day at the Beach*, Davies' *Lady In Danger* is a fun time-waster. Performances are adequate with an easy to follow plot. Plus the music rocks. But the real problem is the ending - it makes no sense! Either they ran out of ideas or time, because no explanation is offered for the final scene. But everything before it stands out nicely, and I'd really like to see more from this group. Fun stuff!

LOST FAITH
1992, Color, 80 min
STARRING: *Joel D. Wynkoop, David Bardsley, David Lurry, Melisa Sanford*
DIRECTOR: *Joel D. Wynkoop*

When his wife is kidnapped and sold into a pornography slave trade, good guy Steve Nekoda bursts into action. With a ferocious tendency for roundhouse kicks, Steve must fight to free his wife and regaining his faith in God almighty!

Kicking ass for 80 straight minutes, Wynkoop writes, directs and stars in this Chuck Norris-like entry of analog cheese. Charismatic and hilarious, Wynkoop betrays his horror persona with an intensely entertaining movie about a good guy gone wild. Light on horror (save an opening dream sequence added at the last minute), *Lost Faith* lights an analog firecracker that never quits. Busting into the kidnapping crime scene, Nekoda pushes until he gets answers. He leaves, then pushes people again. Gangs and thieves get in his way but his roundhouse clears the air. And Nekoda knows that when your VCR's fried, the cable's turned off and the car breaks down, the last thing you need is your wife missing.

Wynkoop (who also choreographed and wrote the music) tailors the film as his vehicle to leading-man status. And it works! Featuring a cameo from filmmaker buddy Tim Ritter, *Lost Faith* is an impressive piece of poverty-row adrenaline that truly delivers the goods. Brew up the popcorn and sit your ass down.

MAXIMUM IMPACT
1992, Color, 62 min
STARRING: *Ken Jarosz, Bill Morrison, Christine Morrison, James Black, Michael Cagnoli*
DIRECTOR: *Lance Randas (J.R. Bookwalter)*

An insurance salesman on business happens upon a prostitution/snuff ring operated by his boss.

A refreshingly serious entry from Bookwalter, cast with team regulars (including James L. Edwards), everyone gleefully playing against type. Both Bill and Christine Morrison (no relation, just same last name) are outstanding as the meticulous killer and an abused slave. Jarosz excells as the *Commando*-like vigilante while Black underplays as the heavy. And disturbing themes are explored with sincerity. A wonderful turn from a director flexing his muscle. Forth in the six pack - Recommended!

  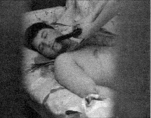 

A MOTHER'S VENGEANCE
1992, Color, 64 min
STARRING: *Claudia Perry, Tracy Moy, Carrie Denito, Debbie Conley, Angel Salerno*
DIRECTOR: *Mitch McGuire*

After a 15 year-old boy accidently drowns at a pool party, the mother and sister take revenge on the girls responsible.

Short and to the point, *A Mother's Vengeance* is a peppy push into psychosis. Alcoholic and already traumatized by her husband's death, the film begins with a mother fractured. Then her son drowns and she blames the four girls who teased him. Cue revenge! Perry and Moy get the most screen time, hamming it up as they coerce the "guilty" before drowning them. It's short but fun vigilante stuff. And the biggest moment is saved for last when a lesbian is (somehow) seduced into a bathtub. Her wrists are slit and the bathwater bleeds red. Share with someone you love.

NIGHTMARE ASYLUM
1992, Color, 69 min
STARRING: *Lori Hassel, Todd Sheets, Matthew Lewis, Jerry Angell, Jenny Admire*
DIRECTOR: *Todd Sheets*

A woman is trapped in a maze-like asylum filled with cannibalistic butchers that eventually turn into demons.

Those familiar with Sheets gore-a-thons will know what to expect here (and yes, it is more of the same). But what separates *Nightmare Asylum* from countless other zombie/demon flicks is context. *Nightmare Asylum* is pure saturated Sheets raging at the walls. Characters are constantly yelling. Buckets of blood literally cover people's bodies. One man squeezes a severed foot into a funnel for another to drink. And Sheets himself gets the last laugh, hilariously spanking Angell with a bloody machete. Filmed in an amusement park's haunted house, shots consist of manic running while dialogue screams twice over (making sure we heard it). Not that that's a bad thing, *Asylum* benefits from its quick pace and restless action thanks to the confined location. And heavily influences of *The Texas Chainsaw Massacre* (and sequels) appear as everyone acts like Chop-Top while driving nails into Hassel's hands. Even the soundtrack feels *Chainsaw* lifted. But watch as craziness gets the best of some actors as they burst into laughter too.

Regular movies establish characters before throwing them into dangerous situations. *Nightmare Asylum* shows everyone trapped and running from the opening frame. Recommended to Sheets enthusiasts.

NIGHTMARE VACATION
1992/2017, Color, 54 min
STARRING: *John Polonia, Matthew Satterly, Maria Russo-Davis, DJ Watts*
DIRECTOR: *John Polonia, Matthew Satterly, Mark Polonia (uncredited)*

Two dudes go to the beach for a weekend. A masked killer tails them, taking victims along the way.

Assembled in 2017 using raw footage from 1992, *Nightmare Vacation* debatably may not qualify for book inclusion. Both John and Matthew sadly passed away years ago, and the film was never completed until Mark used existing footage to create it. Holes in the original photography's plot needed filling, so Mark did the best he could with voice narration. This may have been the only way to make sense of the picture though, as audio loss (and missing sequences) left the narrative vacant. Therefore Mark's efforts are commendable and necessary in bringing this film to a viewing audience. But *Nightmare Vacation* cannot truly be held against other films within the timeframe. We must instead view it as a window into an unfinished project, interpreted and presented with the best of intentions.

With the bulk of footage shot after *Splatter Farm* (and before their mega-hit *Feeders*), *Nightmare Vacation* impresses for what it is. Using other Polonia films of the time, one can imagine what the final product might have resembled had John and Matt finished it themselves. There likely would have been more characters and certainly more deaths.

And their killer would have had more screen time. But dressed in black with a transparent *Sledgehammer*-like mask, what we have is spooky enough. Mark had to simplify certain aspects to find a story (which shows in the final product) but his efforts were successful and wholly appreciated. *Nightmare Vacation* does tell its tale. And this ultimately is a wonderful "workshop version" of an unfinished film, highly attractive for Polonia fans and for those interested in independent filmmaking. But it also serves to remind us that life is short and to never take things for granted.

Pretty impressive stuff for a slasher. Highly Recommended.

PREHISTORIC BIMBOS IN ARMAGEDDON CITY
1992, Color, 68 min
STARRING: *Holly Star, Tonia Monahan, Jenny Admire, Deric Bernier, Veronica Orr*
DIRECTOR: *Todd Sheets*

Continuing where *Bimbos B.C.* left off, a cyborg named Nemesis resurrects the evil Salacious Thatch to reclaim Armageddon City. And with their leader away on business, the Bimbos must band together to fight resistance.

Already known as a zero-budget horror filmmaker, *Bimbos B.C.* became a welcome diversion for Sheets with comedy, babes and sorcery. It remains one of his most accomplished works with sharp focus and pacing. But the same cannot be said here. With blatant references to *Alien 3*, there is a total lack of seriousness throughout the film. Actors deliver lines straight to camera at nausea. A character even tells the audience to *"go make popcorn"* because things are about to get ugly. And inexplicably, Sheets finds the clapperboard on set and blames Bimbo-mentality for leaving it there. Too many moments play for laughs as characters aren't motivated to act. In other words, people want to stand in fields instead of doing things to propel the plot. There's a great deal of charm piggybacked in from the original, but *Armageddon* does nothing with it. And another sequel is promised.

PSYCHO DANCE!
1992, Color, 77 min
STARRING: *Sal Longo, Laura Foutz, Launa Kane, Angela Smith, Autumn Kline*
DIRECTOR: *Gary Whitson*

A psychopath named Charlie is chloroforming and dancing with unconscious women.

An interesting premise keeps *Psycho Dance!* distinctly different from numerous other W.A.V.E. productions. Girls are drugged and then swung around to classical music. Longo plays Charlie, a brute with a panache for wrestling women and handcuffing them in his basement (the character was even successful enough for his own spinoff series *Psycho Charlie Returns*). The females are largely interchangeable, save for Foutz who spends the entire film as Charlie's prisoner, repeatedly asking *"are you crazy?"* And half of the movie focuses on six campers as they setup tent, roast hot dogs and go swimming. But they've only brought one beer (darn the luck) so the men drive back to town, leaving Charlie to the ladies. Smith gets a few good throws in the lake before everyone's drugged and taken back to the basement. Then it's time to boogie as Dave Castiglione appears in the final 2 minutes to make the arrest. *"I guess that was your LAST dance!"* Followed by *Psycho Vampire*. Recommended!

PSYCHO VAMPIRE
1992, Color, 91 min
STARRING: *Sal Longo, Laura Foutz, Autumn Kline, Carol Livingston, Dave Castiglione*
DIRECTOR: *Gary Whitson*

Managing escape, psychopath Charlie fixates on becoming a vampire. Buying a halloween costume and plastic fangs, Charlie enacts revenge on the girls responsible for his arrest.

A direct sequel to *Psycho Dance!*, *Psycho Vampire* furthers the psychotic tendencies of Longo's most gleefully crazy role. Charlie's still obsessed with dancing, but after hypnotically watching a VHS tape of *Sleepover Massacre*, he convinces himself that become a vampire is the best thing to do. And why not? A few bucks spent at the costume shop and we're in business! But the great thing about *Psycho Vampire* is that Charlie really isn't a vampire, and he knows it. He wears the cape and bites nubile necks, but it's an act stretched only as far as it helps subdue women. Longo even pops in the fake fangs mid-struggle, letting viewers see their absurdity. Much of the film uses flashbacks and a lengthy clip of *Sleepover Massacre* to help propel story, but they're important elements to those unfamiliar with the first film. The flashbacks do slow momentum but both films share a wonderful sense of twisted imagination. And the movie ends with a bit of magic that really elevates the proceedings. Fun stuff.

REANIMATOR ACADEMY

1992, Color, 68 min
STARRING: *Steve Westerheit, Connie Speer, Richard Perrin, Benton Jennings*
DIRECTOR: *Judith Priest*

Science student (and member of the Ded-Heads fraternity) Edgar Allan Lovecraft creates a serum that reanimates dead tissue. Testing it, Edgar reanimates a severed head into a joke-telling one-eyed appendage resting in an aluminum tray. Two gangsters learn of Edgar's discovery and force him to reanimate their recently deceased hooker.

And you thought *Re-Animator* was silly!

Smacks hit without sound effects. Guns shoot 30 times without reloading. A serum that turns females into shrews. All this and more in *Reanimator Academy*; like some cosmic mix of *Re-Animator* and *Revenge of the Nerds*. It's a film so bizarrely aimless, one wonders why it exists at all. Leagues away from horror, *Academy* is sketch comedy at its zaniest - and it works! Effortlessly earnest, the film never degrades people as the butt of jokes. Instead it emphasises jokes themselves; badly told zingers rolled out one after the next. Storywise, this is a sideways tale of a student becoming a professor. But it's also about hooker empowerment and punching men's heads off. Surprisingly recommended.

SLAUGHTERED SECRETARIES

1992, Color, 55 min
STARRING: *Sal Longo, Carol Livingston, Amanda Maddison, Clancey McCauley*
DIRECTOR: *G.W. Lawrence (Gary Whitson)*

In 1958, three female secretaries are tormented and killed by Artie the janitor.

Though billed as a period piece, *Slaughtered Secretaries* is really just an excuse to show-case women in stockings. The trio constantly complain about how much work they have, spending most of their time gossiping. Longo plays the janitor/killer, sloshing booze and taking naps on the job. But after the boss cracks the whip, Longo gets to work. Prolonged death by stabbing. Strangulation by telephone. And in the funniest bit, death by vacuum in the mouth. There's a bit of flair as Longo forces the dead (or passed out) girls to play cards in his basement, but much of *Slaughtered Secretaries* is wrapped in those nylon stockings. And yes, they do go way up.

Followed by *Slaughtered Socialites* in 1996.

SORORITY BABES IN THE DANCE-A-THON OF DEATH
1992, Color, 70 min
STARRING: *Laura Fuhrman, Matthew Lewis, Lisa Krueger, J.T. Taube, Holly Starr*
DIRECTOR: *Todd Sheets*

While pledging a sorority, a girl buys a crystal ball to use in a séance with friends. Together they conjure a demon who possesses the girl, then is exorcised by the ball's original (and elderly) owner.

Supposedly a sequel to *Sorority Babes in the Slimeball Bowl-O-Rama* (also produced by DeCoteau), Sheets' *Dance-A-Thon* is an unofficial continuation that leaves a lot to be desired. Is this footage assembled from other projects? No actor stands out and nothing really seems to happen. Gore is surprisingly low considering Sheets' history, so perhaps he was strapped for cash? I do commend the man for making so many films with such little money, but the car feels out of gas here. Filled with *Wayne's World* references and little else, *Dance-A-Thon* inexplicably remains popular thanks to title alone.

TORTURED SOUL
1992, Color, ? min
STARRING: Michael W. Johnson, Steve Bistrum, Carolyn Chambers, Kevin K. Smith
DIRECTOR: Michael W. Johnson

Ike wanted to be just like his older brother Steve... a demented serial killer!

Unavailable for review.

VIOLENT SHIT 2: MOTHER HOLD MY HAND
1992, Color, 74 min
STARRING: *Andreas Diehn (Andreas Schnaas), Anke Prothmann, Claudia Von Bihl*
DIRECTOR: *Andreas Schnaas*

The son of the original killer has been raised (and trained) by his deranged mother to kill. Anyone who steps foot in the woods is decapitated, mutilated or brutalized beyond words.

Returning with another gore filled over-the-top extravaganza, Germany's Schnaas throws every mutilation he can think of into *Violent Shit 2*. Gleefully offensive and hilariously zany, *Shit 2* firmly sticks its tongue deep in its bloody cheeks.

Opening with a drug deal gone bad before descending into the ultimate *Friday the 13th*, Schnaas crafts a film guaranteed to entertain. Framed with a recap, Schnaas wastes little time proving he has matured since his bloody original. The story flows at a great pace while the blood keeps spraying. Characters are always enjoyable and so are the many death scenes (fishing hooks into testicles being the showstopper). And a voyeuristic stop at a Tanning Salon delivers some much needed nudity too. The film even ends with a shoot-out in a local theater! Amazing. And equally impressive considering Schnaas' restraint on comedy, complementing the gore without overriding it. Truly a gem of the genre. Highly Recommended!

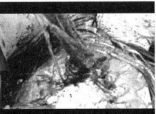

Interview
NICK MILLARD

Nick Millard is an auteur. Entering the film business in the early 1960's, Nick was originally known for sexy "smut" films such as *Sappho '68* and *Darling, Are You Bored With Men?*. Nick briefly turned to horror in the 1970's with *Satan's Black Wedding* and the critically acclaimed *Criminally Insane* starring Priscilla Alden. Action films followed before he reappeared in horror during the mid 1980's, but this time on video. Delivering an astounding seven SOV features within a short amount of time, Nick solidified himself as a capable filmmaker adapting to changes in technology, and as a man passionate about telling stories. Nick is still making movies today.

Though incredibly supportive during the writing of this book, Nick's schedule would not allow for lengthy interviews. Therefore I have pulled quotes from other various interviews, commentaries and online statements as they relate to his SOV output.

This is Nick in his own words.

BEGINNINGS...

There is only one business that is any fun... THE FILM BUSINESS. My father S.S. Millard was a producer on what was called Poverty Row. Nondescript office buildings that rented cramped office space to low budget producers like my father. Located at Sunset and

Gower, in front of Columbia Pictures. He made it off poverty row, and he took me with him. I quit school at age 16, after I finished the sixth grade... I say this with a great deal of pride... I learned to write by reading Hemingway, and the street. Oakland's skid row, the Moulin Rouge burlesque theatre.

In late summer of 1960, my dad S.S. Millard, myself, Carl the bookie and cameraman Robert Taunton left San Francisco to go on location in Virginia City, Nevada. This would be the first feature film I worked on, the title *Tales of Virginia City*. It lit the filmmaking fire in me with a blow torch and dynamite for fireworks. I am 77 now, back than I was 19, that fire has never gone out....never will.

My dad and I were sitting in a coffee shop in Hollywood across the street from Columbia Pictures. It was there that he gave me the best piece of advice I ever got, *"Be handy with a pencil."* My mother took me to the two most important places a mother can take a child... the church and the library. My father taught me to trust no one. He raised me to be a cynic. Did ever a boy have better parrents?

I started in the Film Business in 1960. That was 58 years ago... I will retire when I am dead. Best way for me to go on up to Heaven would be a heart attack, while shooting. I have been in all three parts of the Film Business... I had a theatre in Sacramento, The Royal Theatre at Sixth and K streets... Distribution, domestic and foreign... Production, that is where the fun is, creativity. There were no VHS cassettes or DVDs back in the 1960's. If you wanted to make money you had to shoot on 35mm motion picture film, and get play-dates in theaters. Hollywood was never goot to me, but New York City always was. To make a film, to be a director, it's like being a child all your life. I've never grown up. And when you direct you get to be the child who's in charge of the other children.

It is very important to be a little C R A Z Y, if you are in the Film Business or the arts. Van Gogh was a nut, most of the others as well. So I was forced to make a decision, to get to where I wanted to be I'd have to get a little more nuts. There is a bonus attached... the nuts have all the fun.

[My wife] Irmi is one of the best Film Producers in the Business. I have seen her go into a bar with a Twenty Dollar, talk to the bartender, and get me and two actors in to shoot a dialogue scene. A Hollywood producer cand do the same thing, only she must pickup a check for five thousand dollars for the bartender or owner first. That is why we are still around after more than fifty years... we can do what others cant.

In 1973 I shot *Criminally Insane* and then in 1974 I shot another horror film, *Satan's Black Wedding*. A vampire film. And I wanted to release them both together, you get a little more money from a theater owner (Exhibitors, we called them). So we gave them like a double bill and they'd give you a little better percentage. Instead of 25% you'd get maybe 35% because they had two features to offer the public. Two first run features.

I'm very much influenced by Orson Wells. He was a great director. He makes the present Hollywood directors, with a few exceptions, he makes them look like little kids filming comic books. He's one of my heroes. I've learned a lot from reading books about him and his way of doing things. There's no doubt he was a genius. He died like Brando, he committed suicide with a fork eating too much. Brando was 300 pounds when he died, perhaps the greatest screen actor of all time. And Wells weighed like 300 pounds. It's a slow way to die, you eat yourself to death. But I admired Wells. He made some great films.

Most of my life I've been afraid, not all of it but a lot of it. When I first went to the Cannes Film Festival in 1966, I felt very much out of place. The Introvert. Would like to be an extrovert, to be the life of the party. These days I feel like I own the world, and deserve every damn good thing in it. 77 is a wonderful age. I feel like a million bucks... have not had a cigarette since 1967, or a drink since 1982... don't need 'em, film is my addiction.

CRIMINALLY INSANE 2

It's a remake. If I've got any kind of camera, a video camera, a motion picture camera, I'll make a film with it.

DEATH NURSE

This was made in 1987 and as you all probably know with Medicare today, it's the biggest racket there is. Some hospitals have been caught billing Medicare like three times. I'm not exaggerating. They've caught countless doctors overcharging. The idea came from an actual case. I made some changes to it, it wasn't a nurse. But it was a woman who ran a rooming house. And she was taking in these old pensioners, people getting social security checks. And she murdered them, one by one, and hid the bodies, or buried them I don't remember. But then these social security checks would continue to come to the house and she'd forge the lodger, the dead lodger's signature onto the check. So that's where I got the idea from. Priscilla Alden and I had done about 4 films together before this, so I knew she'd be good for the part. And it's meant to have a little bit of black comedy to it, aside from the gruesome murders. There's a little chuckle here and there. It is a black comedy. It's kinda hard to remember, but I think *Criminally Insane 2* came before this.

My brother-in-law's son Royal played the first victim, and Mr Bedowski. I liked to use my mom because I didn't have to pay her. And I don't think I ended up paying my nephew either. So that's a big advantage, they did it for fun. And Irmi too, she didn't get any money. And I didn't take any either. We're not a rival to Meryl Streep here, we know she's not Meryl Streep and I surely know I'm not Anthony Hopkins or Daniel Day Lewis. Priscilla was a hard worker because when you carry that many pounds, that's strenuous. God she was a real trooper. I'd sometimes ask her to do 4 or 5 takes, and she was always a trooper. She'd do it. Priscilla passed in 2006 and she was 67 and I'm sure through the years the doctors tried to get her to lose weight. She can turn on the charm; a sweet voice, smarmy.

Here's what I like about its ending: it's kind of existentialist. Life has no meaning. So she comes back [to the couch], life has no meaning, what's the difference what happens? We'll just sit here. And a lot of people don't get it. Why doesn't she try to run away or something?

When I sit down, everything I write we put in the picture. I mean, maybe sometimes I've left something out if it's atrocious or bad. I've been doing this for 51 years and if I had a million, the last thing I'd do is make a film. I'd make cheap films. But anybody that would gamble… this is the big casino, making films! Not even the major studios know what the public wants.

Producers love dream sequences. If you got some stock shots you can put in there, they become the dream, the nightmare. It's called the Film Business. The film is the artistic side. The business is the make money and you've got to save money. You can't always spend money. Believe me, Irmi and I can make one dollar do the work of fifty dollars. We can stretch a buck. And the only people that waste money more than Hollywood are the Washington DC Politicians.

I'm proud to say, nobody ever got hurt on one of my sets. When we're making an action film, rule number 1: there's no such thing as an empty gun. That's why actors are dead. On a Nick Millard set, nobody gets hurt. There's no shot. It's only a movie, we can do it over again. We practice perfect gun safety. Even though it's a prop gun, we never point it at anybody. Because as long as you have that rule number 1, there's no such thing as an empty gun.

We finished *Death Nurse* part 1 in 1987, and Irmi and I had been to the American Film Market. Back then, back in the 1980's it was held in February. So we'd been down for that and we made the acquaintance of a man named Bob Brown. He had a company called Video City Productions and he also owned 13 video stores in the San Francisco Bay area. So I screened the film for him. I screened *Death Nurse* part 1 and he was familiar with Priscilla Alden's work from *Criminally Insane*. So right away he liked the film, he wanted it. It's what we call black comedy. It's tongue in cheek. It's not meant to be taken too seriously. He liked the film and the price was right, we know we don't have any Hollywood stars in our films so we price them accordingly. So that a small distributor can make a profit and we make a profit as well. So we had some success with the sale to Bob Brown and we did some foreign right sales: Greece and Spain. So I right away planned to make a sequel.

DEATH NURSE 2

This is what you might call a nice horror film. Now someday, the critics might pick up on this. I'm biased, but I like the film. First of all, because I made money on it. And when you create something it's like a child, in a sense. You love all your children. I love all my films. Even the ones that lost money.

Part 2 was a little bit easier to write because I was into the characters a little bit more. I'm sure with Priscilla also. The first time she played Edith was in part 1, and the actor kind of settles into their role as the film progresses. So it was easier for me to write as well. And I knew that we'd have to start part 2 with the stabbing of the policeman to explain why weren't they arrested. She kills the nosey cop and has Gordon haul his body down to the basement where the rats are at and they eat the poor deceased policeman. And then in terms of writing, I sit down, I don't outline, I just sit there. And A will lead to B, B will lead to C, one scene takes you to another. I enjoy writing.

We shot both *Death Nurse* 1 and 2 with the principles (Priscilla and Albert) together about 3 days all together. The secondary parts in a matter of hours, maybe half a day. It's not a long shooting schedule. These were quickies. If you add up every hour I'd say maybe a week. 5 days, maybe 6. Shot on 3/4 inch. It was pretty good at the time.

[Priscilla] was every inch the professional and enjoyed doing film work. She did a little theatre also so she did always a good job, a professional job. She wouldn't hassle you. She understood the character. And it was my pleasure. The first time [I worked with her] was 1969 on a film called *Severine*. And the last we did together was 2006, a film called *Funeral Parlor*. So that's quite a stretch. What is it, 37 years we worked together. Priscilla, I personally believe, was a genius. Acting is a creative art and I've worked with her, made films, and she just always came high above what I had written. She just would add an extra dimension to it.

What I always liked about Albert [Eskinazi] was he's got a great strong face. He's done a lot of parts for us. Hitman, he's a great hitman. I like an interesting face.

You gotta see, it's tounge in cheek, it's black comedy. It's made to be laughed at. People will say, oh it's not a real nurse or a real doctor. Of course they're not real! It's all pretend. They're homicidal maniacs. That's what they are. He's not a real doctor.

CEMETERY SISTERS

To the best of my recollection, this was shot early 1988.

We had the good fortune to work with two delightful real life sisters, the Simon sisters.

They make the whole picture, in my view because first of all, they have a certain chemistry being real sisters. So they fit together very well. Chemistry is something that directors always want because it's not two strangers acting together, it's two people that have a history together. And they just fit together and they're relaxed and comfortable and real, for lack of a better word. They're real because they're real sisters and they're playing sisters.

I do play parts now and then. My favorite thing is to write and direct. But I will play a small part. Saves money, saves bringing in an actor. The true test for a film is the same test for architecture. Does it look good 20, 25, 50 years later?

THE BLUE ANGEL

Shot on SVHS, then edited to 3/4.

We worked from the book. That film has aged quite well, we shot it late 1991. I tried very hard to get Hemingway's Granddaughter (actress Margaux Hemingway) to play Lola. My plan was to take the film to the Cannes Film Festival and line up three or four interviews per day, playing up the Hemingway name. But we took it to the Cannes, not in competition but in the film market to sell films. Foreign rights. And that was 1992 in May.

I've always got ideas because I'm always thinking cinema. We live, sleep, eat, breathe films at Irmi Films. For entertainment, we watch films. I asked my Dad once, where do you get stories from? And he said, read the newspaper.

IN CONCLUSION...

If your small dreams have not come true, dream bigger... the Gods like daring.

Early to bed. Early to rise. Makes a man healthy, wealthy, and wise.

You are never too old, to be young...

Thank you for all your support, Nick!

Interview
TODD JASON COOK

Defining independent horror in the 1990's, Todd exploded into the genre with the clown-masked revenge favorite *Evil Night*. Showcasing his love for slashers and the supernatural, Todd quickly returned with the killer doll flicks *Demon Dolls* and *Bloody Anniversary*. Zombies prevailed in his heavy metal gut-muncher *Death Metal Zombies* and his trademark glee spills across the screen in every title. But Todd is also known worldwide as the master skateboarder called Falcon, documenting his incredible skill in his newly released documentary *Skateboarding Revelations* (34 years in the making!)

Todd, thank you for giving your time to this interview! In many ways, your films are the epitome of early horror in the 1990's. Fun heavy metal slashers fully aware of their 80's influence. What initially lead you want to make movies?

Wow, that's an HONOR to hear that my films are considered the "epitome" of early 90's horror, thank you so much! They were intentionally produced to be exactly as you described - 80's style horror films with a metal vibe that were very aware and paid tribute not only to studio produced 80's horror but also the camp and "B" movie sub-genres.

My obsession with horror films began when I was 4 years old when I saw films like *Westworld*, *Satan's Triangle* and *House of Seven Corpses*. I watched every horror film that came on TV, from the original b/w vampire, mummy and werewolf re-runs to horror features that made their way to regular television. We got cable in 1979 and I saw *Phantasm*, which blew my mind with originality and alternate worlds. In 1980, one film single-handedly changed my life FOREVER after seeing it: *Friday the 13th*.

Today, thousands of filmmakers cite the same film and/or franchise as their reason for making films. I began making films literally weeks after seeing *Friday the 13th* on cable in 1980... and I knew from that very moment that I was going to do this for the rest of my life, with a life-long goal and dream to direct and act in a *Friday the 13th Part 13* for the major studios some day.

Everyone that knows anything about me know that I can never run out of oxygen talking about *Friday the 13th* and it's sequels and that is because it was and still IS THE driving force behind a lifetime's worth of filmmaking with a plan to turn my dream directing gig into reality! All I talked about in school, every drawing, every school writing project, everything was *Friday the 13th*. I even made tons of what I called "Audio Movies" where I would record on audio tapes, me acting all of the characters and Jason roles in my own *Friday the 13th* "Audio Movies." I acted out entire movies (sometimes in real time) and I played the Manfredini score from my 1982 *Friday the 13th Parts 1-3* vinyl record.

I was acting 24/7. I did it at home, at school and even at friend's houses. I played "characters" from all my favourite horror movies throughout school as well. I would lock into a character and stay in it all day and respond to kids and teachers accordingly. All of the school kids thought I was weird. I told everybody that there would be at least 13 *Friday the 13th* films right after Part 1 came out. I made an audio movie with Jason on a ship in 1981 (which Paramount used for the plot of 1989's *Jason Takes Manhattan*). From 1980-1986, I shot a lot of *Friday the 13th* fan films and original films on Super8 film. I simply grabbed the camera, planned shots and tried to capture what I needed into every frame in order to make films that to me, would feel like they were part of the *Friday the 13th* franchise. I took every film dead seriously as a director and was determined to make every one of these films, whether I had help or had to do them myself. My destiny was plotting and everything I wrote was *Friday the 13th* sequels: *Jason at Crystal Lake in the Dead of Winter* (1988), a telekinetic kid vs. Jason (1985), a oujia-resurrected demon possessed Jason with mind powers (1990), a film that explored Jason's youth (1989)... I came up with all the ideas for my *Friday the 13th* films years before the major studios used the very same ideas and concepts!

in 1989, I finally wrote, directed, produced, edited, scored, filmed, edited and did special fx for my first feature length film: *Friday the 13th Part XIII: The Final Destruction* (1989). This film was my ultimate dream and I pulled off a very ambitious film with the longest final battle in *Friday the 13th* history (over 30 solid minutes). It was based off of the 1985 script I wrote about a telekinetic kid using mind powers to stop Jason. By the time I began filming, *Part VII: The New Blood* had hit theaters using the telekinesis idea, so I adapted the "kid" in my story to be the son of the "Tina" character. Because of the cost of film, I decided to use video simply because it was cheaper. I spent a year and a half filming the movie, piece by piece and when it was done, I watched it a million times and to this day I still watch it every year numerous times because it reminds me of the purpose of my life and also because it serves as a continuous inspiration for every film I do. I want to do *Part 13* for the studios some day (a slightly different story from my original though).

Now that I [had] completed my first full-length film, I went back and made *Friday the 13th Part IX: The New Life* (1991) which was a fan film like *A New Beginning* but still with Jason. 1992 was when I decided it was time to make my first original film for mass distribution.

And in 1992, you made your first feature film *Evil Night*. How did this film come about? Did you already have a distribution plan while shooting it?

I had no plans for the movie other than I knew that I was going to make it. I simply created a production company, got contracts and paperwork together and made sure I had everything I needed to make a professional film with outside actors. We ran a few small ads in papers and the casting was announced on local major radio stations, which led to me watching hundreds of people audition for *Evil Night*.

After a few months of pre-production, we speedily shot the film in 4 weeks with an amazing cast and crew. It took several edits and versions before I was happy with the final version. After the first edit, [the] original film ran too short, I didn't like the "video" look of it and I needed to film additional scenes, which were done in 1994 and again in 1995. Only then was I completely satisfied with the final cut.

There are 3 different versions of *Evil Night* that I edited and I later decided to make them all available. [See Screamtime Films @ www.screamtimefilms.com]

The killer's mask in Evil Night is now iconic. Where did the mask come from?

The mask came from a wholesale dealer catalog from one of our business partnerships in the early 90's. Unfortunately, the mask is no longer produced, so I have been shipping the original mask around to producers such as Chris Seaver (who directed the 2015 *Evil Night* remake) and Jason Harlow (who is doing the long awaited sequel called *Another Evil Night*).

***Evil Night* also starred then-unknown Lisa Forbes, who eventually became Lisa Cook. How did you first meet Lisa?**

Lisa was one of the hundreds who showed up for the auditions. After being cast in the role of "Shannon," she wanted to help out on crew and any other areas and wound up being my assistant for a few shots. Her dream was to be a Scream Queen of the "B" movie genre and Linnea Quigley was her greatest inspiration. After doing *Evil Night*, Lisa and I got married five months later and for me, it was an easy decision to place her as the star in each film in order to create a following for her which worked and she eventually had her own fan club and everything.

Lisa quickly became your regular actress, eventually becoming that Scream Queen with several *Lisa Cook's Nightmares* videos and the Linnea Quigley-like *Deadly Workout* entry. What was it like being married to your main star? Were you the dynamic duo of moviemakers?

It was an amazing time on non-stop filmmaking, appearing at horror conventions and visiting other indie filmmakers like Todd Sheets (*Zombie Rampage*) and Jim Larsen (*Nigel the Psychopath*). We paid direct tribute to a lot of 80's slasher movies and Linnea Quigley movies with films like *Demon Dolls* and *Deadly Workout*.

I've always found it fascinating that you were married, living in such a large house and had such an awesome bedroom filled with horror posters. Your room looked straight out of a video store! Where did you get all those cardboard standees?

The house was a major fixture in my filmmaking life and I utilized it in almost every film I made because it was a film house for me. My old bedroom was covered with 80's horror posters and standees from 1987-2003 when I left. I had collected everything from the local VHS rental stores and since I was also a VHS dealer, I would get horror posters and VHS from the local company that supplied ALL the local VHS rental shops.

A supernatural element plays heavily in almost all of your films. Do you prefer stories with "unexplainable" aspects rather than straight forward killers?

I have always first and foremost been influenced by all the 80's slasher era films. The supernatural element always came from *Carrie*, *Phantasm*, *Scanners* and *Halloween 3*. I always loved the limitless worlds that those films created and I am by nature a "NO RULES" person who likes to make my own original worlds or by combining aspects that were not too common back then.

You also act in your films, often as the main character. Do you enjoy directing and acting at the same time? Which do you ultimately prefer?

I became a director because I was an actor first. I learned how to make films based on that one major passion and goal. I have always been able to act. After decades of acting daily, I have gained the ability to hit the mark with any kind of role because I always viewed my real life as a movie, with every day being a new scene, role etc. With the experiences I have lived, I am now able to channel every emotion with ease and a naturalness which makes me happy because I wanted to be the most versatile actor possible. I worked extremely hard to be able to achieve that and I would love to be able to act in other films more often. I don't really prefer one over the other, I just want to be able to keep making films one way or the other.

1995's *The Dummy* (*Bloody Anniversary*) is credited to director Dante Falconi. Is this your alias? If so, why did you choose an alias?

Dante was pulled out of the air. "Falconi" was a hint towards "Falcon," which is the name I use as a professional skateboarder. I went for an Italian style film (Fulci/Argento style of atmosphere) and the look was really unique for me, so I decided it would be fun to use an alias for that film and *Night of the Clown*.

Several of your films have been available in different versions, some shorter while others containing additional material. Why do different versions exist?

Just like with *Evil Night*, I did several different versions of edits before deciding that I had made a final cut. I thought it would be neat to offer all of the different versions to the true hardcore fans that want to have everything since each version has its own unique feel and style.

You also impressively started your own distribution company in the 90's called Screamtime Films. Was this initially created as a means to distribute your own work? What has your distributor experience been like?

The distribution company began as "Cemetery Cinema" in 1992 and the retail catalog was full of films we all know and love like *Killer Nerd*, *Splatter Farm*, *Zombie Rampage*, and every indie produced horror film that I could find. I simply made my films available through my own label and catalog and slowly but surely, I began to see results. I always knew that it would take 20 years (or more) before the company would have any kind of fanbase, but I kept at it and now I am distributing indie films from filmmakers around the world.

In addition to your filmmaking career, you turned pro in the early 2000's as a professional skateboarder - featured in Tony Hawk DVDs, magazines and several skate films. Incredible! Horror fans should recall you doing a few skateboard tricks in your early films too. Have your successes in the skateboard world and film crossed over? Can we expect a skateboarding slasher in your future?

I think you're the first person to ever mention my pro skateboard career in an interview about my horror films! I have always kept my horror film and skateboarding careers separate. This was done intentionally because I have a major film coming out in 2018 that is now the longest production in film history (34 years in the making)!

In 1984, I began production on *Skateboarding Revelations: Journey to the Final Level*. It's a combo documentary/feature/reality show/art film that follows my skateboarding career (and touches on my horror film and music career) from the 1970's to present day. Anyone who has EVER stepped on a skateboard, made a film or recorded a record album needs to see this film. It applies to EVERYONE and shows how maintaining life-long goals and constantly planting seeds to help those dreams grow will turn them into reality. Since my entire life was recorded since I was born, I wanted to make the ultimate documentary in film history - a film that is 100% real audio/film/video/tv of one person who planned to make this lifelong dream. I began this process in 1984 and it's coming next year. The first trailer was released in 2016 and it landed on every major skateboarding/extreme sports magazine/website/tv channel in the industry. I am truly excited to finally be completing the film soon (after 8 years of daily editing). [*Skateboarding Revelations* has since released and it is incredible. Available @ www.screamtimefilms.com]

Video has been such an important tool for your over the years. But how do you regard today's world of HD smartphones and YouTube? What advice might you offer a young filmmaker just starting out?

Interestingly, I never regarded video as different for making films, other than the appearance. I have never personally liked the look of video, so all of my films were processed to make them have grit, grain and film color schemes so that they have the same nostalgic feel of the 80's era slasher and horror films. Video was cheaper than film, so that became the rationale behind using it for features. Each film still had a budget (ranging from $500 - $15,000 each), but using video helped keep filming costs at a minimum so that monies could be spent elsewhere. I started with real film, then video and now HD formats and they have all be the same process as far as making films, but each has their advamtages/disadvantages. I always felt that I should be able to make a fun and entertaining film regardless of the format or budget and it's still smart to think that way today, especially in an over-flooded indie film market. With the internet and technology in everybody's hands, it is ten thousand times more difficult to stand out in the world of film, no matter how good your film is. I suppose that is why I have chosen to focus on releasing other filmmakers' projects and keep working on my ultimate lifetime-in-the-making film which will show the world how I succeeded with horror movies, music and skateboarding and how I have combined all three in ways that nobody is expecting.

Thank you so much for your time and thoughts, Todd!

Chapter 15
INDEPENDENT REINVENTION (1993)

AGE OF DEMONS
1993, Color, 78 min
STARRING: *Eric Matson, Damon Foster, Becca Torez, Alice Cooper, Butch Portillo*
DIRECTOR: *Damon Foster*

A female cult has killed 100 people and aims to resurrect a demon, but needs a telekinetic head-banger's help to do it. The telekinetic head-banger resists.

Age of Demons is a chore. A ridiculous spoof of martial arts, gang-bangers and *Kamen Rider* films (think *Power Rangers*), Foster tells a tale so excruciatingly bad it's nearly unwatchable. *Age of Demons* is no horror film, yet horrific elements exist (decapitations, gushing squirts of blood). Lightning bolts destroy cars. Gangland war erupts on the streets. And Foster gleefully spits in a woman's face. Opening text informs the viewer that nothing is meant to be taken seriously, particularly the racial slurs. But one wishes Foster did take it serious because he certainly put effort into choreography, effects and story. There's an interesting premise here, undone by its own terrible characters. *Age of Demons* deserves better and the biggest offender is the man who made it. Not to be taken seriously? Remove the nonsense and this could be something worth watching.

BIMBOS IN TIME
1993, Color, 70 min
STARRING: *Tonia Monahan, Jenny Admire, Auggie Alvarez, Mike Hellman, Cathy Metz*
DIRECTOR: *Todd Sheets*

Resurrected yet again because the scriptwriter wanted to (it's admitted in the movie), Salacious Thatch returns and somehow manages to travel back in time. Tailing him is a bunch of Bimbos with little concern for altering history.

Being the third in Sheet's trilogy, hopes were high that *Bimbos In Time* would right the wrongs of *Prehistoric Bimbos In Armageddon City*. I genuinely enjoyed *Bimbos B.C.* but *Prehistoric* muddied the waters with constant self-awareness and breaking of the fourth wall. Sadly, things go even further here (blaming its own existence on terrible writers). The idea of bouncing throughout time is great, and some hilariously interesting scenes occur as Bimbos team up with "The King" (Alvarez as Elvis Presley) and run from huge dinosaurs. But there's no heavy; no villain. Salacious Thatch is a walking joke, recast as a thinner actor stating *"the bimbos blew the fat off me."* At one point, Sheets himself walks on set saying *"this is a family film"* so no violence should be expected. Yet there's still a ton to appreciate, especially after learning that the entire production was shot in 9 days with no money. It's a chase film, complete with a sequence featuring disco geriatrics burning-up the dance floor. And for that alone, I'm letting this slide.

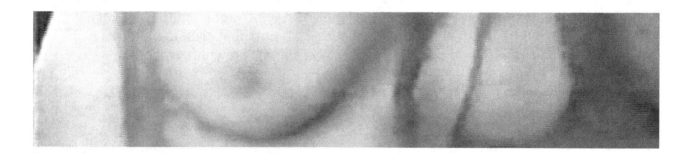

BLOOD SUMMER
1993, Color, 33 min
STARRING: *Michael Man, Sean Fralin, Misty Norway, Diane Angel, Jessica Star*
DIRECTOR: *Matthew Samuel Smith*

Under pressure to evict non-paying tenants at the family trailer park, a teenager cuts off his own thumb and goes crazy. Donning a devil mask, the teen beheads and kills various friends and onlookers.

Though short, Smith's *Blood Summer* is not without style. The film opens abruptly with first-person narration before breaking into action. Blood is lovingly splashed around as the killer grunts his way to psychosis. Yet what makes *Blood Summer* memorable is the wonderful filters used throughout. Reminiscent of *Heavy Metal Massacre*, the killer's rage brings throbbing reds over the screen during kills. The camera plays very fly-on-the-wall at times too, watching as people make-out, sun tan and talk to flowers. 33 minutes later and you'll only wish for more (this could easily stretch to feature-length). Just don't let friends use the bathroom. Recommended!

BLOODTHIRSTY CANNIBAL DEMONS
1993, Color, 71 min
STARRING: *Auggi Alvarez, Jerry Angell, Rodney Joiner, Cheryl Metz, Jody Rovick*
DIRECTOR: *Todd Sheets*

A street gang and their rivals become trapped in an old warehouse theatre. Several characters die, then are horribly brought back to life as flesh-eating creatures. Turns out the theatre is cursed.

Sheets' homage to Lamberto Bava's *Demons* places the director in familiar territory. There's tons of gore and zombie beasties. But what makes *Bloodthirsty* more attractive than most is Angell's starring role. Sporting a huge mullet and the thickest moustache, Jerry Angell embodies the awesome 90's of analog video. He is unique, hilarious, honest, rural and above all, committed. Any film with Angell guarantees a good time. Recommended!

 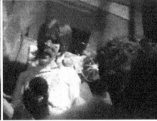  

BLOODY CREEK

1993, Color, 91 min
STARRING: *Gary Whitson, Aven Warren, Terri Cavalier, Sal Longo, Dave Castiglione*
DIRECTOR: *G.W. Lawrence (Gary Whitson)*

A serial killer is loose in the forest.

Framed in flashback as a cop recounts the murders to a reporter, *Bloody Creek* is a nice
entry in the woodsy slasher subgenre. Without giving too much away, the killer's identity is
revealed early. But the real fun is watching the police bungle the investigation as the killer
operates. None of it is terribly exciting (no iconic hockey masks), but a prolonged
mud-tussle and an impressive decapitation keep things rolling. Whitson pulls double duty
again, directing while starring in a major role. And Castiglione shines as the horny park
ranger looking for action (doubling as the red herring in a nightmare sequence). But this is
an early W.A.V.E. title I keep coming back to, ending with a nice twist as the *Blood Creek*
killer rebrands himself. Worth revisiting! Highly Recommended.

BURGLAR FROM HELL

1993, Color, 97 min
STARRING: *Matt O'Connor, Ben Stanski, Barry Gaines, Bryant Sohl, Angela Jackson*
DIRECTOR: *Phil "Chip" Herman*

When a tough-guy burglar breaks into an old woman's house, she kills the bastard and
buries him in the backyard. Years later, friends rent the house for a weekend of booze and
partying. But the friends inadvertently resurrect the burglar with an impromptu séance.
Now the vengeful crook is out for blood.

A wonderfully funny, grungy and occasionally scary entry in early 90's horror, *Burglar From
Hell* is something special. Sohl as the burglar constantly steals the show, chewing each
scene with glee. Sohl rips out throats, pull off arms, tear off shirts and even scoops
intestines from a man's stomach. And that's when he isn't pissing! Honorable mentions go
to Sohl's dick too, freshly reanimated and broken after a struggle (*"Guess I won't be*

needing THAT anymore!"). The film is unashamedly sophomore with camera and effects, but charmingly so. You really feel like Herman's just filming his friends. Mistakes appear too (a tripod in the background and a crewmember walks on set) but they're subtle and possibly intended. Herman's style is very handheld, giving a real-time feel to the picture. And *Burglar From Hell* also tackles racism with a wonderful speech delivered by Gaines. Yet most striking is how natural everything comes across. Performances range from comical to charming and everyone seems to genuinely care for one another (a camaraderie shared with *Blood Lake* and *The Heaping Bouncy Breasts That Smothered a Midget*). This is one of the best comedic SOV horror entries ever made. Plus look for Scream Queen Debbie D as a horny schoolgirl! Required Viewing.

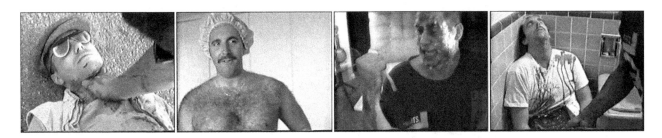

Phil Herman (under umbrella) directing Burglar From Hell (1993)

CHOPS

Academy Awards

by Mark Anthony Hunkel
Fourth Estate entertainment editor

E at your heart out, Stephen King. Amateur filmmaker Anthony Van Deuren of De Pere has got one up on you.

It's been two years since the script for *Chops* was conceived and in six months, Van Deuren and his fellow actors finished the filming. On Feb. 8, those of legal drinking age can witness the one-time showing of the movie at 8 p.m. at the West Pitcher Show in Green Bay. Doors will open at 6:30 p.m., and as a special treat before the showing, the local band Boris the Sprinkler will perform at 7 p.m. Those under 21 can still view the film as it will be

(Chops) simply puts it, "It's about two guys that like to kill."

"They travel from state to state and when the heat starts getting up on them, they take off and go to another town," said Andy Adzima who plays Biscuits.

With the help of Van Deuren's friends playing the characters, most of the movie was filmed in various places in Green Bay with the exception of one scene that was shot in a national forest near Abrahms. "It's a do-it-yourself project," he said, "but we put a lot of work into it."

Chops is actually Van Deuren's fourth hommade movie. His three previous flicks were based on the same theme—horror. "I just like horror movies," he

CHOPS
1993, Color, 122 min
STARRING: *Bronson T. Smith, Andrew Adzima, Scott E. Blavat, David Larson*
DIRECTOR: *Anthony Vandeuren*

Serial killer brothers Chops and Biscuits attack, mutilate and rape unsuspecting victims.

A Wisconsin slasher from the star (and uncredited director) of *Shreck*, *Chops* is hard to nail down. The film begins mid-interview after the brothers have been caught, then spends its runtime showing the killing. Narrative follows the brothers as they attack, lay around and complain about life. But it's the honest portrayals from Smith and Adzima that thankfully drive the film. These guys kill, then live in the victim's apartment afterword. They drink booze, eat popsicles and watch *Last House on Dead End Street* between airings of *"Beavis & Butt-Head."* But then they're bored so it's out to kill again. The film's camcorder work is sufficiently shoddy (with the single in-camera microphone) but this isn't a movie needing production value. Fake punches are seen and fights occur in bathrooms. Blood is splashed around and sex acts are crudely simulated. There's some in-jokes to horror and comparisons to Jeffery Dahmer, but this only helps give the audience context. Vandeuren is making a mid-90's epic about two low-income brutes. And as much as we want to despise them, we can't help but be entertained. Recommended with cans of beans.

Chops actually runs longer than 122 minutes, but the review tape I had cut off mid-scene!

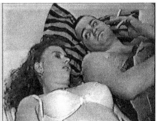

CURSE OF THE SWAMP CREATURE
1993, Color, 84 min
STARRING: *Lonna Cottrell, Sal Longo, Amanda Madison, Clancey McCauley*
DIRECTOR: *G.W. Lawrence (Gary Whitson)*

Two girls set sail to a deserted island and forget to anchor the boat! Stranded, they're soon terrorized by a deformed cannibalistic psychopath determined on make them his next meal.

With its opening sequence on water, *Curse of the Swamp Creature* immediately carries an adventurous tone. This is a W.A.V.E. production with a lot of style. More like an analog *Anthropophagus*, our heroines hilariously stand by as their boat floats away, then compound stupidity by laying in the woods for a night's rest. And it's still daylight! Good thing the deranged psychopath is there, because these girls would have died from exposure. Longo plays the killer adorned in ski-mask, hiding facial Freddy Krueger-like scars that once seen, immediately cause girls to faint. Bodies are tied to a spick and roasted for dinner. And McCauley gets the worst of it, bound to a tree and stripped to her tighty-whities before nipple-flashing the camera. *Curse* also features a plane crash (providing extra snacks for the killer) and everything ends with a muddy quicksand tussle. Pretty, pretty good!

DEAD IN THE POOL
1993, Color, 75 min
STARRING: *Lonna Cottrell, Cristie Clark, Dawn Lewis, Sal Longo, Gary Whitson*
DIRECTOR: *G.W. Lawrence (Gary Whitson)*

A young girl is attacked by a female swim team, leading to her termination when she arrives late to work. Her stepfather continually insults her and worse - he's been sexually abusing her too. But she's not going to take it any longer! Acquiring a gun, the girl shoots, drowns and chokes her attackers in the ultimate form of revenge.

With a straightforward approach, Whitson crafts another winner with *Dead In the Pool*. This is W.A.V.E. Productions operating at their most efficient, with countless wrestling sequences deep in Whitson's pool. Cottrell carries the film alternating between smarmy smiles and cowering the nasty bits, while Whitson himself plays the stepfather (allowing for some control in the abuses). But the quieter moments are more impressive. *Dead In the*

Pool never strays from story or feels overlong, yet several moments occur without dialogue as characters perform their daily routines. The film opens with Cottrell reading a newspaper and all we hear are the turning of pages. Later, girls bask in the sun and all we hear are the birds and wind. It's these little touches that turn *Dead In the Pool* into a time and place; an environment captured on video. Plus the movie is memorable. Highly Recommended.

DEAD IS DEAD 2: THE INCARNATION
1993, B&W, 56 min
STARRING: *Mike Stanley, Diane Busuito, Jose S. Chackunkal, Dave Waszak*
DIRECTOR: *Mike Stanley*

Eric Shepherd is still alive, walking around and avoiding zombies.

Reportedly unreleased (though footage was later added into *Dead Is Dead: The Director's Cut* in 2008), *Dead Is Dead 2* is a hard watch. Not gory, sexy, interesting or eventful, this black and white sequel is a bore. Running less than an hour and at an incredibly slow pace, there just isn't enough plot to carry a story.

DEMON DOLLS
1993, Color, 96 min
STARRING: *Todd Jason Cook, Lisa Cook, Joey Scarborough, Scott Spellman, Rik Deskin*
DIRECTOR: *Todd Jason Cook*

A man conjures life into a doll, which tries to kill him.

Fresh from his overcomplicated (but fun) *Evil Night*, Cook earns a lot of respect with this kooky camcorder follow-up. He directs and is onscreen the entire time. Plus, soon-to-be Scream Queen Lisa Cook is introduced and a number of innovative editing tricks are used throughout. But most importantly, the film never outstays its welcome.

Cook employs mirrors and jump-cuts to keep things moving. A lengthy shower scene (with full frontal female nudity) is employed. Random toys appear to cry. Yet the bulk of the picture is essentially two people walking around a house for an hour and a half. Is it real, or is it Memorex? The Cook's are married (both in real life and the movie), yet Todd inexplicably spends his nights watching horror flicks with his buddy. But all's fair in love and horror because Lisa needs more shower time too. As with *Evil Night*, scenes take place in Cook's real-life bedroom adorned with movie posters, so part of the fun is seeing all the paraphernalia. But there are some issues. A case of serious overacting almost derails the plot. The doll's animation is good (as is the makeup) but the story actually goes nowhere. There are four characters in the entire film and they love binge-watching horror flicks. Yes, they literally sit and watch other movies (which is not very exciting for us). But the end does contain a nice no-budget *Videodrome*-riff so all's forgiven.

A newer director's cut runs 23 minutes shorter, and the film was remade in 2014.

THE FLESH MERCHANT
1993, Color, 100 min
STARRING: *Neil Delama, Margaret Romero, Adam Tucker, Don Stroud, Joe Estevez*
DIRECTOR: *Mike Tristano*

A white sex-slave kingpin is kidnapping and initiating beautiful women from a local bar.

Though unavailable for review, *The Flesh Merchant* has enjoyed a fairly large distribution history (no doubt thanks to mega producer David Sterling's involvement). But more dramatic thriller than horror, the film is reportedly clunky in its action. Estevez has two scenes and Scream Queen Michelle Bauer appears for 10 minutes, pops her top and dies immediately. The plot involves a female detective desperately searching for her sister, who's been abducted by the slave trade. Lots of male chauvinism mixed with muscle guys chloroforming babes to "fill an order" for Don Stroud.

FULLMOON (PLENILUNIO)
1993, Color, 85 min
STARRING: *Martin Cabrera, Ricardo Islas, Ana Cecilia Garcia, Sebastian Rivero*
DIRECTOR: *Ricardo Islas*

A cable access reporter and his pre-teen "helpers" investigate murders that appear to be caused by a werewolf.

Inspired and well paced, Islas' *Fullmoon* is a fun ride. The film mainly follows a group of kids as they discover (and fight off) a werewolf. To this, *Fullmoon* feels like a cross between *Stand By Me* and *The Monster Squad*. Islas keeps his beast off-camera for much of the runtime, building suspense from POV angles and sounds of panting. But in the final act when all is revealed, one can't help but laugh and applaud the ingenuity (the film's white wolf appears to be made of cotton). Suspense is the main draw, highlighted in a sequence involving four young girls rehearsing for a play. The wolf arrives, tears them to shreds and leaves the handicapped girl pissing in her wheelchair. This is a werewolf film done right. Oh, and we get to see a stuttering kid eat a condom on his birthday. Recommended.

GOBLIN
1993, Color, 75 min
STARRING: *Bobby Westrick, Mike Hellman, Jenny Admire, Kim Alber, Dana Cheney*
DIRECTOR: *Todd Sheets*

A young couple move into an old house with a chained-up well outside. Together with friends, they unchain it and open a locked suitcase found in the cellar. Inside the suitcase is a diary which (when read aloud) awakens a goblin that kills and disembowels the group.

More direct than most, *Goblin* benefits from isolated locations and a focused story. The goblin (looking like a wolfman dressed in rags) wields interesting weapons while attacking his victims. There's a sickle to the crotch, a power-drill in the eye and bare hand disembowelments. And our victims are a nice mix of mindless 20somethings only interested in pizza and partying. The film zips along quickly too (which can't be said for all Sheets productions). But *Goblin* does resort to zombie territory with an ending that literally raises the dead because hey, Sheets loves zombies. Yet this is a solid, unpolished splatter flick that entertains because it knows what it is. Just watch out for that power drill! Recommended.

GOROTICA
1993, Color, 60 min
STARRING: *Ghetty Chasun, Dingo Jones, Bushrude Gutterman, Brady Debussey*
DIRECTOR: *Hugh Gallagher*

Two bank robbers steal a diamond. One swallows it for safety but is gunned down by police. The other drags the body to a cemetery where they happen upon Carrie. Aroused by dead bodies, Carrie brings the two home where she proceeds to have sex with the dead thief. Carrie eventually sells the thief's body to another man (infected with AIDS) so he too can have sex with it. But the living thief still needs to get the diamond back.

Shot in three days under original title *Wake the Dead*, *Gorotica* is a brisk piece of perversion from returning director Gallagher. Essentially a showcase for necrophilia (sexual acts or attraction towards corpses, previously seen in Jorg Buttgereit's *Nekromantik* films),

Gallagher brings corpse fucking horrors stateside. Are you ready? Erotically presented, Gallagher wastes no time bringing the plot forward. Chasun (a fearless performance artist at the time) strips and masturbates with a rotten skull while images of dead bodies appear on television. Later as she showers with the dead thief, she (again) wastes no time mounting the stiff in the bathtub. And to this end, the film works extremely well.

Selling the corpse to a man infected with AIDS, erotic interests subvert as infection enters the story. Sex has gone from perverted to disgusting, from erotic to now deadly; yet we cannot look away. The film climaxes in a wild threesome as Chasun adorns herself in leather, then whips the infected man while he penetrates the corpse below. Then the *living* thief arrives. He kills the infected man and becomes exposed to AIDS in the process. The film marvelously showcases Chasun, electrically stealing every minute she's onscreen. And performances are fully committed, letting the audience know they're in for a wild ride. Chasun was apparently discovered by Donald Farmer after witnessing one of her live performances. He then recommended her to Gallagher before casting her himself in *Red Lips*. Highly Recommended.

HALLOWEEN HORRORS
1993, Color, 58 min
STARRING: *Sal Longo, Clancey McCauley, Gary Whitson, Launa Kane, Diana Lea*
DIRECTOR: *G.W. Lawrence (Gary Whitson)*

Under the cover of halloween, a man kidnaps two sisters with intentions to extort $500,000 from their father.

Filmed in 1992, *Halloween Horrors* is more kidnap-for-ransom than anything spooky.

Whitson plays the kidnapper, chaining girls in his torture-like dungeon while he waits for money. Longo plays the father, giving a solid performance (though his age is about the same as his daughters). And the film does find some mileage with its use of halloween costumes and a plastic pumpkin. But this is a ransom movie all the way; pay me or I kill the girls. *Halloween Horrors* never loses the audience with plot twists (some nice ones play out), but its horrific themes rest solely in the title.

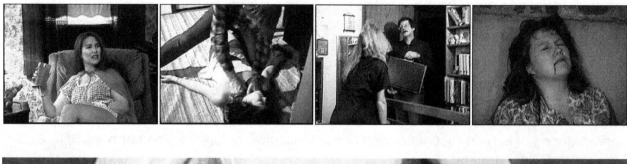

HELLSPAWN
1993, Color, 86 min
STARRING: *Brian Berry, Sebastian Barran, 'Big' Dale Storm, Mark Polonia, Gary LeBlanc*
DIRECTOR: *John Polonia, Mark Polonia*

A woman births a creature so demonic, it kills everyone in the delivery room. Years later, the now-grown creature returns to kill while searching for its father. Only two guys on a paid vacation stand in its way.

Wider in scope than any Polonia film before it, *Hellspawn* is notable for many reasons. Several familiar faces appear including both John and Mark, Mark's wife, Todd Rimatti, Todd Carpenter, Marion Costly and others. Locations feature both of the brothers' homes, while music and sound cues would be continually reused in films to come. But *Hellspawn's* expanded plot deserves attention. Like *Frankenstein*, this creature is really just lonely for compassion. It reads fairy tales and sheds tears. The main characters are old friends but one is secretly coping with a life-threatening condition. And indeed, a strong thread of tragedy runs throughout the picture. This is what matures *Hellspawn* beyond its rubber mask silliness, and elevates it as one of the brothers' best. Technical aspects are improved here too, showcasing creative angles and colored lighting throughout. And the movie is just plain fun. The film apparently didn't perform well with wider audiences though, likely due to limited availability and underexposed advertising. But the film impresses and is certainly worthy of a second look. Highly Recommended.

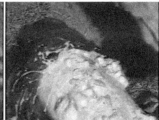

HIGH KICKS
1993, Color, 83 min
STARRING: *Tara Lee-Anne Roth, Dennis Swarthout, Sandy Kay, Kevin Knotts*
DIRECTOR: *Ruta K. Aras*

An aerobics instructor is gang-raped after work. Recovering from her ordeal (and at the behest of her new employee), she trains in the art of kung-fu.

Can *I Spit On Your Grave* be considered horror? Ruta K. Aras would think so, and it certainly contains extremely horrific themes. *High Kicks* uses these themes and turns a gang-raped victim into a lethal weapon. But where *I Spit* presented an uncomfortably protracted and gritty horror, *High Kicks* glosses with a PG-rated shine.

This is not a violent rape film. Unlike *Death Wish*, *Demented* or *Ms. 45*, *High Kicks* is about the awakening of senses. Nowhere is rape glorified, but it seems very sanitized at times. Rape is the catalyst that propels the story (for better or worse), turning victim into kung-fu dispatcher. But the film also doubles as a romance, allowing the victimized to fall in love with her long-haired savior. The rapists are systematically attacked and beaten throughout the movie, leading to a final confrontation where all lessons are learned. But this seems almost like a kids show gone bad. *High Kicks* ultimately uses the same elements as *I Spit*, but emphasizes its romantic action. Is that in bad taste? Perhaps. But the film plays well and hinges on a great performance from Roth (who sadly stopped acting soon after). Average.

MIDNIGHT 2: SEX, DEATH AND VIDEOTAPE

1993, Color, 68 min
STARRING: *Matthew Jason Walsh, Jo Norcia, Chuck Pierce Jr., Sandra Wurzer*
DIRECTOR: *John A. Russo*

In this sequel to 1982's *Midnight*, the surviving son of the devil-worshipping family stalks and kills women while videotaping his actions.

Though official (Russo wrote and directed both entries), *Midnight's* follow-up is a forgettable throwaway representing the worst of sequel cash-ins. J.R. Bookwalter produces and Tempe regulars Norcia, Wurzer and Walsh appear, but it's all for not as the film wallows in abduction, torture and ridiculous narration. *Midnight 2* purports itself to be actual camcorder footage of death, handheld by the killer. Yet it destroys its own illusion with alternate angles and close-ups. Footage from the original appears as Walsh attempts to explain how the films connect (they really don't) but Russo's biggest issue is logic. *Midnight* was a film that needed no sequel. It was a modest horror entry, notable by the names of its participants (Lawrence Tierney, John Amplas) with special make-up by Tom Savini. But here, Russo only has video and a torture chair so he cashes-in for suckers. It's not the first SOV to draw on a forgotten fright flick (*Criminally Insane 2* anyone?) but certainly the most shameless. And at one point, Walsh even states that he's making a sequel to *Silence of the Lambs!* Dreadful.

THE MUMMY'S DUNGEON
1993, Color, 87 min
STARRING: *Sal Longo, Michelle Caporaletti, Christie Clark, Dave Castiglione*
DIRECTOR: *G.W. Lawrence (Gary Whitson)*

A middle-aged creep revives an Egyptian mummy in his house. Advertising in the newspaper, the man poses as a photographer of female models. When women respond, he lures them into his basement and into his mummy's grasp.

Tame on nudity, *The Mummy's Dungeon* feels like a titillation video for Karloff junkies. A porky gentleman welcomes women into his house, takes their picture and lets his mummy work the room. The women constantly faint, so the man chains them to a board. Then our bandaged fiend licks and dry-humps them for fun. And if I haven't already mentioned, I really enjoy W.A.V.E. productions. They're an analog slice of life that doesn't exist much today (though W.A.V.E. has persevered for over 30 years). Yes, girls are chained and slobbered upon. Yes, blood is drooled. Yes, one scene involves a heart. But strangely nothing is graphic or exploited. This is Whitson's genius. He approaches subject matter as it is, allowing sexual violence to mix with passive hilarity. No one's going to see *The Mummy's Dungeon* and be scared of its monster (wonderfully performed by Castiglione). But they will see beautiful girls bound and squirming in various levels of undress. And perhaps that's the point. This is a drive-in movie with a videotaped mindset. Highly Recommended.

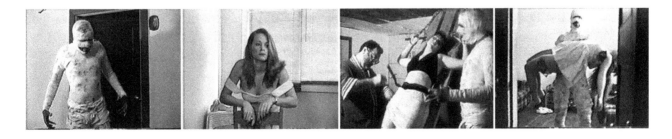

RED SPIRIT LAKE
1993, Color, 69 min
STARRING: *Annabelle Davies, Charles Pinion, Holly Adams, Rick Hall*
DIRECTOR: *Charles Pinion*

When a relative is murdered, the last living heir travels to Red Spirit Lake to spread the ashes. But the property (family owned) has become something of a hot commodity. Murderous developers want it. And the lake appears to be haunted as ghosts of Devil worshippers possess the lands.

Five years after his impressive *Twisted Issues*, Charles Pinion returns to the director's chair in grand style. Artistically framed and colorfully lit, *Red Spirit Lake* challenges the viewer. Aggression pushes the film into a frenzy of character wants and desires. Land developers extort victims by groping their naked breasts. A man burns-up after spending too much time in a sauna. Crack-head housekeepers claim to be abducted by angels and a man dies from a bloody fist-enema. Yet as lurid as it all is, Pinion keeps it real. *Red Spirit Lake* is a beautiful film weaved from a talented man with a message. And perhaps with the exception of the *Dark Romance* volumes, it's crafted in a style rarely seen today. Like *Twisted Issues*, Pinion fills *Red Spirit* with images and themes beyond its literal premise, making repeat viewings a must. This is high-art horror at its best. Recommended.

SCARY TALES
1993, Color, 70 min
STARRING: *Al Darago, Brad Storck, Ilene Zelechowski, Mark Shapiro, Kevin Rogers*
DIRECTOR: *Doug Ulrich, Al Darago*

A ghostly apparition reads three stories to children. "Satan's Necklace" concerns a man transforming into a demon after finding a necklace in the ground. "Sliced in Coldblood" has a man killing his cheating wife before going on a murderous rampage. And finally, "Level 21" is about a man who enters live-action role play when he advances on a computer game.

Bursting with charm, *Scary Tales* gets a lot of things right. Ulrich and Darago zip through their anthology with a zest often missing from the genre. Stories are balanced and filled with impressive special effects. Blood and gore splatter the film with ripped-open skulls and decapitated heads. And "Satan's Necklace" contains a transformation scene reminiscent of *Teen Wolf*. There's fantastic dialogue too, like *"I haven't seen pussy in so long, the crack of dawn looks good to me."* Then a cop grabs his dick twice in 2 minutes. The film is also firmly shot with tripods, lending a great 80's feel (which most 90's entries lack). And best of all, the same actors appear throughout the stories reminiscent of Emmeritus' *Shock Chamber*. *Scary Tales* should make every analog horror fan's wish list. Recommended.

SHATTER DEAD
1993, Color, 82 min
STARRING: *Stark Raven, Flora Fauna, Daniel "Smalls" Johnson, Robert Wells*
DIRECTOR: *Scooter McCrae*

A woman travels through a zombie infested town to reach her boyfriend.

Borrowing heavily from Jean Rollin's *The Grapes of Death*, McCrae's *Shatter Dead* is froth with depressing themes and hopeless characters. But the film's greatest hurdle is it attempts to rewrite established zombie norms. Here, the dead can talk, think and act rationally. Indeed several characters prefer death (dubbed *"folding"*) as it sustains their vanity. And destroying the brain no longer destroys the zombie. But the film's most incredible aspect is its infamous sex scene between Raven (alive) and Johnson (dead). Since being dead doesn't allow for erections, Raven ties a gun to Johnson's waist and fucks it. Graphically. Vaginal penetration appears but there's no beating around the bush, *Shatter Dead* is a depressing tale that takes itself a little too seriously.

  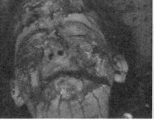 

THINGS

1993, Color, 82 min
STARRING: *Kinder Hunt, Kathleen O'Donnel, Kelly-Jean Dammeyer, Neil Delama*
DIRECTOR: *Dennis Devine, Jay Woelfel, Eugene James*

A philanderer's wife ties-up her husband's mistress and tells her two horrible stories. "The Box" about three prostitutes killed by a mayor's pet, and "Thing in a Jar" about a husband who kills his wife, then is killed by her reanimated body parts.

Things is all over the place. Unlike *Scary Tales* (which assuredly played to its analog senses), *Things* suffers from an identity crisis. Is it a Playboy showcase? A horror anthology? A warning to a cheating spouse? Maybe we shouldn't ask. The film opens with an extremely breezy wraparound. Hunt (as the vengeful wife) impresses with perfect timing and fluidity. Then she wants to tell a story about a slimy creature that attacks everyone except men in hats. Okay. Then she wants to talk about a wife leaving her abusive husband. And just when you think the stories might have relevance to the premise, Hunt whips out her slimy creature and all the mistresses she keeps prisoner in her garage. Huh? Produced by David Sterling, *Things* was a financial hit for the movie mogul. At least three further sequels have materialized. The film is memorable enough, but too drawn out and conflicted with what it wants to be. Its best segment is ultimately the wraparound by director James, shot a year after the two main stories were completed. Average but enjoyable.

TRAPPED!

1993, Color, 91 min
STARRING: *Sal Longo, Michelle Caporaletti, Amanda Madison, Clancey McCauley*
DIRECTOR: *G.W. Lawrence (Gary Whitson)*

A serial rapist is trapping and tormenting women.

More fetish than horror, *Trapped!* illustrates the "customer request" side of W.A.V.E. productions. Four woman inhabit the picture. Each gets snared in a trap, stripped and raped. The cycle only concludes when the rapist is dead. Caporaletti is caught in a bear trap, Madison sticks in glue, McCauley's hung and Christie Clark is caught in the same bear trap (because it worked so well the first time). Movies about rape are usually classified as sexual thrillers, though there's no denying their horrific themes. But rape has often crossed into horror territory (*Henry: Portrait of a Serial Killer*, *I Spit On Your Grave*) when there's a murderous twist or vengeance involved. *Trapped!* features no such twist, though Longo eventually meets his doom via gunshot to the balls. But a heavy, torturous element is present as clothes are stripped by use of a very large knife. Much of the rapes are off-screen (thankfully) and the film sports a higher level of sexual violence than most W.A.V.E. titles. But it's singular focus and repetitive nature are the real issues here.

VIOLENT SHIT 3: INFANTRY OF DOOM
1993, Color, 79 min
STARRING: *Andreas Schnaas, Xiu-Yong Lin, Matthias Kerl, Marc Trinkhaus, Uwe Gruntjes*
DIRECTOR: *Andreas Schnaas*

Three men wash-up on an island after their boat capsizes in the sea. Quickly taken hostage, the men find themselves in a cat and mouse game against mercenaries lead by Karl the butcher. A bloodbath of slaughter follows.

Shot in 1993 and unreleased until 1999 (thanks to shoddy distribution and post-production issues), *Violent Shit 3* is the self-billed conclusion to the *Violent Shit* trilogy. Schnaas out-does himself here, building a world dominated by the Karls and their bloody violence. Indeed there truly was a method behind the *VS2* madness! Now running an empire, both father Karl and Karl junior brutally bask in their royalties with supreme nastiness. Faces are ripped apart, chests are torn open and a crazed doctor appears to be turning men into zombies. At times, the film even feels like a rollicking island adventure plagued with post apocalyptic barbarians! One could easily imagine George Eastman in the lead too, or a producing credited to Joe D'Amato had this been made in Italy. But the film never loses sight of the gore on display (its reason for being). *VS3* is a fantastic conclusion to an otherwise exceptional display of slasher nonsense. It shows directorial growth from Schnaas and restraint when moods need to be tightened. And though originally released in the US as *Zombie Doom*, the film was unique enough that most viewers weren't aware of its *Violent Shit* connection. An epic adventure.

Joel D. Wynkoop and Tim Ritter on Wicked Games (1993)

WICKED GAMES
1993, Color, 80 min
STARRING: *Joel D. Wynkoop, Patricia Paul, Kevin Scott Crawford, Kermit Christman*
DIRECTOR: *Tim Ritter*

After discovering his wife cheating, a man boozes his depression away at a friend's house. But soon, various couples are murdered in town by a knife-wielding maniac wearing a copper mask. Is the man to blame?

An official sequel to 1986's *Truth Or Dare?* (though reportedly reluctant to use the *Truth Or Dare* title, thanks to Madonna's 1991 documentary of the same name), *Wicked Games* is incredible. Shot on video (the original was 16mm), *Wicked Games* uses the same "cheating vengeance" format on all-new characters and it works. Wynkoop steals the show as an aggressive cop with a panache for banging strippers. His presence is unmistakable. And equally impressive is Paul portraying several characters, each sexier than the last. Blood sprays throughout as barbed-wire, machetes, knives and lawn sprinklers are put to gruesome use. And a heavy amount of sleaze permeates with humor and over-the-top performances. Ritter's direction is in top form with precise editing, only besting himself with 1995's *Creep* (arguably his greatest film). But make no mistake, this is 80 minutes of pure Wynkoop and Ritter gold stylistically shot with healthy doses of horror. Required Viewing.

THE WITCHING
1993, Color, 63 min
STARRING: *Auggi Alvarez, Mike Hellman, Frank Dunlay, Dianne O'Connell, Dana Pace*
DIRECTOR: *Eric Black (Matthew Jason Walsh)*

Two guys inadvertently open a door to Hell through their refrigerator, unleashing a witch and her demonic minions.

Produced by Todd Sheets and edited by J.R. Bookwalter (under a Darryl Squatmpump alias), *The Witching* is an interesting picture. Directed by Walsh (also using an alias), the film looks like a Sheets production with comedy in place of gore. Sheets regulars Alvarez,

Hellman and Dunlay appear and all do fine, but the real star is the film's tone. *The Witching* brims with deadpan jokes and bad one-liners (*"let's make like a baby and head out!"*). But the comedic elements and interesting camera tricks belie its poverty-row budget. Impressively, the film contains early computer animation (morphing) as a character transforms into a frog, and explosions occur during the finale. Yet the action is occasionally bogged down with lengthy exposition. *The Witching* is a fun discovery in the long list of forgotten SOV entries. It's no diamond in the rough, but it is an exciting Bookwalter/Walsh collaboration with Todd Sheets support.

ZOMBIE BLOODBATH
1993, Color, 88 min
STARRING: *Auggi Alvarez, Chris Harris, Frank Dunlay, Jerry Angell, Cathy Metz*
DIRECTOR: *Todd Sheets*

A nuclear disaster reanimates dead bodies into flesh-eating zombies. A few friends (and their parents) fight to stay alive.

The pinnacle of Sheets' zombie madness and the first of a trilogy, *Zombie Bloodbath* is not without its problems. Overlong and disorganized, much of the action repeats itself through nameless faces and gore. But while most may falter under these conditions, *Zombie Bloodbath* sings. This is not Sheets' first rodeo, but this is his first attempt at making a real movie.

Already hugely familiar with zombies, Sheets somehow crafts an enjoyable, kick-ass entry in the done-to-death subgenre. The man knows what he's doing. Centered around knowledgeable youths (and eager to please parents), *Bloodbath* puts itself closer to the heart. Who else wouldn't mind watching *Zombie Rampage* after a late night cookout? Beautifully cast with Trustinus regulars, Sheets gathers a regional showcase of stunted line deliveries and massive mullets. And an incredible level of charm. *Zombie Bloodbath* is earnest and true to itself as Sheets' believes this to be his thirteenth video production. Thirteenth! Shot over a couple of months with a cast of 700 (mostly playing zombies), Sheets used numerous video formats to bring this epic to life. Rock and Roll dude! Highly Recommended.

Originally released on Cinema Home Video, *Zombie Bloodbath* was re-edited and shortened by 10 minutes for its Camp Motion Picture DVD release. Bogus!

Todd Sheets (center) and crew on Zombie Bloodbath (1993)

ZOMBIE GENOCIDE
1993, Color, 65 min
STARRING: *Darryl Sloan, Paul Barton, Jason Morrison, Andrew Morrison*
DIRECTOR: *Andrew Harrison, Khris Carville, Darryl Sloan*

Teenagers return from a camping trip to discover their town completely overrun by flesh-eating zombies.

An Irish zombie film with a twist, *Zombie Genocide* is a wonderful slice of juvenile genre love. With direct (and subtle) references to George Romero and his dead films, *Genocide* stands apart from other zombie rip-offs by shining new light on an old story. This is entirely told from the perspectives of four youths; a first-person experience caught in a zombie apocalypse. What would you do if everyone you knew was dead and walking around? Hilarious in execution (yet filled with suspense), it's easy to see shades of what would influence *Shaun of the Dead* a decade later. But *Genocide* stays ahead of the pack with an outrageous ending that could only make Stephen King proud. Burn up the popcorn and check this one out. Required Viewing!

ZOMBIE NIGHTMARE
1993, Color, 88 min
STARRING: *Sal Longo, Aven Warren, Cristie Clark, Amanda Madison, Clancey McCauley*
DIRECTOR: *G.W. Lawrence (Gary Whitson)*

A scientist kidnaps and poisons young women before reanimating them, hoping to learn how to reanimate his cryogenically frozen wife.

An interesting premise, but *Zombie Nightmare* has only one thing on its mind. Get women in that electric chair and shock away! Lingerie clad ladies shuffle and shake to the powers flowing through them, and W.A.V.E. strikes again. Best shaking goes to McCauley, enjoying a slow-mo boobie-jiggle that must be seen to be believed. And Clark pulls double duty as the frozen wife and later as kidnapped victim (without mention of how identical they both look). Warren hilariously lumbers as the face-mangled henchman, while Longo delivers his requisite psycho performance. Some repetition comes with *Zombie Nightmare*, but a standout moment of Warren repeatedly reaching for Madison's breasts (while Longo keeps slapping him away) is laugh out loud. Supreme fun while it lasts. Recommended!

ZOMBIE TOXIN
1993-1996, Color, 69 min
STARRING: *Thomas J. Moorse, Adrian Ottiwell, Lee Simpson, Robert Taylor*
DIRECTOR: *Thomas J. Moorse*

When a bucket of horse parts gets dumped into a nearby river, a zombie toxin is unwittingly unleashed throughout an English countryside.

Like *Bad Taste*, *Zombie Toxin* is a wild and zany gross-out from start to finish. Stylishly shot and loaded with gore, Moorse's breakout epidemic is not to be missed for fans of do-it-yourself cheapies. And with characters as varied as Adolf Hitler, kids wearing googly-eyed glasses and drooling buck-teethed scientists, no one is watching this for the story. Gore is the point as arms are severed by running trains, diseased horse legs are hacked off and pimply assholes spew liquid shit (I kid you not). Moorse and his team reportedly wanted *"side-splitting laughter"* and they got it with their antics. But like the work of Zachary Winston Snygg (*The Bloody Video Horror That Made Me Puke On My Aunt Gertrude*), the unfettered zaniness of it all wears thin quick. Great fun in small doses.

Released in 1996.

 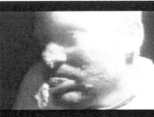  

Interview
PHIL "CHIP" HERMAN

Shooting in and around Queens, New York, Phil "Chip" Herman and his team Falcon Video made a name for themselves. Through determination and a balls-out love of movies, they made SOV slashers and post-apocalyptic video nasties with independent passion. With handheld camcorders and a lot of heart, Phil and his team pushed video entertainment into areas it's rarely gone since. Totally accessible and completely hilarious, Phil's SOV entries have become some of the most fondly remembered films of the genre. *Arena of Death! Burglar From Hell! Jacker!* 30 years later and Phil is still making movies today.

Phil, thank you for giving your time to this interview! What initially inspired you to make movies?

When I was young, I always loved watching old Hammer movies and then the 70's slasher flicks. The final step was when I was terrified yet amazed at a small movie called *Halloween*. That did it. I said *"I want to scare people and have fun!"* Shortly after, I got my first video camera. A Hitachi camcorder. It was the clunky 2 part version. Was a 20lb camera and it attached to an equally heavy VHS portable player. So now nobody in the neighborhood was safe and blood was all over. Friends, neighbors, family members were all being killed. I was living the dream and thought I was freaking amazing. Kids were lined up to be killed by the nutty kid down the block.

I was making a movie every few days. They were only shorts. But had credits, music and FX. Pretty damn good for low budget. I was getting itchy I wanted to do a feature. But not yet!

Phil Herman versus Chip Herman - one in the same?

Oh yes they were. It is simple. It added another name to the credits. It looked like there were more people working on the project than there was. Chip was my nickname givien to me by my mother. In my earlier movies it was used then fazed out when I started doing features with my real name... Philip. Which is, more mature. It's funny because it is a childhood name very few people call me that. Not even my wife does. But is so nice when I hear someone call me Chip cause I know they're an old friend then.

Online credits have often been misleading, which films did you personally direct?

All of them (laughing). The ones you're covering in your book. *Jacker, Burlgar From Hell* and *Hell on Earth: Arena of Death* are mine. I wrote all the stories. *Hell On Earth* though I wrote with my then partner Matt O'Connor. We equally dedicated a half a decade to that movie. I directed the beginning and end and he did the rest with a few exceptions. It was grueling that one. See my movies, I wore all hats. I wrote, casted, directed, edited, produced and starred. But I wanted everyone to keep playing with me so I gave them titles. *Burglar* was 100% mine. I was able to go nuts with that and really pushed the envelope on that one. I gave credit for *Jacker* to Ben. But he pretty much just listened to me and shot the movie and claimed to be director. The only one who I can honestly say directed one of my movies is Barry Gaines when I returned in *Jacker 2*. It got to be too much to do everything and stay in character. The script was very demanding and needed a fresh director. Barry watching from the sidelines all those years stepped up and made me proud.

How was Falcon Video created? Did it include your regular group of Bryant Sohl, Ben Stanski, Barry Gaines?

Hell on Earth: Arena of Death was our first real big movie. We thought it was going to be the next *Omega Man/Road Warrior*. So we said lets become a real company. I chose Falcon Video. My Mom is a big *Star Wars* fan and it played homage to the Millennium Falcon. So we got a lawyer and made Falcon a real company. It was Ben, Matt and I. What a crock of shit that was. We weren't making money and paying at the end of the year to the IRS for corporate taxes. We dissolved and it cost us a pretty penny.

But no matter what, all the boys were always reunited and did what we did best.

We always came together and made fun movies that have endured over the years. Barry, Ben, Bryant, Matt and myself. We were the driving force of Falcon Video. A big driving force now is my buddy Joel D. Wynkoop. He fell in love with *Burglar From Hell*. I had always dreamed of a remake with him as the Burglar. He even auditions in the movie *Tales till the End* for the part. Since then he has been in every one of my movies. We had fans that liked that we always had the same characters. We switched up so we would not be type casted. What was fun is that we never fought or had problems with the stories or characters. Everyone had input and was able to add lib if they pleased. I tried making the characters similar to the actor.

One of your earliest features was billed as a sequel to an original film (that has yet to be released) - *Hell On Earth 2: Arena of Death*. Beginning in 1992 and taking years to complete, was *Hell On Earth* a massive learning experience in independent filmmaking?

It was a lesson to *"Don't bite off more than you can chew."*

We made *Hell on Earth* the original in 30 days. Even that was ambitious and took us off the block. It was all over desolate places with a large cast. It got a cult following and people liked [it]. So we said lets go big. Lets not write with restrictions. Lest write a story and worry about if we can do things later.

We always kidded around and said it was our *Waterworld*. [It's] the problem with movies with a large cast (not getting paid) working in the elements (snow, rain and heat). Filming most of the movie on Parks Department controlled parks. No permits. We broke down walls, had fires, built cells from old bunkers. We took over an abandoned World War II army base. There were times when we had 20 people at a time in "end of the world" mutant garb. There were bird watchers, nature lovers and us. The park police were always on our backs. To make things easier we used to hide our costumes and weapons in this old abandoned bunker. Break up into small groups and meet up in certain areas. The parts were the jail cells were we built all by ourselves. We found bed frames and wired them together with working doors and looked authentic.

The Arena of Death was an abandoned bath house and it became our Arena. One of our members got arrested when we got raided by the park police. Accidently we turned on all the lights in the area during a pivotal fight scene. This movie had so many stories and almost made us never to shoot a movie again. It was too demanding and took a lot of time and energy from our lives. Actors could not take filming long hours with no pay under the elements and dropped out. Friends were lost and minds. We had a meltdown and stopped filming for a bit. It took 6 years but we had a premiere and it has become a cult favorite. I am having problems locating the original. The original master was swept away in Hurricane Sandy and still trying to track down a copy.

***Burglar From Hell* is one of my most favorite films. It's absolutely hilarious! *Jacker* on the other hand, is more mean-spirited and pessimistic. Were the two films designed to contrast each other?**

You hit the nail on the head with that. We filmed the two movies simultaneously. *Burglar* was light hearted fun. *Jacker* was a movie where I said the hero is a villain. You feel for the killer. *Burglar* was a homage to the 80's slasher flicks. *Jacker* was my answer to the headlines. There was a carjacking problem at the time and I said let's do it. I wanted people after the finish of *Jacker* say *"what the hell!"* This dude was a bad ass heartless mutha.... You laughed and had fun with *Burglar*. *Jacker* you sat there and did not feel good or laugh. It was gritty and real. We felt we achieved that. To this day I get offers for remakes on *Jacker* but nothing ever materializes.

Soon-to-be Scream Queen Debbie D's earliest appearance is in *Burglar From Hell*. Do you recall how she was cast?

We saw a photography magazine and there was an ad. We contacted her then manger/photographer Bill Arthur. She had taken acting lessons and was looking into movies. She was a musician at the time. We fell in love with her and after first meeting we knew we had our Heather for *Burglar From Hell*. She was the dream girl. Being tutored by the nerd Bookie. Her role was the most memorable. She was so good we cast her for *Jacker*, and every movie after that! She is the girl next door American sweetheart. You can never work with an actress so dedicated as her.

A similar visual style is shared across your early films, specifically the handheld "caught on camera" feel. It gives urgency to the story. Were things purposely shot handheld?

I chose that way to get into the action. I felt the camera got into the scene. I hated filming on a tripod. It gave a stiff look. I liked the floating of the camera in that sense. We all shot hand held. I feel if you shoot on a tripod it looks like it is being staged. With handheld you can run around and get into the action. To this day I still use that style. I have this cool thing where I can attach the camera to it and it looks like a boomerang. I can run around and really get into the action. But never say "tripod" to me or the crew.

W.A.V.E. Productions regular David Castiglione is credited as editor on *Jacker 2: Descent To Hell*. How did you first meet David? What else have you worked on together?

We had met through WAVE. David had editing experience and the equipment. Barry had the notes and the vision. Barry took the trek from NY to Jersey and for 8 hours and banged out the flick. David is a tremendous talent and good friend. We also worked on *Before I Die*. Plans are in the early stages of doing something with WAVE. We have been friends for over 20 years but never met.

You also have connections with Gary Whitson. Have you ever worked with Gary?

WAVE and I have been dealing with each other for over 20 years. Gary Whitson is a dear friend and really helped me out a lot. He was my distributor for years. He made a lot of money for me. He really put me out there and got me a following. I also shot two segments for features produced by him. We have plans this year for me to act in a feature of his this spring. Gary has been a mentor all these years and don't want it to end, so will be doing things on an off for years to come.... God willing.

How were most of your films distributed during the 1990's? Did you sell direct to viewers through magazine advertisements?

Wow it was rough. What we sold all those years before the internet, was done in one month by our new distributor Chris Woods (The Sleaze Box). He gave new life to what I call the original five. *Burlgar*, *Tales*, *Jacker* 1 and 2, *Before I Die*. But yes it was through magazines like Draculina, Fangoria. Everything was self distribution. It was rough. Very slow going. But WAVE was the beginning of our road to distribution and fan base. We took out ads in all indy fanzines and movie mags.

A rumor has persisted that New Line Cinema was at one time interested in remaking *Burglar From Hell*. Is there any truth to this (and if so, what happened)?

LOL yeah. It was the time of *Nightmare on Elm Street*. Robert Shaye was interested and an associate was in contact with me. It never went past that. I have a letter somewhere but can't find. They will deny but I always felt honored. I think it was the time they went mainstream and the days of *Elm Street* where gone and they were focusing more on big budget flicks.

In closing I would like to thank you. I have been doing this for almost 3 decades, I have not made the million yet. But I have touched a lot of people and have a loyal following. Who would of known that a 16 year old with a VHS camera would still be doing this at 50? My movies still do well at the level there at. I am still shopping around ideas and scripts and still feel a big company (Blumhouse, The Asylum, SpectreVison) to name a few will come calling. Hey how many handheld or remakes can be done? Let's get original and let's face it I have been around longer than them. But if not I had fun and did more than most people can say... I created many movies. I made people laugh, cower and damn I get to be whoever I want to be.

Thank you so much for your time and thoughts, Phil!

"CONRAD BROOKS VS. WEREWOLF"

L)-David "THE ROCK" Nelson("WEREWOLF") attacks
R)-Conrad Brooks in "CONRAD BROOKS VS WEREWOLF"

*CONRAD BROOKS, star of Ed Wood's famous films, is now working with "The Ed Wood of the 90's"- David "THE ROCK" Nelson. *See this collaberation of 2 cult figures spanning 40 years!

*For your VHS copy, send a $14.95 MONEY ORDER TO:

DAVID NELSON
1170 E. Howard ave
Des Plaines, Il 60018

Chapter 16
CONVENTIONS, CUSTOMS & MAIL ORDER (1994)

The 90's were dominated by SOV individuals. The Polonia brothers, Hugh Gallagher, Todd Sheets, Gary Whitson - names that persevered by pushing self-mobilized camcorder productions. Magazine ads and conventions were now the marketplace, selling direct to consumers on an individual basis. Occasionally the odd SOV might still appear on video store shelves, but that was becoming exceedingly rare.

Selling through magazines was profitable in these pre-internet days, particularly if a niche could be established. Gary Whitson's W.A.V.E. Productions were a constant hit (he frankly couldn't turn them out fast enough) and the works of Hugh Gallagher and Carl J. Sukenick were so distinguished, their names alone carried their fanbase. But these were isolated sales sent through the mail without personal contact. Custom orders might occur, where a buyer paid an extra fee to dictate the plot or onscreen action, but a physical distance between buyer and seller still remained.

And then came the conventions.

Surrounded by film starlets and genre advertising, SOV filmmakers got to personally interact with their clientele at conventions - incredibly important to most independents' longevity. For the first time, fans could meet and speak with the directors and stars of their favorite SOV cheapie, and buy more films down the line. Building relationships with viewers ensured future product had homes to go into, and in some cases, it even lead to movies produced literally on the spot. And video's impromptu nature truly knew no bounds.

After shooting a handful of completely original shorts, David "The Rock" Nelson met Conrad Brooks at a Famous Monsters convention in May of 1993. The meeting sparked Nelson to hire Brooks for his first feature film *Conrad Brooks VS Werewolf*. A young woman experessed acting interest to Gary Whitson and Sal Longo at a 1994 Chiller Theatre convention. They immediately started shooting, turning then-unknown Tina Krause into an instantly recognizable Scream Queen that very day. Ron Bonk met his *The Vicious Sweet* lead Sasha Graham while splitting a Chiller table with Kevin J. Lindenmuth. And the list goes on. Conventions became the nucleus where action took place.

But with so many SOV films produced by so many individuals, their presence became harder to track. What if you didn't read Draculina? What if you didn't attend conventions? To combat this, newer magazines were created solely by people trying to sell films. Alternative Cinema was created by the people behind Tempe Video to help sell SOV releases. But everything had to become an opportunity now. Independents couldn't just make their own movies anymore, they had to learn how to advertise them too.

ATTACK OF THE MUTANT ROADKILL & THE VAMPYRE ZOMBIES FROM BEYOND THE GRAVE
1994, Color, 50 min
STARRING: *Dan Malin, Lorraine Lash, John Dulles, Biff St. Hibbins, Brandy Schlush*
DIRECTOR: *Harold Olminsky*

A scientist accidently spills toxins into a small community's lake. Soon, dead animals and deceased townsfolk return to life as bloodthirsty cannibalistic zombies.

More comedy than horror, Olminsky's *Attack of the Mutant Roadkill* is a throwaway venture in zombie-spoof cinema. Everything takes place in a town famous for its roadkill (and a graveyard with Elvis impersonations), so it doesn't take a rocket scientist to see where this is going. Roadkill ends up being fuzzy *Critters*-like furballs (hilariously pulled along with strings) and zombies lumber around moaning *"thank you, thank you very much."* But the fun is constantly interrupted with faux-commercials and a poverty-row host who openly trashes the film. Huh? Charming yet pointless.

CITY OF THE VAMPIRES
1994, Color, 82 min
STARRING: *Matthew Jason Walsh, Anne-Marie O'Keefe, Pam Simmons, Noel Bonk*
DIRECTOR: *Ron Bonk*

A city is overrun by vampires. Mourning the loss of his girlfriend, a reluctant hero seeks revenge against the bloodsuckers who took her. He succeeds with the help of a weapons savvy woman.

Filled with good intentions, *City of the Vampires* aims high. Noteworthy as Ron Bonk's first feature (and shot with a budget of $3500), Bonk would eventually become a legend in the independent community with a slew of successful films released under his distribution company SRS Cinema. But here's where things began with three notable impressions: the film has style, influence and the feeling that there's a better film within itself.

Unfortunately Walsh, who was compelling in *Kingdom of the Vampire* (no relation beyond title), is very dismal here. Is he really just sore about his girlfriend? Do vampires make him cry? We're never really sure, and it's particularly bothersome as he's the main hero. Then we're introduced to Max, a well-armed female Van Helsing. Max has been surviving vamp attacks by boarding herself in a booby-trapped house (complete with garlic at the front door) and Max has weapons. And as Walsh joins her, we can't help but feel like we're following the wrong character. Max has the drive and ability to fight back while Walsh just mopes. And though *City* never quite shakes its 90's Tarantino feel, the craftsman working behind the camera is what really grabs our attention. These are the humble beginnings of a successful filmmaker, producer and distribution kingpin. Like Donald Farmer and the Polonia brothers, Ron Bonk took a chance and started making movies because he desperately wanted to. He met the right people and learned to follow his gut after taking a film seminar. He tried and suceeded, and he has since gone on to direct several award-winning pictures throughout the years (*The Vicious Sweet*, *She Kills*, *House Shark*). This was just his first step learning the ropes, and you can feel his enthusiasm run throughout.

CONRAD BROOKS VS. WEREWOLF
1994, Color, 44 min
STARRING: *Conrad Brooks, Ted Brooks, Henry Bederski, David "Rock" Nelson*
DIRECTOR: *David "Rock" Nelson*

When Henry Bederski is attacked and killed by a werewolf, brothers Conrad and Ted hunt the beast for revenge.

After making a handful of camcorder shorts, David "Rock" Nelson (a former US Marine, street preacher and Golden Glove boxer from 1976 to 1991) embarked on his first feature-length motion picture *Conrad Brooks VS. Werewolf*. Well, a 44 minute feature with 2 hours of bonus content. Get ready to experience *"The Ed Wood of the 90's - and beyond!"*

Hired through a chance meeting at a convention, Nelson enlists B-movie legend Conrad Brooks (*Plan 9 From Outer Space* and several other Ed Wood classics) to play himself hunting a werewolf. Brothers Ted and Henry ride side-saddle since they're part of the deal, and we're off! Amaze yourself with the beauty of analog editing. Scenes play, replay then are chopped up as they play again. Everyone looks at the camera when delivering lines.

Conrad spends half the film carrying a kid's toy gun (*"this Uzi will get him!"*) and the other half changing shirts and swinging a bat. Nelson himself plays the werewolf, growling at everything and anything. And references to *Plan 9*, Ed Wood and Tor Johnson run wild.

This is bottom of the barrel gold.

The film climaxes in a never-ending assault of Conrad's car and random insults. *"This one's for the Marines! This one's for Bela Lugosi!"* And my personal favorite, *"This gun's got no effect!"* as Connie's toy Uzi fails to deliver. Interestingly (and as would be standard in later Nelson pictures), *Conrad VS. Werewolf* does not feature crazed narration over scenes. Live location sounds (crickets, airplanes, birds and shoe scuffs) fill the soundtrack naturally. Dialogue is sparse but effective. And violence, while comical, is surprisingly bloody (it's ketchup). Back-story never happens and nothing should be taken seriously. This is a conflict-only affair with a solid A+ for entertainment. Highly Recommended!

Conrad Brooks and David "Rock" Nelsion

CRYSTAL FORCE 2: DARK ANGEL
1994, Color, 88 min
STARRING: *Paul Bruster, Chris Zawalalski, Betsy Gardner, Gloria Lusiak, Jeff Markle*
DIRECTOR: *James Mackinnon*

A smooth talking minion from Hell bribes a bartender for his soul.

Like *Wicked Games* and *Criminally Insane 2* before it, *Crystal Force 2* is a video sequel to a celluloid original. *Crystal Force* was a 1990 erotic thriller with emphasis on sex. *Crystal Force 2* is a 1994 SOV sequel with emphasis on (you guessed it) sex. But with its lowered SOV production value comes a heightened level of camp with homoerotic undertones. Bruster walks into a bar and talks his way into a job. Not directly, mind you. He whispers around people and sort of makes things happen like a powerful genie. But it's all to work alongside Zawalalski and gain his trust. Why? Zawalalski made a super quick wish to have a barmaid's attention. Bruster appears to make it happen. The film is fairly enjoyable thanks to its overtly cheesy dialogue as characters talk (and talk and talk) to the film's benefit. And the sex scenes are somewhat revealing in what they choose to show. But "fairly enjoyable" leaps into hilarity when viewed as a love story between the two men. At one point, Bruster even convinces Zawalalski to wait in the closet while he gets it on! Vampirism comes up briefly, though the real head-scratcher is the titular crystal. What is it? What does it do? No real answers are given as the men play cards for Zawalalski's soul (girls in wet t-shirts dance in the background). I need a beer and some Chinese take-out. But you need this film.

DAMSELVIS: DAUGHTER OF HELVIS
1994, Color/B&W, 60 min
STARRING: *Sherry Lynn Garris, Brady Debussey, Ghetty Chasun, Portia Jeffries*
DIRECTOR: *John Michael McCarthy*

The birth of a new savior through bikers, blood, babes and rock and roll.

Unavailable for review, this is the first film from John Michael McCarthy. The story is based on the Damselvis comic, which McCarthy created. The film was shot in Memphis and is noteworthy for featuring Ghetty Chasun (who starred in *Gorotica* the previous year). *Damselvis* is often described as a comedic fantasy drama, though horror themes may be present. And one character apparently re-enacts the MGM lion towards the end.

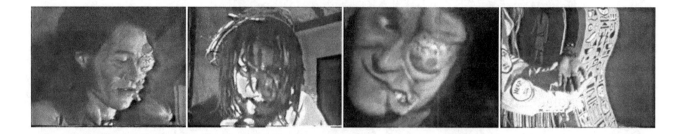

DARK DESCENT
1994-1995, Color, 70 min
STARRING: *James L. Edwards, Ariauna Albright, Theresa Constantine, Jason Burke*
DIRECTOR: *Matthew Jason Walsh, Ron Bonk*

An anthology of two stories: "I've Killed Before" concerning a serial killer and his would-be student, and "Permanent Waves" about a widow haunted by an abusive husband.

Released in 1997, *Dark Descent* is a workman's project. Originally planned much longer, Walsh and Bonk flex directorial muscles in their own dramatic shorts (there is no wraparound). "I've Killed Before" will be familiar to horror audiences, serving as inspiration later expanded into 1997's *Bloodletting*. Edwards and Albright are powerful with a deadly chemistry onscreen. But the flourishing artist is Bonk in "Permanent Waves." Creatively directed, shades of *The Vicious Sweet* surround Constantine's world unraveling into a mini *Repulsion*. Both tales are good but suffer from short runtimes.

DARKEST SOUL

1994, Color, 62 min
STARRING: *Al Darago, Jeff Witte, Heather Brown, Doug Ulrich*
DIRECTOR: *Doug Ulrich*

Best friends Mark and Tommy work a series of dead-end jobs, drink beer and smoking cigarettes. Becoming grave diggers, they find new wealth stealing valuables from corpses.

Though unavailable for review, I first caught a screening of *Darkest Soul* around 2009. I recall one character constantly in a leather-jacket, with the two spending their time smoking at the docks. Mark and Tommy are social outcasts (though one tries to join a popular crowd). The film is enjoyable, sort of *Clerks* without the slapstick. But it really isn't horror.

THE DIVIDING HOUR

1994-1995, Color, 83 min
STARRING: *Michael J. Prosser, Brad Goodman, Greg James, Jillian Hodges, Brian Prosser*
DIRECTOR: *Michael J. Prosser*

A group of men rob a bank. Leaving town, they crash their car and find solace with a girl and her blind/deaf father. But not all is as it seems.

 Co-written, produced and directed by star Michael Prosser, *The Dividing Hour* is an impressive dramatic thriller. Shot on Hi-8 for $7000, the film dealt with a number of problems during production. The shooting location was a 5 hour trip for some cast and crew, which they could only travel on weekends (they had day-jobs). A neighbor in the area would constantly plow his fields, forcing production to stall for noise. A generator was ultimately needed anyway (creating even more noise) so all sound had to be dubbed. And a back road was a tourist route with cars zipping by constantly. But Prosser persisted, adding some impressive computer effects and stop-animation along the way.

The Dividing Hour really isn't a horror film (and really isn't a thriller either) but tension builds thanks to the characters' increasing paranoia. Without spoiling the ending, the film questions whether certain events are actually happening. Characters witness an empty fridge repeatedly supply food. People are killed and later appear uninjured. And strange ghostly beings wander the woods. Is it a dream or drug-fuelled hallucination? A rape occurs and characters are bloodily shot (some in the head), but gore is never emphasized. This is a character piece about fate; decisions leading to permanent outcomes. Sort of a thinking man's purgatory on videotape. Roger Ebert claimed *"it sneaks up on you"* during a 2000 airing of *"Roger Ebert & the Movies,"* co-hosted by Harry Knowles.

After it's rocky production (and post-production headaches), *The Dividing Hour* was completed in 1998 and released in 2000. The film was reportedly re-edited in 2003 for its DVD release.

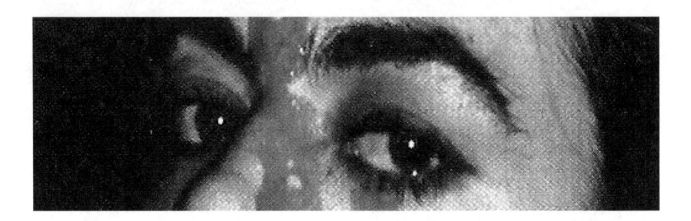

GORE WHORE
1994, Color, 70 min
STARRING: *Audrey Street, Brady Debussey, D'Lana Tunnell, Paul Woodard*
DIRECTOR: *Hugh Gallagher*

An investigator tracks the girl who stole a scientist's experimental formula. But the girl was a dead prostitute who, with the aid of the formula, has now been reanimated with a thirst for blood.

Shot in five days, Gallagher strikes again with a bizarre and sleazy *Re-Animator* riff. And in the right frame of mind, *Gore Whore* can be a lot of fun. There's a high level of comedy here not found in Gallagher's previous films. But the comedy somewhat downplays its tone. Formula injections occur (via a serum-filled black dildo) straight into the ass. The gore whore Dawn is literally called "Dawn of the dead." A grunge band plays Spin the Bottle with Dawn as the bottle. It's a crazy mix with explicit nudity and bloody murders.

The opening (Dawn stripping and biting off a man's penis) works well, but the film quickly pivots into fractured characters and hopeless ambitions. *Gore Whore* feels written as a serious piece; *Gorotica* with added slapstick. But then the comedy pops-in and things just don't gel. Was Gallagher trying to lighten the mood? Hilariously, the film is dedicated to Lorena Bobbitt.

HIGH DESERT
1994, Color, 73 min
STARRING: *Edward B. Glinski, Ron Jason, Tyleen Roberts, Mark Wojcik, Alice Davidson*
DIRECTOR: *Charles T. Lang*

After losing a game of pool to a waitress, Frank and his gang plan revenge. They track the girl to her campsite, kill her boyfriend and rape her. But when Frank double-crosses one of his own, a private war starts between the men.

Taking more from *Wild Riders* than *I Spit On Your Grave*, *High Desert* is a fun biker thriller. Opening with an explosive "trouble on the road" sequence, one might expect another *The Hackers* (or at least a *Hills Have Eyes* clone on wheels). But instead, the film sticks to genre with captive women, booze fuelled chauvinism and extreme potty language. It's entertaining but common to the biker ilk. Yet the use of video is what makes things sizzle. Here, Lang crafts a biker "roughie" on an analog platter. Dolly shots, high angles and cranes all give the film flair. Locations are desert roads, woods and a bar. And performers take risks; riding motorcycles without helmets or safety gear. The film essentially builds to two Vietnam vets with a score to settle (Glinski and Jason). But this is Glinski's film, throwing insults and generally acting like an asshole at all times. Fun with a beer.

HORRORSCOPE

1994, Color, 79 min
STARRING: *Todd Jason Cook, Lisa Cook, Chad Eubanks, Susie Sumner*
DIRECTOR: *Todd Jason Cook*

An anthology of short stories with no wraparound. "La Morte" concerns a guitar player trying to come up with a song name. "Mr. Nice Guy" involves a guy who invites a trio of friends home from a bar, only to murder them. And finally, "The Dummy" is about a girl receiving a ventriloquist doll in the mail, which comes alive and kills her.

With two features under his belt, Todd Cook switches the camcorder back on for *Horrorscope*. And it's incredible. Filled with mid-90's references, regional visits to local bars and an opening scene at a brand new video store, *Horrorscope* earns its accolades. This is a shot on video anthology with all the right moves. And while his previous outings were somewhat muddling, *Horrorscope* knows how to put things right.

Part of the SOV charm is discovering other walks of life. Las Vegas, Tennessee, Oklahoma; movies are memorable thanks to the surroundings they exhibit. And video presents them as is. Dialogue slangs, common haircuts, activities around town; qualities of a community that can't be hidden. All of which *Horrorscope* captures without filter. We're captivated as Cook drives home from a video store, lays around the house and makes a funny drink. He plays guitar, vomits a bit, then calls a friend. And we follow Lisa Cook in the same manner; walking around the house, pouring a drink and calling people on the phone. Then an epiphany happens and we realize our place in the universe: **this is the zenith of shot on video reality**. Watching people do commonly mundane things (living out their lives on camera) is the essence of SOV magic. Doing so within a horror storyline bottles the magic into digestible portions. Take *Blood Lake* with its Oklahoma swagger. Toss in a few beers and you've got one hell of a vacation, but mix in a killer and we're talking horrific nightmare. Well, *Horrorscope* dishes up three boozy vacations with a nightmare twist. And I love it. Wonderfully cheesy, boldly committed and inertly engaging. Highly Recommended!

HUMAN PREY
1994, Color, 73 min
STARRING: *Cliff Drew, Gloria Lusiak, Lena Pointer, Micky Levy, Terry Pohorski*
DIRECTOR: *James Tucker*

A psychologist is mugged after discovering his car broken into. Then his favorite hooker steals his wallet. Now over the edge, the psychologist turns vigilante as he kidnaps hookers and "hunts" them in his private resort.

More dramatic thriller than horror, *Human Prey* nevertheless manages to entertain with bloody knife fights and bound victims. Performances are overly theatrical and stunts are largely kept off-screen. But *Human Prey* so desperately wants to feed its *Most Dangerous Game* plot into its *Falling Down* premise, it can't help but charm. Drew (a cross between Bill Pullman and Michael Moriarty) carries the film well enough, while Pointer is great as the hooker who fights back. Production values are requisitely cheap but there's an overall slickness to the final film. It's short and it delivers. Producer David Sterling cameos too.

JACKER
1994, Color, 87 min
STARRING: *Philip Herman, Patrice Jackson, Barry Gaines, Ben Stanski, Bryant Sohl*
DIRECTOR: *Benjamin Stanski, Philip Herman (uncredited)*

A killer is loose hijacking cars and killing for pleasure. But after he rapes a cop's sister, the officer makes it his personal mission for revenge.

Though credited to Stanski (who was standout hilarious in *Burglar From Hell*), *Jacker* is another dash of New York zaniness from Phil Herman. And returning faces are in abundance too, including another memorable turn from soon-to-be Scream Queen Debbie D. But where *Burglar* excelled with incredible humor and bad taste, *Jacker* is just mean. Herman drives the film, slicing necks and blowing brains out at every turn. He attacks the most vulnerable (unsuspecting young drivers) and relishes in destroying young love. Yikes!

But this is intended; Herman purposefully changed the tone away from *Burglar*. The film features clunky editing and serious continuity issues (hairstyles change as people walk between rooms) but this helps crack the seriousness. *Jacker* is enjoyably nasty. Yet there's a lot of fun here too. Stanski appears as three identical brothers working for the police, comically talking to themselves during an investigation (complete with a porn moustache appropriate for Ron Jeremy). And while violence is abundant, it's Silly Putty bullet holes and watery blood. The rape is handled off-screen and the film ends with an inspired chase and fight sequence. Plus a Barry Gaines directed sequel followed in 1999. Recommended!

Benjamin Stanski and Phil Herman on Jacker (1994)

L.A. AIDS JABBER
1994, Color, 78 min
STARRING: *Jason Majik, Marcy Lynn, Justin Mack, Joy Yurada, Ralph De Leon*
DIRECTOR: *Drew Godderis*

A young man is diagnosed with the AIDS virus. Frantic and angry, he draws his own blood and attacks people with the loaded syringe.

Shot with the same visual indifference as *Las Vegas Bloodbath* (but loaded with *Jacker's* nastiness), *LA AIDS Jabber* (or simply *Jabber*) is an exciting run through the seedy streets of Hollywood. To the film's credit, Majik never suggests sexual orientation as an excuse for his contraction, nor does the film turn preachy over such details. This isn't a docudrama about the perils of unprotected sex. This is a relatively compelling slasher fuelled with fears over a real disease. It's borderline exploitative, but effective nonetheless. Some (possible) behind the scenes issues create for funny moments too, as one character suddenly dies but is mention later as alive. And Majik's angry performance is compelling but weirdly in vein as the end twist is revealed: he didn't actually have AIDS. Huh?!? Then why did the people he attacked suddenly test HIV positive? Nevermind, let's go get a beer.

LOVE IS A STRANGER
1994, Color, 50 min
STARRING: *Christine Cavalier, Dave Castiglione, Champy Frehmel, Sal Longo*
DIRECTOR: *Dave Castiglione*

Fleeing her abusive boyfriend, a woman takes a job with a low-rent photographer. But her new boss is a womanizer with a jealous ex-lover, who wants to kill the competition. A mud wrestle ensues.

Branching into his own video label, W.A.V.E. regular Castiglione directs a tale of jealousy and temptation in *Love Is a Stranger*. And the apple doesn't fall far from the tree. *Love* has W.A.V.E.'s style through and through, complete with familiar faces in front of and behind the camera. The same amateur photography is here too, complete with requisite scenes of lady mud wrestling and undress. But by no means is this a bad thing. Castiglione brings a Jersey coolness to the proceedings with a sharp eye for dream sequences. The audience doesn't suspect the killer for much of the film, mostly thanks to the sleazy characters already surrounding the heroine. Action is hilariously staged (particularly scenes of domestic abuse) and deaths occur when least expected. W.A.V.E. starlet Tina Krause appears in an early cameo (one of her very first appearances) and breasts are exposed during the climactic mud tussle. This is one you won't want to miss. Highly Recommended!

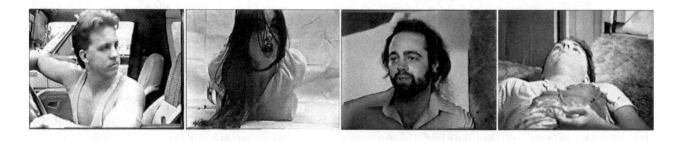

MOONCHILD
1994, Color, 87 min
STARRING: *Auggi Alvarez, Kathleen McSweeney, Dave Miller, Rebecca Rose, Cathy Metz*
DIRECTOR: *Todd Sheets*

A man (who was genetically engineered with DNA from a wolf) escapes imprisonment to search for his son. Lost in a world controlled by a US/Japanese faction called Sodality, the man joins a band of rebels working to overthrow the government.

More post-apocalyptic fantasy than horror, *Moonchild* is Sheets grown up. Indeed, the director's career is often regarded as before and after *Moonchild*; showcasing work as he matures onscreen. Alvarez (a Sheets regular) impresses as leading-man turned werewolf, given much more to do here than usual. From the opening scenes, Alvarez leaps into a moving truck, fistfights numerous thugs, leaps over barb-wired fences and generally kicks ass. Several other regulars appear too, and blood and gore are surprisingly non-existent (yet befitting to the subject matter). The film does indulge in werewolf transformations, keeping tight cuts between drooling fangs and snarling scowls. However, its most impressive aspect is Sheets' tone. This is not a quickie spook-show. *Moonchild* brings gravity to the proceedings with seriousness and believable plot twists. And best of all, you can see everyone's trying their best.

Sheets would continue making horror films post *Moonchild*, but with the maturity he first developed here. And he is still just as active today. Recommended.

MR. ICE CREAM MAN
1994, Color, 66 min
STARRING: *Mack Hail, Henry Weckesser, Jim Mills, Cindy Reed, DeVonn Carral*
DIRECTOR: *Mack Hail*

An ice cream man is stalking and killing kids in a Las Vegas suburb.

In what should be a fun and campy slasher, *Mr. Ice Cream Man* turns into a plodding tale of a man searching for his lost son. Directed by newcomer Hail (who somehow managed to garner impressive reviews in Fangoria magazine), *Mr. Ice Cream Man's* title subverts as the film unfortunately falls flat. Moments of terror are tossed aside with last-minute saves and comic relief. Photography is overwhelmed with endless dolly shots and wide-angle lenses. Children play most of the characters and the film doesn't really capitalize on its premise. Where's the sprinkles?

Two further (and unrelated) ice cream slashers followed with 1995's *Ice Cream Man* starring Clint Howard, and 1997's *Ice Scream* featuring the great Conrad Brooks. Neither connect to Hail's *Mr. Ice Cream Man* (but they could make a nice themed trilogy).

NIGEL THE PSYCHOPATH
1994, Color, 60 min
STARRING: *Jim Larsen, Mike Alves, Rob Hayward, Sam Lipscomb, Brian Lenhart*
DIRECTOR: *Jim Larsen*

A murderous psycho tears through town with a weed-wacker and gas mask. Two assassins are hired to kill him.

Written, produced, directed by and starring young Jim Larsen, *Nigel The Psychopath* is an exercise in teenage mentality. Filled with youth, this is the result of every wary parent who ever gave their kid a camera. Toy guns are brazenly used in public parks. Children have their arms ripped off. Everyone looks into the camera and laughs... but such is the beauty of bargain basement analog wonders. Blood is sparingly used and back-stories are pointless. *Nigel* begins with a 3 minute montage that you'll swear is a trailer. And the killer attacks without rhyme or reason. Cue nature shots. *Nigel* is art from the hands of babes.

NIGHTSTALKER

1994, Color, 127 min
STARRING: *Sal Longo, Lonna Cottrell, Cristie Clark, Clancey McCauley, Dave Castiglione*
DIRECTOR: *Gary Whitson*

A dirty cop is murdering women all over town.

Though filming initially began in 1991, *Nightstalker* plays like a W.A.V.E. highlight reel. And this is not a bad thing. Most of the company's top Screen Queens appear here, from McCauley to Clark and Cottrell to Krause, all gloriously snuffed by Longo in a tour de force killing spree. Girls are tied up while clothes are ripped at knifepoint. Longo methodically carries bodies out back where he can *"bury the trash"* and no one suspects a thing. And some of the murders are particularly sadistic, prolonged by clumsy body-groping of ass cheeks and hips. Then things take a bizarre twist as one victim fights back, revealing herself to be a vampire! Did *Nightstalker* just set up its own sequel? This is a W.A.V.E. epic like no other. Recommended.

  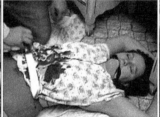 

OZONE

1994, Color, 81 min
STARRING: *James Black, Bill Morrison, Tom Hoover, James L. Edwards, Jerry Camp*
DIRECTOR: *J.R. Bookwalter*

While pursuing drug dealers, Detective Eddie Boone is injected with a new street drug named Ozone. Losing his grip on reality and hallucinating bodily mutations, Eddie finds himself in the center of a mass drug-induced city war, engineered by Ozone's creator.

What a difference a few years make! Bookwalter (who was had become known for such camcorder throwaways as *Chickboxer* and *Humanoids From Atlantis*) ups the ante for low-budget standards in this SOV surprise. Packed with mind-bending action and immense scope, *Ozone* (also known as *Street Zombies*) made Bookwalter a household name. Shot in 1993 with shades of Cronenberg, Bookwalter successfully blends body horror, sensuality and apocalyptic overtones into a scant 80 minutes that never overstays its welcome. With a minimal cast and a $3500 budget, *Ozone's* attention to detail and production quality stands as the benchmark for early 90's video. Obviously, Bookwalter had done his homework.

Performances have also improved, particularly Hoover's (though one could argue he's finally been given good material). Black is charismatic as the lead and carries the picture well. Morrison takes impressive risks, even appearing fully nude onscreen. And Edwards provides charm with his unabashed boy-next-door style... in three separate roles! Special effects are impressively grotesque too, proving that a little slime goes a long way. Ultimately more drug-fuelled thriller than horror, *Ozone* nevertheless leads the way in 90's video nightmares. Recommended.

RANA, QUEEN OF THE AMAZON
1994, Color, 91 min
STARRING: *Pamela Sutch, Tina Krause, Dawn Murphy, Laura Giglio, Sal Longo*
DIRECTOR: *Gary Whitson*

A throwback to 1940's serials, a beautiful jungle-loving Amazonian defends her territory against zombie henchmen, deadly snakes and a Nazi dominatrix named Ilsa Von Todd.

ALTERNATIVE CINEMA

Spring, 1994 • Issue #1 • $3.95

EXCLUSIVE!

OZONE

UNLEASHED

ALSO:
**Spotlight on
Christine Taylor,
star of Imperial
Entertainment's**
Showdown!

**Low-Budget
Production Hell:
The Making of**
The Witching!

**Censorship and
Homemade Gore:
The Films of
Andreas Schnaas!**

**Missouri
Invaded
by Killer B's!**
*Filmmakers Eric
Stanze & Todd
Sheets on
shooting The
Show-Me State*

**Lesbian
Serial
Killers:**
*The creators of
"Killer Nerd"
debut their
third opus:
"Girlfriends"!*

**The New
Horizons
Roger
Corman!**
*40 years, over
175 movies
and still going
strong!*

Inspired, sleazy and totally cornball, *Rana* is one of Whitson's best. Presented in a three story structure, the film never loses pace or becomes boring (and that's with a 9 minute quicksand struggle). Casting is excellent with gorgeously talented women filling the screen. Sutch is Rana and Krause is Von Todd. Stories are presented chronologically with beautiful editing. And fight scenes, though little more than groping, involve hilarious high kicks and upper cuts. There's even an entirely original theme song! *Rana* is a blast from start to finish and the perfect introduction to W.A.V.E. pictures. Highly Recommended.

SAVAGE HARVEST
1994, Color, 72 min
STARRING: *Lisa Morrison, Ramona Midgett, William Clifton, David Berliner, D.J. Vivona*
DIRECTOR: *Eric Stanze*

Six friends clean an old barn on Native American soil. Camping there, the friends find themselves caught in an ancient curse involving demonic spirits and magical stones. Soon they are possessed and turned into fanged flesh-eating zombies.

Essentially an even lower budgeted *Evil Dead* (with a Native American twist), Stanze tackles extreme gore and historical awareness in *Savage Harvest*. But though impressive, the film suffers from excessive exposition and slow pacing. Stanze allows his characters to flourish through dialogue - they talk and talk and talk, and it kind of kills the party. But Rick Fischer (a Mark Polonia doppelganger) delivers a spooky ghost story by campfire and tension builds. The demonically possessed look incredible (showcasing a great Lamberto Bava vibe) and performances eventually win us over. Plus it's always great to see Morrison again. A solid film worthy of repeat viewings.

SORORITY SLAUGHTER

1994, Color, 87 min
STARRING: *Tina Krause, Laura Giglio, Leslie Cummins, Pamela Sutch, Sal Longo*
DIRECTOR: *Gary Whitson, Sal Longo*

A trio of girls prank their neighbor and accidently kill him. But is he really dead? Turns out the man worshiped a demonic god named Radu and achieved eternal life! Now the neighbor takes revenge, sacrificing the girls with his large carving knife.

Wonderful in concept, *Sorority Slaughter* benefits most from its cast of W.A.V.E. regulars. Dave Castiglione and the girls all pose as teenaged misfits lounging on spring break. Longo plays the deadly neighbor in typical Longo style (charmingly brutish) while co-directing with Whitson. And the film entertains. A lengthy car wash sequence involves girls being hosed into a wet t-shirt jamboree, and a nude-less love scene between Castiglione and Krause teases the audience. But the film captures that lazy spring break feeling best of all, making everyone look like their genuinely enjoying themselves. Ah, to be young again! Giglio's first W.A.V.E. appearance too. Highly Recommended (there is no sorority in the story).

TORTURED SOUL 2: IKE & MIKE
1994, Color, ? min
STARRING: *Michael W. Johnson, Steve Bistrum, Kevin K. Smith, Scott Anderson*
DIRECTOR: *Stevin Kassle*

A man tries to avenge the death of his brother at the hands of a serial killer.

Unavailable for review.

VAMPIRE BRIDES
1994, Color, 84 min
STARRING: *Dave Castiglione, Aven Warren, Michelle Caporaletti, Cristie Clark, Sal Longo*
DIRECTOR: *Gary Whitson*

A 500 year-old vampire wants some new brides, but is torn when he'd rather make love to them instead. Thankfully, his zombie/henchman repeatedly abducts women for him to choose.

Vampire Brides is an enjoyable and interesting entry in W.A.V.E.'s cannon of corn. Castiglione portrays the vampire like an old soul looking for romance. He's a lover wanting to make love to women, then orders them away as his fangs takeover. I like it. But sometimes lust overwhelms and he's totally cool with shagging and biting. It's not spelled out for you, but this vamp's torn! Warren gets the thankless role though, having to physically carry everybody (and girls sure do love fainting in this) while W.A.V.E. regular Longo appears for a fantasy marriage. But this is Castiglione's show all the way, giving a great performance as girls are left chained and waiting. Highly Recommended.

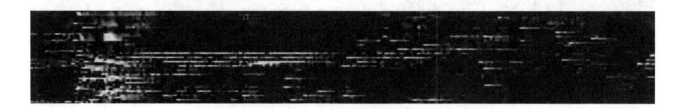

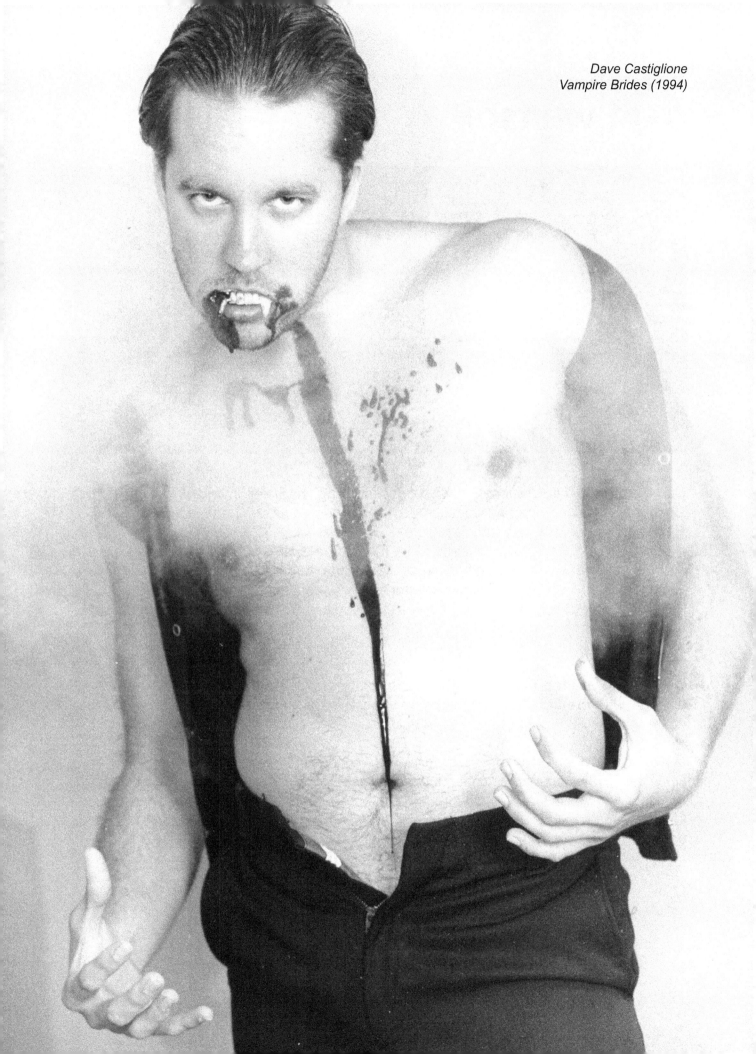

Dave Castiglione
Vampire Brides (1994)

Interview
GARY WHITSON

Gary Whitson is a true visionary and a very interesting character. Originally a high school teacher of Math and Special Education, Gary started his own company in the 1980's making SOV movies with horrific storylines. Known as W.A.V.E. Productions and creating his own homegrown Scream Queens, Gary marketed his films for sale in magazines and horror conventions. Finding immediate success and offering "custom videos" for a paying audience, Gary found his niche and has impressively continued making W.A.V.E. Productions for over 30 years. Most impressively, Gary may indeed be the most prolific SOV filmmaker of all time.

Gary, thank you for giving your time to this interview! You're an incredibly prolific director with credits stretching back into the 1980's. What inspired you to want to make movies?

I have always been of fan of horror movies as well the sci-fi movies of the 50's and 60's. Once the VHS video camera came out and it was affordable and easier to shoot movies, I ran classified ads in local papers for people interested in making movies. Aven Warren, Mike Brady, and Clancey McCauley were three of our original actors. Aven also did our early make-up effects.

What was your first feature film?

Our first movie was called *Sisters* and involved twins, one of which planned to murder the other. But a twist involving daylight saving time ruined her plans. During the course of production, one of the main actors dropped out. We then had to revise the script and a new version was created called *The Valley Strangler*. Both versions are available as a double set. [See W.A.V.E. Productions @ www.wavemovies.com]

What does W.A.V.E. stand for?

Aven Warren and Mike Bradey came up with the first version of the name. It stood for Whitson's Amateur Video Entertainers. It later became Whitson's Amazing Video Entertainers once we began using professional and semi-professional actors. And a later version was simply Whitson's Audio and Video Entertainment. You can take your pick.

One of W.A.V.E.'s unique attributes are your custom videos. Customers can essentially request certain acts or storylines in a film, which you'll produce for a reasonable fee. Were custom videos an essential part of W.A.V.E.'s success? Do you still offer this service today?

Customs were vital at the very beginning. They provided income to cover the cost of equipment, costumes, and the actors. The original idea came from my earlier interest in comic books and doing custom artwork for people. I figured if they would pay for artwork, they might pay to have a script produced. Back in the 80's, there were vanity publishers who would publish your book for a fee and you could then sell it. I thought people who had a script or storyline idea would like to see it come alive on the screen. And back then, we offered a small royalty on the sales. And yes, we still offer the service today from shorts to full length movies.

Another unique offering is your welcoming of new talent. Specifically, customers can audition for future roles in W.A.V.E. productions. How does this process work?

In addition to the ads mentioned previously, we held auditions at a local modeling agency. And we asked for talent from our web site. The biggest turn came when we advertised in Backstage magazine for actors and actresses and received hundreds of responses. We then held auditions at our old studio. Tina Krause was discovered at the Chiller Theatre convention back in 1994.

What was W.A.V.E.'s earliest success? Which film had the most selling impact financially?

In addition to the money from custom tapes, *Sleepover Massacre* was our biggest seller. It was also a custom, but it struck a cord with a lot of people and it sold very well. *Dead North* was also very popular and was a more mainstream thriller and murder mystery than our other titles.

How do you distribute your films? Has it always been through mail order advertisements?

In the beginning, all advertising was placed in genre magazines like Fangoria and others. Then as a mailing list grew, we'd send out mailers to our customers when new movies were available. John Russo of *Night of the Living Dead* fame became interested in our titles and sold them through his Scream Queens Illustrated magazine. Our mother daughter Scream Queens, Christine Cavalier and Terri Lewandowski, appeared in a couple of his features. Then we got an order for the *Psycho Sisters* custom video in 1994. Pete Jacelone who ordered it went all out with selling it and getting it distributed through EI Cinema, as it was called then. EI became interested in all our titles and distributed them throughout the US to video stores everywhere. They continue to sell our movies on their site today. There were other companies that also sold our videos.

Of all the films you've made, which are your favorite? What are your favorite storylines or genre?

I think from the early years my favorites would be *Sleepover Massacre* and *Dead North*. Then *Female Mercenaries On Zombie Island* is another favorite. It's going to be re-released in a special DVD edition by Alternative Cinema in 2018. *Jungle of Screaming Death* is another one that I really like. My favorite storylines either feature mysteries or cliffhanger situations like the old movie serials. *The Perils of Penelope* was shot in chapters where each ending is a cliffhanger.

Walk us through a typical Whitson production. What is your general budget size? How big are your scripts? How many days do you shoot?

Budget size is very small. We're usually talking under $1,000. But we have a studio, all the equipment, and lots of costumes that we already have access to. And usually, we make our money on sales rather than what a customer may pay. Most scripts are pretty short, about 20 pages. We have had ones that have gone as high as 120 pages. Production days can run from 2 to 10, depending on the movie and what's involved. *Hung Jury* was one that took about 10 days of shooting.

W.A.V.E. has also been known to shoot exclusively on video. If you had the means, would you ever choose to shoot on film?

No, I wouldn't want to do film, especially since most movies and TV are now shot using some form of digital format.

Most independent filmmakers begin their careers in unique and varied ways. But in the world of digital video and online streaming, how would you advise a newcomer looking to start in the business today?

Do your own thing. Don't try to make "the great American film" and know success is very difficult. Find your own niche. Decide what you want. If it's to make money, you should do one thing. If it's just a creative outlet, then do another. Someone asked me at a recent convention if I entered film festivals and I said no because it would take away from my way of producing movies. But that doesn't mean a new person shouldn't do it. My objective has always been to be my own boss and not to be dependent on anyone else. That's why I haven't pursued higher budget films. You take more time raising money than making movies. I don't want to do that.

Before you made movies, what were your other professional interests? Did you have a prior career?

I was a Math and Special Ed teacher until I retired to do video full time in 1996. As a hobby, I printed t-shirts and produced comic book fanzines.

And now you are celebrating W.A.V.E.'s 30th year! Congratulations! Anything we should expect to see in the near future?

I'm always working on new titles and new ways of presenting them. I remade both *Dead North* as *The Pinelands Murders* and *Sleepover Massacre* as *Sleepover Massacre: The Curse*. I'm planning a remake of *Female Mercenaries* and may also work on a sequel to *Psycho Sisters* with Pete Jacelone. And I have numerous scripts yet to be shot.

Thank you so much for your time and thoughts, Gary!

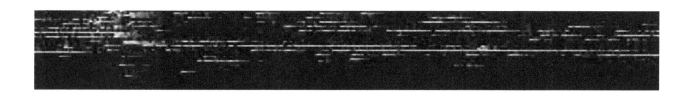

Interview
DAVE CASTIGLIONE

An actor turned director with his own SOV company Sharkey Video, Dave began working with Gary Whitson appearing in numerous W.A.V.E. Productions. Known for playing hunky boyfriends and deranged killers, Dave proved that his charismatic skills were not just in front of the camera with his 1994 directorial debut *Love Is a Stranger*. In 1995, Dave surprised audiences again when he directed the off-the-wall comedy *An Ex-Hooker's Christmas Carol*. Long out of print and hard to find, Dave's SOV films are finally returning to market in lovingly reprinted re-releases from Saturn's Core Audio & Video.

Dave, thank you for giving your time to this interview! You have appeared in numerous early W.A.V.E. Productions in a variety of roles, from lovers to killers. What initially lead you to become an actor?

I really became interested in acting mainly because I had been interested in making movies ever since I was six years old, which is when my father took me to see my first PG rated movie...The Poseidon Adventure. I was totally captivated and amazed. Up until then, I had only seen Disney movies on the big screen. That experience led to my obsession of movie making. At first I would recreate scenes from other movies with my Legos and Hasbro action figures. LOL. But when I turned 12, I found my parent's old 8mm movie camera in the attic one day, and my childhood dreams instantly became a reality! When I was 15, I made my first two horror film shorts on Super8.

How did you originally connect with W.A.V.E. and Gary Whitson?

I met Gary and Sal Longo (his former partner) back in 1989 when I read a local newspaper article and learned that they were holding auditions for a low budget horror movie in my own county and surrounding South Jersey suburbs. That film was *Hung Jury* and was the first real acting role for me of many more to come. The movie was shot in 1990, but I think it took a couple years for them to release it. I remember by the time it came out, I already had several other WAVE movies under my belt.

I remember the audition was the first and only audition I ever did for WAVE. LOL. And I remember Sal seemed most interested in the fact that I was an avid scuba diver, so I was cast in the movie and they rewrote the part of my character so they could incorporate the diving aspect into the story.

Do you remember the W.A.V.E. movie you starred in that was first released?

Hung Jury was the first movie I worked on, but the first WAVE movie I was in that was released was a short called "Corey's Revenge" (I think that was the title). It was a custom tape I believe for one of WAVE's customers. It was how I met Christine Cavalier and the first of many WAVE movies that we starred in together.

How many W.A.V.E. films did you star in?

There are so many WAVE movies, I have lost count over the years. I have also worked with other low budget horror producers such as Phil Herman and had cameos in quite a few of his films. Plus, there were about 10 of my own films that I starred in. So no clue as to how many but oddly only a few show up on IMDB and I don't even know how those ones got there. LOL. I never made an IMDB page myself and not sure how I ended up there but it's pretty cool.

Of all the films you either directed or starred in, which ones are your favorites?

This is a tough one to answer because I have been fortunate to work with so many wonderful people in the business. One favorite of my own movies wasn't a horror movie at all. In fact, it was the opposite... *An Ex Hooker's Christmas Carol* released in 1995. It was my first full length feature that I produced and directed and stars my great friend, Laura Giglio. We had such a blast making that movie. Even though it was a fantasy, comedy, it did have some dark aspects to it. I loved doing that movie because I was great friends with everyone in the cast. It's one of those films that is very near and dear to my heart.

My favorite horror movie to make didn't actually happen until 1998... *Backwoods Marcy* which stars my former wife, Dawn Murphy, who I met while working on *The Agreement*, another WAVE movie. But my favorite WAVE movies to work on were *Hung Jury*, *Bloody Creek*, *The Mummy's Dungeon*, *Vampire Brides*, *Psycho Sisters* and *Sorority Slaughter* parts one and two. Most of these WAVE movies had a large and diverse cast, but I liked doing *The Mummy's Dungeon* because it was the first time I got to work wearing special f/x makeup. And, who wouldn't want to play a horny, old mummy? LOL!

Hung Jury was unique for me being cast in my first acting role with this enormous cast. The only ones I think I saw again after this were Gary and Sal. Most of us had never worked together before, but we all got along great and shooting on location was great fun. We shot some cool scenes on a yacht that belonged to Gary's brother. I don't think WAVE ever attempted a production of that size again, but it was a lot of fun to make. Although I thought *Vampire Brides* was ridiculous, it was a starring role for me, and I got to work with so many beautiful scream queens!

One of my favorite performances of yours is in *Bloody Creek* where you played a horny forest ranger (doubling as the red herring in a nightmare sequence). You've also played various horny teenagers throughout your career, usually scoring with the hottest ladies onscreen. What was it like performing so many love scenes with so many beautiful women?

Yeah I think *Bloody Creek* was the first film when Gary, Sal and I realized my potential to play both a horny teen and an evil villain.

Hung Jury was my first time doing a love scene, and it was with this beautiful blonde, Judy Pasternack (not sure of spelling on last name). Not only was it my first movie, first day of shooting, and the first time doing a love scene, but Judy's mother was also on the set observing the shoot. OMG, LOL... how awkward. But everyone there made light of the situation, including the mom and that made things a lot easier for me to do the scene. What a way to break the ice, though.

After that one, the love scenes got easier and steamier. It wasn't always that exciting because there was Gary and Sal in the room... LOL. Plus, it was tough to get serious and keep from laughing much of the time. However, I can think of a couple times when things felt a little real. LOL. The on-going joke through the years is what Gary and Sal constantly chanted - *"Dave, you should be paying us to be in these movies!"* There were a lot of beautiful women, and some of them I ended up dating. One of them I ended up marrying!

Sometimes in love scenes, an effort is made to conceal nudity from the camera. And sometimes (like the scene in *Sorority Slaughter* between you and Tina Krause) the

effort to conceal is wonderfully hilarious and obvious. Backs are repeatedly turned toward camera. Were some love scenes harder to shoot than others?

LOL. Sometimes but usually it's the choice of the actress, and how much she is comfortable showing or how much Gary and Sal can sneak in there, Hahaha! I think Gary and Sal always tried to get more.

I think *Sorority Slaughter* was Tina's first love scene, and our first one together. I can't remember how it happened that we were so covered up. But ironically, in the sequel we were both totally nude and performed in what I think was one WAVE's most graphic sex scenes. It was so graphic that I remember Tina and some other actresses wanting Gary to re-edit the scene. A lot of people asked me if I got excited and how real was it. I can tell you it was one of the most uncomfortable scenes I ever shot because I was totally naked in front of Tina and a room full of men. Aven Warren (WAVE's makeup artist) was also there arguing with Sal over camera angles. It was utterly bizarre. We never had to re-shoot anything, but I know Gary had to re-edit things on more than one occasion.

In 1994, you branched into directing with your first feature *Love Is a Stranger*. What made you want to direct your own film? Did your experiences as an actor help?

I grew up dreaming of making movies. Once I realized there were others out there locally who were already living the dream, I knew it was possible to realize my dream and possibly market it for others to enjoy. I did learn quite a bit from acting in WAVE movies, and that helped things when it came time to produce my own.

Sal volunteered to help me produce *Love Is A Stranger* which starred Christine Cavalier and myself. We were at the Chiller Theater Expo in North Jersey, and Sal discovered Tina Krause who he enlisted for my movie. By this time we had all ready began production, and Sal shot a scene with Tina. There were schedule conflicts with other cast members, however, and Tina's scenes never made it into the movie's original cut released in 1994, unfortunately. The scenes were later reintroduced into the re-release.

Love Is A Stranger was to be Tina's first feature, but as we all know, Tina went on to star in many WAVE movies and got parts with bigger budget production companies. I remember how lucky I was to finally work with my longtime best friend, Champy Frehmel who played the title character, Landon Love. Christine was the unfortunate victim, and Ivory Blackwood put a very unique and mysterious spin to the character of the seductress, Bebe. Ivory was so good and experienced as a stage actress that I think Christine was actually trying avoid scenes with her, afraid of being upstaged. This led to other cuts of important scenes, and my first feature quickly became a short clocking in at only a 46 minutes for a total running time. Still, I was happy that I was able to wrap on my first Sharkey production.

***Love Is a Stranger* also launched your own video label - Sharkey Video. Did controlling your own work help with video distribution? Was W.A.V.E. a model you tried to follow?**

It helped to a certain extent. But, later on I realized it helped more to network with other producers and collaborate on projects together. This helped get my name out there to a wider audience. I knew WAVE was very successful in the customized horror, fetish genre, but it wasn't really my thing. I was more interested in branching off to do other types of projects. I always loved the suspense aspect to horror/action thrillers. Plus, I loved whenever it was possible to add humor into these otherwise serious plot lines.

What are some of your favorite genres?

I love comedy as much as I love horror and feel that sometimes it's better for both to go hand in hand. It's hard to take many of these outlandish slasher flicks serious, but when you throw in some humor, not only is it more entertaining, I think it gives the audience a chance to breathe a sigh of relief and prepare for the next scare to come.

Do you still act or direct today?

My last film was *Deep Undead* in 2005 but I have not produced anything of my own since then. I have acted in a few independent features and cameos for other producers, but haven't directed anything solo myself. Most recently, I was interviewed and taped for the upcoming *Mail Order Murder* documentary from Saturn's Core Audio & Video.

Do you think it's still possible to earn a living making independent films in today's world of HD cameras and digital downloads?

I think there is a lot more competition out there but also a lot more avenues to choose for marketing and distribution, due to the never ending expansion in internet technologies and cell phone applications. There are probably more possibilities than ever before to make your work known and be successful at filmmaking. I always think *"if only I were a kid again living in this digital age"* and had that childhood motivation and creativity back again.

Thank you so much for your time and thoughts, Dave!

Joel D. Wynkoop and Kathy Willets
Creep (1995)

Chapter 17
BE KIND, REWIND (1995)

Though few knew it at the time, 1995 was one of the last golden years for SOV horror. Technology had so advanced over the past decade, the video of 95 looked nothing like the video of 82. Digital cameras were right around the corner, VHS was soon to be threatened (and replaced) by DVD, Wes Craven's *Scream* would have profound impact on the horror genre, and people again changed the way they watched movies. Imagine buying a movie today when the only content available was the movie itself - blasphemous! No Special Features?!? Yet that was largely VHS. Behind the scenes documentaries and alternate cuts dominate the home viewing world now, accompanied with filmmaker commentaries and cinematic myths explained. But in 1995, these things were still on the horizon.

Public consciousness also entered the genre in ways that hadn't before. A publicity photo of Joel D. Wynkoop and Kathy Willets for *Creep* had to be redone after it was deemed *"in poor taste"* following the murder of Nicole Brown Simpson. Indeed true crimes on television became somewhat more horrific than fiction. Violence (it seemed) was toned down, perhaps in response to MPAA rulings or perhaps to reach a wider audience. *The Sandman* was openly criticized for doing this (attempting to gain more success in family video stores by censoring itself early) which ultimately hindered its popularity. And Horror, it appeared, had gone soft.

But SOV films continued to be made and sold by the dozens. Mainstream horror was somewhat stagnant in 1995, overdosed by the slasher smorgasborg rampant during the 1980's, though some slashers were still coming through. Comedy was the constant now, mixed into various releases to soften offensive thrills. Enjoyable horror entries were still present (mostly from filmmakers who didn't let outside influences affect them), but this was a time of professional burn-out.

Incredibly, the biggest success story came from three of SOV's originators: *Feeders* and the sale to Blockbuster Video. An immeasurable hit tied to the success of 1996's *Independence Day*, Blockbuster picked up the $500 cheapie and gave it mainstream exposure. Jon McBride and the Polonia brothers finally had financial success on their hands - almost a reward for so many years of determination plugging away. And critical acclaim came with Donald Farmer's *Red Lips*, J.R. Bookwalter's *The Sandman* (its imaginative aspects) and Tim Ritter's masterpiece *Creep*.

Yet this was also the year of flash without substance in *Batman Forever*, stylish ick in *Se7en*, and CGI love fests of *Toy Story*, *Casper* and *Jumanji*. And true to those films, some of their influence washed into SOV too. The ropey unknowns of SOV horror soon gave way to comic relief and stylized angles, losing its underground edge.

ADDICTED TO MURDER
1995, Color/B&W, 91 min
STARRING: *Mick McCleery, Laura McLauchlin, Sasha Graham, Bernadette Pauley*
DIRECTOR: *Kevin J. Lindenmuth*

A vampire woman befriends a boy who eventually becomes a serial killer. But his victims aren't random. The man kills to help his fanged friends feed, wanting to join their blood-drinking lifestyle.

Named *"Best Outlaw Movie"* by Cinefantastique magazine in 1996, *Addicted to Murder* accurately represents the genre prior to Wes Craven's influential mega-hit *Scream*. Dreary and melodramatic, the film wallows in black and white flashbacks, warped visuals and a fractured chronology.

Horror in the early/mid 90's was struggling with an identity crisis. The excess of the 80's was gone, major studios had lost their bite and the genre was essentially at its lowest point. Independents were almost solely keeping horror alive and clichéd storylines were reintroduced with new focus. Scooter McCrae's *Shatter Dead* is a good example, using a tired zombie premise to focus on one character's journey. And like *Shatter Dead*, *Addicted to Murder* presents its hero as neither good nor evil, yet doomed to succumb to their own inner demons. This ultimately makes the story about fate. *Addicted to Murder* is a horrific fate from which there is no escape. And it is important to note the influence of 1991's *Silence of the Lambs* Oscar wins, redirecting horror into mainstream psychological dramas. *Silence of the Lambs* won Best Picture! Audiences reveled in fractured characters compelled by inner turmoil. Characters that were doomed to live out their demons onscreen. And with this film, you get that. *Addicted to Murder* impresses with its very low budget and noteworthy performances (particularly from Graham). But the film does not play as well today. *Scream* revolutionized the genre, poking fun at itself while reintroducing the slasher formula to a whole new generation (which eventually lead to remakes). And while they're only a year apart, *Addicted to Murder* feels more art-house than anything scary.

Recommended with a fine glass of wine.

BLOOD SLAVES OF THE VAMPIRE WOLF
1995, Color, 105 min
STARRING: *Don Miller, Annette Perez, Jennifer Knight, Conrad Brooks, Michael Hooker*
DIRECTOR: *Conrad Brooks*

A vampire woman needs blood to stay beautiful. Together with her zombie-slaves, they attack unsuspecting victims during the night.

Though released in 1996, *Blood Slaves of the Vampire Wolf* delivers none of the b-movie magic suggested by Brooks' involvement. And credited as his directorial feature-length debut, Brooks makes every mistake in the book. Dialogue is mumbled and spoken far away from recorders. Auto-focus continually swirls unattended. Lengthy scenes are shot without coverage. Close-ups are haphazardly used from previous scenes. And worst of all, no one tries to tell a story.

Legendary actor Conrad Brooks is a funny man. I like his style, and most films benefit from his involvement. Conrad speaks with an engaging tone! His physical movements are often comical and distinct! So why he thought shambling around as a mute was a good idea, I'll never know. The man doesn't allow himself to act, which is why *Blood Slaves* is so frustrating. Scenes run without purpose. And the only positive is the opening rubber bat "soaring" through town (which we ought to see more of). But this was apparently a teaching film for Brooks, as his next picture *Jan-Gel: The Beast From the East* (1999) will forever shine as the best of his career. So consider *Blood Slaves* a trial run.

BLOODSCENT
1995, Color, 81 min
STARRING: *Mandy Leigh, Julie Wallace, Nicole Mentz, Bill Randolph, Laura Hamilton*
DIRECTOR: *Bill Randolph*

A woman digs up the golden skull of a vampire in her garden. Soon, she is fantasizing about a skinless bloodsucker as her friends turn into vampires.

Though actually 75 minutes (and extended by bloopers), *Bloodscent* is a well made video entry in camcorder cheapness. Obviously shot in someone's house, Leigh and others happily provide enough skin to thrust the story forward. Girls take showers, baths and change clothes often. Nudity is fairly rampant with wardrobes consisting of skimpy dresses and bikinis. And everyone's ass sticks out when climbing on or off a bed. The golden skulls are nicely crafted and the red stuff splatters frequently. Plus the dialogue is hilariously stunted and the soundtrack parties to 90's soft rock metal. Worthy of repeat viewings.

BLOODY ANNIVERSARY
1995, Color, 91 min
STARRING: *Lisa Cook, Todd Jason Cook, Brian Truitt, Jerry McGhee, Angela Watkins*
DIRECTOR: *Dante Falconi (Todd Jason Cook)*

Celebrating their anniversary, a young couple visits a fortune teller. But when they inadvertently insult the psychic, a curse is put upon them in form of a killer ventriloquist dummy. Now the couple must fight to stay alive as the doll kills everyone they know.

Also known as *The Dummy*, Cook returns to killer doll territory with the gleeful *Bloody Anniversary*. Previously seen in a *Horrorscope* short, Cook's emotionless doll goes full range here and to great effect. Through careful camera angles, the dummy walks, climbs, looks around and stabs people with ease. *Child's Play* references stand out (including a *Child's Play 2* standee in Cook's bedroom) and supernatural elements appear nicely. Cook's dummy teleports from one house to another for kills. And unlike Chucky, this dummy never speaks or tells jokes. *Bloody Anniversary* is a fun ride from a director improving with each cinematic entry. Fantastic! A belated sequel came in 2016.

CREEP

1995, Color, 85 min
STARRING: *Joel D. Wynkoop, Patricia Paul, Kathy Willets, Tom Karr, Asbestos Felt*
DIRECTOR: *Tim Ritter*

Convicted serial killer Angus Lynch escapes from police custody, killing everyone he meets. Eventually joining his stripper sister, the two embark on a short murder spree of innocent victims.

Directed by independent Florida-based favorite Ritter, *Creep* is a masterpiece of deranged psychosis. Commanding the film is Wynkoop, giving a manic performance both frightening and hilarious. Wynkoop ranges from murderous lip-curling sneers to cry-laughing naked in a bathtub. And indeed, *Creep* feels epic. Yet the film does not rest on Wynkoop alone.

Returning *Wicked Games* actress Patricia Paul is excellent as the calmly cop haunted by past demons. She delivers hilarious one-liners while dishing vigilante justice out to scum. And one would be remiss without mentioning Willets, lending her name and "talents" to the show. Known as *"Florida's Naughty Nympho,"* Willets was arrested in 1992 for prostitution. During trial, her husband was later revealed to have secretly videotaped her encounters, one with the town's mayor. She eventually turned newfound notoriety into a porn career, but Ritter appears to have nabbed the best deal of the bunch (capitalizing on her celebrity). Willets scrapes by as a performer, but her rock-hard implants are the main attraction and no, they don't move. In addition, Tom Karr (producer of 1974's *Deranged*) provides a nice complimentary performance, proving that not all monsters are boisterous. But it's Ritter's direction that comes out on top, showing everyone why he's the master of independent cinema.

Creep has enjoyed several releases over the years, occasionally re-edited or shortened. But the original unrated version is still the best. Highly Recommended.

DEATH METAL ZOMBIES

1995, Color, 110 min
STARRING: *Lisa Cook, Bill DeWild, Todd Jason Cook, Milton Rush, Mike Gebbie*
DIRECTOR: *Todd Jason Cook*

A group of stoners enter a radio contest, winning a private recording from their favorite band. But the tape turns everyone into murderous zombies! Now the girl who had to work late struggles to stay alive, learning death-metal's secrets before it's too late.

Inexcusably long, *Death Metal Zombies* has good ideas buried under a mess of tomfoolery. Also known as *Deadrock Zombies*, *Death Metal* starts strong before losing itself among its titular menace.

Shot in 1994 and opening with soapy breasts in the shower, Cook lays his cards on the table. This is a filmmaker who has grown over the years, advancing his features with maturity and gusto. He stylishly introduces his characters, spending 10 minutes cutting between people and places overrun with heavy-metal music. Finally we break into dialogue and the plot gets rolling. A dream sequence features Cook's band live onstage (demonstrating his love for metal isn't just lip service). But once the coveted tape arrives and everyone plays it, story drops. Turns out the band's leader is a Satanist wanting everyone to be his zombies. And the zombies talk and control objects through telekinesis. Ingeniously, the tape itself also becomes the bad dude's undoing when played backwards. But the film's problem is a lack of direction once the zombies arrive. Characters wander aimlessly for far too long. Lengthy scenes with nameless faces play just so they can die. Zombies talk about *"getting"* so-and-so but never commit the deed, and the film doesn't really know how to end (showcasing an old woman post-credits yelling *"it's over!"*).

Ultimately, Cook may have agreed with some of this. A re-edited, 83 minute "Anniversary Edition" was released in 2005 containing a new ending.

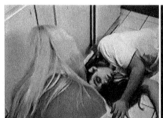   

DEMONSOUL
1995, Color, 82 min
STARRING: *Kerry Norton, Eileen Daly, Daniel Jordan, Janine Ulfane, Drew Rhys-Williams*
DIRECTOR: *Elisar C. Kennedy (Elisar Cabrera)*

Haunted by visions of a red haired woman performing sacrifices on an alter, Erica enlists a crackpot hypnotherapist to help restore her sanity. Unfortunately it brings the red haired woman into the real world! Now Erica is an intermittent vampire hungry for blood.

A British production shot entirely in London, *Demonsoul* is a relatively restrained adventure. Placing emphasis on violent sexuality and gothic themes, Cabrera's bloodsucking thriller has more in common with *Interview With a Vampire* than most traditional fright flicks. And like *Interview*, *Demonsoul* suggests that vampirism is an ancient form of Satanism brought to modern times through one's undying soul. Sexuality is tied to blood, resulting in heavy breathing and orgasmic squeals while drinking. But more impressive is the quality shown in this video production. Like *Shatter Dead*, video equipment has advanced greatly since the days of *Blood Cult*. Indeed this image could easily be mistaken for 16mm, lending *Demonsoul* a visual professionalism not found in most SOV titles. Performances are good (especially from Norton) and the film benefits from a nice level of nudity. But again like *Interview*, this is more thriller than horror; more romantic mystery than shocks. Mildly Recommended.

EXPLODING ANGEL
1995, Color, ? min
STARRING: *Gunnar Hansen, Amy Lindsay, Jan Fawcett, Scott Shaw, Paul Locklear*
DIRECTOR: *Hugh Gallagher*

Unavailable for review. An unreleased feature from the director of *Gorgasm*, *Exploding Angel* appears noteworthy for Gunnar Hansen's involvement. Hansen (Leatherface in 1974's *The Texas Chainsaw Massacre*) appears to play a character of significance, though the only trailer available has music dubbed over his lines. The film takes place in some kind of warehouse or garage. Women are pursued by thugs dressed in black. A dual rape (or sexual assault) occurs, then a man yells *"you better come out, bitch."* Visuals have a strong Tarantino vibe with trench coats, sunglasses and a guy sporting a ponytail. Possibly a drug or human trafficking thriller.

FATAL DELUSION
1995, Color, 104 min
STARRING: *Sal Longo, Tina Krause, Michelle Caporaletti, Laura Giglio, Gary Whitson*
DIRECTOR: *Sal Longo*

A serial killer with a hatred towards women kills his psychiatrist and assumes the identity.

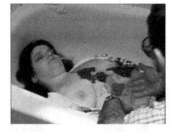 Firing on all cylinders, Sal Longo's *Fatal Delusion* is a fun body-count picture with heart. Impressively written and directed by Longo (who also plays the killer), *Fatal* wastes little time getting to the good stuff. Haunted by the horrors of Vietnam, Longo traps, strips, stabs and disembowels victims with glee. One scene hilariously features newly torn-out guts being flushed down a toilet. Another involves Longo stating (with deadpan delivery) *"I'm the crazy serial killer and you're the helpless victim."* Priceless! Blood is charmingly slopped into wounds and gore is present, though the real draw is the physical struggles between killer and victims. Crotch shots, simulated choking, bra-less breasts wiggling under thin shirts; it's all here in typical W.A.V.E. fashion. But everything zings with a wonderful tongue-in-cheek approach. And the beautiful Tina Krause plays three separate characters (all doomed to die) in her premiere film debut. Definitely worth seeking out! Highly Recommended.

FATAL DELUSION

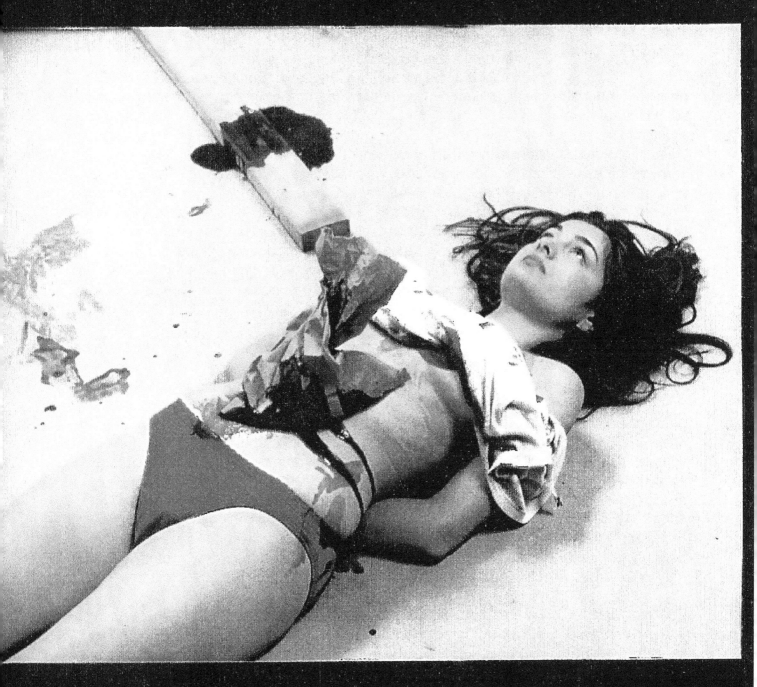

HIS DELUSION MEANS DEATH

FEEDERS

1995, Color, 65 min
STARRING: *John Polonia, Jon McBride, Maria Davis, Melissa Torpy, Todd Carpenter*
DIRECTOR: *Mark Polonia, John Polonia, Jon McBride*

Two men driving to the beach inexplicably happen upon an alien invasion.

 Originally filmed in 1994 as a low-key invasion cheapie, *Feeders* eventually became the brothers' and McBride's most successful film (after substantial recuts). Opening with an astronaut investigating a downed space signal, *Feeders* quickly introduces its alien menace before the main titles. Characters are established and killed, leaving our two nonchalant "heroes" investigating with corny dialogue and exaggerated reactions. Endless shots of the pair running through the woods appear, as do such memorable moments as McBride nearly slamming his own ass in a car door and Polonia blowing smoke directly into camera. The entire film has a "cut and paste" feel, building scenes clearly out of footage shot at different times in different locations (with different cameras), such as the meeting of Polonia and Torpy at the gas station and Carpenter seeing flying objects in the woods. The aliens, famously small and built without mouths, run rampant through the town devouring a host of Polonia regulars. Blood is hilariously kept to a minimum, while skulls are childishly shown with googly eyes still in their sockets. Spacecrafts look like golden desk lamps and cosmic entities are clearly pictures filmed out of a book. Yet it all works! And if the film was originally released in this version, SOV fans would continue to appreciate the Polonias for their die-hard approach to crackerjack filmmaking (and probably wonder what the hell Jon McBride was doing in this mess).

But fate had other plans...

Prompted by Davis (Mark's wife) and convinced that *Feeders* was still redeemable, the Polonia machine took another pass at their alien opus. Utilizing cutting-edge Amiga graphics and an upbeat opening tune, *Feeders* was revamped into legendary status. The astronaut opening with nixed in favor of mysterious Polonia narration. Desk lamp spaceships became spinning metallic discs. And most impressively, certain sequences were reshot for greater emphasis. All footage of Davis and Torpy was scraped and re-filmed with different character outcomes. Computer effects (well, Microsoft Paint) was added to allow body parts to appear mangled. And through it all, the film was tighter cut with a zesty pep. It's still the same *Feeders*, but now wonderfully enhanced with a new dollar store gusto. Running 69 minutes, the Polonia's shopped their newly refurbished motion picture to hopeful distributors... and fell into the stars.

The year was 1996 and *Independence Day* was the biggest movie on the planet. And while *Independence Day* had sophisticated special effects, a colossal climax and Will Smith, it shared one thing in common... it had aliens! So, unbelievably finding themselves in the right place at the right time, the Blockbuster Video chain agreed to distribute *Feeders* based solely on its intergalactic villains. And with Blockbuster Video stores all across America and Canada, this meant a lot of alien-hungry customers were going to be renting. And they did! Thousands of copies were generating unknown thousands of dollars for the video chain, billing *Feeders* as *"the #1 independent rental of 1996!"* But that the film is actually good, is the icing on the cake. In its revamped form, *Feeders* is a brisk and wonderfully hilarious adventure of B-movie proportions. It's cheapness in production (littered with amateur performances) has become a constant source of laughs for audiences hungry on heartfelt cinema. And just when you think the film can't get any sillier, the boys go for broke in the final minutes with world domination.

Feeders is ultimately much more than a tale of alien invaders, it's the tale of a video revolution riding the coattails of Hollywood's finest. Required Viewing.

HORRORGIRL
1995, Color/B&W, 50 min
STARRING: *Ghetty Chasun, Lena Miara, Doug Walker, Scott Vehill, Wendell Walker*
DIRECTOR: *Raoul Vehill*

A death-metal punk band needs cash to pay the rent. They even steal their pizza! But thankfully there's a band competition at the local club with cash winnings. Only problem is, their lead guitarist is a witch who accidently summons a demon while high on drugs. Now the trio must mentally "enter" another dimension to defeat the demon and win the cash.

Mixing both video and 8mm film, *Horrorgirl* is a hoot. Hilariously deadpan and extremely blunt, Vehill presents an antisocial goth-punk music video wrapped in narrative nirvana. Leading the team is Chasun, the beautifully charismatic artist best known from *Gorotica*. Chasun gives sex appeal a whole new meaning here, providing a strong and dominating performance that absolutely makes the film. Chasun is the "horrorgirl" with fishnet tights, black-chained shirts and painted face. Lengthy musical acts appear while absurd green screens and cocaine (spilled on nipples) surround the climax. And throughout the chaos, Vehill never loses focus. Wonderfully entertaining. Shut up and do it.

   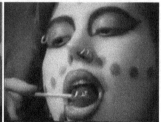

LISA COOK'S NIGHTMARES
1995, Color, 83 min
STARRING: *Lisa Cook, Todd Jason Cook*
DIRECTOR: *Todd Jason Cook*

Horror actress Lisa Cook falls asleep. She dreams of situations involving a lack of clothes and being killed by a knife, a gun, a whip and other various weapons.

A series of vignettes, *Lisa's Nightmares* feels like Todd Cook's secret fantasies. But in reality, the film appears to have originated as a series of fan-ordered custom tapes. Lisa exercises then gets killed. Lisa takes a shower then gets killed. Lisa takes a dump then gets killed (I kid you not). Shots of Lisa "sleeping" between scenes stylize the picture, lending an almost Italian feel to the proceedings. But the saving grace is the mock-interview Lisa provides in the finale, sharing her interest in horror and how a fan's belly fetish slowly became her own. The film ends with a short message of thanks to the "Lisa Cook Fan Club" and incredibly, there are at least four more volumes to go. Love never dies!

MARK OF THE DEVIL 666
1995, Color, 96 min
STARRING: *Mick Wynhoff, Karen Dilloo, Jason P. Collum, Michele Fredericks, Lee Worrell*
DIRECTOR: *Jason P. Collum*

A cop and a reporter work to solve a wave of brutal killings. The case is cracked after the reporter rents a bunch of horror films, discovering that the murders were grizzly re-enactments of famous scenes.

Though filmed in 1994, *Mark of the Devil 666* is a fun trip through the eyes of amateur filmmaking. Much of the film takes place in a video store straight out of *Video Violence*. People watch scenes from other movies (*Mark of the Devil, The Slumber Party Massacre, Alice Sweet Alice*) which are filmed directly off television sets. Dialogue is muffled or spoken away from microphones and everything plays like a fan film for the genre. Wynhoff (*America's Deadliest Home Video*) gives a moody performance but the bulk of the film rests with Dilloo as the nosy reporter. Trips to the video store are the highlight; the camera strolling through shelves hypnotically nostalgic. Much of the violence is regrettably off-screen, but this is a thriller worth investigating. Recommended.

MOTHER'S DAY: WHAT A HORROR!
1995, Color, 88 min
STARRING: *Chris Laffin, Steve Sorrentino, Jesse Volt, Sue Matier, Shirlena Vandyne*
DIRECTOR: *Mike Russo*

Two elderly ladies (men in drag) watch a television program full of snooty woman (more men in drag). Singing corpses resurrected by aliens follow.

Is this horror? Don't bet your life.

Like a bad skit on *"Saturday Night Live,"* *Mother's Day* is a major turn-off. Bizarrely shot with a number of beefy men in dresses, one wonders what audience this was intended for. "Women" passed their prime wax about everything bothering them, only to meet their doom in incredibly unfunny ways. *Mother's Day* feels like a spoof of people we don't know. The plot essentially follows snobby man-in-drag Sylvia as she undergoes hypnosis. With doctor's orders, she tries to recall events she "may" have hallucinated. Everything revolves around mother's day. Then some dead people lip-sync to *"Devine Thing"* by Soup Dragons.

This isn't a film for the horror genre. It's not even for the general public! But as an offbeat bonkers production with unknown motivations, it's a shot on video entry for the most determined viewers. Proceed with caution.

NATHAN'S GIFT: NIGHT STALKER
1995, Color, ? min
STARRING: *David McGrady, Malcolm Farquhar, Warren Johnson*
DIRECTOR: *?*

Unavailable for review. As the video box proclaims, *"Some gifts can be a curse! The Night Stalker sought his revenge, but Nathan had the Power, and Herne the hunter had not ridden for five hundred years!"*

ORIGINAL SINS
1995, Color, 108 min
STARRING: *Cheryl Clifford, Angelique De Rochambeau, Faustina, Ivo Ing, Scooter Macrae*
DIRECTOR: *Howard Berger, Matthew Howe*

Three devoted Christian girls believe they see Jesus. Convinced they've been chosen for immaculate conception, the trio kidnap a door-to-door hippie. The girls mount him, drink his blood and eat his flesh before crucifying him on a homemade cross. Later when one of the girls dies, a heavy-metal band mounts the dead girl to hopefully resurrect the Devil. It works.

While the above summary captures the narrative beats, *Original Sins* is far more interesting than any religious-themed horror outing. The film is packed with humor and ridiculous insanity; masterfully directed by Berger and Howe. Epic in story, the film impresses by never becoming preachy. Clifford, De Rochambeau and Faustina are sinfully electric as the trio with perversions both hilarious and disturbing. And the film shifts midway with the resurrection of the Devil, wonderfully achieved via stop-animation and an obviously fake rubber mask. But all bets are off towards the end as Jesus is revealed to actually be an alien looking for love! Obviously there's a lot going on here, which (predictably) found the film banned in the UK. But this is not a film debating the merits religion. It's a hilarious document of ridiculous conclusions by people wanting to believe. And its bizarrely entertaining.

  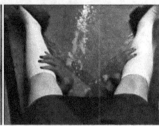 

THE PACT
1995, Color, 75 min
STARRING: *Dawn Corbin, Brett Edenton, Deanna Day, Jack Wareing, Joe Marino*
DIRECTOR: *Brad Sykes*

A young woman inherits an old house that belonged to her grandmother. Haunted by it and warned of evil doings, the woman discovers a spirit-possessed mirror within.

Shot in the summer of 1995 (and unreleased until 2013), *The Pact* is Sykes feature film debut. But unfortunately, it deflates under its own premise. A woman haunted by sleepwalking visions and spooky mirrors rarely builds tension, but what's impressive here is Sykes' gusto and creativity. Opening with unique camera angles, *The Pact* demonstrates a first time director gaining traction. Performances are generally weak (save for Corbin) but unintentional hilarity comes from Edenton's deadpan delivery and crazy hairdo. The starting point for Sykes' career.

PSYCHO SISTERS
1995, Color, 91 min
STARRING: *Pamela Sutch, Christine Taylor, Tina Krause, Peter Kerr, Chris Monroe*
DIRECTOR: *Pete Jacelone, Sal Longo, Gary Whitson*

Three adult sisters (already traumatized by their rapist-father abandoning them) are attacked and raped by three hoodlums. Two girls manage to get away but the third is strangled to death. Years later, the surviving sisters enact revenge on all males via seduction, castration and strangulation.

As with most W.A.V.E. productions, *Psycho Sisters* is a fetish film dressed in horrific themes. But while adapting the rape/revenge angle, *Psycho's* three directors are more interested in choking girls than anything else. Is that a relief? The film contains no nudity yet practically every character is stripped, tied and suffocated. Blood is used sparingly. Violence is largely off-screen. Three directors are credited, yet camerawork seems like the work of one. Most W.A.V.E. productions are harmless endeavors meant to satisfy some particular fetish. Hangings, stabbings, strangulations; they have a recipe. But *Psycho Sisters* feels like it should be a softcore sex-romp about chicks keeping cut-up dicks in a closet. It's not. But the film is fun with a lot of ropes and panties.

Psycho Sisters was remade in 1998 (co-written by James L. Edwards).

Ghetty Chasun and Michelle Bauer
Red Lips (1995)

RED LIPS

1995, Color, 76 min
STARRING: *Ghetty Chasun, Michelle Bauer, Mandy Leigh, Danny Fendley, Jasmine Pona*
DIRECTOR: *Donald Farmer*

Caroline needs money and selling blood ain't paying the bills. So when a doctor offers $100 a day to undergo experimental testing, Caroline jumps at the chance. But the tests turn her into a bloodthirsty vampire!

Featuring the electric Chasun as Caroline, *Red Lips* is an impressively emotional film from Donald Farmer. And loaded with lesbianism and neck biting, Farmer reaches beyond standard curse films of the genre. Yes, Chasun accepts her newfound bloodlust a little too quickly, but the tone shifts as the film develops. Bauer is introduced and the two share a whirlwind romance. Bauer also accepts Chasun's fanged ways and even aids in her daily snacks. But when one victim's pimp comes looking, Bauer tragically dies. Chasun grieves with a heartfelt performance belying the film's poverty-row ambitions, proving once and for all how talented this lady is. And B-movie icon George Stover appears in cameo (as does Farmer himself). Final moments include Chasun screaming for her lost love on the shores of New York's harbor as *Red Lips* displays a maturity not found in Farmer's earlier work. Sequels followed in 1996 and 2005. Required Viewing.

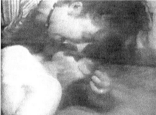

THE SANDMAN

1995, Color, 90 min
STARRING: *A.J. Richards, Rita Gutowski, Terry J. Lipko, Matthew Jason Walsh*
DIRECTOR: *J.R. Bookwalter*

Gary, a writer living in a trailer park, desperately tries to finish his new novel. But he's plagued by insomnia, his cousin wants to crash on his couch and his girlfriend won't talk to him anymore. Now a demon haunts the dreams of Gary's friends and neighbors. And everyone is dying in their sleep.

Though filmed in late 1994, *The Sandman's* origins come from a 1990 script written by

Matthew Jason Walsh. Hot off *Ozone* and unsure of what to do next, Bookwalter recalled Walsh's script and helped flesh it out for production. Inspired by the *Nightmare on Elm Street* premise (though careful not to mimic it), *The Sandman* became an interesting take on a supernatural night stalker. And a lot of mileage comes from the film's location. The insulated trailer park wonderfully allows for colorful characters and a unique world. But in resuscitating the 1990 script, Bookwalter attempted to rewrite it as a more "Blockbuster friendly" financial hit. *"The first things to go were the brief nudity and ample gore of the original version"* states Bookwalter, thinking this would make the film accessible to a wider audience. But Bookwalter also cast the film through an audition process rather than returning to his usual troupe of actors (an approach which inevitably rubbed some the wrong way). The film also credits future SRS Cinema founder and filmmaker Ron Bonk as director of photography and indeed, the film is impressively shot. *The Sandman* himself resembles something of a Jawa mixed with the *Boardinghouse* demon, so great nostalgia appears with the chills. And performances are strong across the board, bringing life to a story about sleeping.

Shot on SVHS for around $20,000, this was also Bookwalter's first venture into digital post-production (adding digital effects on a Macintosh with Adobe Premiere). A fun movie, playing well and fully aware of what it is. Recommended.

SAVAGE VOWS
1995, Color, 72 min
STARRING: *Armand Spasto, Mark Polonia, Kelly Ashton, Adam Bialek, Jackie Hergen*
DIRECTOR: *Robert S. Dennis (Bob Dennis)*

When a man's wife dies in a car crash, he invites friends to stay with him in a private cabin. But an uninvited guest arrives too, killing the group with various sharp knives.

The history of *Savage Vows* is rather interesting: Bob Dennis owned a video store which stocked a wide selection of horror films, including several by the Polonia brothers. In walks Mark Polonia and he and Bob get to talking. Turns out Bob's always wanted to make a horror movie so Mark agrees to help. Their collaboration results in *Savage Vows*. True story. This is the beginning of the Dennis-Polonia connection.

Filmed on a consumer-grade camcorder with heavy doses of Polonia knowhow, Dennis' *Savage Vows* is a diamond in the rough. Taking the plot of *The Big Chill* and mixing it with an Argento giallo, Dennis entertains while philosophizing on life, death and relationships. Smart choices are made too, such as introducing characters post-accident (relationships at their boiling points with characters unguarded). The killer operates through black leather gloves and point-of-view camerawork. Gore ranges from average to excellent, particularly during a nasty graveyard scene. And the real star is Mark Polonia, playing a man questioning his wife's fidelity while coping with his own inadequacies. There's also a midday visit to Bob's video store, nicely delivering referential nostalgia (and reminding viewers just how much we've lost over the years). But the film contains a lot of trickery as things aren't always as they seem. A character driven slasher with its heart on its sleeve. Recommended!

THE SNUFF FILES
1995?, Color, 69 min
STARRING: *Christy, Loren*
DIRECTOR: *?*

Four vignettes consisting of women being killed, stripped and groped. "The Chase" involves a girl arriving at a photographer's garage. "Exercise Break" has a girl killed in a hotel room, then being fondled by a supposed friend. "Ransom" involves a failed gunpoint ransom. "Harem Execution" features the honor killing of an Arabic dancer.

With an opening "Club Dead presents" credit, little is known about *The Snuff Files'* production. Three of the four vignettes were filmed in the same location. The same actors appear in more than one story. Stunted editing and the director's voice can be heard between takes. Blood and violence is comically presented and nudity is prime focus. And similar camerawork between stories suggest that one director is responsible. No copyright appears (it merely ends) so year of production is a best guess (somewhere between 1993-1995 based on the vehicles, fashions and early cellular phones). The film does very little to titillate and makes no effort to entertain, though a final screen states "for entertainment purposes." *The Snuff Files* wants to present a series of true-life attacks on unsuspecting women, yet is filmed with staged action and rehearsed sequences. For example: the camera follows one woman as she knocks on a door, then cuts to inside as the door opens.

And the camera's point-of-view is always from a third party, not subjective or isolated from the action. The wide-legged full nudity of the women is impressive, but the film's structure kills its snuff aspect before it starts. Hilariously, a "Coming Attractions" segment appears at the end consisting of the same actors (in the same locations) being killed in all new ways. Forgettable.

VAMPIRE WOMAN
1994-1996, Color, 282 min
STARRING: *Janet Lynn, David "Rock" Nelson, Herbert Bussewitz, Jerry Diehl*
DIRECTOR: *David "Rock" Nelson*

A vampire woman is running loose attacking people throughout Chicago. Detective "Rock" Nelson is assigned to investigate, but he doesn't believe in vampires.

Filmed over a period of two years (with the bulk shot in 1995), *Vampire Woman* is David "Rock" Nelson's magnum opus. Inexplicably running over 4 hours and 40 minutes, *Vampire Woman* roams aimlessly as Nelson sleeps, eats, watches monster movies and smokes before (finally) pursuing his bloodsucker. And the film is transformative too, bridging the gap between the mellow passiveness of *Conrad Brooks VS. Werewolf* and the schizophrenic randomness that would soon dominate Nelson's career. In short, there's a lot of "Rock" in this little story.

 Sporadically narrated by the man himself, *Vampire Woman* delivers premise without plot. Things begin well enough, with people actually attempting to act (and sly references to Hugh Gallagher). But then we're thrown into a never-ending mix of Lynn hissing into camera and point-of-view shots of "victims" falling to the floor. Hilariously, Nelson himself doubles for Lynn (presumably since she wasn't always available) complete with cape and wig, masking half his face like Lugosi's double in *Plan 9 From Outer Space*. Nelson/Lynn continually hiss at band members, children and cats, reminding us that you're never too old to have fun. And though eating isn't the endurance test it soon would become (and as all later Nelson films will feature), it does dominate a fair amount of screen time. But the most cringe-worthy

sequence in this "everything and the kitchen sink" patchwork is Nelson's late brother Keith's stand-up routine. Filmed live in a bar (and edited with single shots of Nelson laughing at every joke), things go from painful to extreme as terrible jokes (being terribly delivered) turn into a shouting match with surly patrols. But while this may sound like the film's downfall, it's actually Nelson's saving grace. Against all odds, Nelson presents his movies (warts and all) from the heart. He's out there making art, sometimes completely by himself, and it's entertaining, wild and wonderful. Does it matter if the jokes land?

Like most endurance tests, it's not about the finish line but rather how you got there. Nelson understands this better than anyone. And while *Vampire Woman* could stand to lose about 2 hours of nonsense, there's still a whole lot to love here. Recommended!

Janet Lynn and David "Rock" Nelson in Vampire Woman (1994-1996)

THE VEGETABLE MONSTER FROM OUTER SPACE (O MONSTRO LEGUME DO ESPACO)
1995, Color, 77 min
STARRING: *Loures Jahnke, Onesia Liotto, Jorge Hippler, Marcos Braun, E.B. Toniolli*
DIRECTOR: *Petter Baiestorf*

An alien with vegetable-like DNA escapes from his scientist captor, killing men while attempting to mate with females.

A Brazilian horror/comedy gross-out, *Vegetable Monster* feels like two films thrown together. The main story of the alien lose in the countryside is wonderful, surely the draw for most audiences. But the film doesn't really take place on Earth. Instead, the film surrounds itself in a pseudo-Earth where competing religious sects (one of which practices necrophilia) dominate the countryside. More time is spent showing cannibalism, vomit slurping, shit-eating, intestine fondling and corpse fucking than anything the alien does, which is a shame. We want to take this alien seriously, but Baiestorf would rather see how far he can gross-out the audience. And does any of the cannibalism, shit-eating or necrophilia matter to the story? Nope. I had high hopes for *Vegetable Monster*, something akin to *Zombie 90: Extreme Pestilence* or *Bad Taste*. But instead I got a waste of time.

WRITER'S BLOCK: TRUTH OR DARE 2
1995, Color, 96 min
STARRING: *Joey Michitson, Candace Rose, Robyn Allen, Jeffrey C. Hawkins*
DIRECTOR: *Chris LaMont*

A writer desperate for ideas adapts a murderer's diary into a best-selling novel. Hungry for credit, the killer torments the writer by killing his loved ones.

Awkwardly also known as *Writer's Block Truth Or Dare 2: Playing For Keeps*, this is no sequel to Tim Ritter's classic. *Truth Or Dare?* was a murderous turn on an innocent game that nicely continued in *Wicked Games* (the real *Truth Or Dare?* sequel). But in *Writer's Block*, the killer becomes so by watching *Wicked Games* on videotape. A fun premise to be sure, but it's quickly cast aside by melodramatic nonsense and uninteresting conflict. Is the audience supposed to care that the writer adapted his story? The film wants us to believe that a killer's diary is a book, but it's anything but. A book is fleshed out; dramatic with a beginning, middle and end. *Writer's Block* ultimately requires stupidity to be interesting because writers adapt things into books all the time. So the real drama should be lack of credit where credit's due, yet characters overreact to this idea. The worst is the wife, who all but screams for a confrontation when presented with the diary. Why? And why is nobody snooty enough to brush it off? In all seriousness, who cares? The problem lies in the writing. Only the uncredited killer should care, but he's too busy playing games with publishers and editors.

Writer's Block could have been the penultimate SOV horror film with a killer motivated by watching SOV horror. Instead, it's just stupid.

ZOMBIE BLOODBATH 2: RAGE OF THE UNDEAD
1995, Color, 93 min
STARRING: *Dave Miller, Kathleen McSweeney, Nick Stodden, Jody Rovick, Jerry Angell*
DIRECTOR: *Todd Sheets*

Three escaped convicts take refuge in a farmhouse. Teens run out of gas and seek help at the same house. Now held prisoner, fate intervenes as dead bodies rise from their graves, hungry for human flesh.

 More *Night of the Living Dead* (and less *Zombie Bloodbath*), Sheets' sequel is wonderfully paced with interesting plot twists. The film opens with a 1940's Satanic cult, differentiating itself from countless zombie copycats. And the surprises keep coming. Indeed, the living dead themselves don't actually appear until the 30 minute mark. So characters are important in *ZB2* because they run the show. Too often (particularly with zombie films) the undead force characters to adapt or succumb to carnage. Zombies can often appear like a one trick pony in this respect: they arrive, they swarm, they bite whatever they can (the essence of the modern zombie). But *ZB2* surprises with unique situations and unpredictable characters. The worst of the murderous convicts becomes the most valiant. Tormented

teens give their lives to save others. And a bounty-hunter defends everyone's life until losing his own. These characters make the film far more interesting than simple zombie attacks, and show Sheets has matured as a director. Familiar faces appear, but Angell (again) steals the show as a gas station robber. Paired with genre favorite Matthew Jason Walsh, Angell ranges from cruel to hilariously crazy, giving the film its edge. And while gore is present, enough restraint is shown to give it impact.

Controversially, the film ends with footage of Bill Clinton and Saddam Hussein. The word *"Devil"* is spliced into the picture, stating *"This feature is produced with the hope that we have left you with a thought or two about the state of the human race. In many ways we are already zombies...as a race, we humans always try and blame something else for our problems when in reality, it is a fact that we are killing ourselves. We as a race are killing our forests and natural resources, but far worse, we are destroying us. Think about it."*

Sheets at his most political.

ZOMBIE HOLOCAUST
1995, Color, 114 min
STARRING: *Pamela Sutch, Tina Krause, Laura Giglio, Kathy Steel, Sydney Nice*
DIRECTOR: *Gary Whitson*

In the future (2008), a female scientist will perfect the art of brain transplants. She will control a tribe of female mercenaries and secretly, the male leaders will have their brains transferred into younger bodies. Men will be condemned as mindless cannibals and the only hope for freedom will come from a lady assassin. And the future is NOW!

A high concept W.A.V.E. production. Most will wonder why there isn't any nudity (seriously, this film is ripe for a skin-fest), but *Zombie Holocaust* delivers with blood and shaky boobs like you wouldn't believe. And they're glorious. Machetes are used, pitchforks disembowel, mud wrestling occurs and an electric chair is put to good use. The showstopper is Dawn Murphy who (somehow) manages to tuck herself into a large pot for boiling. And another girl is roasted over an open fire as fat men slice the skin from her bones. This is *The Mummy's Dungeon* times 10. But true to Whitson's style, camera never excels beyond his "point and shoot" approach while costumes revolve around t-shirts and tube socks. Shirts are wet and soaked without bras underneath. Girls repeatedly faint or are drugged unconscious. And bottoms are everywhere. An epic opus! Recommended.

The film was later re-edited, rescored and re-titled as *Female Mercenaries On Zombie Island*. Incredibly, a sequel was also produced in 2008 starring most of the original cast.

 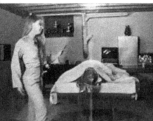  

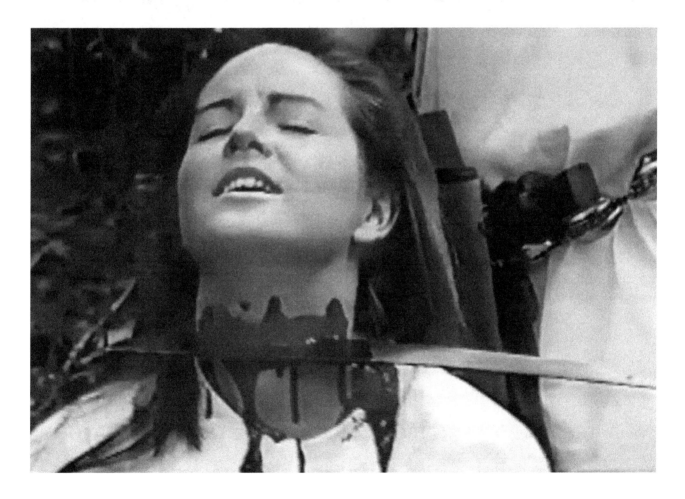

Interview
DAVID "THE ROCK" NELSON

A former US Marine and Golden Glove boxer from 1976 to 1991, David "The Rock" Nelson is a force to be reckoned with. Originally shooting hilarious shorts before advancing into his own features, Rock often casts family and friends to be pitted against various rubber monsters in his "monsta movies." More classical villains appear too (such as Frankenstein's monster, the wolfman and a whole bunch of vampires) as Rock personally performs, directs, edits and narrates his work into a hypnotic horror nirvana. There's nothing quite like a David "The Rock" Nelson picture, and he was given the *"Ed Wood of the 90's"* title to prove it.

Rock graciously accepted this opportunity for interview, and in true Rock form, he responded with answers to his own questions. Provided here is some of what I received, including written statements from several of his recorded interviews.

DAVID "THE ROCK" NELSON - THE MAN, THE MYTH, THE LEGEND

Yes, YES!!! I was thinking about this last night, that the image you posted was not for a movie, but for your Book. So, to remind me to contact you, I wrote a note & stuck it in my gym shoe (one that I wear daily) saying to: "Send Richard MOGG photos of *Vampire Woman* and *Conrad Brooks VS. Werewolf*, etc!" So, I will download those & send to you now, with info on those movies. I'll start that now, while I'm listening to classic 1968 soundtrack suites of the original *Planet of The Apes!* I love that music.

Well hello my fiends! It's me, your fiend David "The Rock" Nelson and I got my nice hot java here, I'm going to stir it in my WGN cup that I got for free at WGN, must watch news. I'm on their show now every Halloween for five minutes since 1997. I was writing them for three and a half years, three times a year, hand written letters, and I wrote every station in Chicago, and after three and a half years of letter writing, writing WGN like three-four times a year, keep telling them about my new movie I'm doing. I made Xerox pictures. I made Xerox pictures at Kinkos and I made my own letterhead with a typewriter and I enlarged the lettering with the Xerox machine, and I made the lettering bigger. It said *"David The Rock Nelson: Film director, actor, ex-Marine"* blah blah blah, and then two pictures of me taken down here in my dungeon, my basement (my basement of bloody horror).

Anyway, the Psychotronic Film Society gave me my first official website back in 1995. They made me an honorary member of the Chicago Psychotronic Film Society, formed by Michael Flores who named me "Ed Wood of the 90's" back in November 1992 (before I did *Conrad Brooks VS Werewolf*, before I met Conrad Brooks). Then in 1993, I met Conrad Brooks at the Famous Monsters Convention in May of 1993 at the Sheraton Hotel, Crystal City Sheraton in Arlington Virginia.

CONRAD BROOKS VS WEREWOLF

So I met Conrad at the Famous Monsters Convention. I go up to his table and this guy goes *"Hey, I'm Conrad Brooks"* and I'm thinking *"Who are you?"* and he goes *"Yeah I'm in the worst movie of all time, Plan 9 From Outer Space, by Ed Wood"* and I'm like *"Okay, but what's so great about Ed Wood?"* I didn't know that much about him, but I had heard his name because Flores had already given me the name "Ed Wood of the 90's" (later he changed it to "Ed Wood of the 21st Century.") So Conrad says *"Hey Rocky, you make your own movies right?"* and I go *"yeah"* and he goes *"I'd like to be in your pictures."* This is the day after the Famous Monsters Convention, May 1993 and we're sitting in the lobby. He buys me a Hershey with almonds (I don't know how he knew that was my favorite candy bar). So on my way home on a bus trip, on a napkin (the only thing I had to write on) I wrote the script for *The Werewolf of Baltimore*. And I wrote it on both sides. The original title was *Werewolf of Baltimore* but I changed it to *Conrad Brooks VS Werewolf* so people would know there's a star in it.

I filmed it in 4 days.

This was my 7th time playing a werewolf! My 1st time was in my "fiend" & Prez of our "Monster CLUB" (that I came up with for us to start, at age 7, in spring of 1964) Don Stillwaugh's Super8 3-minute movie, where I was roaming the grounds of a real "castle" in Fox River Grove, IL. And then Don shot me, using his 8-ring cap-gun! He then did a gradual "transformation" on me, showing me change back to a human. His Dad, Don Stillwaugh, Sr, who filmed the movie, is the architect who designed both our high school ("Maine SOUTH H.S" in Park Ridge, IL & "Maine NORTH H.S.") which was used in the 1980's movie *The Breakfast Club* and his name is in the credits! However, the reel was lost before it was developed & I never saw the finished movie. However, I've been "Making-UP" for that in "SPADES", for OVER '26"-YEARS & BEYOND, as I've been steadilly "Cranking"-OUT my own FUN "MONSTA"(Monster) Movies!

Oh, my 1st "Werewolf" Movie was a Monster-Comedy, "Werewolf Vs. Sodom INSANE", where the WEREWOLF battles a "parody" of a certain terrorist, who only seems to hunt-down "Monsters", Haah-Haaah! That was videotaped by me, as my late brother Keith's old video-camera was mounted on a tripod, recording the fight scenes between the werewolf (me wearing a used $20 werewolf mask and $12 werewolf gloves) and Sodom (also played by me, wearing a funny mask and my old Marine camoflauge uniform)! My little brother Phil "doubled" as Sodom in the "fight scenes," as we "wrestled" and he threw the snow-balls at me off camera, when werewolf and sodom threw snow-balls at each other! "Haaah!" That's on my "David ROCK Nelson Volume 1 'MONSTER' Movies"(1991-'93)!

My 2nd Werewolf movie on video was a Winter, 1991 shot-on-video short-film "Werewolf Meets TOR!" That one is only 10-minutes long and videotaped on a tripod, as BIG Mike Johnson wore my $16 "TOR" Johnson mask (by Don Post) and I wore my $20 werewolf mask and we wrestled and boxed at each other in front of the former "CRASH Palace" Bar (now "DELILAH's" Chicago Bar), during a meeting and "FREE" Sat. Nite Video screening of "The PsychoTronic Film Society!"

My 3rd and 4th shot-on-video "Werewolf" Movies were on my "David ROCK Nelson Volume 2 'MONSTER' Movies"(1992)! Those two were the 9-minute, shot in 3 & 1/2 hours, in 92-degree sunny, humid weather "Werewolf Vs. DRACULA" starring Gregg "OZZIE" Ozimek, the one who named me "The ROCK" (in 1989) and taught me boxing, in his first role EV-UH(ever), as the werewolf and me as Dracula! Then, also on my "Vol. 2 Monster Movies" video compilation was "DR. Johnson Meets The WEREWOLF!" It was originally going to be titled "Werewolf Vs. Frankenstein" but Big Mike "Frankenstein" Johnson wasn't available when I was going to do the "Werewolf Vs. Frankenstein" fight scenes at an old, abandoned, "Haunted"-looking house and the ruins of an old, Gothic-or-Victorian-style Niteclub. Big Mike was never around when I wanted to do those scenes at those locations and eventually the old, "haunted" house and ruins of the old niteclub were totally "demolished." R.I.P. old "Haunted" house & old "SPOOKY"-looking Niteclub (called "The ROMAN House" on N. Milwaukke Ave near LIbertyville, IL).

My next "Werewolf" movie was "SON of werewolf" (1993), a 25-minute movie on my "Vol. 3 Monster Movies" for 1993-'94, on a double-bill with my hoot (Hit?!) "MUMMY, A.D. 1993!" Then, I did the 44-minute featurette, *Conrad Brooks VS Werewolf*, my 6th Werewolf Movie!

Hope this is enough info for you and your Book! ...It's probably "Tooooo" Muh, "Haaaah, haaah!!!"

VAMPIRE WOMAN

Hi again, Richard! And NOW, without any further ado, is my 2 & 1/2 years in-the-making, 4-Hour & 38-minute SUPER-length feature, *Vampire Woman!* My late brother Keith's big, Sony camcorder stopped working immediately after videotaping International "Ghost-Hunter" Richard T. CROWE's scenes in the "haunted" "International CINEMA Museum" in October. 1994! I had to sweep floors at "Handy Andy" for two and a half weeks to earn enough for a new 8mm Video camcorder, to finish the movie *Vampire Woman*, which I finally finished video-editing on Sept. 6th, 1996! It is now on a 2-disk DVD, available from me. That former "International Cinema Museum" is on ERIE St., three blocks west of Wells St. where "HOOTERS" is located, in Downtown Chicago. The Prez of Chicago's "PsychoTronic Film Society," Mike Flores is also in some scenes with the now late, great International "Ghost-Hunter" Richard Crowe and we "celebrated" afterwards three blocks away, at "HOOTERS" (NW corner of ERIE St. and Wells) as I bought us a 50-piece "Three Mile Island" hot, spicy chicken wings, with blue cheeze dressing, an order of "curly-fries" and two pitchers of "RED DOG" Brew, all for $35. My treat to them for being in my movie! Richard Crowe said to me: *"Just buy us a big order of chicken wings and a pitcher or two of 'Red DOG' Beer and we'll do the movie!"* Janet "Vampire Woman" and I attended his wake & funeral in 2011 R.I.P. Richard Crowe, "Ghost-Hunter!"

[When] Detective ROCK (Dir. David ROCK Nelson) chases "VAMPIRE Woman"(JANET) through the "haunted" cemetery, we wanted to do a few more scenes the next day, but saw a police squad car parked at the entrance right where we did the scenes the day before. So, I kept driving and we did those "other" scenes in another, abandoned, "secluded" old cemetery I found, about 7-miles away! We used that other cemetery often, after that.

I shot all my movies on 8mm [video]. Regular video 8, not Hi8, with my 8mm camcorder. I still edit on the VHS video (the master), and then I make a DVD copy, and then I make a couple copies on DVD and run off copies from a DVD copy. Your "FIEND," David ROCK Nelson, B-"Monster"-comedy Moviemaker/Actor 26-Years & BEYOND & former MARINE Corporal "OO-Rah" Nelson (served 1976-'80) in U.S. Marine Corps. SEE ya! -ROCK!

Thank you so much for your time and thoughts, Rock!

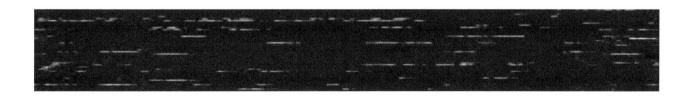

Interview
RON BONK

Writing his own ticket, Ron gained technical know-how and skill after attending a filmmaking seminar and creating his own instructional video *"What a Deal!"* in 1992. Launching into his first feature *City of the Vampires* in 1993, Ron quickly connected with J.R. Bookwalter, shooting several shorts and serving as Director of Photography on Bookwalter's *The Sandman*. Ron's critically acclaimed break-out film *The Vicious Sweet* came in 1997, followed by *Strawberry Estates*, *Clay* and *Ms. Cannibal Holocaust*. But Ron's greatest legacy has been his long-running distribution company SRS Cinema LLC (also known as SubRosa Studios). Over the past 25 years, Ron has become one of the leading moguls of independent genre film distribution worldwide. And still an active filmmaker today, Ron has also created award winning films such as *She Kills* and his hilarious horror thriller *House Shark*, playing to rave reviews at festival screenings.

Ron, thank you for giving your time to this interview! What initially lead you to become a filmmaker?

When I was growing up, I loved acting out movies. Or make up my own stories and acting them out with kids in the neighborhood. My mom used to babysit a couple kids from across the street and they would go see movies before we did. And they were the kids who would see something 7 or 10 times and tell you the entire plot before you had a chance to see it. So we'd act out these movies and it was just so much fun. I remember in high school briefly considering becoming a filmmaker, but I thought it was too high of a mountain to try and climb. I didn't want to have to go out to California. And even if I tried to venture out on it on my own, everyone I talked to said it was minimum $100,000 and I'd have to shoot on film. So I started pursuing other degrees and the whole college process. But I looked at my future and knew I wasn't going to enjoy the mundane. I wanted to be creative and I wanted to tell my own stories. So I decided to throw it aside and really pursue filmmaking. And then I found out that there were movies being made on analog video. And I found out about people like Eric Stanze who were shooting on S-VHS and it looked good! Yeah, it was a little bit grainy and a bit dark. But they were making legitimate stories and it was awesome to sort of control your own destiny. Tell the stories you wanted and not be under someone else's control. And films could literally be done for a few thousand, if not a few hundred dollars. So I eventually got a camera and pursued it.

Were you influenced by any films or filmmakers?

I was at this John Russo filmmaking seminar and he was talking about different things with guest speakers he had there. And one of the guests was J.R. Bookwalter who was shooting movies on S-VHS and distributing them. J.R. played *Kingdom of the Vampire* and I saw how he treated the story seriously. Sure it was campy and performances were somewhat over the top, but the story didn't poke fun at itself. And between that and films I had seen like *The Scare Game* and some of Tim Ritter's stuff, I was really impressed. There can be good work done, even if you're shooting with a camcorder available to the average consumer.

Was the seminar held before you did *"What a Deal!"*? How did that project come about?

Yes, it was before I did *"What a Deal."* What happened was I was working antiques and went down to Florida to avoid the bad weather up in New York. So I was in Florida and had gotten my camera and was really eager to make a movie. So I wondered what I could shoot and my Dad had written this book on the antique business. Buying and selling antiques. So I took that and cast some local people and shot some re-enactments. I cut it all together when I got back to New York (maybe cut a little while I was down in Florida) and got it out there. It did really well but I knew special interest topics weren't what I wanted to do. I wanted to do stories; fiction. So I had written a couple scripts and decided to pursue *City of the Vampires* because it was the script I didn't like as much. I knew it was kind of going to be my film school and I was going to go out and learn how to make a movie. Even though I knew it wasn't going to come out very good, I still had that vision that it's going to be the greatest. But it came out horrible. Part of the problem was that I did every single crew job. I was doing special effects, sound, lighting, just everything. But it was a learning process.

How much time had passed between the seminar and making your own feature?

I started shooting *"What A Deal"* almost right after. They were both in 1992 and I shot *City of the Vampires* in 1993. So it all happened pretty fast. In 1994, I was shooting an anthology and J.R. asked me if I wanted to work on *The Sandman*. *The Sandman* was shot around 1994-1995, I think. And I remember I wrote *The Vicious Sweet* in 1996.

Did you meet everyone from Tempe at the Russo seminar?

Only J.R. I met there, I think. Matthew Jason Walsh, who ended up playing the lead in *City of the Vampires* after I recast it, I saw in *Kingdom of the Vampire*. But I didn't actually meet him until he came to Syracuse to shoot *City*. I would meet Tim Ritter when I would go down to Florida and was always amazed how tall he was.

Jack (John Russo, everybody calls him Jack) and I have become long time friends. I see him at conventions all the time now. We'll grab dinner, we'll catch up, he'll come out to Syracuse. He's a big supporter of my work and will always give me great quotes on the stuff. He's the closest thing I have to a mentor in this business. For years, Jack would tell me that I was the only one from the seminar who did anything. That I was the one success story. But now there's also Zane Hershberger, who was working on his own stuff before working on *The Barn* and directing and producing.

From your very first film, you've always strived to have really in-depth characters.

Thank you. I try to put a lot of thought into them. Even if they're comedic. Some of the stuff didn't come out as good as I hoped, but they've gotten better over time.

Being your first feature, what did you learned from making *City of the Vampires?*

First, not to do all the jobs. Definitely. You do need the help, even if it's just one or two hard working people. And people are going to work hard if they believe in the project and are on set. That was probably the biggest thing. But I made a lot of amateur mistakes on *City*. We would shoot night stuff and I was convinced I didn't need powerful lighting. We'd shoot in these buildings that didn't have electricity. We'd use car headlights to light stuff because I didn't have the budget for a generator. And by the time you'd go down a couple generations editing deck to deck (or camera to deck), it would drop down in quality so quick. But you learn. Whatever didn't work the first time, you try to fix it in the next.

When (or why) did you start thinking about creating your own video label?

I didn't think about that until after *City of the Vampires*. When I had *City* done and I knew it wasn't an amazing piece of cinema, I didn't want to just turn it over to someone and never see it again. J.R. was leaving the distribution business (he would leave and come back) but he was scaling back on titles and the only other company was Dead Alive, who had a horrible reputation for not paying filmmakers. So I thought my next step was learning the distribution side of things. I had done it already with *"What a Deal"* but a lot of those sales came from a couple of good reviews I had in key publications. So I got some advice from J.R. and pursued it, yet a lot of it was learning and trying on the spot. See what worked and what didn't, and people started seeing *City of the Vampires* out there. That's how Tim Ritter contacted me. He saw I was doing distribution and contacted me about these movies he was doing: *Killing Spree*, *Wicked Games* and *Creep*. And when I signed those, I sold them pretty quick to Germany. We ended up splitting that money and I used my half to make *The Vicious Sweet*.

And then I saw the internet becoming something and looking around on that, there was only Scorched Earth online selling movies. But they just had this catalogue that wasn't dedicated to any type. So I said I'd make a site that was dedicated to B movies and started www.b-movie.com. And being the first on the internet with movies like that really helped develop the distribution. I wasn't necessarily owning the rights to all the movies selling on the site, but I was sub-distributing. Basically buying wholesale off of other filmmakers and reselling them on the site. I had some W.A.V.E. titles and they sold great. Other companies too that also did custom work. So between doing my own distribution and movies I signed or owned rights to, I was able to build the distribution up.

Why did the company change names over the years?

I started off selling City Home Video and then I incorporated into SubRosa Studios. Later, I was trying to up the level of movies I was releasing to have more mainstream success, I started SRS Cinema. Sort of the elite indie movies. And it was easier to just get everything under one banner. I would do offshoots that were in-name only like SRS Underground (or was it SRS Unbound?) but that didn't really help. They just became harder to track. So I eventually said *"I'm just going to make this all SRS Cinema."* I only brought the SubRosa line back when we started doing VHS again because it's fun. Sometimes SubRosa seems to have a bigger following than SRS because people remember it. SubRosa was the company during the peak of VHS. But now everything just comes out under SRS.

So after *City of the Vampires* came *Dark Descent*?

It was pretty much the next year following *City*. I had shot the "Permanent Waves" segment and I had an idea for the "Strawberry Estates" segment, but we shot another short after *The Sandman* called "I've Killed Before." That ended up becoming *Dark Descent* [an anthology]. But *Dark Descent* was going to be 4 shorts, only when I wrote the "Strawberry Estates" script, it was feature length and I didn't want to cut it down. And once I worked on *The Sandman*, it pretty much killed off the anthology. So I came back to "Strawberry Estates" with the intent of shooting that as a feature.

And how did *The Sandman* come about?

Well I remember shooting the "Permanent Waves" segment when J.R. contacted me. Offering if I'd like to come out and DP *The Sandman* (shoot as Director of Photography). So we did that and I stayed out there a bit. I enjoyed working with Matthew Jason Walsh and the intent was to kind of start our own production company. Matt would come back to Syracuse with me for a while too, but I wasn't able to get things going. I had to kind of get re-established and get an income coming in. It was only for a short amount of time, maybe 2 or 3 months, then he eventually decided to head back home. And a year after that, I was in production on *The Vicious Sweet*.

The reason he hired me for *The Sandman* was because, despite the problems I had on *City*, I pushed through it. I was determined to finish it and that impressed J.R. enough that he asked me to come out. With *The Sandman*, he wanted to be more hands off instead of running the camera and doing in the lighting. Someone else to do that so he could focus on direction.

Any memorable stories from *The Sandman's* production?

We were shooting in a trailer park that had gangs and I think drug issues too. The cops had to be called in after one of our lead actors got in a fight with one of the local gang members. Our guy peeled out in his car and got mud on the gang member's jacket, or something like that. The cops came in and were really surprised we were shooting in there. They called it "Death Park!"

***The Vicious Sweet* has often been regarded as your "breakout film." Was it a financial success also?**

I think it was the first one people looked at and thought it was okay. *City of the Vampires* has fans today for some reason, but I don't think anyone was a fan of it back then. I remember the Polonia brothers telling me they liked it, but I was more mortified by it. I used it to learn distribution and then I shelved it. Took it off the market. *The Vicious Sweet* didn't sell as well as *City,* but I think a lot of it has to do with the art. It was better received, but I don't think I took advantage of the momentum that *Vicious Sweet* started. I produced *Gut Pile* but I didn't direct it. And I shelved *Strawberry Estates* and didn't reshoot it for a few years.

The film notably stars Scream Queen Sasha Graham as the lead. Did casting her bring extra attention to the production?

Well any of the Scream Queens help bring in more fans, but Sasha had a different fan base because she didn't do nudity. So there were the Scream Queens on one extreme who had fans because they did tons of nudity, some in the middle who did nudity but were really good actors, and some on the other end who didn't do nudity but had a quality of acting. Sometimes the no nudity ones had a smaller fan base than the ones who did nudity, but having her name certainly helped. She had been in Kevin Lindenmuth's movies and some others, but I don't know how much she was really out there at the time that I cast her. She was out there for sure, but I remember a whole bunch of roles she did after we did *Vicious*. The *Addicted To Murder* sequels, the *Alien Agenda* films, *Bloodletting*; things like that.

How did you first meet Sasha Graham?

Kevin and I would split a table sometimes at Chiller and he had her come out and sit at the table. She had done the first *Addicted To Murder* and would sign for it. I was having trouble in writing, deciding what the lead character would be like and after I met her, I pictured her in the lead [for *Vicious*]. So right after the convention, I was able to go home and get the script done. I went to Kevin and asked about having her auditioning just to see if she was interested in the role. But for whatever reason, she didn't end up coming out to audition. So I cast Debbie Rochon. Debbie loved it and wanted to do it, but kept having scheduling conflicts. We kept having to cancel and push things back. So Debbie and I were really good friends at the time and I finally said *"I'm never going to get this movie made"* and I had to recast. She understood completely and I finally went back to Kevin about casting Sasha. And this time, Sasha did get in contact with me and was interested. So she got on a train but didn't actually read the script until she was on the train. And she loved the script, loved the character and was really eager to play it.

What's your opinion on shot on video movies?

I like that they tell different stories that you won't find anywhere else. Look at the Polonia brothers' work or Tim Ritter's or so many others. Despite the budgets, you can tell they just love B movies and just love slasher movies. The Polonia brothers were making stuff in their teens that is still so inspiring today. Their cool shots and the stuff they'd do, I mean jeez! I wish I could have done stuff like that when I was young. And you can see all the homages in their work. I remember Chris Seaver would send me his early shorts and they were using all these characters that were copyrighted. Jason Vorhees and Michael Myers. But it was always inspiring to see how much these guys loved horror movies. They loved them so much, they wanted to do their own stories. And it was very relatable for me.

Among the hundreds of titles released by SRS Cinema, you also notably represent *Midnight 2: Sex, Death and Videotape.* **Was that through your relationship with John Russo?**

Midnight 2 was part of an acquisition. Russo wanted to sell his library and I was doing some foreign rights sales for him. And I had approached a guy who was buying some movies off me. Well the guy who was buying had slowed down over the course of a year and finally stopped. Closed up shop or something. So I went back to Jack and said that maybe I'd be interested in picking some of the titles up. *Midnight 2* was the only feature in there, the rest were make-up or special interest stuff (*Scream Queens Illustrated, Monster Make-up With Dick Smith, Tom Savini Horror FX, Drive-In Madness* and others). Jack just wanted to sell those off.

In your (expert) opinion, how has distribution changed over the years?

Well it's actually changed from VHS being the main media to VHS being a niche thing. It's developed to different physical media (DVD and Blu-ray) to the ultimate dream for movie fans: being able to dial-up the internet and find almost anything they want without having to wait. A lot of people still like to have the physical copy and all the bonus features, but say one night you want to watch *The Vicious Sweet.* Well it's available on Vimeo for like $1.99, giving you 24 hours to watch it. You don't have to spend extra to buy it and wait however long for it to ship. You can literally watch it right now. So that sort of stuff has changed. But distribution is a constantly changing model. Whenever you think you've figured it out, it'll change. So you just have to stay very up-to-date on it and alert. Even when I think I'm up on it, I'll see numbers shrinking and then I'll find out there's been another vast change.

A couple years ago, I learned that main retailers don't want the comic art anymore. Wal-Mart, Best Buy, Family Video; they want real images on it. They say comic doesn't translate to their buyers. So what retail wants doesn't always match what (I'm told) fan's want. So for *She Kills*, we had to redo the art to get into Family Video. Make it look super slick and Hollywood-like just to be able to get it into stores.

Horror always remains popular but within it, there's different subgenres. And sometimes those come in and out of popularity. For years, erotic vampire titles were red hot. I would stock every single one I could on the website because you'd be guaranteed 20-30% sales right off the top. But now, I can never sell erotic vampire movies the way I used to. They've died off. Bigfoot movies were big for a while, but they've teetered off. There just comes a time when the market gets saturated with something. And not just by independents but by the major studios. So things will come and go, but they usually come back too.

Again in your (expert) opinion, what advice might you offer today's filmmakers just starting out?

In terms of production, tell the story you want to tell. Too many times, people make something (a found footage film, a slasher film, a zombie film) because they're popular but they're not really passionate about the story. So they'll turn out something that might look slick but has no heart. And that really does hurt the bottom line because throwing a bunch of money in a film does not solve the filmmaking riddle. Go out and make whatever you want to make and make it the very best you can. Try to get the best equipment, try to shoot at least HD, get really good sound; make every aspect you can the best. Get the best actors you can. Try to think out your shots. Do the best lighting you possibly can do. Try to get a good special effects person because everybody loves practical effects. Just make it the very best you can because then, the audience will find it.

And you have to be your own PR guy; you have to promote it. You can't just think someone's going to take it and run for you. You have to do that yourself because no one will believe in your project as much as you do. So think of it as a 2 part process: making the movie and releasing the movie. But really go out and study films and study the art of filmmaking. Don't do shots just because they look cool. Try to make something where the camera manipulates the audience as part of the story.

Is there still an open market today for filmmakers hoping to get their movie out?

Yeah, I'm always looking for new stuff. Sometimes if there's a down-turn in the market (or I just need a break) I might not be releasing much, but I'm usually releasing 1 or 2 titles a month. And I'm still always looking for new product. If you've got a cool movie and it has some good gore effects, some solid production value with a lot of heart in it, I would be interested for sure.

And what's the best way these filmmakers can get in touch with you?

Email me at srscinema.com or the SRS Cinema Facebook page!

Thank you so much for your time and thoughts, Ron!

FANGORIA'S
Weekend
OF
HORRORS

Chapter 18
HORROR FOR SALE

Before *Boardinghouse* had its impact and before *Sledgehammer* saw release, a wise Charles Band saw an opportunity and pounced. Video stores were popping up everywhere and before you could say *"What should we watch tonight?,"* Charles was going to tell you.

Meagerly produced and quickly assembled, Band created *Filmgore*: a video clip show of the most gruesome films available, hosted by the Mistress of the Dark herself. Elvira (Cassandra Peterson) talked up the movies, commenting on their panache (much as she did on her cable television program *"Movie Macabre"*), only the violence was uncensored. *Filmgore* was big, hard and forbidden... and it made people rent. More clip shows followed, and just as the format became a tool for up and coming producers looking to make a movie, it also became a means to market, advertise and (surprisingly) educate a horror audience.

Instructional videos were everywhere throughout the decade, from how to carve a table, to when to feed your fish. But as the videos dovetailed into horror for horror purposes, we took notice. Video was frequently used for clip shows, sometimes creatively so as with *Terror On Tape* or *Prevues From Hell*, but usually with the basic intent to advertise films. After all, these were suppliment videos to movies already on video. But the idea that cassettes would be manufactured with the sole purpose to sell more cassettes was extraordinary. As previously discussed in Chapter 6, *Blood Cult* had exploded upon the masses like a giant awakening. Video suddenly became legitimate and people realized *"Hey! I can do that!"* But another release came (from the most unlikeliest of places) that created almost as much impact.

Fangoria magazine famously began documenting their horror conventions in 1985, producing their own video called *Fangoria's Weekend of Horrors*. The video was a smash hit. Essentially memorializing a convention, the hour-long tape supplements itself with comments and interviews from horror's biggest names of the day. Others companies expanded on Fangoria's approach by focusing on horror topics or genre icons. Eventually, horror celebrities were even paid to star in "how-to" and educational tapes themselves, bringing in audiences solely on the promise that the topic somehow related to the genre. But even when it came to simple topics like revenge, horror was being sold on video in every way imaginable. Some of it was sleaze dressed up, but the majority of titles were scrapes at the barrel using every last good idea producers had to turn a buck. And for sheer huckster bravado, it worked.

These were the Special Interest videos of the genre, the shameless horrors for sale.

FANGORIA'S WEEKEND OF HORRORS

1986, Color, 59 min
STARRING: *Kerry O'Quinn, Wes Craven, Tobe Hooper, Clu Gulager, Robert Englund*
DIRECTOR: *Mike Hadley, Kerry O'Quinn*

A lively edited document of a mid-80's horror convention, complete with filmmaker and celebrity interviews.

 One of the most nostalgic videos amongst slasher fans, *Weekend of Horrors* was initially designed to document the rising popularity of fan conventions. Science fiction conventions had already been popular, but horror had not featured prominently as the main attraction until a partnership between Creation Entertainment and Fangoria magazine. Created in 1979, Fangoria (an offshoot of Starlog publications) was initially designed to focus on fantasy films before shifting entirely to an all-horror format by issue #7. And by the mid-80's, Fangoria dominated newsstands as the greatest horror magazine worldwide. Complete with on-set articles, bloody pictures and celebrity interviews, Fangoria took its successful recipe into the home video market; partnering to host horror conventions and produce relevant material for a hungry audience.

And this is the fruits of their labor.

Filmed during some of its earliest ventures, *Weekend of Horrors* brought viewers into the main event as honored guests. Fan observations hit before larger insights came from Wes Craven, Robert Englund and more (all appearing somewhat dazed by the interest). Trailers and film clips surrounded the talking heads, most of which were brand new at the time (*Troll, A Nightmare On Elm Street 2*). Elvira (Cassandra Peterson) appeared to answer a few candid inquiries, Tobe Hooper awarded some independent filmmakers and a live auction was held amongst patrons. More familiar faces appeared too (Clu Gulager, Rick Baker, Dick Miller) and everything ended with a wonderfully homemade costume contest. Emphasis was placed on popular fantasy over slashers (lots of *A Nightmare on Elm Street*), but this document has become an exciting time-capsule for when practical special effects still reigned supreme. *Weekend of Horrors* is an excellent, nostalgia filled memoir to a time when horror knew no bounds. Required Viewing!

   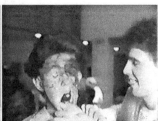

FILMGORE
1983, Color, 120 min
STARRING: *Elvira (Cassandra Peterson)*
DIRECTOR: *Ken Dixon*

Elvira hosts a bunch of film clips.

First appearing as the host of television's *"Movie Macabre"* in 1981 (a program playing various horror films), Elvira (Peterson) became an iconic sensation almost overnight. With her witty remarks, tongue-in-cheek approach and revealing figure, horror fans fell in love with the "Mistress of the Dark." So to see her host a 2 hour video was her next logical step. *Filmgore*, a release most memorable to horror fans of the early 80's, featured the bloodiest clips from some of the most notorious horror films available (several of which were banned in Britain's Video Nasties scandal). *Blood Feast*, *The Texas Chainsaw Massacre*, *Driller Killer*, *Drive-In Massacre*, *Snuff* and more; all here to impress and disgust the most jaded viewer. Elvira is only briefly appears throughout, leaving clips to dominate the runtime. But her smiling beauty and smarmy winks go a long way. *Filmgore* exists mostly as a historical piece today, presenting dated clips of films now widely available in lavishly remastered prints. But for some, *Filmgore's* legendary status will never die.

GORGON VIDEO MAGAZINE
1989, Color, 70 min
STARRING: *Michael Berryman, Wes Craven, Linnea Quigley, Lloyd Kaufman*
DIRECTOR: *Stuart Shapiro, Evan Pendell, Modi, Patricia Wadsley, Alex Winter*

Host Michael Berryman (in full *Hills Have Eyes* getup) introduces viewers to a series of interviews with horror filmmakers and stars.

Taking cue from Fangoria magazine's foray into home video, Gorgon showcases a collection of on-set interviews, film reviews and a musical spotlight on the band Gwar. Horror icon Berryman provides an adequate (if not hilarious) delivery of telegraphed lines direct to camera while superimposed over various film clips. Indeed the whole affair feels like a visual magazine, complete with momentary cartoons separating the articles. The real interest is the on-set visit to Wes Craven's *Shocker* (where he claims *"total control over every aspect of production"*) and a sit down chat with "Queen of the B's" Linnea Quigley. The Troma Team also gets their own chance to shine, complete with a young Kaufman sporting a dark, unkempt beard. Gorgon is best regarded as a celebration of 80's low budget horror (complete with sneak peeks of *Henry: Portrait of a Serial Killer*) that will surely bring a smile to fans old enough to remember. The video was also successful enough to warrant another volume, which was quickly produced and shelved. Recommended.

GORGON VIDEO MAGAZINE #2

1989, Color, 90 min
STARRING: *Michael Berryman, Stuart Gordon, Penn Gillette, Screaming Mad George*
DIRECTOR: *Adam Cohen, Paul Bacca, Stuart Shapiro, Modi, Patricia Wadsley, Joe Horne*

More of Michael Berryman introducing interviews with horror filmmakers, makeup artists and magicians.

Billing itself as a "Halloween Edition" (though sparingly focused on halloween), *Gorgon 2* tries and fails to live up to the original entry. Berryman tweaks and mugs for the camera constantly. Segments are cut tighter and run shorter, yet the video is extended to cover more ground. The lengthy interviews of *volume 1* are kept minimal here, allowing only Gordon and Screaming Mad George to deliver worthwhile musings. And the most bizarre inclusion is magicians (on-stage illusionists) Penn and Teller who offer a backstage pass to a rat-involved stage trick. *Gorgon 2* feels like a rushed production, hastily assembled with footage that was possibly intended for *volume 1*. And if it weren't for the Gordon and George segments, I'd be tempted to let it rest in video Hell. Only for purists.

HORROR F/X

1989, Color, 38 min
STARRING: *Tom Savini, John Russo, Lia Savini*
DIRECTOR: *Paul McCollough*

Makeup legend Tom Savini (alongside daughter Lia) is interviewed by writer/director John Russo.

Looking to ride the success of Fangoria's initial *Scream Greats* entry, *Horror F/X* entertains thanks to the wonderfully candid material. Savini shares several behind-the-scenes moments of his impressive career, charmingly joking with his daughter between tales. Yet the real star is the live on-set footage from Savini's personal collection. Choice moments from his more famous creations are seen, undressed and unfinished. A few years have passed since *Scream Greats* too, so *Monkey Shines* and *The Texas Chainsaw Massacre 2* are nicely touched upon. *Horror F/X* largely plays towards those interested in special makeup effects (which was everybody during the 1980's) but hangs on Savini's charisma too.

Later released as *Tom Savini: Horror Effects*.

HOW TO GET... REVENGE!

1988, Color, 49 min
STARRING: *Linda Blair, Gregory Itzin*
DIRECTOR: *Bob Logan*

Horror actress Linda Blair hosts an instructional video describing several ways to damage people's property, reputations and relationships with others.

A household name since her demonically possessed appearance in 1973's *The Exorcist*, Blair continued her tormented portrayals with leads in 1974's *Born Innocent* and 1975's *Sarah T- Portrait of a Teenaged Alcoholic*. Incredible work that frequently cast her in victimized roles, Blair's talents were often overshadowed by the haggard roles she played. An *Exorcist* sequel and the spooky slasher *Hell Night* only solidified things, before numerous appearances in WIP (woman in prison) films had Blair constantly raped and ridiculed onscreen. Revenge was often the WIP climax, and it also played heavily in her excellent *Savage Streets* from 1984. Therefore, it was wholly appropriate to have Blair host a revenge-themed documentary. And she doesn't disappoint.

Showcasing her comedic side, Blair jokes with a charm perfectly natural for the subject matter. Attractively dressed in blouse and skirt, Blair banters with commentators as she openly narrates the video. *How to Get Revenge* even lands a few jokes, opening with Blair reading from the Bible (an *Exorcist* reference). And as for the techniques described, some are pretty farfetched while others are shockingly attainable. Occasionally, even Blair seems caught off-guard by the dastardly tactics being taught! The participants showcased are quite obviously actors (Itzin purporting to be a cop) but it's all part of the fun. Surely such a video would never be produced today, but *How to* is a wonderful throwback to a time when pay phones were untraceable and mail was easily stolen from mailboxes. Recommended.

INVASION OF THE SCREAM QUEENS
1992, Color, 82 min
STARRING: *Michelle Bauer, Brinke Stevens, Mary Woronov, Elizabeth Kaitan*
DIRECTOR: *Donald Farmer*

Several B-movie actresses are interviewed candidly.

Released in 1992, *Invasion of the Scream Queens* is a series of relatively unfiltered chats with horror actresses of the time. The heart of the program lies in the participants' honesty, particularly Woronov as she shares her love of painting. But much of the runtime is happy smiles and positivity. Everyone feels genuine, except Monique Gabrielle (who breaks into laughter throughout). Common topics include how they first started acting and thoughts on nudity. Basically a talking heads program, warmly engaging thanks to the people involved.

Invasion's producers famously found themselves sued for copyright infringement after using the image of Michelle Bauer on the videocassette cover. The image had originated from the film *Hellroller*, though producers claimed that rights were purchased from the photographer. Litigated on *"The People's Court,"* Judge Wapner surprisingly ruled in *Invasion's* favor and the case was lost.

Judge Wapner on "The People's Court"

LINNEA QUIGLEY'S HORROR WORKOUT
1989, Color, 60 min
STARRING: *Linnea Quigley, B. Jane Holzer (Cynthia Garris), Victoria Nesbitt, Jeff Bowser*
DIRECTOR: *Hal Kennedy (Kenneth J. Hall)*

Screen Queen Linnea Quigley takes a long shower, dons a studded bikini and does aerobics. Later she aerobicises with zombies and a masked killer (who gruesomely slays her friends).

Capitalizing on Quigley's celebrity (often naked and butchered in films like *Return of the Living Dead, Silent Night Deadly Night* and *Creepozoids*), *Horror Workout* is little more than an advertising piece for other films. Linnea reminisces while clips from *Sorority Babes in the Slimeball Bowl-O-Rama* and *Nightmare Sisters* dominate the show. Finally 10 minutes in, the "workout" starts in studded bra and black leather boots. Young men are clearly the target audience, though women are encouraged to join with quips like *"I don't know what this move is, but it sure feels good"* and *"this one's great for the guys... I mean thighs."* But Quigley's untouchable as she's genuinely entertaining throughout. Some childhood footage of the star dancing and playing guitar offer substance, but this is mostly played for laughs. A clip tape meant to sell videos (and it worked).

LISA COOK'S DEADLY WORKOUT
1994, Color, 39 min
STARRING: *Lisa Cook*
DIRECTOR: *Todd Jason Cook*

Todd Cook's wife and lead actress shines in her own workout video.

Inspired by *Linnea Quigley's Horror Workout* (with a reference to Linnea in the opening), Lisa Cook's is a fun quickie for interested parties. Lisa gets chased by the *Evil Night* clown, changes into lingerie and offers a short interview on camera. Then it's aerobics time with some very revealing crotch shots. Short, sweet and to the point.

MAD RON'S PREVUES FROM HELL
1987, Color, 84 min
STARRING: *Nick Pawlow, Ron Roccia, Michael Townsend Wright, Anthony Kelly*
DIRECTOR: *Jim Monaco*

Nick Pawlow and his undead ventriloquist dummy host a slew of horrific trailers for a bunch of zombies.

A compilation video framed in a theater, *Prevues From Hell* is still enjoyable 30 years later. Like *Terror On Tape* before it, *Prevues* frames its advertisements with fun nostalgic interplay between viewer and host. Pawlow and his dummy struggle to play trailers for a flesh-hungry audience. Dubbed Happy Goldsplatt, the rotted doll operated by Pawlow is essentially a joke telling, one-man performance. And it's funny. At one point, Happy states that he *"must be Jewish"* because the end of his dick is missing, to which Pawlow responds that it may have rotted off. Makeup is impressive (technically better than several of the films being advertised) and the zombies have a nice *Day of the Dead* look. The trailers may be prints, but the wraparounds are all glorious video. Recommended!

NAKED HORROR
1995, Color, 42 min
STARRING: *Kelly Smith, Jasmin St. James, Melissa Silver, Stacy Warfel, Debbie D*
DIRECTOR: *Jack Redd*

A horror convention's security guard watches a trio of babes strip and dance with horror statues. The guard later fantasizes that he too was a monster receiving the strip tease.

Seemingly made on a whim, *Naked Horror* feels like a zero-budget Playboy tape with stolen footage of a fan-expo. Nothing makes sense as girls bare silicone breasts across the screen. Screen Queens inexplicably see statues of the *Predator*, *The Exorcist's* Regan McNeil and Stan Winston's *Pumpkinhead* before stripping and stroking the latex beasts. Later as a guard (watching via hidden camera) dreams of wearing a rubber mask, the girls strip exclusively for him. That's the extent of this man's desires I guess (or at least, the extent of Redd's naughty footage). But you don't have to be a rocket scientist to see that *Naked Horror* is really just a nudie tape hiding under a horror banner. This is something for teenage boys to rent when mom thinks it's a horror film.

  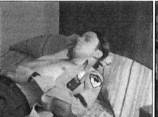 

SCREAM GREATS #1: TOM SAVINI, MASTER OF HORROR EFFECTS

1986, Color, 53 min
STARRING: *Tom Savini, George A. Romero, Greg Nicotero, Taso Stavrakis, Nancy Savini*
DIRECTOR: *Damon Santostefano*

An in-depth, charismatic look at special makeup effects artist Tom Savini.

Coming at the peak of Savini's popularity, Fangoria's *Scream Greats* was a hugely influential video for splatter fans and a brilliant behind-the-scenes look at the man who was almost as famous as the monsters he created. *Scream Greats* became an immediate success for the horror magazine and it's easy to see why. Savini opens with the statement *"sometimes I feel like an assassin,"* before casually explaining how he has realistically sliced teens and disemboweled zombies. Many of his most famous effects are touched upon, complete with behind-the-scenes personal footage, in-studio testing and Savini's narration to demonstrate creative processes. And all of it is fascinating. Savini's then-assistants Nicotero and Stavrakis contribute with personal stories, and a squib blood-effect is tested on then-wife Nancy. *Scream Greats* also unknowingly captured lightning in a bottle, as this was produced just after *Day of the Dead's* release (arguably still his most impressive work to date). *Day* and *Dawn of the Dead* are featured heavily, as is *Friday the 13th: The Final Chapter*, *The Burning*, *The Prowler*, *Martin*, *Knightriders* and Savini's directed episode of *"Tales From the Darkside."* Yes, there are some overlooked titles (and *Friday the 13th 2* and *3* appear though Savini did not work on them), but this is an incredible companion piece to the splatter films produced throughout the decade and the man most synonymous with their violence. Required Viewing.

SCREAM GREATS #2: SATANISM AND WITCHCRAFT

1986, Color, 57 min
STARRING: *Paul Valentine, Ed Warren, Lorraine Warren, Hans Holzer, Richard Donner*
DIRECTOR: *Damon Santostefano*

Fangoria's second *Scream Greats* entry focuses on Satanism as a religion and practices of modern day witchcraft.

An interesting documentary utilizing both popular film clips and interviews, *Scream Greats #2* offers a fairly unbiased look into the realm of Satanism. High priests and self proclaimed witches are interviewed, as are paranormal investigators Ed and Lorraine Warren (famous for their *Amityville Horror* investigation and present day's *Conjuring* films). But as intriguing as the subject is, *Scream Greats #2* feels a little off the mark. It's Fangoria produced but feels more suited for the History channel. *The Omen* and *Rosemary's Baby* are used for reference, but the film feels motivated to portray Satanism in a positive light. And perhaps it is, but not when showcased alongside horror films. Ultimately entertaining but with misguided political motivations. *Scream Greats #2* would be the series' final volume.

SCREAM QUEEN HOT TUB PARTY
1991, Color, 50 min
STARRING: *Brinke Stevens, Michelle Bauer, Monique Gabrielle, Kelli Maroney*
DIRECTOR: *Bill Carson (Fred Olen Ray), Arch Stanton (Jim Wynorski)*

Five of the top B-movie Scream Queens are invited to a deserted mansion. There, they host a Ouija séance and reminisce in a medium-sized hot tub.

Infinitely rewatchable and hilariously self-aware, *Hot Tub Party* knows its target audience. Bauer, Stevens and the rest of the girls lovingly make fun of themselves quoting the do's and don'ts of Queendom (while delivering the T&A). Such tips as how to properly have a nudity-filled shower, or dance with a chainsaw (while naked) add practicality to the excitement. But the real stars are the personalities between the vixens. Everyone seems to be genuinely enjoying themselves, regardless of role competition or attitudes. The film also acts as a compilation featuring several clips from the actresses' movies. But wait for the final moments before popping those tops - it's a soapy party of five where everybody's invited!

SPLATTER: ARCHITECTS OF FEAR
1986, Color, 78 min
STARRING: *Paul James Saunders, Chris Britton, Amber Wendleborg, Doug Cawker*
DIRECTOR: *Peter Rowe*

A pseudo-documentary about grizzly special effects implemented on a horror movie set.

Narrated by Britton (yet occasionally hosted by Saunders), *Splatter* is a product of its time. Slasher films had saturated the market by 1986, adopted by mainstream studios and produced direct to video by independents. Tom Savini had become a household name (with credits in *Friday the 13th*, *Dawn of the Dead* and *The Burning*) and Fangoria was the number one choice for blood-hungry magazine readers. It was only a matter of time before "how to" videos entered the marketplace and *Splatter* jumped at the chance.

Bookending itself with a film-within-a-film presentation, *Splatter* entertains while it educates. It allows audiences an unfettered look at real behind-the-scenes wizardry, while crafting a fictional story around a mangled crewmember. Fang (as everyone calls him) is a sharp toothed, mullet-sporting hunchback passionate about gore. He bites the heads off mice and eats latex fingers. And *Splatter* build his character as a real flesh-eater on set too because... well, why not? It's the gory make-up emphasized here, complete with multiple camera angles showing how it all comes together. Logic takes a nap as gore comes in fully edited sequences, then deconstructs itself with narration and outtakes. To this, *Splatter* is a quaint peek at independent filmmaking in the 80's. But focusing on a fake post-apocalyptic movie (also dubbed *Splatter*) is a head scratcher. Why not use behind-the-scenes footage of a real established movie? Or perhaps make *Splatter* into a full length movie all its own? The answer lies in the PG rating, achieved thanks to a clause in the Canadian Ratings Board (which has since been rewritten). As the producers saw it, *Splatter* would surely garner an X had it been a straight motion picture. But crafting itself as an "Educational video" meant censoring was not required because this was for education. So the ruse was launched. The producers created a fake film within the film and it worked! *Splatter* acquired its PG status by default, even though spread-eagle asses and plaster-rubbed breasts occur onscreen. And it was all in the name of art as the Canadians tried to *"out do"* the Americans. Today, *Splatter* remains an antiquated footnote in analog's impressive shelf-life; a feature-length documentary about the making of a film that doesn't exist. Seriously ahead of its time and well worth revisiting. Highly Recommended!

TERROR ON TAPE

A COMPILATION OF THE MOST TERRIFYING SCENES FROM 20 OF THE SCARIEST HORROR MOVIES EVER MADE.

Hosted by...
Cameron Mitchell

TERROR ON TAPE

1985, Color, 84 min
STARRING: *Cameron Mitchell, Michelle Bauer, Mark Fenske, Tim Noyes*
DIRECTOR: *Robert A. Worms III*

Legendary actor Cameron Mitchell (appearing as a white haired ghoul) operates a video store, scaring his customers by previewing the bloodiest moments from rentable horror films.

Essentially a compilation of horror titles available from entertainment company Continental Video, *Terror On Tape* goes the extra mile by filming new segments for a video store wrap-around. Unlike later compilations such as *Slashermania* (featuring randomly assembled clips with no introduction), *Terror On Tape* stands as nostalgic bliss for a time when selling was an art. For those old enough to remember, walking into a video store and chatting up employees was often how people discovered movies. *Terror* brings back that experience in spades. And while its choices of which clips play may be questionable, *Terror* also wins points by not settling for overused trailers. Mitchell wonderfully hams things up (complete with whipping stick) while sexy horror queen Bauer impresses as the customer demanding satisfaction. Ultimately *Terror* is an advertising piece designed to make Continental titles rent (a motive extinct in today's digital world) but the hard sell still entertains. And while all films showcased were originally shot on film, Mitchell's deadly video store is awesome analog all the way.

Recommended.

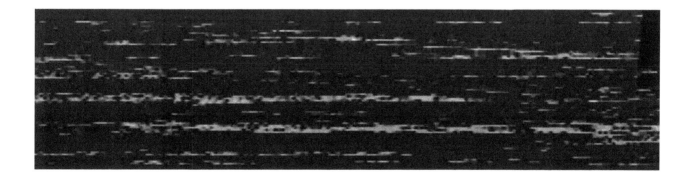

Chapter 19
RECOMMENDATIONS FROM FANS

As a special treat, I have cultivated the top recommendations from some of SOV's biggest fans. Though this book attempts to document every SOV horror feature prior to 1996, I recognize that a large number of these films may be totally alien to the viewing public. What if readers had never seen a shot on video horror film? Where should prospective viewers begin?

Thankfully with the aid of the following participants, there's a place to start. SOV movies are as dear to them as they are to me, and I hope you enjoy their personal stories and note the films they responded to. SOV horror may ultimately be about cheap thrills, but it's also about an unbound love for the genre.

So tuck in... because their nightmares will soon become your own.

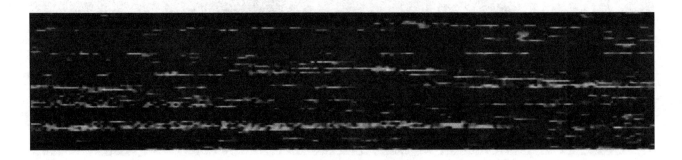

Tony Masiello

When I was coming of age in the late 80's and early 90's, the video store was a magical place. The shelves were lined with colorfully painted box art that had enticing titles and lurid taglines that were all designed to grab your attention and your money. Most video rental stores were Mom and Pop operations that would carry the latest Hollywood trash and the cheapest of independent productions. It was like the wild west, where a copy of *Conan the Barbarian* would be next to *Cannibal Campout*. Half of the displays were movies that you may have never heard of, but if it had appealing box art with a clever tagline you were going to fork over your $1.50 to rent it. Video distributors were wise to this fact and often employed seedy tactics to get your to rent their tape. Sometimes they would change a movie's title and shoot new box art so the consumer would be none the wiser that they were renting a title they had already watched.

Due to this boom and equal playing field for Hollywood and independent films, some true entrepreneurs said *"Wait I can make a movie too and get it in video stores and actually make a profit!"* Armed with affordable video cameras, a exploitive idea, some friends, and Karo syrup many aspiring filmmakers starting shooting their own backyard blockbusters that actually made it into video stores. All you needed was that shiny box art and a good tagline! What would cost one filmmaker one million dollars to make, would cost another ambitious filmmaker one thousand dollars, and the video store consumer would be unaware of this until after they rented and watched the video. The video store was at such a peak in this era. They were struggling to keep up with the demand of consumers who wanted more product to fill their hungry VCR's. Back then it was common for VHS tapes to cost on average about $100 a tape. So some smaller (and smarter) distributors dropped the prices on their titles so the stores would be more likely to buy their product to stock their shelves.

These factors led to one of the most interesting eras in movie history: the Direct to Video Shot On Video horror films of the early 80's and 90's. In 1983 Sony released the first consumer camcorder (even though video technology had existed for many years prior) which changed everything. Now anyone (who had a lot of money to blow) could purchase their own camera and make their own movie. With the independent features typical cost to produce, it was a risky venture for any amateur filmmaker. However, the camcorder changed the playing field, and the SOV horror movie was born.

As a young boy growing up in this prolific time where I had easy access to Jason Voorhees brutally dispatching teens, I became obsessed with going to the video store to get my daily dose of horrific gore. Soon after I got my first video rental store membership, I began renting any horror film that looked like it was filled to the brim with flesh and gore. I wanted to see every horror movie that I could possibly get my hands on, it was like an obsession. I don't really recall the first SOV horror movie I saw but I know I was pretty disappointed when I did first see one. I felt ripped off at the time due to the video look and cheap production values, I felt like it was not a real movie but something I could have made in the backyard with my friends.

Back in those days small independent labels like Tempe, Salt City, Cinema Home Video, and EI Independent Cinema would cold call video stores by offering lurid titles at discounted rates. It was at one my of favorite local video stores where I first discovered an SOV gem, *Redneck Zombies*. This horror comedy featured tons of outlandish gore scenes and a goofy sense of humor that was right up my alley. I soon starting looking for similar movies and discovered that most of these small, gory, backyard epics were released by the same companies, which ultimately made it easy to pick up other similar titles. Another avenue to find these weird obscure flicks was in the back of horror magazines.

After watching a fair share of SOV movies I started to think that this was something I could do too. My best friend had a video camera and soon after we started making our own horror shorts like "The Hand" and its sequel "The Foot." We had no idea what we were doing but we had fun coming up with effects shots and covering our friends in blood and gore. We would edit our little micro-masterpieces using two VCR's daisy linked together. It was very difficult editing in this manner and you had to have perfect timing to get the edits just right. It wasn't until the advent of mini DV cameras that real non-linear editing and the quality of our shorts improved. There was also a boom in shot on DV horror movies coming from companies like Dead Alive Productions, Brain Damage Films, Alternative Cinema and Vista Street Pictures. That is when I finally realized this could be a real thing. I could actually make my own video movies, get them distributed, and possibly make some money doing it.

I decided to go school to study Digital Video Production, and soon after enrolling I started making many fake trailers and shorts. The early SOV and DV movies inspired me so much to try and work in the movie industry. Even though some of them have poor acting, no production values, and shoddy effects, most of them had weird crazy scripts that were not afraid to take chances. Ultimately these films showed the huge amount of heart and determination put into them. These weren't Hollywood cash in movies like most the other direct to video movies. These were movies that were made by horror fans turned horror filmmakers.

I currently work in the film industry and have been lucky enough to have worked on many big Hollywood movies like *The Transformers* and *Shrek* films. However, while that was my day job, I spent my nights working for free doing visual fx on low budget horror films for the likes of Todd Sheets, Chris Seaver, Brett Kelly, and Ron Bonk. I even directed a short for the SOV anthology *Hi-8*. This was an honor, as I was the only non veteran to direct a short for it. My short, "The Tape," was a love letter to the genre that inspired me to jump into filmmaking. Since then, I have had the opportunity to work with many of my SOV idols such as Tim Ritter, Donald Farmer, etc. I even started making a documentary on the subject that I hope to complete in the near future. SOV's have changed the way filmmaking was, and changed my life to the point where I will forever be grateful for all the great movies and people behind them. Long live SOV horror!

Having watched and re-watched nearly every shot on video horror film in existence, there are a handful that have stood the test of time and inspired me throughout my life. Whether it is because the gore effects were awesomely grotesque, the script was intelligently written, or the overall production seemed masterful for the low budget used, all this films had on things in common. Heart.

My Top 5 SOV's In Order of Release

Sledgehammer (1983)

The granddaddy of SOV's. A group of friends rent a little house for a party weekend. Unbeknownst to them, a 7ft tall supernatural sledgehammer killer is on the prowl. *Sledgehammer* is an SOV that transcends the horror genre and is almost transgressive with its approach to the horror subject matter. There are tons of slow motion scenes to pad the film's running time that actually work to create a weird and creepy atmosphere, great 80's synth score, a real intimidating killer (7 ft tall Doug Matley), and some very claustrophobic hallway scenes. Director David A. Prior's (*Killer Workout, Deadly Prey*) first movie is a great example of what can be done with a two bedroom apartment, some friends, and a lot of heart.

Black Devil Doll From Hell (1984)

One of the most unique and engaging SOV movies of all time. A religious woman purchases a ventriloquist dummy from a second hand shop despite some cryptic warnings from the shopkeeper. When she arrives home she starts having sexual fantasies about the doll and eventually has a sexual relationship with it. The next thing you know she is on a search for sexual gratification from any man she can find. The problem is that none of them live up to her little wooden lover. Directed by African American Chester Novell Turner in 1983, *BDDFH* is one of the first commercially released SOV's for the home video market. There's bad acting, directing, effects, casio soundtrack and puppet sex. Despite its shortcomings this movie does not disappoint as it is another SOV that almost transcends the genre into transgressive territory. It has an odd charm that will keep you going back for repeat viewings.

A Taste for Flesh and Blood (Flesh Eaters From Outer Space) (1989)

Shot in 1989 but not released until 1997, Warren Disbrow Jr's New Jersey lensed epic is a great example of what can be done on a very limited budget. This movie has so much gore you would swear it was made in Germany. A space mission accidentally brings back a cargo containing a giant flesh-eating alien. The alien costume is really awesome looking and there are kills pretty much every 10 minutes. Another SOV that was re-edited for its DVD release, the Brain Escape VHS tape release is the only way to go as it has more nudity and gore than the DVD release by Troma.

Las Vegas Bloodbath (1989)

A guy walks in on his wife having an affair with a cop and offs her. He then decides that all women are whores and goes on a massacre. Eventually ending up at a house full of lady oil wrestlers to feed his blood lust. *LVBB* is another movie that needs to be seen to believed. You got some horribly great dialogue, squishy special effects, and a fetus ripping scene that you will not forget once you've seen it. *LVBB* was originally released by Dead Alive Home Video which is pretty hard to come by these days. A rough cut somehow made it onto DVD in the 2000's and unfortunately this is the version most people have seen. The rough cut makes for a real tough viewing experience as there is a 20 minute long scene of the oil wrestlers just talking - major snoozefest. The Dead Alive Home Video version is edited tighter, making the pace better and has some additional gore scenes not seen in the dvd cut. I highly recommend seeking out the Dead Alive version.

Goblin (1993)

I've been fortunate enough to work with many SOV filmmakers over the years and one of the nicest of them all is Todd Sheets. Though he is not proud of this movie, like many other SOV's on my list this one has a charm you can't not deny. The story is simple. A newlywed couple buys a farmhouse and invite a bunch of friends over to party but they accidently release the GOBLIN, a cannibal demon who really has a thing for playing with guts. Probably one of the goriest SOV's of the era, this thing has Fulci written all over it. It reminds me of Andreas Schnaas's *Violent Shit* as far as the level of gore goes. The kills are all over the top and are borderline gorenography. Must for all SOV gorehounds.

Honorable Mentions

Blood Lake (1987) - Great 80's style slasher

Video Violence (1987) - A classic of the genre

Splatter Farm (1987) - Couldn't skip the Polonia Brothers

Night of the Living Babes (1987) - I really really REALLY like Michelle Bauer movies

The Hackers (1988) - Regional shocker in the vein of Mother's Day

Redneck Zombies (1989) - My gateway drug

The Witching (1993) - It's horrible, but I love it

Gore Whore (1994) - My favorite of the Hugh Gallagher Gore Trilogy

Wicked Games (1994) - Ritter is one of the best writers/directors in the genre, one of his best

Red Lips (1995) - Ghetty Chasum and Michelle Bauer as lesbian vampires. Oh my!

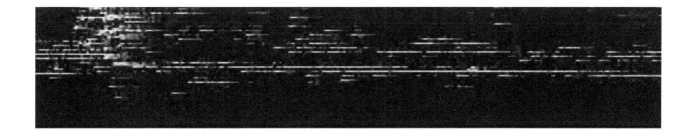

Tony Newton

I'm a writer and filmmaker who owes a debt to SOV films and the horror genre. Every film project I've worked on has its roots set in SOV horror. Films I've made and worked on like the Troma *Grindsploitation* film series, the VHS documentary *VHS Lives: A Schlockumentary* which touches heavily on SOV films and a homage to the genre in Brad Twigg's *Frames of Fear* horror anthology which I directed a segment entitled "The Night Demon" (along with Richard Mogg who directed the segment "Format of the Dead").

My love of this amazing genre of film stems from trying to track down and spending my youth watching these low budget splatter offerings on VHS. They were made with heart and most of all passion.

In the UK, trying to find an SOV film in the late 80's and early 90's was harder than getting crack from your grandmother. We would trade tapes and mainly get these from collectors fairs where you could pick up foreign horror films including SOV and German splatter films. As I got older, I would spend more money and more time tracking these cult SOV titles down. I always collected VHS and there is nothing better than owning a shot on video film actually on video tape.

I think you have a defining moment when you realize that big budget stars filling blockbusters aren't all there is out there! I was kind of brainwashed by the TV when I was a kid. I wouldn't watch a film that didn't have a star like DeNiro, Stallone or Van Damme in it, though that could have been being forced to sit through hours of true movies thinking all low budget films were like that.

I remember watching *The Toxic Avenger* for the first time on VHS. This film didn't have big stars or even a huge budget. Not only was I in love with indie horror from that moment on but a friend also lent me David A. Prior's *Deadly Prey* on VHS. Damn this was a film that was like *Rambo* but with Z-list actors, more ham and cheese than a toasted sandwich, but at the same time pure VHS heaven. That led me to my first viewing of a true SOV horror film *Sledgehammer* also directed by David A. Prior (who later made the cult classic *Killer Workout*). Not only was I hooked from then onwards but David A. Prior is still one of my favourite directors. I adore that guy, he was not only a pioneer but such a nice guy as well who always had time to chat about his work and his love of cinema.

Once I realized there were films that featured more blood, more gore and a great sense of humour, delivering the goods the way we wanted it, without big budgets, big named stars - a true indie film, that was it. [In] my youth (and to be honest up until now and beyond), there [has been] nothing I like more than tracking down SOV VHS films.

SOV films broke the rules and made new ones along the way. I love SOV horror films with a passion and always will. Not everyone gets them, not everyone loves them but for those who do, they are a feast for the eyes and candy for the soul!

I still collect SOV films on every format but nothing compares to putting a SOV video in the VCR player and pressing the PLAY!

My Top 5 SOV Picks!

Blonde Death (1983)
Director: James Dillinger

Originally titled *American Perversions* and rumored to be shot for under $2000 American dollars, *Blonde Death* is a tour de-force of sex, drugs and violence. This film is a middle finger directly up to the establishment. The film's punk aesthetic shines throughout. Tammy transforms from a virginal teen to a drug fuelled psycho in this shot on video slice of cult VHS heaven. The director James Dillinger is writer and playwright James Robert Baker. I'm a huge fan of Baker's work and his novel "Fuel Injected Dreams" is outstanding. Baker's directorial debut in the mid 1970's was "Mouse Klub Konfidential," a film about a mouseketeer who starts working as a gay bondage photographer. This was a short film. He then went on to direct the feature *Blonde Death* in the early eighties. Baker was a writer of transgressive fiction, his work was controversial and reception of his novel "Tim and Pete" in the early 1990's was disliked by critics. After "Tim and Pete," he found it impossible to get his work published and in 1996 he published a book online as a way to get his work out there. Baker killed himself by asphyxiation in 1997. The stress of not getting his work published and money problems were rumored to be the cause.

Since Baker's death, he has become somewhat of an cult icon with his work getting a much wider audience. *Blonde Death* is an amazing film. I'm a lover of exploitation and SOV films full of sex, drug use and violence, but it was James Baker's witty, razor sharp dialogue that stole the show here for me. Much like [a] precursor [to] John Waters, the mix of exploitation and on point dialogue wins throughout. *"Tammy is 18 years old, sexually frustrated and ready to blow!"* Well the actual tagline is *"Meet Tammy, The Teenage Time bomb, Eighteen years of bottled-up frustration are about to explode!"* I think my tagline has a better ring to it! Though does sound more like a porn film! The film is very hard to get hold of on VHS as it never had a wide VHS release, although the film was bootlegged like crazy in both the 80's and 90's. I remember being sent a bootleg copy from a friend saying *"You have to see this movie it's killer!"* Bleeding Skull and Mondo released a limited edition VHS version which was transferred direct from the original 1" master tapes, (try your hardest to track one of these down), though the VHS version is long since sold out. This is a killer SOV film that will cure the cravings of any SOV or VHS fan. Grace your VCR player with this nihilistic beast!

Sledgehammer (1983)
Director: David A. Prior

I adore this film. Not only was this the first ever horror SOV film I ever watched, but it's one of my all time favorites for so many reasons. Some shot on video films look crisper and cleaner than others. This film has a certain aesthetic all of its very own. This is true SOV here. A bloody slasher in the true stalk and slash style, okay by the early 80's we were knee deep in teen slasher films, [but] by 1983 this film was different enough to stand out from the crowd. Not only do you feel like you just smoked weed while watching it due to the almost psychedelic colors onscreen, but you get sucked into David A. Prior's nightmare. Ted Prior is the muscle bound wanna be hero in this slasher. A group of teens fall victim to a masked sledgehammer wielding psychopathic killer who picks the teens of one by one. This film has some innovative kills, lots of blood all rounded up nicely with some great cinematography and a great atmosphere.

Boardinghouse (1982)
Director: John Wintergate

This is a cracking film. A little gem of a movie, balls out, all out craziness, weird effects, a guy who looks like Malcolm McDowell if he was on blow who has telekinetic powers - oh and most important of all, a swimming pool! I love this film. Everything from the dialog, the acting, the laugh out loud scenes and sheer campness of the whole production. There aren't many horror films that aren't comedy that you can be freaked out and scared one minute, and the next be rolling on the floor laughing. In *Boardinghouse* you can and will! The first time I saw *Boardinghouse* to be honest, I thought it was a porno movie. If the characters started to have full on sex you wouldn't be surprised at all. This film is like a SOV comfort blanket for me, that's why it has to go in my top 5 SOV film list. Even the cheesy blood style after effects! Hell Yeah! Don't you dare stay in this boardinghouse! Well except for the killings, it looks [like] a bloody good laugh to be honest!

The Video Dead (1987)
Director: Robert Scott

[Okay it's not a video movie, but it looks like a video movie!] I'm a lover of zombie films. The first time I watched George A. Romero's *Night of the Living Dead,* I was hooked and became literally obsessed by the zombie genre. So it was such a treat to find *The Video Dead*. To be honest I think I'm in love with the cover more than I am the film itself. In the UK, it was released by Medusa on good old VHS, I remember seeing the cover on the shelf in my local video store and actually ended up buying that same copy in the reduced bargain bin much later. *The Video Dead* was one of those films I would rent on repeat so when I finally got to own this film, I was in heaven. Zombies coming out of the TV. WOW! Much before *The Ring. The Video Dead* scared kids shitless across the globe. This film has a kind of Michael Jackson's "Thriller" quality to it. It doesn't take itself too seriously. I like the white melt look of the zombies. The zombies coming out of the TV is just so iconic, you got to love this movie! I still have my VHS copy on display to this very day!

Splatter Farm (1987)
Directed by: Mark Polonia, John Polonia, Todd Michael Smith

I love the Polonia brothers' films and without a doubt, *Splatter Farm* has to be my favorite of their work. This film is quite long for a SOV film, one you can really get your teeth into! I love the premise when brothers spend the a summer vacation with their aunt. They find out more than they bargained for when they find the aunt's farm hand is a sick sadistic killer (though the aunt has a few secrets up her sleeve of her own!) I think the Polonia Brothers were like 17 or something when they made this movie. WOW! It's so freaking cool on every level, I love everything about *Splatter Farm*. The Polonia Brothers are SOV legends! This film is a cult classic with just the right amount of blood and gore and a superb creepy horror atmosphere created by the directors! It will shock you and make you squirm with fear! A SOV must see!

Ross Snyder

Greetings analog aficionados! My name is Ross Snyder. I am a film journalist and distributer from New Jersey, and the co-director of the documentary *"Mail Order Murder: The Story Of W.A.V.E. Productions."* Back in 2014, I started a label called Saturn's Core Audio & Video as a means to distribute and shine a spotlight on some of my most beloved SOV films by reissuing them solely on the VHS format. Truth be told, I've spent the better part of my life renting, watching, collecting, chronicling, and marvelling at shot on video feature films and I've enjoyed every brain-melting moment of it. Had I spent an equivalent amount of time writing about the Czech New Wave or the New German Cinema movements (both of which I adore), it's possible that I would have been published more than I have over the years. However, it's doubtful that I would have had anywhere near as much fun or been subjected to the bizarre images and colorful cast of characters that I've encountered during my journeys into the wilds of the analog jungle.

My introduction to the world of camcorder films started, like most film fanatics my age, at the video store. My parents purchased their first VCR in 1987 and the horror sections of the mom and pop video stores of my youth became the exploring grounds for my burgeoning movie obsession. This was the utopian age when the VCR had become a common household appliance and the independent rental stores were hungry for titles to feed to their growing clientele. In the same way that one of Mario Bava's supernatural, surrealist, gialli could be crudely recut and sold to American drive-ins as an *Exorcist* rehash a decade earlier, the hucksterism of film distributors was back in full swing and they were beyond ecstatic to unload their most unscrupulous wares onto video stores shelves nationwide. This thankfully led to a glorious era where backyard camcorder epics like Jon

McBride and Tom Fischer's *Cannibal Campout* could sit on the shelf right next to an Academy Award nominated, major studio film like Brian DePalma's *Carrie* and harmoniously share equal real estate. To my delight, The Video Warehouse store in my town carried an ample array of shot on video titles, and I religiously rented and enjoyed films like *Video Violence* 1 & 2, *Blood Cult*, *Death Row Diner*, *The Ripper*, and *Attack of the Killer Refrigerator*. As a child of the 80's, I grew up on a steady diet of MTV and public access cable programming, so using video as a means of storytelling was not a major issue or foreign concept to me. I quickly fell in love with this strange sub-genre of movie making for a multitude of reasons. First off, was the purity of the filmmaking. For the first time in the history of American cinema, average folks from places far outside of Hollywood could purchase a camcorder from their local Sears, gather their friends or relatives, and tell their stories on video with little or no money and without the fear of interference from producers, studio executives, or test market research groups. If the director wanted to see a ventriloquist doll come to life and perform cunnilingus on a nude, middle aged women or just have his friends wash a car for 18 minutes of screen time then so be it. The demand in the marketplace even afforded some of these features, originally created for fun and with no intention for distribution, to be picked up by fly-by-night video companies, shipped to rental stores, and thrust into the hands of confused customers.

Secondly, was the peculiar documentary aspect of these narrative features. Even when underground legend George Kuchar switched to video in the late 80's to chronicle his Weather Diaries (a bizarre series of vacation films that placed the filmmaker in the direct path of imminent weather catastrophes), his aesthetic was not too far removed from the sprawling monster movies of Illinois filmmaker David "The Rock" Nelson, who spent an equal amount of screen time interacting with his parents, consuming junk food, and talking directly into the camera about his life as he did on furthering the narrative of his movie. Whether it's an attempt at a slasher movie or a gothic vampire melodrama, we learn a lot about the everyday life and eccentricities of the filmmaker and participating actors just by watching. And much like average television viewers obsession with reality TV programs, I find great joy and elation in observing these folks in their natural habitat, playing pretend in a perfect snapshot of that space and time when they decided to go out and try to make a movie.

Lastly, is what I like to refer to as the "local color" aspect of shot on video filmmaking. While most mainstream films are shot in California or utilize elaborate sets to recreate a certain exotic geography, SOV films instead act as a unique travelogue of everyday banality in regions all across the globe. As a man who is not very well traveled, my distorted view of many unfamiliar locations is solely informed by what I've seen in SOV movies. When I think of the German countryside for example, my mind immediately wanders to the films of Andreas Schnaas and his marauding killers and zombies. The sunny tropics of Florida will always be synonymous to me with the films of Tim Ritter and his sweaty and sun burnt cast of crazies. And the early works of the Polonia Brothers seem to have captured the rotted old barns and general isolation of rural Pennsylvania in a nutshell.

As the 90's came and mainstream horror became increasingly stagnant, I moved away from fawning over Fangoria and quickly discovered a new crop of underground film magazines such as Alternative Cinema, Draculina, Independent Video, and Film Threat Video Guide. It was through these periodicals that I discovered that shot on video filmmaking was still a widely viable and thriving entity and I promptly began sending away money orders for the tapes I saw advertised and reviewed within the pages. It was around this same time that I started attending the local Chiller Theatre convention, which in the early to mid 90's, contained an unfathomable smorgasbord of video obscurities, where all the tapes I had read about (and hundreds more) were available right at my fingertips. This second wave of 90's SOV filmmaking seemed to culminate into a somewhat unified scene with movie makers from all over the country connecting, collaborating, and promoting each other's work. Many of my mail order and convention film discoveries from this era were just as game changing and eye opening as my initial video store revelations of the late 80's.

Richard asked me to compile a list of my Top 5 favorite SOV films from the era covered in this book. These are by no means listed in any particular order or ranked by their cultural significance to the overall history of video features. Just my Top 5 personal favorites for those who have exhausted their options of celluloid lensed horror and are looking to dip their toes into the shallow end of the analog pool so to speak. So here it goes:

Video Violence (1987)

Shot in Frenchtown and Boundbrook New Jersey, theatre director and video store owner Gary P. Cohen crafted the quintessential SOV opus with the sole intention of stocking it on his own rental shelf. A feature shot on 3/4" U-Matic video and set in Cohen's actual rental store, it chronicles a town of denizens who concoct their own real murder features on video, after tiring of the mainstream titles available to them. It comments on media violence, celebrity obsession, video store culture, and the snuff myth, all while blithely lampooning the entire burgeoning shot on video filmmaking movement.

Splatter Farm (1987)

Wellsboro, Pennsylvania's notorious identical twin directing team of Mark and John Polonia had already spent the bulk of their childhood making dozens of short, backyard horror productions before teaming up with local friend and fellow filmmaker Todd Smith to create their most infamous SOV feature. Probably the least technically sound film on this list, the boys more than made up for it by taking the narrative into unfathomably, transgressive extremes. Scenes of full frontal male nudity coupled with simulated acts of geriatric incest, male anal fisting, and severed head fellatio were primarily unheard of in 1987 and still leave a gut-wrenching sour taste behind 30 years later. Unfortunately for many completists, the only way to access the full uncut version of the film as described above is on the original, scarce Donna Michelle VHS release.

Redneck Zombies (1987)

Lensed in the backwoods of rural Delaware and Maryland, latter-day Troma FX guru Pericles Lewnes launched his career by directing and starring in this ultra-violent, live-action, Warner Brothers cartoon on video. One of the torchbearers of the backyard zombie movie genre, it's often overlooked due to its relatively easy accessibility. Troma has steadily kept the film in general release, leaving many to neglect it while searching for more elusive video oddities.

Ozone (1994)

In February of 1994, the camcorder movie scene changed forever in my mind with the release of director J.R. Bookwalter's stunning, John Capenter-esque, sci-fi drug parable. After toiling away on a series of quickly made, director-for-hire SOV features for producer David DeCauteau in his native Akron, Ohio, Bookwalter sought to break away and construct a passion project to reclaim his directorial integrity. Utilizing a fluent steady cam, dolly moves, crane shots, and some of the earliest examples of digital morphing FX in indie film history, J.R. showed us that with both time and talent, anything is possible even on the most meager of budgets.

Savage Harvest (1994)

Prolific St. Louis, Missouri video auteur Eric Stanze cut his teeth with this ambitious, Native American themed, *Evil Dead*-style, demonic possession romp set against the actual backdrop of the Great Flood of '93 (a real life debilitating disaster that crippled parts of America's Midwest). Elaborate practical effects, extreme chainsaw violence, a memorable monster, and some genuine atmospheric scares make for a rollicking good time that frequently warrants repeat viewings.

Part of the fun of chronicling this genre of DIY filmmaking is the ample opportunity for continuous discovery. It seems like almost every other day I'm discovering another new movie from this era that was formerly unbeknownst to me. So much video product was distributed solely through fan conventions and fanzine classified ads that the full breadth of what existed in the marketplace at the time is almost unfathomable. I'm certain that decades from now, we will still be unearthing shot on video features from this period that were hitherto unknown. With that in mind, I'd like to introduce another list for the more seasoned video fanatics. A Top 5 of still relatively unknown (or under appreciated) shot on video features for those who have devoured their way to bottom of the barrel but are still hungry for more analog nourishment.

Hell On Earth 2: Arena Of Death (1992)

One of the most ambitious, amateur SOV epics of all time, this 2 hour, post-apocalyptic, action film shot on the desolate shores of Rockaway Beach, NY by Falcon Video partners Phil Herman and Matt O'Connor was started in 1986 and took 6 gruelling years to complete. Boasting one arrest, numerous broken bones, and nearly 100 cast members, it's an eye-opening testament to the payoff of sheer unadulterated tenacity.

Blood Summer (1993)

Tallahassee Florida's resident underground madman Matthew Samuel Smith's trailer park set slasher film falls somewhere between the hypnotic monotony of Tim Boggs' *Blood Lake* and a fly-on-the wall documentary of stoned, southern teens shown through the lens of Harmony Korine.

Plenilunio (Full Moon) (1993)

Stephen King meets early Todd Sheets in this crude Uruguayan werewolf film from director Ricardo Islas, in which a group of teens who hang out at a cable TV station studio try and battle a lycanthrope that resembles a giant stuffed animal.

No Resistance (1994)

One of the most original science fiction films of the 90's is an obscure, rarely discussed, $7000, S-VHS feature from Houston, Texas. Tim Thomson's bleak, dystopian, cyberpunk action thriller has enough original ideas for 10 feature films and plays out like a neo-noir film directed by Jim Van Bebber.

Hung Jury (1994)

A passion project from Gary Whitson's W.A.V.E. Productions (New Jersey's infamous kings of custom video features) *Hung Jury* is a nearly 2 hour, head scratching, island-set, slasher whodunnit revolving around a family revenge plot, a murder mystery cruise, and a multitude of painfully prolonged death sequences. It features a huge non-thespian cast, some underwater photography, and the greatest post-coital weight-lifting axe massacre in cinema history.

Happy hunting.

Chris Yardley

My passion for shot on video horror started because of Super 8mm horror.

Back in the early 1990's I was living in a small village in Scotland. Our local video store was about a mile away and the only way I could keep up-to-date with all the new horror releases was through The Dark Side Magazine; a UK based genre publication that catered for folks obsessed with video nasties, sci-fi schlock and exploitation cinema. There was no easy internet access; no eBay; no Amazon; and the British Board of Film Classification (BBFC) was still censoring horror movies right, left and centre.

As young horror fanatic I was just beginning to learn the mechanics of film making and I was looking at low budget movies to show me the ropes. I watched as many Roger Corman productions as I could get my hands on; I obsessed over movies by Lucio Fulci, Ruggero Deodato, and Lamberto Bava that I hadn't even seen yet. The one thing that struck me most was that even so-called low budget movies where still way out of my league; even Andy Milligan movies where way out of my league in regards to budget. I thought to myself; if I don't have the cash to shoot movies then I can at least write screenplays; all I need for that is paper and a word processor.

Then I picked up the Oct/Nov 1994 edition of The Dark Side Magazine.

On the front cover was a close up Cinzia Monreale as the blind girl, Emily, from Lucio Fulci's masterpiece *The Beyond* (1981). Inside there was an article titled: "The Mad Butcher of Long Island." This article would change my outlook on film making forever.

The article was about a guy called Nathan Schiff who shot movies on Super 8mm with titles such as *The Long Island Cannibal Massacre*, *Weasels Rip My Flesh*, *They Don't Cut the Grass Anymore* and *Vermillion Eyes*. He made these movies with his friends for practically nothing. This blew my mind.

Up to that point when I thought about how movies were made, I thought you'd need a studio behind you and at the very least hundreds of thousands of dollars. Here was a guy who had made movies with his buddies for pennies and was now being interviewed in The Dark Side Magazine. I wouldn't actually get to see Nathan Schiff's films until years later; but in the mean time I obsessed over the fantastically gory photos and read the article about a hundred times. My mind was racing with the possibilities: If he could do it then so could I. But there was still one slight problem. I didn't have a Super 8mm camera or the means to get one. Fuck!

So I continued writing screenplays; hoping that one day they would get made. A few years after reading the article about Nathan Schiff, I was in my local Tower Records shopping for horror flix when I stumbled upon a movie called *Invasion for Flesh and Blood* directed by Warren F. Disbrow. The movie was released on VHS by a company known as Screen Edge. The plot sounded right up my alley: big rubber alien monsters tearing people apart. I'm in. So I bought the movie and took it home. One of the great things about Screen Edge VHS tapes was that on the reverse side of the cover they would give you some behind the scenes info on the movie and the director. It was there that I found out that *Invasion for Flesh and Blood* was shot on video.

I popped the video into the video recorder not knowing what to expect. It was another mind blowing experience. Warren F. Disbrow had written, directed, edited, photographed and produced the movie with help from his father Warren F Disbrow Sr. Disbrow Sr. had also helped construct the sets and the props. And it was all shot on glorious video tape. I needed to find more movies like this.

Over the next few years I was able to get my hands on more Screen Edge titles such as Ronnie Sortor's *Ravage*, J.R Bookwalter's *Ozone* and Scooter McRae's *Shatter Dead*, which was financed entirely from Scooter's $250 a week wages, with the entire production costing around $4000 bucks. These movies showed me that I didn't need hundreds of thousands of dollars or fancy film equipment to make movies; all I needed was a VHS camcorder and a few like minded friends. I started to collect as many shot on video movies as I could get my hands on. Over the years I have amassed about 150 titles.

Here are some of my favorites...

Cannibal Campout (1988)
Produced and Directed by Jon McBride and Tom Fisher

I like this movie because it doesn't take itself too seriously and it has some great micro budget gore effects. Jon McBride also made the 1989 shot on video classic *The Woodchipper Massacre*, which isn't as gory as it sounds but is also a fun watch.

Video Violence (1987)
Directed by Gary P Cohen

Video Violence, in my opinion, is probably one of the best SOV movies out there and shows what is possible with a VHS camcorder and a dedicated crew. It's one of the more professionally produced shot on video titles and I highly recommend checking it out along with the 1988 sequel, *Video Violence 2*.

Splatter Farm (1987)
Written, Produced and Directed by Mark Polonia, John Polonia and Todd Smith

I think *Splatter Farm* was made for exactly zero dollars. Mark and John Polonia are two geeky looking teenagers running around an old farm getting up to all kinds of insane debauchery. They even get their aunt in on the act, having her indulge in all manner of necrophilic shenanigans. Hilarious stuff and highly recommended.

Ozone (1994)
Directed By J.R Bookwalter

Another very well produced SOV movie with great atmosphere and some nifty special effects. The whole movie reportedly cost $5000 bucks; amazing considering how good it looks.

Sledgehammer (1983)
Directed by David A. Prior

The first shot on video slasher movie (John Wintergate had directed *Boardinghouse* in 1982, but I don't know if you could call that a slasher movie; a mind expanding trip into the depths of madness is more like it if you watch the 157 minute long directors cut). *Sledgehammer* has a nice, eerie atmosphere and has more slow motion than the average John Woo movie; if the whole film was played at normal speed it would probably only last half an hour. *Sledgehammer* also has a great synth score which adds to its fever dream like quality. Well worth checking out.

And Honorable Mention goes to...

555 (1988)
Produced and Directed by Wally Koz

Every 5 years, within 5 days of each other, the killer strikes! *555* has a Herschell Gordon Lewis *Blood Feast* vibe running through it, from the way shots are composed, right down to the awesome, ultra gory splatter effects. Shot on video gold and well worth a watch.

The reason why I love shot on video horror movies so much is that they made me realize that I wasn't the only crazy bastard out there who thought they could make a film for no money. There were groups of dedicated film makers in the same situation I was; who didn't let lack of budget or lack of actors put them off. They created a micro budget analog underground, and stuck a middle finger up to Hollywood. They would make their movies on their terms using whatever means necessary. I like that kind of attitude.

Long live shot on video horror.

Attack of the KILLER Refrigerator

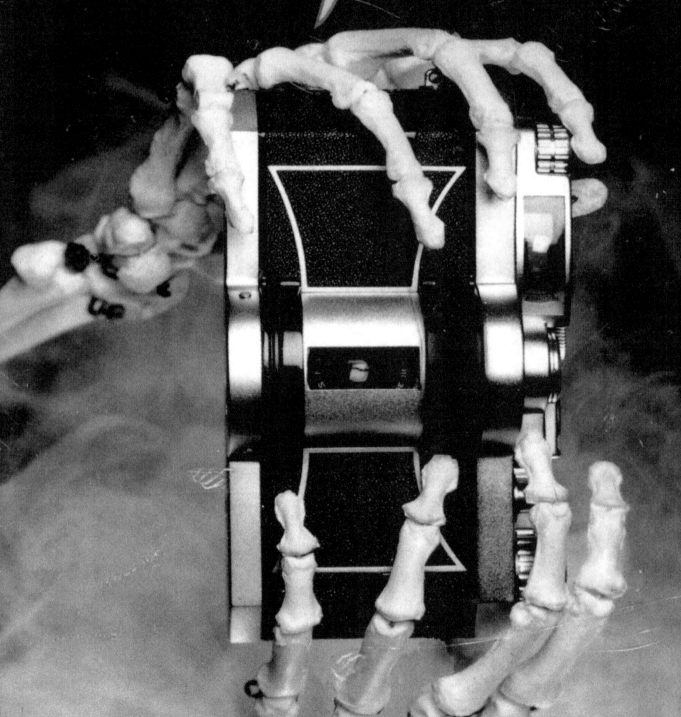

Chapter 20
I WANT TO WRITE YOU A LETTER...

Dear readers - you made it!

If you're seeing this entry, then your brains have not yet melted to the floor. But what have we learned? That over the course of 13 years, independent filmmakers bested professionals at their own game. With the tools in hand (and a complete lack of training), consumers made their own movies of rural panache and heartfelt dedication. They used video, achieved mass distribution and eventually took over the format.

David beat Goliath on videocassette.

And things didn't end after 1995.... As the decade wore out, more and more DV productions appeared with further sophistication. Sometimes they were hilariously inept like *Sick-O-Pathetics*, sometimes uniquely thrilling like *Sinistre* (or sometimes insanely bizarre like *Zombies Invade Pittsburg*). But their ernest passion continued. Today, we enjoy independent productions on Vimeo and YouTube as second nature. Want to be a filmmaker? You can make films literally on your iphone. Remember what Tim Ritter said about *Clown* and Eli Roth? Connections are happening all the time, provided you have an idea and the determination to tell it. And SOV is where it all began.

Video went through major changes during the 1982-1995 crossover and they weren't all technical. In its infancy, video was largely used by semi-professional companies with distribution access into video stores. By the 90's, video was almost completely abandoned to independents using hand-to-hand sales. Video *became* the tool of independence as it became the format of the people. And through that independence came all the wonderful things we value in movie watching today: unpredictability, passion and heart. Were the films gory and full of blood? You bet. Voyeuristic and clinging with nudity? We hoped. Unrelenting and made to engage? Definately. But they were also real attempts at telling stories unhinged by Hollywood's rules. Any character could (and often would) die in SOV titles. Runtimes could be infinately padded or abruptly cut short. Graphic violence wouldn't pull any punches and storylines could freely mix genres. SOV even eventually became unexpected gifts throughout the 2000's, crystalizing itself in higher definitions more than ever before. And the impact of these films can still be felt in the industry today.

Independents broke the chains off Hollywood's door and nothing could stop them.

One of the most noteworthy stories told in David "The Rock" Nelson's interview was how he wrote *Conrad Brooks VS Werewolf* (*The Werewolf of Baltimore*) on a napkin. Sounds too silly to be true, but it's the real deal. This demonstrates that movie plots need only be simple (or perhaps, not necessary at all) to succeed. Style and timing is what makes a movie. Stories are important, but how many slashers have used the same "killer in the woods" tale with repeated success? If you're a filmmaker, then make the film you want to make. With a simple plot of revenge, Nelson took what he had (Conrad and a mask) and turned it into memorable entertainment. Want proof? Here's the napkin...

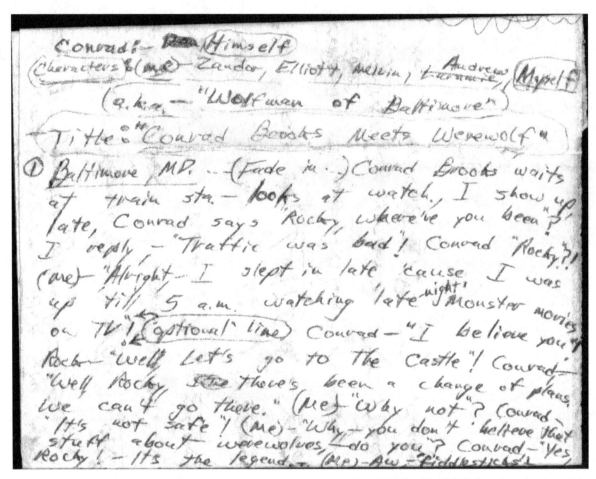

David "The Rock" Nelson's actual napkin

When I started this journey, I had already written and shot several motion pictures. My fourth film *Massage Parlor of Death*, was designed as a love-letter to the SOV genre. But after spending years hunting, watching and reviewing all the films in this book, my love for the genre has surprisingly enhanced. Watching SOV horror has become like visiting an old friend (and I always hope to meet a new one around the corner). These were movies made by struggling storytellers who incidently loved telling stories. And through their untrained efforts came wholly unique works of art. Therefore, SOV horror means something far more than just movies shot on videotape: it means independent expressions sharing love for a genre.

Could *any* SOV film ultimately be bad?

I sit here at the end of this journey (in my underwear, in a broken chair) contemplating the first time I rented *Boardinghouse*. And I realize, I have become the image that first burned into my mind so many years ago: a man, staring into an abyss, wearing only his tighty-whities. And I wonder if (in some way) the knowledge John Wintergate possessed in *Boardinghouse* has somehow now passed on to me; bulk accumulated from watching a world shot on video. Is telekinesis around the corner? SOV cassettes surround me. They adorn my walls on homemade shelves. And all I can do is look to the next Saturn's Core release or DVD announcement of another long lost title coming back for sale. Like a metaphysical awakening, I realize I've come full circle. Sniff, ha ha!

I hope my reviews have provided insight on a genre that has remained silent for far too long. And I hope you have been inspired (as I have) reading and learning from the interviews contained within. Hearing from the masters that *"you can do it too,"* is truly remarkable. They know what they're talking about - these men and women took hold of a new format and made it their own with little to no training. **Independence lies in video**; pick up a camera and try it yourself. Take everything serious, even the silly stuff (make it seriously silly). Do your best and try your hardest. And at the end of the day, distribution can be found if you reach for it. The tools to make your own movie are in your hands, you just need to charge the batteries.

Stop. Rewind. Eject,

Richard Mogg
RickMoe Productions

Behind the scenes on Demon Queen (1986)

INDEX OF FILMS

Death Row Diner (1988), 164-165
Demon Dolls (1993), 328
Demon Queen (1986), 81, 86-88, 468-469
DemonSoul (1995), 393
Devil Snow [see Neighborhoodz (1991)]
Dinastia Sangrienta [see Bloody Dynasty (1987)]
Disgusting Spaceworms Eat Everyone!! (1989), 209
Dividing Hour, The (1994), 359-360
Doctor Bloodbath [see Butcher Knife (1987)]
Dominion (1992), 287
Dream Stalker (1991), 259-260
Dummy, The [see Bloody Anniversary (1995)]
Dungeon of Death (1989), 210

E

El Espiritu del Zombie [see Southern Shockers
    (1985)]
El Monje Loco [see Mad Monk, The (1984)]
Escape From the Insane Asylum (1986), 81, 88-89
Evil Night (1992), 288
Exploding Angel (1995), 393-394
Eye of Satan, The (1988), 165
Eyewitness Murders (1988), 166

F

Fangoria`s Weekend of Horrors (1986), 426-429
Fatal Delusion (1995), 394-395
Fatal Images (1989), 210-211, 464
Feather Pillow (1988), 167
Feeders (1995), 17, 387, 396-397
Female Mercenaries On Zombie Island [see Zombie
    Holocaust (1995)]
Filmgore (1983), 15, 427, 430
Fine Art, The (1992), 289
Flesh Eaters From Outer Space [see Taste For Flesh
    and Blood, A (1989)]
Flesh Merchant, The (1993), 329
Fullmoon (1993), 329

G

Galaxy of the Dinosaurs (1992), 289-290
Ganjasaurus Rex (1987), 122
Ghost Stories: Graveyard Thriller (1986), 89-90
Goblin (1993), 330
Gore Whore (1994), 360-361
Gorgasm (1990), 236-237
Gorgon Video Magazine #1 (1989), 430-431
Gorgon Video Magazine #2 (1989), 431
Gorotica (1993), 330-331
Greedy Terror [see Shock Chamber (1985)]

Groundhog`s Day Massacre, The (1986), 90
Groundhog`s Day Massacre 2, The (1990), 237
Gunblast (1986), 81, 91

H

Hackers, The (1987), 122-123
Halloween Horrors (1993), 331-332
Hallucinations (1986), 81, 92
Heaping Bouncy Breasts That Smothered a Midget,
    The (1988), 168
Heavy Metal Massacre (1989), 211-212
Hell On Earth 2: Arena of Death (1992), 290-291
Hellroller (1992), 291-292
Hellspawn (1993), 332-333
High Desert (1994), 361
High Kicks (1993), 333
Holy Moly (1991), 260-261
Hook of Woodland Heights, The (1988), 168-169
Horror F/X (1989), 432
Horrorgirl (1995), 397-398
Horrorama [see Scarlet Fry's Horrorama (1989)]
Horrorscope (1994), 362
Houseboat Horror (1989), 212
Housegeist [see Boardinghouse (1982)]
How to Get... Revenge! (1988), 432-433
How to Slay a Vampire (1992), 292-293
Human Prey (1994), 363
Humanoids From Atlantis (1992), 282, 293-294
Hung Jury (1990-1994), 238

I

Into Darkness (1992), 294-295
Into the Darkness (1986), 81, 93-94
Invasion For Flesh and Blood [see Taste For Flesh
    and Blood 2: Raising Hell, A (1991)]
Invasion of the Scream Queens (1992), 433-434

J

Jabber [see LA AIDS Jabber (1994)]
Jacker (1994), 363-364
Jungle Trap (1990), 238-239

K

Killer Nerd (1991), 261-262
Kingdom of the Vampire (1991), 262-263

L

LA AIDS Jabber (1994), 365
Lady in Danger (1992), 295
Las Cenizas de Crowley [see Crowley's Ashes (1990)]

Las Vegas Bloodbath (1989), 213-214
Last Day at the Beach (1990), 240
Last Season, The (1987), 123-124
Linnea Quigley's Horror Workout (1989), 435
Lipstick and Blood (1986), 95
Lisa Cook's Deadly Workout (1994), 436
Lisa Cook's Nightmares (1995), 398
Lost Faith (1992), 296
Love Is a Stranger (1994), 365-366

M

Mad Monk, The (1984), 15, 39
Mad Ron's Prevues From Hell (1987), 427, 436-437
Madhouse (1991), 263-264
Mac-10 [see Gunblast (1986)]
Mama's Home [see Captives (1987)]
Mark of the Beast (1986), 67
Mark of the Devil 666 (1995), 399
Maximum Impact (1992), 297
Miami Vendetta (1986), 95-96, 477
Midnight 2: Sex, Death and Videotape (1993), 334
Moonchild (1994), 366-367
Mother's Day: What a Horror! (1995), 399-400
Mother's Vengeance, A (1992), 298
Mountain Fury (1990), 241
Mr. Ice Cream Man (1994), 367-368
Mummy's Dungeon, The (1993), 335
Mutant Massacre [see Alien Beasts (1991)]
Mutant Massacre 2 [see Alien Beasts (1991)]

N

Naked Horror (1995), 437
Nathan's Gift: Night Stalker (1995), 400-401
Neighborhoodz (1991), 264-265
Niagara Strip (1987), 67-68
Nigel the Psychopath (1994), 368
Night Feeder (1988), 169-170
Night of Terror [see Escape From the Insane Asylum (1986)]
Night of the Living Babes (1987), 124
Night Ripper! (1986), 81, 96-97
Nightmare Asylum (1992), 298-299
Nightmare Vacation (1992-2017), 20, 299-300
Nightstalker (1994), 369

O

O Monstro Legume do Espaco [see Vegetable Monster From Outer Space, The (1995)]
Original Sins (1995), 400, 402
Ozone (1994), 369-370

P

Pact, The (1995), 402
Phantom Brother (1989), 214-215
Pieces of Darkness (1988), 16, 170-171
Plenilunio [see Fullmoon (1993)]
Prehistoric Bimbos in Armageddon City (1992), 19, 300-301
Price of Vengeance (1985), 68
Psycho Dance! (1992), 301-302
Psycho Sisters (1995), 403
Psycho Vampire (1992), 302

R

Rana, Queen of the Amazon (1994), 370, 372
Reanimator Academy (1992), 303
Red Lips (1995), 387, 404-405
Red Spirit Lake (1993), 336
Redneck Zombies (1987), 125-126
Revenge of the Mercenaries [see Bounty Hunters, The (1985)]
Ripper, The (1985), 47-49, 81
Rumbo a la Oscuridad [see Into Darkness (1992)]

S

Sandman, The (1995), 387, 405-406
Satan Place: A Soap Opera From Hell (1988), 171
Satan's Storybook (1989), 215-216
Savage Harvest (1994), 372
Savage Vengeance (1988), 20, 172-173
Savage Vengence [see Savage Vengeance (1988)]
Savage Vows (1995), 406-407
Scare Game, The (1990), 241-243
Scarlet Fry's Horrorama (1989), 216-217
Scary Tales (1993), 336-337
Scream Dream (1989), 217-219
Scream Greats #1: Tom Savini, Master of Horror Effects (1986), 438-439
Scream Greats #2: Satanism and Witchcraft (1986), 438-440
Scream Queen Hot Tub Party (1991), 440
Sed de Venganza [see Bloody Dynasty (1987)]
Sexandroide (1987), 127
Shatter Dead (1993), 337
Shock Chamber (1985), 69
Shreck (1990), 242, 244-245
Sisters (1987), 128
Slaughtered Secretaries (1992), 303-304
Sledgehammer (1983), 14-15, 28-30, 41, 427
Sleepover Massacre (1989), 218
Snake Movie, The [see Copperhead (1983)]

INDEX OF DIRECTORS

Howard, John, 97-98
Howe, Matthew, 400, 402

I

Islas, Ricardo, 109, 119, 159, 167, 232-233, 294-295, 329
Ittenbach, Olaf, 205, 284-285

J

Jacelone, Pete, 403
James, Eugene, 338
Johnson Jr. III, J., 170-171
Johnson, Michael W., 305

K

Kassle, Stevin, 374
Keller, George, 209
Kennedy, Elisar C. [see Cabrera, Elisar]
Kennedy, Hal [see Hall, Kenneth J.]
Kent-Watson, David, 94, 165
Klus, Rita, 268
Koz, Wally, 159-161

L

LaMont, Chris, 410-411
Lang, Charles T., 266, 361
Larsen, Jim, 368
Lawrence, G.W. [see Whitson, Gary]
Levinson, Gary J., 291-292
Lewis, Christopher, 15, 41-43, 47-48
Lewis, Herschell Gordon, 4
Lewnes, Pericles, 109, 126
Lindenmuth, Kevin J., 246-247, 268, 353, 388
Logan, Bob, 432-433
Longo, Sal, 259, 353, 373, 394, 403

M

Mackinnon, James, 357
MacMillan, Will, 83
Makichuk, Jim, 67-68, 70-71
Martin, Ollie, 212
Matsui, Rodd, 207-208
McBride, Jon, 17, 159, 162-163, 223-224, 387, 396-397
McCarthy, John Michael, 357-358
McCleery, Mick, 268
McCollough, Paul, 432
McCrae, Scooter, 337
McCubbin, Peter, 70
McGuire, Mitch, 298

Michael, T, 175-176
Millard, Nick, 81, 91, 109, 112-113, 117-121, 159, 164, 283, 306-311
Miller, Patricia, 207-208
Mills, Christopher, 259-260
Modi, 430-431
Monaco, Jim, 436-437
Moorse, Thomas J., 345

N

Nelson, David "The Rock", 353, 355-356, 408-409, 414-417, 465
Nicholson, James I., 233-234

O

O'Quinn, Kerry, 428
O'Conner, Matt, 290-291
Oaks, Joe, 46-47
Oldham, Samuel, 207-208
Olminsky, Harold, 90, 237, 354
Ottaviano, Ron, 211-212
Ozanix, Lance, 260-261

P

Payton, Leland, 34
Pendell, Evan, 430-431
Perez, Jack, 256-257
Pinion, Charles, 159, 173, 175, 336
Pischiutta, Bruno, 64-65
Plummer, Scott, 286
Polonia, John, 17, 41, 45-46, 81, 84-85, 87, 92, 109, 129-130, 292-293, 299-300, 332-333, 353, 387, 396-397
Polonia, Mark, 17, 41, 45-46, 52-61, 81, 84-85, 87, 92, 109, 129-130, 292-293, 299-300, 332-333, 353, 387, 396-397
Priest, Judith, 303
Prior, David A., 14, 29-30
Prosser, Michael J., 359-360

R

Ramirez, Alfred, 171
Randas, Lance [see Bookwalter, J.R.]
Randolph, Bill, 389-390
Ray, Fred Olen, 440
Redd, Jack, 437
Reynolds, Ursi, 122
Ricaud, Michel, 127
Rico, Luis Quintanilla, 111
Rider, Michael, 215-216

Miami
VENDETTA

IN 1980 CASTRO
EMPTIED HIS JAILS...
THEY CAME TO AMERICA
WITH A VENGEANCE.

WORLD PREMIERE ON VIDEO!

BIBLIOGRAPHY

CHAPTER 1

About Copyright Law. Accessed August 30, 2018. https://www.mplc.org/copyright.

"Betacam." Wikipedia. Accessed June 3, 2018. https://en.wikipedia.org/wiki/Betacam.

"Betamovie." Wikipedia. Accessed June 2, 2018. https://en.wikipedia.org/wiki/Betamovie.

Boardinghouse. Directed by John Wintergate. USA: Code Red DVD, 2008. DVD: Audio Commentary with Director John Wintergate and Film Star Kalassu.

"Boardinghouse (film)." Wikipedia. Accessed March 16, 2018. https://en.wikipedia.org/wiki/Boardinghouse_(film).

Bsgtrekfan88. "Oscars 90 Years Montage." YouTube. Accessed April 6, 2018. https://www.youtube.com/watch?v=WuC2r8OMt0c.

"E.T. the Extra-Terrestrial." Wikipedia. Accessed August 30, 2018. https://en.wikipedia.org/wiki/E.T._the_Extra-Terrestrial.

Greenberg, Joshua M. From Betamax to Blockbuster. Cambridge, MA: MIT Press, 2008.

"HEARINGS." Margaret Newsham: Source for First Echelon Report. Accessed July 2, 2018. https://cryptome.org/hrcw-hear.htm.

Sony BMC-100. Accessed June 2, 2018. http://www.totalrewind.org/cameras/C_BMC1.htm.

"The Betamovies Page!" BetaInfoGuide Homepage. Accessed July 2, 2018. http://www.betainfoguide.net/BTMpage.htm.

"Video Rental Shop." Wikipedia. Accessed June 3, 2018. https://en.wikipedia.org/wiki/Video_rental_shop.

CHAPTER 2

"About Living Life to the Fullest." SHAZER EVERQUAR. Accessed March 3, 2018. https://shazereverquar.wordpress.com/about/2/.

"Boardinghouse (1982)." IMDb. Accessed March 16, 2018. https://www.imdb.com/title/tt0083670/.

"DVD." Wikipedia. Accessed June 3, 2018. https://en.wikipedia.org/wiki/DVD.

Feeders. Directed by Mark Polonia, John Polonia, and Jon McBride. USA: Sub Rosa Studios, LLC, 2004. DVD: Interviews with Mark Polonia, John Polonia and Jon McBride.

Fisher, Bob. "The Emerging New Film/Video Interface." American Cinematographer, June 1981, 570 .

Haberfelner, Mike. "An Interview with Gary Whitson, Director of The Sleepwalker Strangler, Head of WAVE Productions." (re)search My Trash. April 2010. Accessed November 18, 2017. http://www.searchmytrash.com/articles/garywhitson(4-10).shtml.

"Monty Python Live at the Hollywood Bowl." Wikipedia. Accessed March 16, 2018. https://en.wikipedia.org/wiki/Monty_Python_Live_at_the_Hollywood_Bowl.

Sledgehammer. Directed by David A. Prior. USA: Intervision Picture Corp., 2011. DVD: Audio Commentary with Director David A. Prior.

Sledgehammer. Directed by David A. Prior. USA: Intervision Picture Corp., 2011. DVD: Interview with Director David A. Prior.

Thrower, Stephen. Nightmare USA: The Untold Story of the Exploitation Independents. Godalming: FAB Press, 2008.

Ziemba, Joseph. "From Betacam To Big Box: Shot-On-Video Trash In The 1980s (Part I)." BLEEDING SKULL From Betacam To Big Box ShotOnVideo Trash In The 1980s Part I Comments. Accessed August 3, 2011. http://bleedingskull.com/from-betacam-to-big-box-shot-on-video-trash-in-the-1980s-part-i/.

CHAPTER 3

Boardinghouse. Directed by John Wintergate. USA: Code Red DVD, 2008. DVD: Audio Commentary with Director John Wintergate and Film Star Kalassu.

"Boardinghouse (1982)." IMDb. Accessed March 16, 2018. https://www.imdb.com/title/tt0083670/.

Thrower, Stephen. Nightmare USA: The Untold Story of the Exploitation Independents. Godalming: FAB Press, 2008.

CHAPTER 4

""Blonde Death": A Transgressive No-budget Frenzy of Sex, Drugs and Violence." Night Flight. Accessed July 6, 2018. http://nightflight.com/blonde-death-a-transgressive-no-budget-frenzy-of-sex-drugs-and-violence/.

"Blödaren (1983)." IMDb. Accessed August 2, 2018. https://www.imdb.com/title/tt0302356/.

Cotenas, Eric. "Suffer Little Children." DVD Drive-In. Accessed August 14, 2018. http://www.dvddrive-in.com/reviews/n-s/sufferlittlechildren83.htm.

Dixon, Ninja. "Blödaren (1983)." Ninja Dixon. Accessed August 2, 2018. http://ninjadixon.blogspot.com/2012/02/blodaren-1983.html.

Sledgehammer. Directed by David A. Prior. USA: Intervision Picture Corp., 2011. DVD: Audio Commentary with Director David A. Prior.

Sledgehammer. Directed by David A. Prior. USA: Intervision Picture Corp., 2011. DVD: Interview with Director David A. Prior.

"Sledgehammer (Video 1983)." IMDb. Accessed March 22, 2018. https://www.imdb.com/title/tt0244800/.

Wooley, John. Shot in Oklahoma: A Century of Sooner State Cinema. Norman, OK: U. of Oklahoma P., 2011.

CHAPTER 5

Black Devil Doll From Hell. Directed by Chester N. Turner. USA: Massacre Video, 2013. DVD: Audio Commentary with Director Chester N. Turner and Film Star Shirley L. Jones.

Black Devil Doll From Hell. Directed by Chester N. Turner. USA: Massacre Video, 2013. DVD: Interview with Director Chester N. Turner and Film Star Shirley L. Jones.

"El Monje Loco (1984)." IMDb. Accessed July 26, 2018. https://www.imdb.com/title/tt0359708/.

CHAPTER 6

Blood Cult. Directed by Christopher Lewis. USA: VCI Entertainment, 2006. DVD: Audio Commentary with Director Christopher Lewis.

Blood Cult. Directed by Christopher Lewis. USA: VCI Entertainment, 2006. DVD: Interview with Director Christopher Lewis.

"Blood Cult (Video 1985)." IMDb. Accessed July 27, 2018. https://www.imdb.com/title/tt0136735/.

Church of the Damned. Directed by Mark Polonia, John Polonia, Todd Rimatti. USA: Sub Rosa Studios, LLC, 2015. Blu-Ray: Audio Commentary with Director Mark Polonia.

Church of the Damned. Directed by Mark Polonia, John Polonia, Todd Rimatti. USA: Sub Rosa Studios, LLC, 2015. Blu-Ray: Introductory Exposition by Director Mark Polonia.

Just Desserts the Making of "Creepshow". Directed by Michael Felsher. USA: Red Shirt Pictures, 2016. Blu-Ray: Special Feature "Scream Greats Volume One: Tom Savini, Master of Horror Effects" Audio Commentary with Tom Savini and Michael Felshner.

The Ripper. Directed by Christopher Lewis. USA: VCI Entertainment, 2006. DVD: Audio Commentary with Director Christopher Lewis.

The Ripper. Directed by Christopher Lewis. USA: VCI Entertainment, 2006. DVD: Interview with Director Christopher Lewis

"Twisted Illusions (Video 1985)." IMDb. Accessed December 20, 2017. https://www.imdb.com/title/tt0376278/.

Ziemba, Joseph. "From Betacam To Big Box: Shot-On-Video Trash In The 1980s (Part I)." From Betacam To Big Box ShotOnVideo Trash In The 1980s Part I Comments. Accessed August 3, 2011. http://bleedingskull.com/from-betacam-to-big-box-shot-on-video-trash-in-the-1980s-part-i/.

Wooley, John. Shot in Oklahoma: A Century of Sooner State Cinema. Norman, OK: U. of Oklahoma P., 2011.

CHAPTER 7

"Lionel Shenken." IMDb. Accessed January 2, 2018. https://www.imdb.com/name/nm0791564/.

Theodin.co.uk, Philip Beel. "Canuxploitation Article: Every Six Minutes: The Story of Emmeritus." Canuxploitation! Accessed April 5, 2017. http://www.canuxploitation.com/article/emmeritus.html.

CHAPTER 8

"About Camp." Black River Farm and Ranch - Summer Horse Camp for Girls. Accessed August 30, 2018. http://www.blackriverfarmandranch.com/about/.

"CARDS OF DEATH (BSV-001)." From Betacam To Big Box ShotOnVideo Trash In The 1980s Part I Comments. Accessed August 12, 2018. http://bleedingskull.com/cards-of-death-bsv-001/.

Channel 13. Directed by Mark Polonia and John Polonia. USA: Sub Rosa Studios, LLC, 2014. DVD: Audio Commentary with Director Mark Polonia.

Demon Queen. Directed by Donald Farmer. USA: Massacre Video, 2012. DVD: Interview with Director Donald Farmer.

Hallucinations. Directed by Mark Polonia, John Polonia, Todd Rimatti. USA: Sub Rosa Studios, LLC, 2015. Blu-Ray: Audio Commentary with Director Mark Polonia.

"Mondo & Bleeding Skull Video Present: CARDS OF DEATH." Mondo. Accessed August 12, 2018. https://mondotees.com/blogs/news/16993703-mondo-bleeding-skull-video-present-cards-of-death.

Spine. Directed by John Howard and Justin Simonds. USA: Massacre Video, 2015. DVD: Audio Commentary with Co-Director Justin Simonds and Actor R. Eric Huxley.

Victims! Directed by Jeff Hathcock. USA: Slasher Video, 2017. Blu-Ray: Interview with Director Jeff Hathcock.

CHAPTER 9

"1987's Hottest TVs, VCRs, Stereos, Cellular Phones & More." Click Americana. Accessed August 2, 2018. https://clickamericana.com/media/ephemera/1987-tv-vcr-stereo-walkman-phones.

Cemetery Sisters. Directed by Nick Millard. USA: Slasher Video, 2013. DVD: Audio Commentary with Director Nick Millard and Producer Irmi Millard

Criminally Insane. Directed by Nick Millard. USA: Retro Sock-O-Rama, 2005. DVD: Interview with Director Nick Millard.

Death Nurse. Directed by Nick Millard. USA: Slasher Video, 2012. DVD: Audio Commentary with Director Nick Millard and Producer Irmi Millard.

Death Nurse. Directed by Nick Millard. USA: Slasher Video, 2012. DVD: Interview with Director Nick Millard.

"List of Horror Films of 1987." Wikipedia. Accessed September 02, 2018.
https://en.wikipedia.org/wiki/List_of_horror_films_of_1987.

Masiello, Tony. "Genesis of Donald Farmer's Cannibal Hookers by Tim Ritter." SOV HORROR.
Accessed April 22, 2018. http://www.sovhorror.com/2014/01/genesis-of-donald-farmers-cannibal.html.

Redneck Zombies. Directed by Pericles Lewnes. USA: Troma Entertainment Inc., 2008. DVD: Audio
Commentary with Director Pericles Lewnes and Producer Ed Bishop.

Redneck Zombies. Directed by Pericles Newnes. USA: Troma Entertainment Inc., 2008. DVD: Interview with
Director Pericles Lewnes.

Splatter Farm. Directed by Mark Polonia, John Polonia, Todd Rimatti. USA: Camp Motion Pictures, 2007.
DVD: Commentary with Directors Mark Polonia and John Polonia.

Tales from the Quadead Zone. Directed by Chester T. Turner. USA: Massacre Video, 2013. DVD: Audio
Commentary with Director Chester T. Turner and Film Star Shirley L. Jones.

"VCR Prices Rising, But Features Improving." Tribunedigital-chicagotribune. Accessed August 30, 2018.
http://articles.chicagotribune.com/1986-10-03/entertainment/8603140673_1_vhs-hi-fi-vhs-vcrs-prices.

Victims! Directed by Jeff Hathcock. USA: Slasher Video, 2017. Blu-Ray: Interview with Director Jeff Hathcock.

Video Violence. Directed by Gary P. Cohen. USA: Camp Motion Pictures, 2007. DVD: Audio Commentary with
Director Gary P. Cohen.

CHAPTER 10

555. Directed by Wally Koz. USA: Massacre Video, 2016. DVD: Interview with Special Effects Artist Jeffery
Lyle Segal.

Cannibal Campout. Directed by Jon McBride. USA: Camp Motion Pictures, 2007. DVD: Audio Commentary
with Director Jon McBride.

Death Nurse 2. Directed by Nick Millard. USA: Slasher Video, 2013. DVD: Audio Commentary with Director
Nick Millard and Producer Irmi Millard.

"From Betacam To Big Box: Shot-On-Video Trash In The 1980s (Part II)." BLEEDING SKULL From Betacam
To Big Box ShotOnVideo Trash In The 1980s Part I Comments. Accessed August 3, 2011.
http://bleedingskull.com/from-betacam-to-big-box-shot-on-video-trash-in-the-1980s-part-ii/.

"NIGHT FEEDER (BSV-004)." BLEEDING SKULL From Betacam To Big Box ShotOnVideo Trash In The
1980s Part I Comments. Accessed August 12, 2018. http://bleedingskull.com/night-feeder-bsv-004/.

Savage Vengeance. Directed by Donald Farmer. USA: Massacre Video, 2013. DVD: Audio Commentary with
Director Donald Farmer.

Venus Flytrap. Directed by T Michael. USA: Massacre Video, 2014. DVD: Audio Commentary with Producer Kevin M. Glover and Actor Steve Malis.

Venus Flytrap. Directed by T. Michael. USA: Massacre Video, 2014. DVD: Interview with Producer Kevin M. Glover and Actor Steve Malis.

Video Violence 2. Directed by Gary P. Cohen. USA: Camp Motion Pictures, 2007. DVD: Audio Commentary with Director Gary P. Cohen.

"Wally Koz." IMDb. Accessed July 28, 2018. https://www.imdb.com/name/nm0468751/.

CHAPTER 11

Dead Silence. Directed by Hugh Gallagher. USA: Sub Rosa Studios, LLC, 2016. DVD: Audio Commentary with Director Hugh Gallagher.

Masiello, Tony. "Interview - Las Vegas Blood Bath FX Artist David Dalton." S.O.V. the True Independents: A Visual History of Shot on Video Horror Films from the 80's and 90's. Accessed April 22, 2018. http://www.sovhorror.com/2014/05/interview-las-vegas-blood-bath-fx.html.

The Violent Shit Collection. Accessed September 03, 2018. http://mondo-digital.com/violentshitseries.html.

Verhoskan. "Disgusting Space Worms Eat Everyone (1989)." ZMDB Search Forum. Accessed June 1, 2018. http://www.zmdb.org/indie/1297-Disgusting_Space_Worms_Eat_Everyone_(1989).htm.

Werbeck, Kai-Uwe. "The State vs. Buttgereit and Ittenbach: Censorship and Subversion in German No-Budget Horror Film." Journal of the Fantastic in the Arts27, no. 3 (2016): 435-51. https://pages.uncc.edu/kai-werbeck/wp-content/uploads/sites/285/2018/08/8-Werbeck-Article-JFA-No-Budget-German-Horror.pdf.

Woodchipper Massacre. Directed by Jon McBride. USA: Camp Motion Pictures, 2007. DVD: Audio Commentary with Director Jon McBride.

CHAPTER 12

Facebook. www.facebook.com.

Dark Harvest. Directed by James I. Nicholson. USA: Intervision Picture Corp., 2017. DVD: Interview with Actor Patti Negri.

Death by Love. Directed by Alan Grant. USA: Intervision Picture Corp., 2017. DVD: Interview with Director Alan Grant.

Gorgasm. Directed by Hugh Gallagher. USA: Sub Rosa Studios, LLC, 2016. DVD: Audio Commentary with Director Hugh Gallagher.

KJLindenmuth. "Vampires & Other Stereotypes Movie Trailer." YouTube. Accessed March 28, 2018. https://www.youtube.com/watch?v=kkbSRE5_5Sw.

Lindenmuth, Kevin J. Making Movies on Your Own: Practical Talk from Independent Filmmakers. Jefferson, NC: McFarland, 1998.

"Mondo & Bleeding Skull Video Present: JUNGLE TRAP." Mondo. Accessed August 30, 2018. https://mondotees.com/blogs/news/mondo-bleeding-skull-video-present-jungle-trap-soundtrack-vhs-dvd.

CHAPTER 13

America's Deadliest Home Video. Directed by Josh Schafer. USA: Camp Motion Pictures, 2016. DVD: Audio Commentary with Director Josh Schafer.

Dream Stalker. Directed by Alan Grant. USA: Intervision Picture Corp., 2017. DVD: Interview with Actor Mark Dias.

Facebook. www.facebook.com.

Invasion for Flesh and Blood. Directed by Warren F. Disbrow. USA: Troma Entertainment Inc., 2005. DVD: Audio Commentary with Director Warren F. Disbrow.

Killer Nerd. Directed by Mark Steven Bosko and Wayne A. Harold. USA: Troma Entertainment Inc., 2004. DVD: Audio Commentary with Filmmakers.

Kingdom of the Vampire. Directed by J.R. Bookwalter. USA: Tempe Video, 2007. DVD: Audio Commentary with Director J.R. Bookwalter.

Lindenmuth, Kevin J. Making Movies on Your Own: Practical Talk from Independent Filmmakers. Jefferson, NC: McFarland, 1998.

Zombie Cop. Directed by J.R. Bookwalter. USA: Tempe Video, 2007. DVD: Audio Commentary with Director J.R. Bookwalter.

CHAPTER 14

Chickboxer. Directed by Scott Plummer. USA: Tempe Video, 2007. DVD: Audio Commentary with Producer J.R. Bookwalter.

Galaxy of the Dinosaurs. Directed by J.R. Bookwalter. USA: Tempe Video, 2007. DVD: Audio Commentary with Director J.R. Bookwalter.

Humanoids from Atlantis. Directed by J.R. Bookwalter. USA: Tempe Video, 2007. DVD: Audio Commentary with Director J.R. Bookwalter.

Masiello, Tony. "Interview - Evil Night Actor Rik Deskin." S.O.V. the True Independents: A Visual History of Shot on Video Horror Films from the 80's and 90's. Accessed April 22, 2018. http://www.sovhorror.com/2014/05/interview-evil-night-actor-rik-deskin.html.

Nightmare Vacation. Directed by John Polonia, Matthew Slatterly, Mark Polonia. USA: Sub Rosa Studios, LLC, 2017. Blu-Ray: Audio Commentary with Director Mark Polonia.

"People's Court Hellroller vs Judge Wapner." YouTube. Accessed July 29, 2018. https://www.youtube.com/watch?v=-GgYGHIHE_k.

Werbeck, Kai-Uwe. "The State vs. Buttgereit and Ittenbach: Censorship and Subversion in German No-Budget Horror Film." Journal of the Fantastic in the Arts27, no. 3 (2016): 435-51. https://pages.uncc.edu/kai-werbeck/wp-content/uploads/sites/285/2018/08/8-Werbeck-Article-JFA-No-Budget-German-Horror.pdf.

CHAPTER 15

Gorotica. Directed by Hugh Gallagher. USA: Sub Rosa Studios, LLC, 2016. DVD: Audio Commentary with Director Hugh Gallagher.

The Violent Shit Collection. Accessed September 01, 2018. http://mondo-digital.com/violentshitseries.html.

Zombie Bloodbath. Directed by Todd Sheets. USA: Camp Motion Pictures, 2007. DVD: Audio Commentary with Director Todd Sheets.

CHAPTER 16

Gore Whore. Directed by Hugh Gallagher. USA: Sub Rosa Studios, LLC, 2016. DVD: Audio Commentary with Director Hugh Gallagher.

Lindenmuth, Kevin J. Making Movies on Your Own: Practical Talk from Independent Filmmakers. Jefferson, NC: McFarland, 1998.

"Mack Hail." IMDb. Accessed July 15, 2018. https://www.imdb.com/name/nm1109374/.

"Mr. Ice Cream Man (Video 1996)." IMDb. Accessed August 30, 2018. https://www.imdb.com/title/tt0323307/.

Ozone. Directed by J.R. Bookwalter. USA: Tempe Video, 2003. DVD: Audio Commentary with Director J.R. Bookwalter and Actor James Black.

"Roger Ebert & the Movies | TV Guide." TVGuide.com. January 2000. Accessed September 01, 2018. https://www.tvguide.com/tvshows/roger-ebert-the-movies/episodes/444285/2/.

Watt, Mike. "Jillian Hodges." Hollywood Is Burning. Accessed August 30, 2018. http://www.oocities.org/hollywoodisburning/jillian.html.
Originally published in GC Magazine, ED. John Keeyes

CHAPTER 17

"Addicted to Murder." Brimstone Media Productions, LLC. Accessed June 20, 2018. https://www.lindenmuth.com/movie_atm1.shtml.

Carlin, Shannon. "How 'Scream' Changed The Way We See Women In Horror Movies." Bustle. Accessed June 20, 2018. https://www.bustle.com/articles/200788-how-scream-changed-the-way-we-see-women-in-horror-movies.

"DVD." Wikipedia. Accessed June 3, 2018. https://en.wikipedia.org/wiki/DVD.

Feeders. Directed by Mark Polonia, John Polonia, and Jon McBride. USA: Sub Rosa Studios, LLC, 2004. DVD: Interviews with Mark Polonia, John Polonia and Jon McBride.

Graham, Jeff Dylan. "Adventures of a B-Movie Actor." B-independent.com On-line Cult-film Entertainment: Articles. Accessed September 01, 2018. http://www.b-independent.com/articles/graham2.htm.

"How Scream Changed the Formula for Slasher Movies." AMC. 2008. Accessed August 25, 2018. https://www.amc.com/talk/2009/01/stacie-ponder-25.

Matthau, Charles. "How Tech Has Shaped Film Making: The Film vs. Digital Debate Is Put to Rest." Wired. Accessed September 01, 2018. https://www.wired.com/insights/2015/01/how-tech-shaped-film-making/.

The Sandman. Directed by J.R. Bookwalter. USA: Tempe Video, 2006. DVD: Liner Notes.

The Sandman. Directed by J.R. Bookwalter. USA: Tempe Video, 2006. DVD: Audio Commentary with Director J.R. Bookwalter and Line Producer James L. Edwards.

CHAPTER 18

"Fangoria." Wikipedia. Accessed June 3, 2018. https://en.wikipedia.org/wiki/Fangoria.

"People's Court Hellroller vs Judge Wapner." YouTube. Accessed July 29, 2018. https://www.youtube.com/watch?v=-GgYGHIHE_k.

Splatter: Architects of Fear. Directed by Bill Smith. USA: Slasher Video, 2014. DVD: Audio Commentary with Director Bill Smith, Cannibal Cam, & Jesus Terán.

Splatter: Architects of Fear. Directed by Bill Smith. USA: Slasher Video, 2014. DVD: Interview with Director Bill Smith.

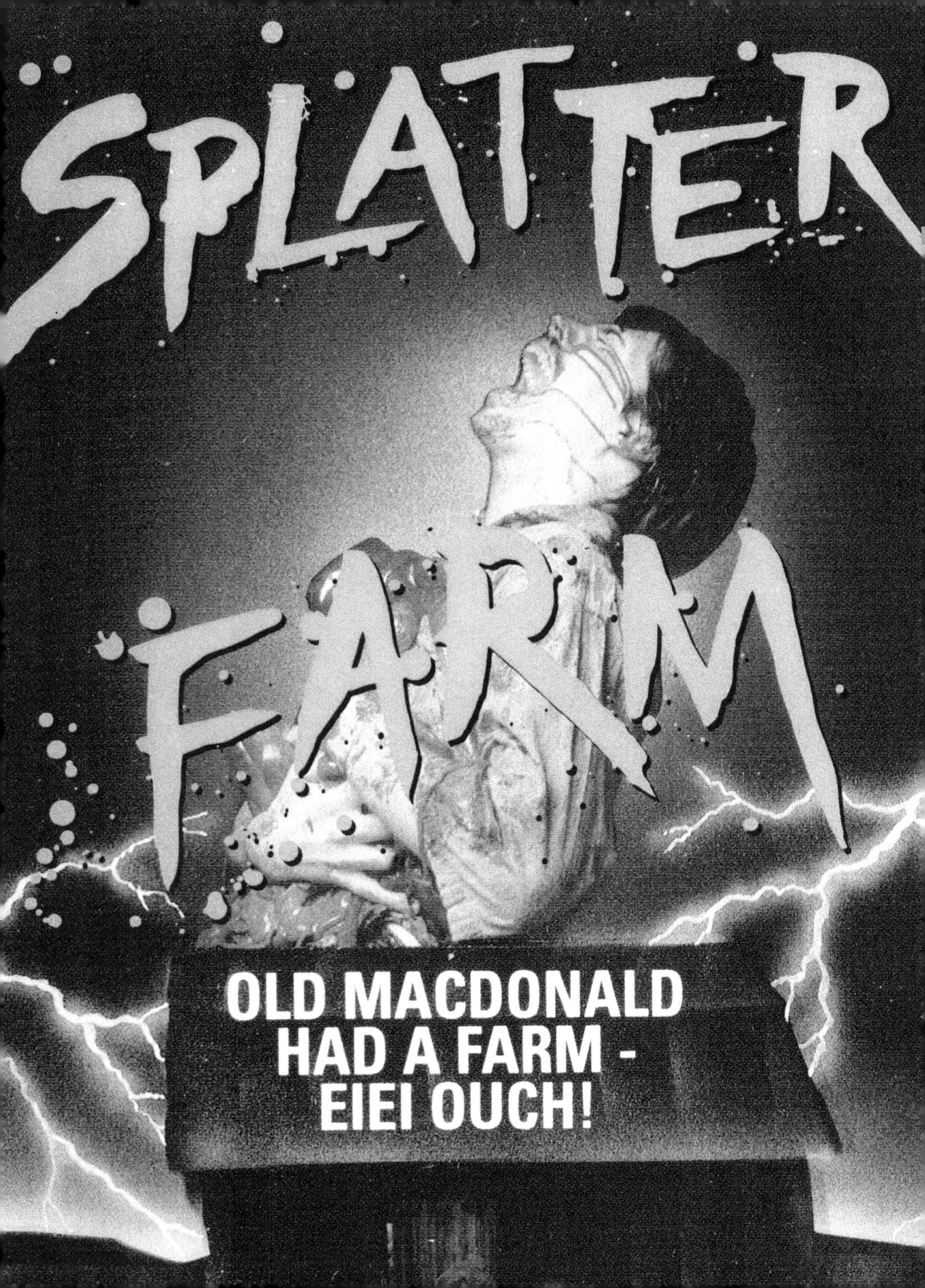

SPLATTER

FARM

**OLD MACDONALD
HAD A FARM -
EIEI OUCH!**

Richard Mogg is an independent film producer and director.

He is the writer/director/producer of *Easter Bunny Bloodbath, Teenage Slumber Party Nightmare, Bigfoot Ate My Boyfriend* (featuring Lloyd Kaufman) and the infamous *Massage Parlor of Death* (voted *"#1 Worst Movie of 2015"* by zombiesdontrun.net). He has presently directed 9 feature-length films, many of which are available on Amazon, Barnes & Noble and other fine retailers worldwide, and distributed through SRS Cinema, Gatorblade Films, Briarwood Entertainment and Screamtime Films. Richard has also appeared frequently in VHS collecting and moviemaking documentaries, including *VHS Lives: A Shockumentary, VHS Lives 2: Undead Format,* and *Penny Pinchers 2: Scenes From the Underground.*

This is his first book.

IN ADDITION: New releases of older SOV films are happening all the time! Stay vigilant and watch for them. Perhaps we'll discover more lost titles together as the years go by...

CPSIA information can be obtained
at www.ICGtesting.com
Printed in the USA
BVHW011912050819
555124BV00007B/189/P